T0235915

Lecture Notes in Computer Science 12024

More information about this series at http://www.springer.com/series/7410

Maryline Laurent · Thanassis Giannetsos (Eds.)

Information Security Theory and Practice

13th IFIP WG 11.2 International Conference, WISTP 2019
Paris, France, December 11–12, 2019
Proceedings

 Springer

Editors
Maryline Laurent ⓘ
Telecom SudParis
Evry, France

Thanassis Giannetsos ⓘ
Technical University of Denmark
Lyngby, Denmark

ISSN 0302-9743   ISSN 1611-3349   (electronic)
Lecture Notes in Computer Science
ISBN 978-3-030-41701-7   ISBN 978-3-030-41702-4   (eBook)
https://doi.org/10.1007/978-3-030-41702-4

LNCS Sublibrary: SL4 – Security and Cryptology

This Springer imprint is published by the registered company Springer Nature Switzerland AG
The registered company address is: Gewerbestrasse 11, 6330 Cham, Switzerland

Preface

It was our great pleasure to organize the 13th International Conference on Information Security Theory and Practice (WISTP 2019), held December 2019 at Conservatoire National des Arts et Métiers (CNAM) in Paris, France. This year marked the 13th edition of the conference, and we were thrilled to continue fostering collaboration among researchers and practitioners to discuss the various facets of cyber- and information-security. WISTP covers a wide range of topics on theoretical and practical aspects of security and privacy, as well as experimental studies of fielded systems, and thus benefits the cyber-security community by encouraging the emergence of novel research avenues of the aforementioned areas. The conference considered all complex facets and double-edged sword aspects of the cyber-security ecosystem, in particular, how new security algorithms and technologies can impact the security posture of existing and future ICT systems.

The WISTP 2019 call for papers attracted submissions from 24 countries, from a wide variety of academic and corporate institutions. In total, we received 42 valid submissions, of which 12 papers were selected as full papers and 2 were accepted as short papers after a double-blind review by our Program Committee comprised of 44 members, leading to a full acceptance rate of 28.5% and an overall acceptance rate of 33.3%. These papers cover a wide range of topics on the pressing challenges of security and privacy, including authentication, software security, threats and attacks, post-quantum cryptography, security analysis and proofs, and combining theoretical expertise and practical experiments that rely on emerging technologies (like Blockchain) with direct application of and impact on emerging domains of Internet of Things.

Two papers received extra praise: "Fault Injection Characterization on modern CPUs - From the ISA to the Micro-Architecture" by Thomas Trouchkine, Guillaume Bouffard, and Jessy Clediere received the Best Student Paper Award; and "Threat Analysis of Poisoning Attack against Ethereum Blockchain" by Teppei Sato, Mitsuyoshi Imamura, and Kazumasa Omote received the Best Paper Award.

The program also included two invited talks by David Naccache (ENS, France) on "How to Compartment Secrets - Trust Everybody, but Cut the Cards -" and Pascal Paillier (CryptoExperts, France) on "Homomorphic encryption for deep learning: a revolution in the making."

Putting together WISTP 2019 was a team effort. We first thank all the authors for the quality of their submissions. We are grateful to the Program Committee who worked very hard in reviewing papers and providing valuable feedback to authors. In addition, we would like to thank the General Chairs, Wojciech Mazurczyk from Warsaw University of Technology (WUT), Poland, and Samia Bouzefrane from Conservatoire National des Arts et Métiers (CNAM), France, for their valuable support and help with the planning and organization of the conference, as well as the Steering Committee, especially Damien Sauveron from the University of Limoges, France, for their continuous efforts in making the event evolve throughout the years. Finally, special thanks to the Local Organizing Committee, Yulliwas Ameur (CNAM, France), Abou-Bakr Djaker (University of Oran, Algeria), Xiaotian Fu (CNAM, France), Thiziri Saad (CNAM, France), and Mamoudou Sangaré (CNAM, France) for hosting the conference in a beautiful and historical location.

We also want to thank the IDfix project, whose support helped to keep registration fees as low as possible and for providing great prizes to the best paper awards winners, as well as the IFIP WG 11.2: Pervasive Systems Security for their continued confidence in the organization of the WISTP editions.

January 2020   Maryline Laurent
                                                              Thanassis Giannetsos

Organization

Program Committee Chairs

Maryline Laurent	Télécom SudParis, France
Thanassis Giannetsos	Danmarks Tekniske Universitet, Denmark

Steering Committee

Angelos Bilas	University of Crete, Greece
Olivier Blazy	University of Limoges, France
Konstantinos Markantonakis	Royal Holloway University of London, UK
Joachim Posegga	University of Passau, Germany
Jean-Jacques Quisquater	Catholic University of Louvain, Belgium
Damien Sauveron	University of Limoges, France
Chan Yeob Yeun	Khalifa University, UAE

Program Committee

Raja Naeem Akram	Royal Holloway University of London, UK
Claudio Ardagna	University of Milan, Italy
Kadri Benamar	University of Tlemcen, Algeria
Olivier Blazy	University of Limoges, France
Samia Bouzefrane	Conservatoire National des Arts et Métiers, France
Xavier Bultel	University of Auvergne, France
Serge Chaumette	University of Bordeaux, France
Liqun Chen	University of Surrey, UK
Céline Chevalier	University of Pantheon-Assas Paris II, France
Emmanuel Conchon	University of Limoges, France
Mauro Conti	University of Padua, Italy
Gabriele Costa	IMT Lucca, Italy
Tassos Dimitriou	Computer Technology Institute, Greece
Ruggero Donida Labati	University of Milan, Italy
Sara Foresti	University of Milan, Italy
Thanassis Giannetsos	Danmarks Tekniske Universitet, Denmark
Johann Groszschaedl	University of Luxembourg, Luxembourg
Yong Guan	Iowa State University, USA
Nesrine Kaaniche	The University of Sheffield, UK
Süleyman Karda	Batman University, Turkey
Mehmet Sabir Kiraz	De Montfort University, UK
Ioannis Krontiris	Huawei Technologies, Germany
Andrea Lanzi	University of Milan, Italy
Albert Levi	Sabanci University, Turkey

Olivier Levillain	Télécom SudParis, France
Javier Lopez	NICS Lab, Spain
Sjouke Mauw	University of Luxembourg, Luxembourg
Keith Mayes	Royal Holloway University of London, UK
Alessio Merlo	University of Genoa, Italy
Antonios Michalas	Tampere University of Technology, Finland
Jiaxin Pan	Norwegian University of Science and Technology, Norway
Joachim Posegga	University of Passau, Germany
Kouichi Sakurai	Kyushu University, Japan
Pierangela Samarati	University of Milan, Italy
Siraj A. Shaikh	Coventry University, UK
Dave Singelee	Catholic University of Louvain, Belgium
Denis Trcek	University of Ljubljana, Slovenia
Umut Uludag	TUBITAK-BILGEM-UEKAE, Turkey
Paulo Verissimo	University of Luxembourg, Luxembourg
Anjia Yang	Jinan University, China
Stefano Zanero	Politecnico di Milano, Italy
Gongxuan Zhang	Nanjing University of Science and Technology, China

Additional Reviewers

Angèle Bossuat	Eleonora Losiouk
Stefano Cecconello	Shahid Mahmood
Luca Demetrio	Ameer Mohammed
Atif Hussain	Paolo Montesel
Elif Bilge Kavun	Enrico Russo
Rhys Kirk	Korbinian Spielvogel
Felix Klement	Federico Turrin
Huimin Lao	Andrea Valenza
Yuxian Li	Axin Wu
Stefano Longari	Yuriy Zacchia Lun

Sponsor

Contents

Cybersecurity

Internet of Things

Invited Paper

How to Compartment Secrets

Trust Everybody, but Cut the Cards

Gaëlle Candel[1,3], Rémi Géraud-Stewart[2,3(✉)], and David Naccache[3]

[1] Ingenico Labs, 28 boulevard Grenelle, 75015 Paris, France
gaelle.candel@ingenico.com
[2] Ingenico Labs, 9 Avenue de la Gare, 26300 Alixan, France
remi.geraud@ingenico.com
[3] DIENS, ENS, CNRS, PSL University, 45 rue d'Ulm, 75230 Paris cedex 05, France
{gaelle.candel,remi.geraud,david.naccache}@ens.fr

Abstract. Secret sharing splits a secret s into ℓ shares in such a way that $k \leq \ell$ shares suffice to reconstruct s. Let $\rho_{i,j}$ be the probability that shareholder i disclose their share to shareholder j, with $0 \leq i, j < n$.

Given $k \leq \ell \leq n$, to whom ℓ individuals should we hand shares, if we wish to minimize the probability that one of them reconstitutes s?

1 Introduction

Queen Elizabeth I stated *"Do not tell secrets to those whose faith and silence you have not already tested"*. Given the relative faith in the audience, how can we calculate the overall disclosure risk? This paper provides an answer to this question.

Secret sharing splits a secret s into "shares", distributed among n participants. Under certain conditions – the sharing scheme's *access structure* – this secret s can be reconstructed (e.g. from enough shares). In the simplest case, we may require all shares to be combined [Sha79, Mig82, Bla79]. A more interesting access structure requires that at least k shares among n are required. Constructions for different access structures are known [DD94].

In this paper we are given a table:

$$\rho = \{\rho_{i,j}\}_{0 \leq i,j < n}$$

where $\rho_{i,j}$ is the probability that shareholder i will leak their share to shareholder j. Because of this leakage mechanism, it is possible that eventually one of the shareholders gets enough shares to reconstruct s. Our goal is to evaluate the probability p_{col} that any third party's reconstructs s, an event called "collapse".

The most general setting, where we can produce exactly ℓ shares, is motivated by a real-life data escrow scenario: given n data centers we wish to select ℓ of them to hold shares of a k-out-of-ℓ secret sharing, so that collapse probability is minimal. However, as we will discuss below this is a challenging problem, that is best approached in several steps. We therefore discuss two simplified versions of the problem first:

© IFIP International Federation for Information Processing 2020
Published by Springer Nature Switzerland AG 2020
M. Laurent and T. Giannetsos (Eds.): WISTP 2019, LNCS 12024, pp. 3–11, 2020.
https://doi.org/10.1007/978-3-030-41702-4_1

- $\ell = k = n$ *and* $0 \le \rho_{i,j} \le 1$: Given $n, \boldsymbol{\rho}$, compute p_{col}.

The optimal strategy resides in the access structure. To see why, consider the simplest n-out-of-n setting in which all shares are necessary recover s.

The optimal choice in this situation (assuming $0 < \rho_{i,j} < 1$) is to give a share to everyone. The proof is immediate: adding a share to the game multiplies collapse probability by a factor < 1; p_{col} can be computed with the tools of Sect. 2.

- $\rho_{i,j} \in \{0, 1\}$: Given $n, \boldsymbol{\rho}$, compute p_{col} and potentially avoid giving shares to participants not affecting p_{col}.

The case $\rho_{i,j} \in \{0, 1\}$ allows a more parsimonious distribution of shares: we distribute a share per strongly-connected component of the graph defined by $\rho_{i,j}$. Thus the general problem can be solved by condensing the graph (this is done in linear time) and handing a share to each representative of a strongly-connected component. If there are fewer shares than connected components, we have $p_{\mathrm{col}} = 0$. If there are more, then depending on k we can have $p_{\mathrm{col}} = 0$ or 1. This process is detailed in Sect. 3.

1.1   Notations and Hypotheses

Let $n > 2$ be the number of possible shareholders. Let $[n]$ denote the set $\{0, \ldots, n-1\}$. The cardinality of a set X is denoted $|X|$. If p is a probability, we write $\overline{p} = 1 - p$. U_i will denote shareholder i.

For any $i, j \in [n]$ we denote by $\rho_{i,j}$ the probability that U_i shares all he knows with U_j. We say in that case that U_i and U_j *collude*. Collusion is transitive: U_i can send its share x_i to U_j, who then transmits it (along with x_j) to U_ℓ — even if U_i and U_ℓ abstain from direct interactions. Note that $\rho_{i,j}$ may differ from $\rho_{j,i}$.

2   Collapse Probability

In this section we explain how to compute the collapse probability, defined as the probability that *at least one* shareholder can reconstruct the secret (e.g. by gathering enough shares).

Definition 1 (Saturation, $G^{\pm}$). *A labeled directed graph G is saturated if all labels are equal to 1. Saturated graphs are in one-to-one correspondence with unlabeled directed graphs. We say that an edge is saturated if it is labeled 1, and is unsaturated otherwise. Unsaturated edges of G can be ordered (e.g. by lexicographic order), and we denote by $G^{+(i \to j)}$ (resp. $G^{-(i \to j)}$) the graph obtained by saturating (resp. removing) the first unsaturated edge of G, denoted $i \to j$.*

Definition 2 (Evaluation at a Random Graph). *Let f be a function taking as input a directed graph and returning an element in some (fixed) vector space.*

Let G be a labeled *directed graph, with edges labels in* $[0,1]$. *We define*

$$\widehat{f}(G) = \begin{cases} f(G) \\ \quad \textit{if } G \textit{ is saturated} \\ \ell_{i,j}\widehat{f}\left(G^{+(i\to j)}\right) + \overline{\ell_{i,j}}\widehat{f}\left(G^{-(i\to j)}\right) \\ \quad \textit{for the unsaturated edge } i \to j \textit{ labeled } \ell_{i,j} \end{cases}$$

which we call the evaluation *of f at G.*

Definition 3 (Root-Directed Spanning Tree). *Let G be a directed graph. G has a* Root-Directed Spanning Tree *(RDST) if there is a vertex R such that, for every other vertex S, G has a directed path from S vertex to R.*

Remark 1. Note that if G has an RDST, then G is connected, so that connectivity is a necessary condition. Note also that if G is strongly connected, then it has an RDST, so that strong-connectivity is a sufficient condition. Both properties can be established in linear time.

Note that G has this property if and only if $G^\bullet$ has it, so that without loss of generality we may assume we are working on a condensed graph. Such a graph is acyclic which makes it possible to logarithmically check efficiently the presence of an RDST.

Example 1 ((n,n)-secret sharing). The (n,n)-collapse function $L^{(n,n)}$ takes a directed acyclic graph G as input, and returns 1 if G has a root-directed spanning tree, and 0 otherwise. Therefore, collapse probability for this access structure only depends on the graph ρ defined by the values of $\rho_{i,j}$, and is $p_{\text{col}}^{(n,n)} = \widehat{L}^{(n,n)}(G)$.

Example 2 ((n,n)-secret sharing, n = 3). Consider $n = 3$ and write $a = \rho_{0,1}$, $b = \rho_{1,2}$, $c = \rho_{2,0}$ all other probabilities being 0. The collapse probability is $p_{\text{col}} = ab + bc + ca - 2abc$. Note that the expression is symmetric in a, b, c, and $0 \le p_{\text{col}} \le 1$. A worked-out computation is given in Appendix A.

The following remark gives a computer-friendly representation of p_{col}:

Remark 2. Let $e_1, e_2, \ldots, e_\ell$ be the edges' labels in G, and for any ℓ-bit string $x = (x_1, \ldots, x_\ell)$, let $u_i(x_i) = (1 - x_i)e_i + (1 - e_i)x_i$ and $u(x) = \prod_i u_i(e_i)$. Then any collapse probability is of the form

$$p_{\text{col}} = \sum_{x \in X} u(x)$$

where X is a set of ℓ-bit strings, corresponding to edge saturations associated with an RDST graph. In Eq. 2, with $e_i = (a, b, c)$, we have $X = \{011, 101, 110, 111\}$.

Example 3 ((n,n)-secret sharing, n = 4). (Same as above, but with an additional edge in the reverse direction). $X = \{1111, 1101, 1011, 1010, 1001, 0111, 0101, 0011\}$.

3   Optimal Solution When $\rho \in \{0, 1\}$

The minimal collapse probability is achieved when every participant has a share. It is possible to be slightly more efficient using the following notion:

Definition 4 (Condensation). *Let G be a directed graph. A strongly con-nected component of G is a sub-graph in which there is a path in each direction between each pair of vertices. The condensation of G is the directed acyclic graph $G^\bullet$ obtained by contracting strongly connected components.*

We apply condensation to the graph G whose vertices are $[n]$ and whose edges are those edges $(i \to j)$ such that $\rho_{i,j} = 1$. Tarjan's algorithm [Tar72] computes the condensation of a graph in $O(n + e)$, where n is the number of vertices and e the number of edges, i.e. $e = |\{i, j \in [n] \mid i \neq j, \rho_{i,j} = 1\}|$. By design, all elements in an equivalence class have exactly the same knowledge (they share their knowledge with probability 1).

Thus it suffices to give a share per representative of each equivalence class, and the optimal solution is attained by giving a share to every vertex in $G^\bullet$ (which is at most n). Henceforth, we denote by n the number of vertices in the condensed graph, unless stated otherwise.

If there are fewer shares than connected components, we have $p_{col} = 0$. If there are more, then we attempt to distribute them uniformly. Let g denote the number of strongly-connected components in $G^\bullet$, then if $\ell/g < k$ we have $p_{col} = 0$. Otherwise $p_{col} = 1$.

4   Optimal Solution for Monotone Secret Sharing

In threshold secret sharing, the secret is recovered as soon as any k shares among n are known. Recent work [BDIR18] shows that high-threshold instances of Shamir's secret sharing scheme are secure against local leakage when the under-lying field is of a large prime order and the number of parties is sufficiently large.[1]

As mentioned in the introduction, the minimal collapse probability is achieved when $k = n$; in some settings there exists a value $k < n$ with the same leakage probability.

Definition 5 (Access Structure). *An access structure on $[n]$ is a predicate on subsets of $[n]$.*

A secret sharing scheme has access structure P if it allows reconstructing s for any subset of $[n]$ satisfying P, and does not allow reconstruction for any subset not satisfying P. This generalizes the threshold construction discussed previously, which corresponds to $P : S \mapsto (|S| \leq k)$.

---

[1] Contrast this with the fact that for some protocols full recovery of a multi-bit secret is possible by leaking only one bit from each share [GW17].

Definition 6 (Monotone Access Structure). *An access structure P is monotone [Toc15] if $\forall A \geq B$, $P(A) = 1 \Rightarrow P(B) = 1$.*

In particular, threshold access structures are monotone; the argument made that a minimal leakage probability is achieved by handing shares to all participants applies immediately to monotone access structures.

5 Finding Optimal Strategies

Exact computation of p_{col}. The algorithmic complexity of computing $\widehat{L}$ on a graph with n vertices is $O\left(2^{n^2}\right)$ using a direct implementation of the recursive algorithm corresponding to Definition 2. Indeed there are $n(n-1)/2$ edges to consider and each of them leads to a twofold branch in the evaluation of $\widehat{L}$. Using classical memorization techniques is it possible to reduce this cost. This is illustrated in the explicit computation of Appendix A.

Optimal Strategy. The previous algorithm gives a computable (if inefficient) way to find optimal strategies for small graphs, by exhausting subsets of $\{1, \ldots, n\}$ of size ℓ and computing the collapse probability for each of them. In the simplest case, $k = \ell = n$, there are n such subsets to be tested, whereas in the worst case, $k \approx n/2$ there are of the order of 2^{2n}. As a result, in practice it becomes intractable to compute general solutions for $n > 6$.

6 Heuristic Solutions

Sampling heuristic. One heuristic argument consists in replacing all probabilities in $\boldsymbol{\rho}$ by the nearest integer (0 or 1), so that the efficient algorithm in that case can be used. We propose a slightly more refined approach: let $0 < \eta < 1$ and h_η the function that sends x to 0 if $x \leq \eta$ and 1 otherwise. Applying h_η entrywise to $\boldsymbol{\rho}$ with $\eta = 0.5$ we fall back on the previous heuristic. For every value of η, we get a certain partition of the resulting graph G into strongly connected components. We are then interested in those components that are *stable* as we vary η. Indeed, any chose of η corresponds to an over- or an underestimation of the true leakage probabilities. We may assume $\eta \in \{i/m \mid i = 1, 2, \ldots, m-1\}$ for some integer m, consider the graphs G_η resulting from applying h_η to $\boldsymbol{\rho}$, and rank the vertices in G by the *number of strongly-connected components* that they belong to as we vary η. A vertex that remained in a single component all along ("stable") will be given many shares, whereas a vertex that often switched components ("unstable") will be given fewer shares, if any.

Furthermore, for every value of η, we get a collapse probability $p_\eta \in \{0, 1\}$: by averaging these values we can hope to obtain an approximation $p_\approx = \mathbb{E}_\eta[p_\eta]$ of the true collapse probability p_{col}.

7   Numerical Example

Consider the following (completely arbitrary) leakage matrix:

$$\rho_{i,j} = \begin{cases} 1 & \text{if } i = j \\ |\cos(1 - 2i + 3j^2)\sin(-4 + 5i^2 - 6j^3)| & \text{otherwise} \end{cases}$$

We can compute optimal strategies exactly for $n = \ell = 4$ and $k = 1, 2, 3, 4$ shares. The results are given in Table 1 and confirm that the scenario minimizing p_{col} corresponds to $k = \ell = n$. The heuristic algorithm finds that U_3 is the most stable vertex, followed by U_1, U_2, and U_0 in that order. It therefore produces the same strategy on this example.

Table 1. Optimal strategies, given as a list of i such that U_i gets a share, for $n = \ell = 4$ as a function of k.

k	Winning strategy	p_{col}	$p_\approx$	Number of strategies
1	None	1.0	1.0	4
2	[1, 3]	0.79695	0.79695	10
3	[1, 2, 3]	0.73182	0.73182	20
4	[0, 1, 2, 3]	0.71852	0.71852	35

However, it seems out of reach to perform exact computations for graphs larger than $n = 6$. Instead, we turn to the heuristic algorithm discussed in the previous section to address larger scenarios. Note that for small values of n, the exact and heuristic algorithms produce identical results.

Taking $n = 1000$, $\ell = 100$, $k = 15$ and the same ρ as above, we get $p_\approx = 0.9859$. Using $k = \ell = 100$ instead, we get $p_\approx = 0.9839$. The heuristic algorithm's running time grows roughly quadratically with respect to n, so we expect instances of size $n \approx 100{,}000$ to be within reach.

8   Conclusion

The problem of distributing a secret amongst leaking shareholders is defined, along with the "collapse probability" which measures how likely it is that at least one shareholder reconstructs the secret. We show that this probability measures the likelihood of having a root-directed spanning tree (RDST) in a realisation of the underlying graph's condensation, and provide an algorithm to compute this probability. Unfortunately a direct implementation of this exact algorithm is computationally expensive; we therefore provide an efficient (but unproven) heuristic to find optimal distribution strategies (i.e. that minimises the collapse probability).

Given n potential shareholders, a leakage matrix ρ, and ℓ shares of which k suffice for reconstruction, these algorithm tell us whom to hand the shares.

Future Work. The problem as stated is motivated by a distributed storage scenario; a "non-monotone" access structure [LMC15] may allow for a thriftier distribution of shares, assuming it is computationally difficult for the adversary to test all subsets of the shares they have collected.

Complementary to our work, but beyond the scope considered here, is the question of obtaining a reasonable estimate for the matrix ρ — what does this matrix look like in the real world? — as well as the consequences of having imperfect knowledge of this matrix on the predicted results. For instance, in the explicit computation of Appendix A, an uncertainty δ in the values of (a, b, c) results in an uncertainty $O(\delta^2)$ in p_{col}. Can this be treated in more generality?

There are also several interesting directions in which it would make sense to extend our model, which may lead to simplifications. For instance, restrictions to some families of structured graphs (e.g. grids) may allow for more efficient algorithms (or even closed-form expressions, although that seems unlikely). Alternatively, rather than minimising secret reconstruction, we may wish to *maximise* it, maybe only for a selected subset of shareholders.

Finally, precise bounds on the heuristic algorithm's errors (or maybe, better approximation algorithms) are needed.

A   Detailed Computation For (3, 3)

We denote [XYZ] $= \widehat{L}(\mathtt{graph[XYZ]})$ for the following graphs:

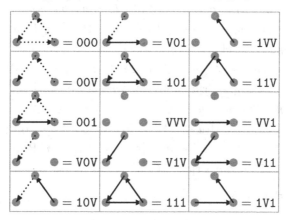

The collapse probability is:

$$
\begin{aligned}
p = \widehat{L}(\rho) &= \texttt{[000]} = \overline{a}\,\texttt{[00V]} + a\,\texttt{[001]} \\
&= \overline{a}(\overline{b}\,\texttt{[V0V]} + b\,\texttt{[10V]}) + a(\overline{b}\,\texttt{[V01]} + b\,\texttt{[101]}) \\
&= \overline{a}(\overline{b}(\overline{c}\,\texttt{[VVV]} + c\,\texttt{[V1V]}) + b\,\texttt{[10V]}) + a(\overline{b}\,\texttt{[V01]} + b\,\texttt{[101]}) \\
&= \overline{a}b\,\texttt{[10V]} + a\overline{b}\,\texttt{[V01]} + ab\,\texttt{[101]}) \\
&= \overline{a}b(\overline{c}\,\texttt{[1VV]} + c\,\texttt{[11V]}) + a\overline{b}\,\texttt{[V01]} + ab\,\texttt{[101]} \\
&= \overline{a}bc + a\overline{b}(\overline{c}\,\texttt{[VV1]} + c\,\texttt{[V11]})) + ab\,\texttt{[101]} \\
&= \overline{a}bc + a\overline{b}c + ab\,\texttt{[101]} \\
&= \overline{a}bc + a\overline{b}c + ab(\overline{c}\,\texttt{[1V1]} + c\,\texttt{[111]}) \\
&= \overline{a}bc + a\overline{b}c + ab \\
&= ab + bc + ca - 2abc
\end{aligned}
$$

B   Detailed Computation With The Heuristic Algorithm

We apply the heuristic algorithm to the same graph as in the previous section.

The collapse probability is 1 whenever any two edges are saturated, and 0 otherwise. In other terms, using that $\Pr[A \vee B] = \Pr[A] + \Pr[B] - \Pr[A \wedge B]$ and $\Pr[A \wedge B] = \Pr[A]\Pr[B \mid A]$, we have:

$$
\begin{aligned}
p_\eta &= \Pr[(a < \eta \wedge b < \eta) \vee (a < \eta \wedge c < \eta) \vee (c < \eta \wedge b < \eta)] \\
&= \Pr[a < \eta]\Pr[b < \eta] + \Pr[a < \eta]\Pr[c < \eta] + \Pr[c < \eta]\Pr[b < \eta] \\
&\quad - \Pr[a < \eta]\Pr[b < \eta]\Pr[c < \eta] \\
&\quad - \Pr[(a < \eta \wedge b < \eta) \wedge ((a < \eta \wedge c < \eta) \vee (c < \eta \wedge b < \eta))] \\
&= \Pr[a < \eta]\Pr[b < \eta] + \Pr[a < \eta]\Pr[c < \eta] + \Pr[c < \eta]\Pr[b < \eta] \\
&\quad - \Pr[a < \eta]\Pr[b < \eta]\Pr[c < \eta] \\
&\quad - \Pr[a < \eta \wedge b < \eta]\Pr[(a < \eta \wedge c < \eta) \vee (c < \eta \wedge b < \eta) \mid a < \eta \wedge b < \eta] \\
&= \Pr[a < \eta]\Pr[b < \eta] + \Pr[a < \eta]\Pr[c < \eta] + \Pr[c < \eta]\Pr[b < \eta] \\
&\quad - 2\Pr[a < \eta]\Pr[b < \eta]\Pr[c < \eta]
\end{aligned}
$$

Sampling over η this gives:

$$
p_\approx = \mathbb{E}_\eta[p_\eta] = ab + ac + bc - 2abc
$$

matching the result obtained in the previous section.

References

[BDIR18] Benhamouda, F., Degwekar, A., Ishai, Y., Rabin, T.: On the local leakage resilience of linear secret sharing schemes. In: Shacham, H., Boldyreva, A. (eds.) CRYPTO 2018. LNCS, vol. 10991, pp. 531–561. Springer, Cham (2018). https://doi.org/10.1007/978-3-319-96884-1_18

[Bla79] Blakley, G.R.: Safeguarding cryptographic keys. In: Proceedings of the National Computer Conference, vol. 48, (1979)

[DD94] Dawson, Ed., Donovan, D.M.: The breadth of Shamir's secret-sharing scheme. Comput. Secur. **13**(1), 69–78 (1994)

[GW17] Guruswami, V., Wootters, M.: Repairing Reed-Solomon codes. IEEE Trans. Inf. Theory **63**(9), 5684–5698 (2017)

[LMC15] Liu, J., Mesnager, S., Chen, L.: Secret sharing schemes with general access structures. In: Lin, D., Wang, X.F., Yung, M. (eds.) Inscrypt 2015. LNCS, vol. 9589, pp. 341–360. Springer, Cham (2016). https://doi.org/10.1007/978-3-319-38898-4_20

[Mig82] Mignotte, M.: How to share a secret. In: Beth, T. (ed.) EUROCRYPT 1982. LNCS, vol. 149, pp. 371–375. Springer, Heidelberg (1983). https://doi.org/10.1007/3-540-39466-4_27

[Sha79] Shamir, A.: How to share a secret. Commun. ACM **22**(11), 612–613 (1979)

[Tar72] Robert Endre Tarjan: Depth-first search and linear graph algorithms. SIAM J. Comput. **1**(2), 146–160 (1972)

[Toc15] Tochikubo, K.: New secret sharing schemes realizing general access structures. JIP **23**(5), 570–578 (2015)

Authentication

A Lattice-Based Enhanced Privacy ID

Nada EL Kassem[1($\boxtimes$)], Luís Fiolhais[2], Paulo Martins[2], Liqun Chen[1],
and Leonel Sousa[2]

[1] University of Surrey, Guildford, UK
{n.elkassem,liqun.chen}@surrey.ac.uk
[2] INESC-ID, Instituto Superior Técnico, Universidade de Lisboa, Lisbon, Portugal
luis.azenhas.fiolhais@tecnico.ulisboa.pt, paulo.sergio@ist.utl.pt,
las@inesc-id.pt

Abstract. The Enhanced Privacy ID (EPID) scheme is currently used
for hardware enclave attestation by an increasingly large number of platforms that implement Intel Software Guard Extensions (SGX). However,
the scheme currently deployed by Intel is supported on Elliptic Curve
Cryptography (ECC), and will become insecure should a large quantum computer become available. As part of National Institute of Standards and Technology (NIST)'s effort for the standardisation of post-
quantum cryptography, there has been a great boost in research on lattice-
based cryptography. As this type of cryptography is more widely used,
one expects that hardware platforms start integrating specific instructions that accelerate its execution. In this article, a new EPID scheme
is proposed, supported on lattice primitives, that may benefit not only
from future research developments in post-quantum cryptography, but
also from instructions that may extend Intel's Instruction Set Architecture (ISA) in the future. This paper presents a new security model for
EPID in the Universal Composability (UC) framework. The proposed
Lattice-based EPID (LEPID) scheme is proved secure under the new
model. Experimentally compared with a closely related Lattice-based
Direct Anonymous Attestation (DAA) (LDAA) scheme from related art,
it is shown that the private-key size is reduced 1.5 times, and that signature and verification times are sped up up to 1.4 and 1.1 times, respectively, for the considered parameters, when LEPID is compared with
LDAA. Moreover, the signature size compares favourably to LDAA for
small and medium-sized communities.

1 Introduction

The Enhanced Privacy ID (EPID) scheme is a fundamental part of the security
model underpinning Software Guard Extensions (SGX)'s functioning [9]. It gives
the ability to attest that a hardware enclave was successfully established on an
Intel platform.

EPID can be seen as Direct Anonymous Attestation (DAA) with different
linkability requirements [5]. The DAA scheme was built having the Trusted Plat-

© IFIP International Federation for Information Processing 2020
Published by Springer Nature Switzerland AG 2020
M. Laurent and T. Giannetsos (Eds.): WISTP 2019, LNCS 12024, pp. 15–31, 2020.
https://doi.org/10.1007/978-3-030-41702-4_2

form Module (TPM) standard in mind. In this context, the TPM holds a representation of the host machine state, and wishes to provide a verifier with a signature of the state representation, without revealing their identity. During an offline phase, an issuer provisions the TPM and the host with membership credentials. Based on this cryptographic material, the TPM and the host jointly prove that they belong to the DAA community in zero-knowledge, while producing the above-mentioned signature. Unlike other privacy-preserving systems, like group signatures, DAA does not support the property of traceability, wherein a group manager can identify the signer from a given signature.

Alternatively, the DAA provides two approaches to prevent a malicious signer from abusing their anonymity. Firstly, when a private-key is leaked, anyone can check whether a specific DAA signature was created under this key or not. Secondly, two DAA signatures created by the same signer may or may not be linked from a verifier's point of view. The linkability is controlled by a parameter called basename. When the same basename is used by the same signer for two signatures, they are linked; otherwise they are not. However, there are situations where this model does not suffice to prevent malicious actions. For instance, should an attacker corrupt a TPM and obtain the private-key without ever publishing it, there is no way to revoke it. While this latter problem can be mitigated by having TPMs use the same basename whenever they access a certain service, this option removes the anonymity for all uses with the same basename.

EPID is a more general scheme than DAA and thus does not split signers into TPMs and hosts, but also targets the creation of anonymous signatures. An EPID scheme consists of an issuer, signers, verifiers and a revocation manager. Like with DAA, one can check whether a certain signature was generated by a leaked private-key. Nonetheless, the ability to link signatures with the same basename is removed. Instead, whenever a signer is corrupted, they may be revoked by including one of their signatures as part of a revocation list. As a result, EPID is capable of revoking corrupted signers from the system, even when their private-key is kept hidden, whilst providing maximum privacy for the platforms. Enhanced Privacy ID signatures can also be constructed on the top of group signatures that allow members of a group to anonymously sign messages on behalf of the group, with the added property that a group manager can revoke the credentials of a misbehaving or compromised group member.

A post-quantum EPID scheme has been proposed in [3] built on hash and pseudorandom functions. More concretely, the EPID credential corresponds to a hash-based signature generated by the issuer, and proofs-of-knowledge are constructed from the Multi-Party Computation (MPC) in the head technique from Ishai et al. [8]. While [3] achieves signature sizes in the order of MBs, execution times are not considered. The main goal of this article is not to outperform [8], but rather to ignite research on lattice-based EPID partially propelled by the National Institute of Standards and Technology (NIST)'s effort on post-quantum cryptography standardisation [16]. By basing our construction on lattices, future versions of EPID might leverage the research resulting from this standardisation process to improve their efficiency. Moreover, since post-quantum cryptography is still in its infancy, it might be useful for implementers to consider multiple security assumptions, to mitigate the effects of cryptanalysis against one of them.

Lattices have proven to be a flexible tool in constructing cryptographic schemes, with applications ranging from digital signatures to public-key encryption and zero-knowledge proofs, while offering post-quantum security [1,2,13]. One expects that as this type of cryptography matures, an increasing number of platforms exploiting EPID ship with accelerators for lattice-based constructs [15]. Herein, by building from a recently proposed DAA scheme [10], the range of cryptographic constructs supported by lattice-based cryptography is extended to EPID. The LEPID signature size compares favourably to Lattice-based DAA (LDAA) for small and medium-sized communities.

Organisation: The next section introduces the lattice-based hard problems and the two building blocks that support the proposed LEPID scheme, namely the LDAA scheme from [10] and the Zero Knowledge Proof of Knowledge (ZKPoK) of Ring-Learning With Errors (Ring-LWE) secrets from [2]. Section 3 presents a new security model for EPID in the UC framework. The novel LEPID scheme is proposed in Sect. 4 and proven secure in Sect. 5. The performance of the LEPID scheme is discussed in Sect. 6. Finally, Sect. 7 concludes the paper.

2   Preliminaries

Throughout this paper we will use the polynomial rings $\mathcal{R}_q = \mathbb{Z}_q[X]/\langle X^n + 1 \rangle$, where $\mathbb{Z}_q$ is the quotient ring $\mathbb{Z}/q\mathbb{Z}$ and n a power of 2. We use names in bold, like $\boldsymbol{a}$, both to denote elements of $\mathcal{R}_q$ and their coefficient embeddings in $\mathbb{Z}_q^n$. $\|\boldsymbol{a}\|_\infty$ represents the infinity norm of a polynomial $\boldsymbol{a}$, $\|\boldsymbol{a}\|_\infty = \max_i |a^i|$, and $\|\boldsymbol{a}\| = \sqrt{\sum_{i=1}^n (a^i)^2}$ where the a^i are the coefficients of $\boldsymbol{a}$. $\hat{A} = (\boldsymbol{a}_1, \ldots, \boldsymbol{a}_m)$ denotes a vector where m is a positive integer and $\boldsymbol{a}_1, \ldots, \boldsymbol{a}_m$ are polynomials. $\|\hat{A}\|_\infty$ denotes the infinity norm of $\hat{A}$, defined as $\|\hat{A}\|_\infty = \max_i \|\boldsymbol{a}_i\|_\infty$. B_{3d} represents the set of vectors $\boldsymbol{u} \in \{-1, 0, 1\}^{3d}$ having exactly d coordinates equal to -1, d coordinates equal to 0, and d coordinates equal to 1. We represent a challenge set by $\mathcal{C} = \left\{ X^{c_v}, |c_v \in \{0, 1, \ldots 2n - 1\} \right\}$, where $\bar{\mathcal{C}}$ denotes the set of differences $\mathcal{C} - \mathcal{C}$ except 0. $\mathcal{D}_s^h$ represents the discrete Gaussian distribution of standard deviation s, s.t. $\Pr_{\boldsymbol{x} \leftarrow \mathcal{D}_s^h}[\|\boldsymbol{x}\| > \sqrt{2h}s] \leq 2^{-h/4}$. We define the following rejection sampling algorithm from [14] to avoid the dependency of $\boldsymbol{z}$ on the secret $\boldsymbol{b}$, $\texttt{rej}(\boldsymbol{z}, \boldsymbol{b}, \xi)$: Let $u \leftarrow [0, 1)$; if $u > 1/3 \exp\left(\frac{-2\langle \boldsymbol{z}, \boldsymbol{b} \rangle + \|\boldsymbol{b}\|^2}{2\xi^2} \right)$ return 0, else return 1, with ξ representing a standard deviation of some distribution.

Definition 1. (The Ring Short Integer Solution Problem (Ring-SIS$_{n,m,q,\beta}$)[17]). *Given m uniformly random elements $\boldsymbol{a}_i \in \mathcal{R}_q$ defining a vector $\hat{A} = (\boldsymbol{a}_1, \boldsymbol{a}_2, \ldots, \boldsymbol{a}_m)$, find a nonzero vector of polynomials $\hat{Z} \in \mathcal{R}_q^m$ of norm $\|\hat{Z}\|_\infty \leq \beta$ such that: $f_{\hat{A}}(\hat{Z}) = \sum_{i \in [m]} \boldsymbol{a}_i \boldsymbol{z}_i = \boldsymbol{0} \in \mathcal{R}_q$. The Ring Inhomogeneous Short Integer Solution (Ring $-$ ISIS$_{n,m,q,\beta}$) problem asks to find $\hat{Z}$ of norm $\|\hat{Z}\|_\infty \leq \beta$, and such that:$f_{\hat{A}}(\hat{Z}) = \boldsymbol{y} \in \mathcal{R}_q$ for some uniform random polynomial $\boldsymbol{y}$.*

Definition 2. (The Ring Learning With Error Problem (Ring-LWE) [18]). *Let χ be an error distribution defined over $\mathcal{R}$ and $s \leftarrow \mathcal{R}_q$ a uniformly random ring element, the Ring-LWE distribution $A_{s,\chi}$ over $\mathcal{R}_q \times \mathcal{R}_q$ is sampled by choosing $\boldsymbol{a} \in \mathcal{R}_q$ uniformly at random, randomly choosing the noise $\boldsymbol{e} \leftarrow \chi$ and outputting $(\boldsymbol{a}, \boldsymbol{b}) = (\boldsymbol{a}, \ \boldsymbol{sa} + \boldsymbol{e} \mod q) \in \mathcal{R}_q \times \mathcal{R}_q$. Let $\boldsymbol{u}$ be uniformly sampled from $\mathcal{R}_q$. The decision problem of Ring-LWE asks to distinguish between $(\boldsymbol{a}, \boldsymbol{b}) \leftarrow A_{s,\chi}$ and $(\boldsymbol{a}, \boldsymbol{u})$ for a uniformly sampled secret $s \leftarrow \mathcal{R}_q$. The search Ring-LWE problem asks to return the secret vector $s \in \mathcal{R}_q$ given a Ring-LWE sample $(\boldsymbol{a}, \boldsymbol{b}) \leftarrow A_{s,\chi}$.*

2.1   Lattice-Based Direct Anonymous Attestation

The DAA scheme proposed in [10] can be split at a high level into three parts. In a first part, a TPM-host pair with identifier $\mathsf{id} = (\mathsf{id}_1, ..., \mathsf{id}_\ell) \in \{0,1\}^\ell$ joins a DAA community. This consists of the TPM sampling small $\hat{X}_t = (\boldsymbol{x}_1, \dots, \boldsymbol{x}_m) \in \mathcal{R}_q^m$, and sending $\boldsymbol{u}_t = \hat{A}_t \hat{X}_t$ to the issuer, where $\hat{A}_t \in \mathcal{R}_q^m$ is part of the issuer's public-key. A signature proof of knowledge based on [12], showing that $\boldsymbol{u}$ is well formed is also sent, along with a link token that prevents two TPMs from having the same secret-key. Using its private-key, the issuer then samples small $\hat{X}_h = (\boldsymbol{x}_{m+1}, \dots, \boldsymbol{x}_{3m}) \in \mathcal{R}_q^{2m}$ such that $\hat{A}_h \hat{X}_h = \boldsymbol{u} - \boldsymbol{u}_t$, where $\hat{A}_h = [\hat{A}_\mathcal{I} | \hat{A}_0 + \sum_{i=1}^{l} \mathsf{id}_i \hat{A}_i] \in \mathcal{R}_q^{2m}$, and $\boldsymbol{u} \in \mathcal{R}_q$, $\hat{A}_\mathcal{I} \in \mathcal{R}_q^m$ and $\hat{A}_i \in \mathcal{R}_q^m$ $\forall i \in \{0, \dots, l\}$ are part of the issuer's public-key. The vector $\hat{X}_h$ is sent back to the host. After this process, the TPM and host own small key-shares satisfying

$$[X_t | X_h][\hat{A}_t | \hat{A}_h] = \boldsymbol{u}. \tag{1}$$

In a second part, the TPM and the host jointly generate a signature with respect to a message μ. The signature corresponds to a tuple (nym, bsn, π), where nym is a link token, bsn is the basename, and π is a signature-based proof:

$$\pi = \mathsf{SPK}\Big\{ \mathsf{public} := \{\mathsf{pp}, \mathsf{nym}, bsn\}, \mathsf{witness} := \{\hat{X} = (\boldsymbol{x}_1, \dots, \boldsymbol{x}_{3m}), \mathsf{id}, \ e\} :$$

$$\boldsymbol{u} = \hat{X}[\hat{A}_t | \hat{A}_h] \bmod q \ \wedge \ \|\hat{X}\|_\infty \leq \beta \ \wedge \ \mathsf{nym} = \mathcal{H}(bsn)\boldsymbol{x}_1 + e \bmod q \ \wedge \ \|e\|_\infty \leq \beta \Big\}(\mu)$$

demonstrating not only (1) but also that $\mathsf{nym} = \mathcal{H}(bsn)\boldsymbol{x}_1 + e \mod q$, where $\mathcal{H}$ is a random oracle mapping bsn to a polynomial and e is small.

A final part deals with signature verification. First, π is verified. Then, the verifier iterates over the list of revoked private-keys, consisting of the elements $\boldsymbol{x}_1^{(i)}$ of the $\hat{X}_t^{(i)}$ in (1) of the corrupt signers. In the case that $\|\mathsf{nym} - \mathcal{H}(bsn)\boldsymbol{x}_1^{(i)}\|_\infty$ is small, the signature has been generated by the i-th revoked user and is rejected. Similarly, two signatures (nym, bsn, π) and $(\mathsf{nym}', bsn, \pi')$ having the same basename are linked when $\|\mathsf{nym} - \mathsf{nym}'\|_\infty$ is small.

2.2   Zero Knowledge Proof of the Ring-LWE Secrets

The technique presented in [2] will herein be used to modify the LDAA and support the more effective revocation method of EPID. This techniques allows one to efficiently prove in zero-knowledge possession of s and e, with $2s$ and $2e$ being short, such that $2y = 2as + 2e$, for public a and y. Random $r_s, r_e \leftarrow \mathcal{D}_s$ are initially produced, and $t = ar_s + r_e$ is computed. A challenge $c = H(t) \in \{0, 1, \ldots, 2n - 1\}$ is generated and $s_s = r_s + X^c s$, $s_e = r_e + X^c e$ are outputted in response with probability $P(s_s, s_e)$, where P is chosen in a way that prevents s_s and s_e from depending on the prover's secret inputs.

3 UC Based Security Model for EPID

The security model for the DAA [7] has been modified by replacing linkability with a revocation interface, adding the signature revocation check from [6], and introducing other modifications that results in a new EPID security model in the UC framework. Our new security definition is given in the UC model with respect to an ideal functionality $\mathcal{F}_{\mathsf{EPID}}^l$. In UC, an environment $\mathcal{E}$ should not be able to distinguish with a non-negligible probability between two worlds: the real world, where each party in the EPID protocol Π executes its assigned part of the protocol and the network is controlled by an adversary $\mathcal{A}$ that communicates with $\mathcal{E}$; and the ideal world, in which all parties forward their inputs to $\mathcal{F}_{\mathsf{EPID}}^l$, which internally performs all the required tasks and creates the party's outputs. A protocol Π is said to securely realise $\mathcal{F}_{\mathsf{EPID}}^l$ if, for every adversary $\mathcal{A}$ performing an attack in the real world, there is an ideal world adversary $\mathcal{S}$ that performs the same attack in the ideal world.

An EPID scheme should satisfy: (i) unforgeability, i.e. no adversary can output a valid signature on a message μ without knowing the signer's secret key; (ii) correctness, i.e. honestly generated signatures are always valid; and (iii) anonymity, i.e. even for a corrupt issuer, no adversary can tell whether two honestly generated signatures were produced by the same signer. The UC framework allows us to focus on the analysis of a single protocol instance with a globally unique session identifier sid. $\mathcal{F}_{\mathsf{EPID}}^l$ uses session identifiers of the form $sid = (\mathcal{I}, sid')$ for some issuer $\mathcal{I}$ and a unique string sid'. In the procedures, functions CheckTtdHonest and CheckTtdCorrupt are used that return '1' when a key belongs to a honest signer that has produced no signature, and when a key belongs to a corrupt user such that there is no signature simultaneously linking back to the inputted key and another one, respectively; and return '0' otherwise. We label the checks that are done by the ideal functionality in roman numerals.

$\mathcal{F}_{\mathsf{EPID}}^l$ **Setup:** On input (SETUP, sid) from the issuer $\mathcal{I}$, $\mathcal{F}_{\mathsf{EPID}}^l$ verifies that $(\mathcal{I}, sid') = sid$ and outputs (SETUP, sid) to $\mathcal{S}$. $\mathcal{F}_{\mathsf{EPID}}^l$ receives from the simulator $\mathcal{S}$ the algorithms Kgen, sig, ver, identify and revoke. These algorithms are responsible for generating keys for honest signers, creating signatures for honest signers, verifying the validity of signatures, checking whether a signature was generated by a given key, and updating the revocation lists respectively. $\mathcal{F}_{\mathsf{EPID}}^l$ stores the algorithms, checks that the algorithms ver, identify and revoke are deterministic [Check-I], and outputs (SETUPDONE, sid) to $\mathcal{I}$.

$\mathcal{F}^l_{\text{EPID}}$ **Join:**

1. JOIN REQUEST: On input (JOIN, $sid, jsid$) from a signer $\mathcal{M}_i$, create a join session $\langle jsid, \mathcal{M}_i, \text{request} \rangle$. Output (JOINSTART, $sid, jsid, \mathcal{M}_i$) to $\mathcal{S}$.
2. JOIN REQUEST DELIVERY: Proceed upon receiving delivery notification from $\mathcal{S}$ by updating the session record to $\langle jsid, \mathcal{M}_i, \text{delivery} \rangle$. If $\mathcal{I}$ or $\mathcal{M}_i$ is honest and $\langle \mathcal{M}_i, \star, \star \rangle$ is already in Member List ML, output $\perp$ [Check II]. Otherwise, output (JOINPROCEED, $sid, jsid, \mathcal{M}_i$) to $\mathcal{I}$.
3. JOIN PROCEED: Upon receiving an approval from $\mathcal{I}$, $\mathcal{F}^l_{\text{EPID}}$ updates the session record to $\langle jsid, sid, \mathcal{M}_i, \text{complete} \rangle$. Then it outputs (JOINCOMPLETE, $sid, jsid$) to $\mathcal{S}$.
4. KEY GENERATION: On input (JOINCOMPLETE, $sid, jsid, tsk$) from $\mathcal{S}$.
   - If the signer is honest, set $tsk = \perp$, else verify that the provided tsk is eligible by performing the following two checks that are described above: CheckTtdHonest(tsk)=1 [Check III]; CheckTtdCorrupt(tsk)=1 [Check IV].
   - Insert $\langle \mathcal{M}_i, tsk \rangle$ into Member List ML, and output JOINED.

$\mathcal{F}^l_{\text{EPID}}$ **Sign:**

1. SIGN REQUEST: On input (SIGN, $sid, ssid, \mathcal{M}_i, \mu, \boldsymbol{p}$) from the signer on a message μ with respect to $\boldsymbol{p}$, the ideal functionality aborts if $\mathcal{I}$ is honest and no entry $\langle \mathcal{M}_i, \star \rangle$ exists in ML, else creates a sign session $\langle ssid, \mathcal{M}_i, \mu, \boldsymbol{p}, \text{request} \rangle$ and outputs (SIGNSTART, $sid, ssid, \mathcal{M}_i, l(\mu, \boldsymbol{p})$) to $\mathcal{S}$.
2. SIGN REQUEST DELIVERY: On input (SIGNSTART, $sid, ssid$) from $\mathcal{S}$, update the session to $\langle ssid, \mathcal{M}_i, \mu, \boldsymbol{p}, \text{delivered} \rangle$, and output (SIGNPROCEED, $sid, ssid, \mu, \boldsymbol{p}$) to $\mathcal{M}_i$.
3. SIGN PROCEED: On input (SIGNPROCEED, $sid, ssid$) from $\mathcal{M}_i$, $\mathcal{F}^l_{\text{EPID}}$ updates the records $\langle ssid, \mathcal{M}_i, \mu, \boldsymbol{p}, \text{delivered} \rangle$, and outputs (SIGNCOMPLETE, $sid, ssid, \text{KRL}, \text{SRL}$) to $\mathcal{S}$, where KRL and SRL represent the key and the signature revocation lists respectively.
4. SIGNATURE GENERATION: On input (SIGNCOMPLETE, $sid, ssid, \sigma$, KRL, SRL) from $\mathcal{S}$, if $\mathcal{M}_i$ is honest then $\mathcal{F}^l_{\text{EPID}}$ will:
   - Ignore an adversary's signature σ, and generate the signature for a fresh or established tsk.
   - Check CheckTtdHonest(tsk)=1 [Check V], and store $\langle \mathcal{M}_i, tsk \rangle$ in DomainKeys.
   - Generate the signature $\sigma \leftarrow \text{sig}(tsk, \mu, \boldsymbol{p})$.
   - Check ver($\sigma, \mu, \boldsymbol{p}, \text{KRL}, \text{SRL}$)=1 [Check VI], and check identify($\sigma, \mu, \boldsymbol{p}, tsk$) = 1 [Check VII].
   - Check that there is no signer other than $\mathcal{M}_i$ with key tsk' registered in Members or DomainKeys such that identify($\sigma, \mu, \boldsymbol{p}, tsk'$)=1 [Check VIII].
   - For all $(\sigma^*, \mu^*, \boldsymbol{p}^*) \in \text{SRL}$, find all $(tsk^*, \mathcal{M}^*)$ from Members and DomainKeys such that identify($\sigma^*, \mu^*, \boldsymbol{p}^*, \star, tsk^*$) = 1
     • Check that no two distinct keys tsk^* trace back to σ^*.
     • Check that no pair $(tsk^*, \mathcal{M}_i)$ was found.
   - If $\mathcal{M}_i$ is honest, then store $\langle \sigma, \mu, \mathcal{M}_i, \boldsymbol{p} \rangle$ in Signed and output (SIGNATURE, $sid, ssid, \sigma, \text{KRL}, \text{SRL}$).

$\mathcal{F}^l_{\mathsf{EPID}}$ **Verify**: On input $(\mathsf{VERIFY}, sid, \mu, \boldsymbol{p}, \sigma, \mathsf{KRL}, \mathsf{SRL})$, from a party $\mathcal{V}$ to check whether σ is a valid signature on a message μ with respect to $\boldsymbol{p}$, KRL and SRL, the ideal functionality does the following:

- Extract all pairs $(tsk_i, \mathcal{M}_i)$ from the DomainKeys and ML, for which identify$(\sigma, \mu, \boldsymbol{p}, tsk_i) = 1$. Set $b = 0$ if any of the following holds:
  - More than one key tsk_i was found [Check IX].
  - $\mathcal{I}$ is honest and no pair $(tsk_i, \mathcal{M}_i)$ was found [Check X].
  - An honest $\mathcal{M}_i$ was found, but no entry $\langle \star, \mu, \mathcal{M}_i, \boldsymbol{p} \rangle$ was found in Signed [Check XI].
  - There is a key $tsk^* \in \mathsf{KRL}$, such that identify$(\sigma, \mu, \boldsymbol{p}, tsk^*) = 1$ and no pair $(tsk, \mathcal{M}_i)$ for an honest $\mathcal{M}_i$ was found [Check XII].
  - For matching tsk_i and $(\sigma^*, \mu^*, \boldsymbol{p}^*) \in \mathsf{SRL}$, identify$(\sigma^*, \mu^*, \boldsymbol{p}^*, tsk_i) = 1$.
- If $b \neq 0$, set $b \leftarrow \mathrm{ver}(\sigma, \mu, \boldsymbol{p}, \mathsf{SRL}, \mathsf{KRL})$. [Check XIII]
- Add $\langle \sigma, \mu, \boldsymbol{p}, \mathsf{KRL}, \mathsf{SRL}, b \rangle$ to VerResults, and output $(\mathsf{VERIFIED}, sid, b)$ to $\mathcal{V}$.

$\mathcal{F}^l_{\mathsf{EPID}}$ **Revoke**: On input (tsk^*, KRL), the ideal functionality replaces KRL with $\mathsf{KRL} \cup tsk^*$. On input $(\sigma^*, \mu^*, \mathsf{SRL})$, the ideal functionality replaces SRL with $\mathsf{SRL} \cup \sigma^*$ after verifying σ^*.

4 The Proposed LEPID Scheme

The DAA scheme proposed in [10] is herein modified so as to support the security model described in Sect. 3. We give a general overview of the proposed Lattice-based EPID (LEPID) scheme in Subsect. 4.1 before proceeding with the details in Subsect. 4.2.

4.1 High Level Description of the LEPID Scheme

The first part of the DAA protocol described in Subsect. 2.1 is herein mirrored, with the exception that the TPM and the host are fused into a single signer. In particular, the issuer makes one further polynomial $\boldsymbol{b}$ available in Procedure 1. When requesting to join a DAA community in Procedure 2, the signer with identifier id $= (\mathrm{id}_1, ..., \mathrm{id}_\ell) \in \{0,1\}^\ell$ samples a small $\hat{X}_t = (\boldsymbol{x}_1, ..., \boldsymbol{x}_{m+1}) \in \mathcal{R}_q^{m+1}$ and sends $\boldsymbol{u}_t = [\boldsymbol{b} | \hat{A}_{\mathcal{I}}] \hat{X}_t \bmod q$ to the issuer, along with a link token $\mathsf{nym}_{\mathcal{I}} = \mathcal{H}(bsn_{\mathcal{I}})\boldsymbol{x}_1 + \boldsymbol{e}_{\mathcal{I}}$ and a zero-knowledge proof $\pi_{\boldsymbol{u}_t}$ from [10] showing that $\boldsymbol{u}_t$ is well formed. Upon receiving this message, the issuer uses $\mathsf{nym}_{\mathcal{I}}$ to check that no other signer has the same $\boldsymbol{x}_1$, verifies $\pi_{\boldsymbol{u}_t}$ and samples small $\hat{X}_h = [\hat{X}_{h_1} | \hat{X}_{h_2}] = (\boldsymbol{y}_2, ..., \boldsymbol{y}_{2m+1}) \in \mathcal{R}_q^m \times \mathcal{R}_q^m$ such that $\hat{A}_h \hat{X}_h = \boldsymbol{u} - \boldsymbol{u}_t \bmod q$, with $\hat{A}_h = [\hat{A}_{\mathcal{I}} | \hat{A}_0 + \sum_{i=1}^l \mathrm{id}_i \hat{A}_i] \in \mathcal{R}_q^{2m}$. $\hat{X}_h$ is sent back to the signer, that updates their key as $\hat{X} = (\boldsymbol{x}_1, \forall_{i=(2,...,m+1)} \boldsymbol{x}_i := \boldsymbol{x}_i + \boldsymbol{y}_i, \forall_{i=(m+2,...,2m+1)} \boldsymbol{x}_i := \boldsymbol{y}_i)$ in Procedure 3.

Signatures are generated in Procedures 4 and 5 as in Subsect. 2.1 for the DAA, but the basename is always chosen at random, generating link tokens $\mathsf{nym} = \boldsymbol{p}\boldsymbol{x}_1 + \boldsymbol{e} \bmod q$ for a uniformly random $\boldsymbol{p}$, and the proof-of-knowledge π

is as described in the Appendix of the full version of this paper [11]. In particular, this allows one to maintain linkability in the case of leaked private-keys, whilst maintaining full anonymity. In addition, when signing a message, the signer is presented with a list of signatures from revoked users and proves in zero-knowledge that their underlying x_1 was not used to produce any of those signatures. We achieve this by firstly randomising the $(\mathsf{nym}_i^* = p_i^* f_i + l_i, p_i^*)$ pairs from the list of revoked signatures, where f_i corresponds to the x_1 polynomial of the i-th revoked user and l_i has small norm, as

$$d_i = \mathsf{nym}_i^* q_i + l_i''' \tag{2}$$

$$o_i = p_i^* q_i + l_i' \tag{3}$$

for small q_i, l_i''' and l_i' sampled from a Gaussian distribution. Note that $d_i = o_i \cdot f_i + e_i$ for a small e_i. The signature includes not only d_i and o_i, but also $k_i = o_i x_1 + l_i''$ along with a zero-knowledge proof of the construction of d_i, o_i and k_i. This zero-knowledge proof is an adaptation of the one described in Subsect. 2.2, the details of which can be found in the Appendix of the full version of this paper [11].

Signature verification in Procedure 6 is similar to that of the DAA, with the difference that now the proof of the shape of d_i, o_i and k_i is verified, and the norm of $d_i - k_i$ is assessed to ascertain whether the x_1 used to produce the signature under verification is the same as the one used to produce the i-th revoked signature. Finally, the community revocation manager may revoke users by updating the list of revoked private-keys (KRL) or the list of signatures of revoked users (SRL) using Procedure 7.

4.2   Detailed Description of the LEPID Scheme

We now present our LEPID scheme in detail. We start by recalling some standard functionalities that are used in the UC model of the DAA [7]:

- $\mathcal{F}_{\mathsf{CA}}$ is a common certificate authority functionality that is available to all parties.
- $\mathcal{F}_{\mathsf{CRS}}$ is a common reference string functionality that provides participants with all system parameters.
- $\mathcal{F}_{\mathsf{auth}}^*$ is a special authenticated communication functionality that provides an authenticated channel between the issuer and the signer.

The LEPID scheme includes the Setup, Join, Sign, Verify and Revoke procedures that are as follows.

Procedure 1 (Setup). $\mathcal{F}_{\mathsf{CRS}}$ creates the system parameters: $\mathsf{sp} = (\lambda, t, q, n, m, \mathcal{R}_q, \beta, \ell, r, s, \xi)$, where λ, t are positive integer security parameters, β is a positive real number such that $\beta < q$, ℓ is the length of the users' identifiers, and r, s and ξ represent standard deviations of Gaussian distributions.

Upon input (SETUP, sid), where sid is a unique session identifier, the issuer first checks that $sid = (\mathcal{I}, sid')$ for some sid', then creates its key pair. The Issuer's public key is $\mathsf{pp} = (\mathsf{sp}, \boldsymbol{b}, \hat{A}_\mathcal{I}, \hat{A}_0, \hat{A}_1, \ldots, \hat{A}_\ell, \boldsymbol{u}, \mathcal{H}_0, \mathcal{H}, H)$, where $\hat{A}_\mathcal{I}, \hat{A}_i (i = 0, 1, \ldots, \ell) \in \mathcal{R}_q^m$, $\boldsymbol{b}, \boldsymbol{u} \in \mathcal{R}_q$, $\mathcal{H}_0 : \{0,1\}^* \to \{1,2,3\}^t$, $\mathcal{H} : \{0,1\}^* \to \mathcal{R}_q$, and $H : \{0,1\}^* \to \{0,1,2,\ldots,2n-1\}$. The Issuer's private key is $\hat{T}_\mathcal{I}$, which is the trapdoor of $\hat{A}_\mathcal{I}$ with $\|\hat{T}_\mathcal{I}\|_\infty \leq \beta$.

The issuer initialises the Member List $\mathsf{ML} \leftarrow \emptyset$. The issuer proves that his secret key is well formed in $\pi_\mathcal{I}$, and registers the key $(\hat{T}_\mathcal{I}, \pi_\mathcal{I})$ with $\mathcal{F}_{\mathsf{CA}}$ and outputs (SETUPDONE, sid).

Procedure 2 (Join Request). On input query (JOIN, $sid, jsid, \mathcal{M}$), the signer $\mathcal{M}$ forwards (JOIN, $sid, jsid$) to $\mathcal{I}$, who replies by sending $(sid, jsid, \rho, bsn_\mathcal{I})$ back to the signer, where ρ is a uniform random nonce $\rho \leftarrow \{0,1\}^\lambda$, and $bsn_\mathcal{I}$ is the issuer's base name. The signer $\mathcal{M}$ proceeds as follows:

1. It checks that no such entry exists in its storage.
2. It samples a private key: $\boldsymbol{x}_1 \leftarrow \mathcal{D}_s$ and $(\boldsymbol{x}_2, \ldots, \boldsymbol{x}_{m+1}) \leftarrow \mathcal{D}_r^m$. Let $\hat{X}_t = (\boldsymbol{x}_1, \ldots, \boldsymbol{x}_{m+1})$ correspond to $\mathcal{M}$'s secret key with the condition $\|(\boldsymbol{x}_2, \ldots, \boldsymbol{x}_{m+1})\|_\infty \leq \beta/2$ and $\|\boldsymbol{x}_1\|_\infty \leq \beta$. $\mathcal{M}$ stores its key as $(sid, \hat{X}_t)$, and computes the corresponding public key $\boldsymbol{u}_t = [\boldsymbol{b}|\hat{A}_\mathcal{I}]\hat{X}_t \bmod q$, a link token $\mathsf{nym}_\mathcal{I} = \mathcal{H}(bsn_\mathcal{I})\boldsymbol{x}_1 + \boldsymbol{e}_\mathcal{I} \bmod q$ for some error $\boldsymbol{e}_\mathcal{I} \leftarrow \mathcal{D}_s$ such that $\|\boldsymbol{e}_\mathcal{I}\|_\infty \leq \beta$, and generates a signature based proof:

$$\pi_{\boldsymbol{u}_t} = \mathsf{SPK}\Big\{\mathsf{public} := \{\mathsf{pp}, \boldsymbol{u}_t, bsn_\mathcal{I}, \mathsf{nym}_\mathcal{I}\}, \mathsf{witness} := \{\hat{X}_t = (\boldsymbol{x}_1, \ldots, \boldsymbol{x}_{m+1}),$$

$$\boldsymbol{e}_\mathcal{I}\}, \boldsymbol{u}_t = [\boldsymbol{b}|\hat{A}_\mathcal{I}]\hat{X}_t \bmod q \wedge \|\hat{X}_t/\boldsymbol{x}_1\|_\infty \leq \beta/2 \wedge \|\boldsymbol{x}_1\| \leq \beta$$

$$\wedge \mathsf{nym}_\mathcal{I} = \mathcal{H}(bsn_\mathcal{I})\boldsymbol{x}_1 + \boldsymbol{e}_\mathcal{I} \bmod q \wedge \|\boldsymbol{e}_\mathcal{I}\|_\infty \leq \beta\Big\}(\rho).$$

3. It sends $(\mathsf{nym}_\mathcal{I}, \boldsymbol{u}_t, \pi_{\boldsymbol{u}_t})$ to the issuer by giving $\mathcal{F}_{\mathsf{auth}}^*$ an input (SEND, $\mathsf{nym}_\mathcal{I}$, $\pi_{\boldsymbol{u}_t}, sid, jsid$).

$\mathcal{I}$, upon receiving (SENT, $\mathsf{nym}_\mathcal{I}, \pi_{\boldsymbol{u}_t}, sid, jsid, \mathcal{M}$) from $\mathcal{F}_{\mathsf{auth}}^*$, verifies the proof $\pi_{\boldsymbol{u}_t}$ and makes sure that the signer $\mathcal{M} \notin \mathsf{ML}$. $\mathcal{I}$ stores $(jsid, \mathsf{nym}_\mathcal{I}, \pi_{\boldsymbol{u}_t}, \mathcal{M})$, and generates the message (JOINPROCEED, $sid, jsid, \mathsf{id}, \pi_{\boldsymbol{u}_t}$), for some identity $\mathsf{id} \in \{0,1\}^\ell$ assigned to $\mathcal{M}$, and not used before by any joined member.

Procedure 3 (Join Proceed). If the signer chooses to proceed with the Join session, the message (JOINPROCEED, $sid, jsid$) is sent to the issuer, who performs as follows:

1. It checks the record $(jsid, \mathsf{nym}_\mathcal{I}, \mathsf{id}, \mathcal{M}, \pi_{\boldsymbol{u}_t})$. For all $\mathsf{nym}_\mathcal{I}'$ from the previous Join records, the issuer checks whether $\|\mathsf{nym}_\mathcal{I} - \mathsf{nym}_\mathcal{I}'\|_\infty \leq 2\beta$ holds; if yes, the issuer further checks if $\boldsymbol{u}_t = \boldsymbol{u}_t'$. If the equality $\boldsymbol{u}_t = \boldsymbol{u}_t'$ holds, the issuer will jump to Step 4 returning $\hat{X}_h = \hat{X}_h'$, if not the issuer will abort. Note that this double check will make sure that no two EPID keys will include the same $\boldsymbol{x}_1$ value.

2. For all $\text{nym}_{\mathcal{I}}^*$ in the Issuer's Revocation record IR, the issuer checks whether the equation

$$\|\text{nym}_{\mathcal{I}} - \text{nym}_{\mathcal{I}}^*\|_\infty \leq 2\beta$$

holds, if yes the issuer aborts.

3. It calculates the vector of polynomials $\hat{A}_h = [\hat{A}_{\mathcal{I}}|\hat{A}_0 + \sum_{i=1}^{\ell} \text{id}_i \hat{A}_i] \in \mathcal{R}_q^{2m}$.

4. It samples, using the issuer's private key $\hat{T}_{\mathcal{I}}$, a preimage $\hat{X}_h = [\hat{X}_{h_1}|\hat{X}_{h_2}] = (\boldsymbol{y}_2, ..., \boldsymbol{y}_{2m+1}) \in \mathcal{D}_r^m \times \mathcal{D}_s^m$ of $\boldsymbol{u} - \boldsymbol{u}_t$ such that $\hat{A}_h \hat{X}_h = \boldsymbol{u}_h = \boldsymbol{u} - \boldsymbol{u}_t \mod q$ and $\|\hat{X}_{h_1}\|_\infty \leq \beta/2$ and $\|\hat{X}_{h_2}\|_\infty \leq \beta$.

5. The issuer adds $(\text{nym}_{\mathcal{I}}, \text{id}, \mathcal{M}, \pi_{\boldsymbol{u}_t})$ to his data base, and sends $(sid, jsid, \hat{X}_h)$ to $\mathcal{M}$ via $\mathcal{F}_{\text{auth}}^*$.

When $\mathcal{M}$ receives the message $(sid, jsid, \hat{X}_h)$, it checks that the equations $\hat{A}_h \hat{X}_h = \boldsymbol{u}_h \mod q$ and $\boldsymbol{u} = \boldsymbol{u}_t + \boldsymbol{u}_h$ are satisfied with $\|\hat{X}_{h_1}\|_\infty \leq \beta/2$ and $\|\hat{X}_{h_2}\|_\infty \leq \beta$. It stores $(sid, \mathcal{M}, \text{id}, \hat{X}_h, \boldsymbol{u}_t)$ and outputs (JOINED, $sid, jsid$). $\mathcal{M}$ then computes $\hat{X} = (\boldsymbol{x}_1, \forall_{i=(2,...,m+1)}\boldsymbol{x}_i := \boldsymbol{x}_i + \boldsymbol{y}_i, \forall_{i=(m+2,...,2m+1)}\boldsymbol{x}_i := \boldsymbol{y}_i)$, where $\|\hat{X}\|_\infty \leq \beta$.

Procedure 4 (Sign Request). Upon input (SIGN, $sid, ssid, \mathcal{M}, \mu$), the signer does the following:

1. It makes sure to have a Join record $(sid, \text{id}, \hat{X}, \mathcal{M})$.
2. It generates a sign entry $(sid, ssid, \mu)$ in its record.
3. Finally it outputs (SIGNPROCEED, $sid, ssid, \mu$).

Procedure 5 (Sign Proceed). When $\mathcal{M}$ gets permission to proceed for $ssid$, the signer proceeds as follows:

1. It retrieves the records $(sid, \text{id}, \pi_{\boldsymbol{u}_t})$ and $(sid, ssid, \mu)$.
2. $\mathcal{M}$ samples a random polynomial $\boldsymbol{p}$ and computes the polynomial $\text{nym} = \boldsymbol{p}\boldsymbol{x}_1 + \boldsymbol{e} \mod q$, for an error term $\boldsymbol{e} \leftarrow \mathcal{D}_s$ such that $\|\boldsymbol{e}\|_\infty \leq \beta$. $\mathcal{M}$ then generates a signature based knowledge proof π.

$$\pi = \mathsf{SPK}\Big\{\text{public} := \{\text{pp}, \text{nym}, \boldsymbol{p}\},$$

$$\text{witness} := \{\hat{X} = (\boldsymbol{x}_1, ..., \boldsymbol{x}_{2m+1}), \text{id}, \boldsymbol{e}\} :$$

$$[\boldsymbol{b}|\hat{A}_h]\hat{X} = \boldsymbol{u} \; \wedge \; \|\hat{X}\|_\infty \leq \beta \; \wedge \; \text{nym} = \boldsymbol{p}\boldsymbol{x}_1 + \boldsymbol{e} \; \wedge \; \|\boldsymbol{e}\|_\infty \leq \beta\Big\}(\mu).$$

The details of the proof π are presented in the Appendix of the full version of this paper [11].

3. The signer proves that it is not using any of the keys that produced a revoked signature $(\sigma_i^*, \boldsymbol{p}_i^*, \text{nym}_i^*)$ in the signature revocation list (more details about the proof can be found in the Appendix of the full version of this paper [11]).
   - Let $\text{nym}_i^* = \boldsymbol{p}_i^*\boldsymbol{f}_i + \boldsymbol{l}_i$, where $(\boldsymbol{f}_i, \boldsymbol{l}_i)$ were used before to create nym_i^* by some $\mathcal{M}_i^*$ that generated a revoked signature $\sigma_i^* \in \text{SRL}$. $\mathcal{M}$ proceeds as follows:
     - $\boldsymbol{q}_i, \boldsymbol{l}_i', \boldsymbol{l}_i'', \boldsymbol{l}_i''' \leftarrow \mathcal{D}_s$

- $o_i = p_i^* q_i + l_i'$, $k_i = o_i x_1 + l_i''$, $d_i = \mathsf{nym}_i^* q_i + l_i'''$
- $r_{x_1}, r_e, r_{q_i}, r_{l_i'}, r_{l_i''}, r_{l_i'''} \leftarrow \mathcal{D}_s$
- $t_{\mathsf{nym}} = pr_{x_1} + r_e$, $t_{o_i} = p_i^* r_{q_i} + r_{l_i'}$,
  $t_{k_i} = o_i r_{x_1} + r_{l_i''}$, $t_{d_i} = \mathsf{nym}_i^* r_{q_i} + r_{l_i'''}$.

  - Calculates the challenge $c_v = H(t_{\mathsf{nym}} | t_{o_i} | t_{k_i} | t_{d_i} | \mu) \in \{0, 1, 2, \ldots, 2n - 1\}$.
  - The following responses are computed:
    - $s_{x_1} = r_{x_1} + X^{c_v} x_1$, $s_e = r_e + X^{c_v} e$, $s_{q_i} = r_{q_i} + X^{c_v} q_i$,
      $s_{l_i'} = r_{l_i'} + X^{c_v} l_i'$, $s_{l_i''} = r_{l_i''} + X^{c_v} l_i''$, $s_{l_i'''} = r_{l_i'''} + X^{c_v} l_i'''$.

      Abort if any of these rejection samples outputs 1:
    - $\mathsf{rej}(s_{x_1}, X^{c_v} x_1, \xi)$, $\mathsf{rej}(s_e, X^{c_v} e, \xi)$, $\mathsf{rej}(s_{q_i}, X^{c_v} q_i, \xi)$,
      $\mathsf{rej}(s_{l_i'}, X^{c_v} l_i', \xi)$, $\mathsf{rej}(s_{l_i''}, X^{c_v} l_i'', \xi)$ or $\mathsf{rej}(s_{l_i'''}, X^{c_v} l_i''', \xi)$.

4. Finally, $\mathcal{M}$ outputs $\sigma = (\pi, \mathsf{nym}, o_i, k_i, d_i, s_{x_1}, s_e, s_{q_i}, s_{l_i'}, s_{l_i''}, s_{l_i'''}, c_v, \mathsf{KRL}, \mathsf{SRL})$.

Procedure 6 (Verify). Let KRL denotes the revocation list with all the rogue signer's secret keys x_1^*. Upon input $(\mathsf{VERIFY}, sid, \sigma, \mu, \mathsf{KRL}, \mathsf{SRL})$, the verifier proceeds as follows:

1. It checks the zero-knowledge proof regarding the statement: $\{[b|\hat{A}_h]\hat{X} = u \wedge \|\hat{X}\|_\infty \leq \beta \wedge \mathsf{nym} = p x_1 + e \mod q \wedge \|e\|_\infty \leq \beta.\}$
2. For all $x_1^* \in \mathsf{KRL}$, if $\|p x_1^* - \mathsf{nym}\|_\infty \leq \beta$ the verifier outputs 0.
3. For all $\sigma_i^* = (\pi_{\mathsf{nym}_i^*}, \mathsf{nym}_i^*, p_i^*) \in \mathsf{SRL}$, the verifier
   (a) computes:
     - $t'_{k_i} = o_i s_{x_1} + s_{l_i''} - X^{c_v} k_i$, $t'_{d_i} = \mathsf{nym}_i^* s_{q_i} + s_{l_i'''} - X^{c_v} d_i$,
       $t'_{o_i} = p_i^* s_{q_i} + s_{l_i'} - X^{c_v} o_i$, $t'_{\mathsf{nym}} = p s_{x_1} + s_e - X^{c_v} \mathsf{nym}$.
   (b) checks $c_v \stackrel{?}{=} H(t'_{\mathsf{nym}} | t'_{o_i} | t'_{k_i} | t'_{d_i} | \mu)$ and that all the following norms satisfy $\|s_{x_1}\|_\infty, \|s_e\|_\infty, \|s_{q_i}\|_\infty, \|s_{l_i'}\|_\infty, \|s_{l_i''}\|_\infty, \|s_{l_i'''}\|_\infty \leq \beta + \sqrt{n}\beta$.
4. For all $\sigma_i^* = (\pi_{\mathsf{nym}_i^*}, \mathsf{nym}_i^*, p_i^*)$, the verifier checks $2\|d_i - k_i\| < \Gamma$, where Γ is a function of β. If $2\|d_i - k_i\| < \Gamma$ the verifier outputs 0, otherwise 1.

Procedure 7 (Revoke). On input $(\mathsf{Revoke}, sid, x_1^*, \mathsf{KRL})$ or $(\mathsf{Revoke}, sid, \sigma^*, \mu^*, \mathsf{SRL})$, the revocation manager adds x_1^* to KRL or σ^* to SRL after verifying σ^*.

5 A Sketched Security Proof for LEPID

In this section, we provide a sketch of the security proof of the LEPID scheme. A detailed security proof is presented in the Appendix of the full version of this paper [11]. A variant of the sequence of games of [7] is presented, showing that no environment $\mathcal{E}$ can distinguish the real world protocol Π with an adversary $\mathcal{A}$, from the ideal world $\mathcal{F}_{\mathsf{EPID}}^l$ with a simulator $\mathcal{S}$. Starting with the real world protocol game, we change the protocol game by game in a computationally indistinguishable way, finally ending with the ideal world protocol.

Game 1. This is the real world protocol.

Game 2. An entity C is introduced, that receives all inputs from the honest parties and simulates Π for them. This is equivalent to Game 1.

Game 3. C is split into $\mathcal{F}$ and $\mathcal{S}$. $\mathcal{F}$ behaves as an ideal functionality, receiving all inputs and forwarding them to $\mathcal{S}$, who simulates the real world protocol for honest parties. $\mathcal{S}$ sends the outputs to F, who forwards them to $\mathcal{E}$. This game is similar to Game 2, but with a different structure.

Game 4. $\mathcal{F}$ now behaves differently in the setup interface. It stores the algorithms for the issuer $\mathcal{I}$, and checks that the structure of *sid* is correct for an honest $\mathcal{I}$, aborting if not. In case $\mathcal{I}$ is corrupt, $\mathcal{S}$ extracts the secret key for $\mathcal{I}$ and proceeds in the setup interface on behalf of $\mathcal{I}$. Clearly $\mathcal{E}$ will notice no change.

Game 5. $\mathcal{F}$ now performs the verification and key revokation checks instead of forwarding them to $\mathcal{S}$. There are no protocol messages and the outputs are exactly as the real world protocol. However, the verification algorithm that $\mathcal{F}$ uses does not contain any key or signature revocation checks. $\mathcal{F}$ can perform this check separately, so the outcomes are equal.

Game 6. $\mathcal{F}$ stores in its records the members that have joined. If $\mathcal{I}$ is honest, $\mathcal{F}$ stores the secret key *tsk*, extracted from $\mathcal{S}$, for corrupt platforms. $\mathcal{S}$ always has enough information to simulate the real world protocol except when the issuer is the only honest party. In this case, $\mathcal{S}$ does not know who initiated the join, and so cannot make a join query with $\mathcal{F}$ on the signer's behalf. Thus, to deal with this case, $\mathcal{F}$ can safely choose any corrupt signer and put it into Members. The identities of signers are only used for creating signatures for honest signers, so corrupted signers do not matter. In the case that the signer is already registered in Members, $\mathcal{F}$ would abort the protocol, but $\mathcal{I}$ will have already tested this case before continuing with the query JOINPROCEED. Hence $\mathcal{F}$ will not abort. Thus in all cases, $\mathcal{F}$ and $\mathcal{S}$ can interact to simulate the real world protocol.

Game 7. (Anonymity). In this game, $\mathcal{F}$ creates anonymous signatures for honest platforms by running the algorithms defined in the setup interface. Let us start by defining Game $7.k.k'$. In this game $\mathcal{F}$ handles the first k' signing inputs of $\mathcal{M}_i$ for $i < k$ using algorithms, and subsequent inputs are forwarded to $\mathcal{S}$ who creates signatures as before. We note that Game $7.0.0 =$ Game 6. For increasing k', Game $7.k.k'$ will be at some stage equal to Game $7.k + 1.0$, this is because there can only be a polynomial number of signing queries to be processed. Therefore, for large enough k and k', $\mathcal{F}$ handles all the signing queries of all signers, and Game 7 is indistinguishable from Game $7.k.k'$. To prove that Game $7.k.k'+1$ is indistinguishable from Game $7.k.k'$, suppose that there exists an environment that can distinguish a signature of an honest party using $tsk = \boldsymbol{x}_1$ from a signature using a different $tsk^j = \boldsymbol{x}_1^j$, then the environment can solve the Decision Ring -LWE Problem.

The first $j \leq k'$ signing queries on behalf of $\mathcal{M}_k$ are handled by $\mathcal{F}$ using the algorithms, and subsequent inputs are then forwarded to $\mathcal{S}$ as before. Now suppose that F outputs the tuples $(\mathsf{nym}^j, \boldsymbol{p}^j, \boldsymbol{o}_i^j, \boldsymbol{k}_i^j, \boldsymbol{d}_i^j, \boldsymbol{s}_{x_1}^j, \boldsymbol{s}_e^j, \boldsymbol{s}_{q_i}^j, \boldsymbol{s}_{l_i'}^j, \boldsymbol{s}_{l_i''}^j, \boldsymbol{s}_{l_i'''}^j, c_v^j, \mathsf{SRL})$ for $j \leq k'$, with $\mathsf{nym}^j = \boldsymbol{p}^j \boldsymbol{x}_1 + \boldsymbol{e}^j$, for an error term $\boldsymbol{e}_j \leftarrow \mathcal{D}_s$, and the remaining proofs are honestly generated. The $j = k' + 1$-th query for $\mathcal{M}_k$ is as follows: $(\mathsf{nym}^{\mathcal{S}}, \boldsymbol{p}^{\mathcal{S}}, \boldsymbol{o}_i^{\mathcal{S}}, \boldsymbol{k}_i^s, \boldsymbol{d}_i^{\mathcal{S}}, \boldsymbol{s}_{x_1}^{\mathcal{S}}, \boldsymbol{s}_e^{\mathcal{S}}, \boldsymbol{s}_{q_i}^{\mathcal{S}}, \boldsymbol{s}_{l_i'}^{\mathcal{S}}, \boldsymbol{s}_{l_i''}^{\mathcal{S}}, \boldsymbol{s}_{l_i'''}^{\mathcal{S}}, c_v^{\mathcal{S}}, \mu^{\mathcal{S}}, \mathsf{SRL})$. $\mathcal{S}$ is challenged to decide if $(\mathsf{nym}^\mathcal{S}, \boldsymbol{p}^\mathcal{S}, \boldsymbol{o}_i^\mathcal{S}, \boldsymbol{k}_i^s, \boldsymbol{d}_i^\mathcal{S}, \boldsymbol{s}_{x_1}^\mathcal{S}, \boldsymbol{s}_e^\mathcal{S}, \boldsymbol{s}_{q_i}^\mathcal{S}, \boldsymbol{s}_{l_i'}^\mathcal{S}, \boldsymbol{s}_{l_i''}^\mathcal{S}, \boldsymbol{s}_{l_i'''}^\mathcal{S}, c_v^\mathcal{S}, \mu^\mathcal{S}, \mathsf{SRL})$ is chosen from a Ring LWE distribution for some secret $\boldsymbol{x}_1$ or uniformly at random. $\mathcal{S}$ proceeds in simulating the signer without knowing the secret $\boldsymbol{x}_1$. $\mathcal{S}$ can answer all the H queries, as $\mathcal{S}$ is controlling $\mathcal{F}_{\mathsf{CRS}}$. $\mathcal{S}$ sets: $\boldsymbol{t}_{k_i}^\mathcal{S} = \boldsymbol{o}_i^\mathcal{S} \boldsymbol{s}_{x_1}^\mathcal{S} + \boldsymbol{s}_{l_i''}^\mathcal{S} - X^{c_v^\mathcal{S}} \boldsymbol{k}_i^\mathcal{S}$; $\boldsymbol{t}_{d_i}^\mathcal{S} = \mathsf{nym}_i^* \boldsymbol{s}_{q_i}^\mathcal{S} +$ $\boldsymbol{s}_{l_i'''}^\mathcal{S} - X^{c_v^\mathcal{S}} \boldsymbol{d}_i^\mathcal{S}$; $\boldsymbol{t}_{o_i}^\mathcal{S} = \boldsymbol{p}_i^* \boldsymbol{s}_{q_i}^\mathcal{S} + \boldsymbol{s}_{l_i'}^\mathcal{S} - X^{c_v^\mathcal{S}} \boldsymbol{o}_i^\mathcal{S}$; $\boldsymbol{t}_{\mathsf{nym}}^\mathcal{S} = \boldsymbol{p}^\mathcal{S} \boldsymbol{s}_{x_1}^\mathcal{S} + \boldsymbol{s}_e^\mathcal{S} - X^{c_v^\mathcal{S}} \mathsf{nym}^\mathcal{S}$; and, finally, $c_v^\mathcal{S} \; : \; = H(\boldsymbol{t}_{\mathsf{nym}}^\mathcal{S} | \boldsymbol{t}_{o_i}^\mathcal{S} | \boldsymbol{t}_{k_i}^\mathcal{S} | \boldsymbol{t}_{d_i}^\mathcal{S} | \mu^\mathcal{S})$. For $i > k' + 1$, $\mathcal{S}$ outputs the tuples $(\mathsf{nym}^j, \boldsymbol{p}^j, \boldsymbol{o}_i^j, \boldsymbol{k}_i^j, \boldsymbol{d}_i^j, \boldsymbol{s}_{x_1}^j, \boldsymbol{s}_e^j, \boldsymbol{s}_{q_i}^j, \boldsymbol{s}_{l_i'}^j, \boldsymbol{s}_{l_i''}^j, \boldsymbol{s}_{l_i'''}^j, c_v^j, \mu^j, \mathsf{SRL})$, with $\mathsf{nym}^j = \boldsymbol{p}^j \boldsymbol{x}_1^j + \boldsymbol{e}^j$ mod q, for some freshly generated secret $\boldsymbol{x}_1^j$ and error term $\boldsymbol{e}^j \leftarrow \mathcal{D}_s$. For each case, $\mathcal{M}_k$ can provide a simulated proof as follows. $\mathcal{S}$ sets $\boldsymbol{t}_{k_i}^j = \boldsymbol{o}_i^j \boldsymbol{s}_{x_1}^j + \boldsymbol{s}_{l_i''}^j - X^{c_v^j} \boldsymbol{k}_i^j$; $\boldsymbol{t}_{d_i}^j = \mathsf{nym}_i^* \boldsymbol{s}_{q_i}^j + \boldsymbol{s}_{l_i'''}^j - X^{c_v^j} \boldsymbol{d}_i^j$; $\boldsymbol{t}_{o_i}^j = \boldsymbol{p}_i^* \boldsymbol{s}_{q_i}^j + \boldsymbol{s}_{l_i'}^j - X^{c_v^j} \boldsymbol{o}_i^j$; $\boldsymbol{t}_{\mathsf{nym}}^j = \boldsymbol{p}^j \boldsymbol{s}_{x_1}^j + \boldsymbol{s}_e^j - X^{c_v^j} \mathsf{nym}^j$; and, finally, $c_v^j \; := H(\boldsymbol{t}_{\mathsf{nym}}^j | \boldsymbol{t}_{o_i}^j | \boldsymbol{t}_{k_i}^j | \boldsymbol{t}_{d_i}^j | \mu^j)$.

Thus, any distinguisher between Game 7.$k.k'$ and Game 7.$k.k' + 1$ can solve the Decision Ring LWE Problem.

Game 8. $\mathcal{F}$ now no longer informs $\mathcal{S}$ about the message and $\boldsymbol{p}$ that are being signed. If the signer $\mathcal{M}$ is honest, then $\mathcal{S}$ can learn nothing about the message μ and $\boldsymbol{p}$. Instead, $\mathcal{S}$ knows only the leakage $l(\mu, \boldsymbol{p})$. To simulate the real world, $\mathcal{S}$ chooses a pair $(\mu', \boldsymbol{p}')$ such that $l(\mu', \boldsymbol{p}') = l(\mu, \boldsymbol{p})$. An environment $\mathcal{E}$ observes no difference, and thus Game 8 = Game 7.

Game 9. If $\mathcal{I}$ is honest, then $\mathcal{F}$ now only allows members that joined to sign. An honest signer will always check whether it has joined before signing in the real world protocol, so there is no difference for honest signers. Therefore Game 9 = Game 8.

Game 10. When storing a new $tsk = \boldsymbol{x}_1$, $\mathcal{F}$ checks $\mathsf{CheckTskCorrupt}(tsk) = 1$ or $\mathsf{CheckTskHonest}(tsk) = 1$. We want to show that these checks will always pass. In fact, valid signatures always satisfy $\mathsf{nym} = \boldsymbol{p}\boldsymbol{x}_1 + \boldsymbol{e}$ where $\|\boldsymbol{x}_1\|_\infty \leq \beta$ and $\|\boldsymbol{e}\|_\infty \leq \beta$. By the unique Shortest Vector Problem, there exists only one tuple $(\boldsymbol{x}_1, \boldsymbol{e})$ such that $\|\boldsymbol{x}_1\|_\infty \leq \beta$ and $\|\boldsymbol{e}\|_\infty \leq \beta$ for small enough β. Thus, $\mathsf{CheckTskCorrupt}(tsk)$ will always give the correct output. Also, due to the large min-entropy of discrete Gaussians the probability of sampling $\boldsymbol{x}_1' = \boldsymbol{x}_1$, and thus of having a signature already using the same $tsk = \boldsymbol{x}_1$, is negligible, which implies that $\mathsf{CheckTskHonest}(tsk)$ will give the correct output with overwhelming probability. Hence Game 10 = Game 9.

Game 11. (Completeness). In this game, $\mathcal{F}$ checks that honestly generated signatures are always valid. This is true as sig algorithm always produces signatures passing through verification checks. Those signatures satisfy $\mathsf{identify}(tsk, \sigma, \mu, \boldsymbol{p}) = 1$, which is checked via nym. $\mathcal{F}$ also makes sure, using its internal records Members and DomainKeys that honest users are not sharing the same secret key tsk. If there exists a key $tsk' = \boldsymbol{x}_1'$ in Members and DomainKeys such that $\|\mathsf{nym} - \boldsymbol{p}\boldsymbol{x}_1'\|_\infty \leq \beta$, then this breaks search Ring-LWE.

Game 12. Check-IX is added to ensure that there are no multiple tsk tracing back to the same signature. Since there exists only one pair $(\boldsymbol{x}_1, \boldsymbol{e}_\mathcal{I})$, $\|\boldsymbol{x}_1\|_\infty \leq \beta$, $\|\boldsymbol{e}_\mathcal{I}\|_\infty \leq \beta$, satisfying $\mathsf{nym}_\mathcal{I} = \mathcal{H}(bsn_\mathcal{I})\boldsymbol{x}_1 + \boldsymbol{e}_\mathcal{I}$, two different signers cannot share the same $\boldsymbol{x}_1$, thus any valid signature traces back to a single tsk.

Game 13. (Unforgeability). To prevent accepting signatures that were issued by the use of join credentials not issued by an honest issuer, $\mathcal{F}$ further adds Check-X. This is due to the unforgeability of Boyen signatures [4].

Game 14. (Unforgeability). Check-XI is added to $\mathcal{F}$, preventing the forging of signatures with honest tsk and credentials. If a valid signature is given on a message that the signer has never signed, the proof could not have been simulated. $\boldsymbol{x}_1$ would be extracted and Ring-LWE would be broken. So Game 14 = Game 13.

Game 15. Check-XII is added to $\mathcal{F}$, ensuring that honest signers keys are not being revoked. If an honest signer is simulated by means of the Ring-LWE problem instance and a proper key KRL is found, it must be the secret key of the target instance. This is equivalent to solving the search Ring-LWE problem.

Game 16. $\mathcal{F}$ now performs signature based revocation when verifying signatures. $\mathcal{F}$ checks that there is no $(\sigma^*, \mathsf{nym}^*, \boldsymbol{p}^*) \in \mathsf{SRL}$ such that for some matching tsk_i and $(\sigma^*, \mu^*, \boldsymbol{p}^*) \in \mathsf{SRL}$, we have $\mathsf{identify}(\sigma^*, \mu^*, \boldsymbol{p}^*, tsk_i) = 1$. By the soundness of the proof presented in the Appendix of the full version of this paper [11], this check will always pass with overwhelming probability.   □

6   Experimental Results

Let $q \geq 2$ represents an integer modulus such that $q = poly(n)$. For correctness, we require the main hardness parameter n, to be large enough (e.g., $n \geq 100$) and $q > \beta$ as both being at least a small polynomial in n. We also let $m = O(\log q)$ as in [17]. A concrete choice of parameters can be as follows: $n = 512$, $l = 32$, $q = 8380417$, $m = 24$, and $\beta = 275$.

Both LDAA and LEPID were implemented in C, emulating all entities in a single machine. The code was compiled with gcc 4.8.5 with the -O3 and -march=native flags and executed on an Intel i9 7900X CPU with 64 GB running at 3.3 GHz operated by CentOS 7.5. The obtained experimental results can be found in Table 1. Note that the measured times for signing and verification do not take into account transfer times between the entities or object creation and destruction.

By construing the signer as a single entity instead of two as in the LDAA, the proposed LEPID scheme achieves a reduction of the private-key size of 1.5 times. While the comparison in signatures sizes between both schemes yields favourably for the proposed LEPID scheme with a small amount of rejected users, as the number of users in the SRL increases, its signature size increases linearly at a rate of 18 kB per rejected user (9 polynomials and an integer). When the SRL contains 500 users, the LEPID signature size closely matches that of the

Table 1. Experimental results for the proposed LEPID and LDAA [10] for $n = 512$, $q = 8380417$, $l = 32$, $m = 24$ and $\beta = 256$ obtained on an Intel i9 7900X

Scheme	Private-key (kB)	Signature (MB)	Signing Time (s)	Verification Time (s)
LDAA	147	847	541	129
LEPID (no revoked users)	100	836	361	114
LEPID (100 users in SRL)	100	838	371	117
LEPID (500 users in SRL)	100	845	372	119
LEPID (1000 users in SRL)	100	854	374	121

LDAA scheme. Should LEPID signing be implemented on a device with limited computational resources like the TPM, its constrained memory resources and the cost of data transfer might limit its application to small and medium-sized communities. In particular, if one considers a revocation rate of 0.1%, LEPID signatures will compare favourably in size to LDAA signatures for communities with fewer than 500,000 users.

The signing time in the LEPID scheme is dominated by the signature based knowledge proof π. The addition of the SRL , and consequently of 13 polynomial multiplications per rejected user, shows no meaningful impact in the final signing time, where LEPID maintains a speedup of 1.4 over the LDAA scheme. Likewise, in the verification time, the additional 2 polynomial multiplications per rejected user incurred by the SRL are negligible compared to the verification of π. Hence, the proposed LEPID scheme achieves a speedup of 1.1 when compared with the LDAA scheme across both small and medium rejection lists. For the computational complexity introduced by the SRL to be meaningful, the number of rejected users must be in the order of millions. Once more, the proposed LEPID scheme shows improved signature and verification times for small and medium communities when compared with the LDAA.

7   Conclusion

While EPID plays a determinant role in the security of SGX, the scheme currently deployed by Intel will become insecure in the event that a large-scale quantum-computer is produced. Herein, a novel EPID scheme is proposed, supported on lattice-based security assumptions, and achieving presumed quantum resistance. A security model for EPID is presented for the first time in the UC framework, and the proposed scheme is proven secure under this model. When compared with a closely related LDAA scheme from related art, the proposed LEPID achieves a reduction in the private-key size of 1.5 times, and of the signature and verification times of 1.4 and 1.1 times, respectively, when no users have been revoked. It is furthermore shown, experimentally, that the overhead introduced by the more effective revocation method of LEPID is minimal for small to medium-sized communities. Finally, it is expected that the proposed LEPID may benefit from theoretical developments and hardware accelerators that result from the increased interest that lattice-based cryptography has gathered in the last few years.

Acknowledgements. This research was supported by European Unions Horizon 2020 research and innovation programme under grant agreement No. 779391 (FutureTPM), and by national funds through Fundação para a Ciência e a Tecnologia (FCT) with references UID/CEC/50021/2019 and FCT Grant No. SFRH/BD/145477/2019.

References

1. Baum, C., Damgård, I., Oechsner, S., Peikert, C.: Efficient commitments and zero-knowledge protocols from ring-sis with applications to lattice-based threshold cryptosystems. IACR Cryptol. ePrint Arch. **2016**, 997 (2016)
2. Benhamouda, F., Camenisch, J., Krenn, S., Lyubashevsky, V., Neven, G.: Better zero-knowledge proofs for lattice encryption and their application to group signatures. In: Sarkar, P., Iwata, T. (eds.) ASIACRYPT 2014, Part I. LNCS, vol. 8873, pp. 551–572. Springer, Heidelberg (2014). https://doi.org/10.1007/978-3-662-45611-8_29
3. Boneh, D., Eskandarian, S., Fisch, B.: Post-quantum EPID signatures from symmetric primitives. In: Matsui, M. (ed.) CT-RSA 2019. LNCS, vol. 11405, pp. 251–271. Springer, Cham (2019). https://doi.org/10.1007/978-3-030-12612-4_13
4. Boyen, X.: Lattice mixing and vanishing trapdoors: a framework for fully secure short signatures and more. In: Nguyen, P.Q., Pointcheval, D. (eds.) PKC 2010. LNCS, vol. 6056, pp. 499–517. Springer, Heidelberg (2010). https://doi.org/10.1007/978-3-642-13013-7_29
5. Brickell, E., Camenisch, J., Chen, L.: Direct anonymous attestation. In: Proceedings of the 11th ACM Conference on Computer and Communications Security, CCS 2004, New York, NY, USA, pp. 132–145. ACM (2004)
6. Camenisch, J., Chen, L., Drijvers, M., Lehmann, A., Novick, D., Urian, R.: One TPM to bind them all: fixing TPM 2. 0 for provably secure anonymous attestation. In: Proceedings of IEEE S&P 2017 (2017)
7. Camenisch, J., Drijvers, M., Lehmann, A.: Universally composable direct anonymous attestation. In: Cheng, C.-M., Chung, K.-M., Persiano, G., Yang, B.-Y. (eds.) PKC 2016, Part II. LNCS, vol. 9615, pp. 234–264. Springer, Heidelberg (2016). https://doi.org/10.1007/978-3-662-49387-8_10
8. Ishai, Y., Kushilevitz, E., Ostrovsky, R., Sahai, A.: Zero-knowledge from secure multiparty computation. In: Proceedings of the Thirty-ninth Annual ACM Symposium on Theory of Computing, pp. 21–30. ACM (2007)
9. Johnson, S., Scarlata, V., Rozas, C., Brickell, E., Mckeen, F.: Intel® software guard extensions: EPID provisioning and attestation services. White Pap. **1**, 1–10 (2016)
10. Kassem, N., et al.: More efficient, provably-secure direct anonymous attestation from lattices. Future Gener. Comput. Syst. **99**, 425–458 (2019)
11. EL Kassem, N., Fiolhais, L., Martins, P., Chen, L., Sousa, L.: A lattice-based enhanced privacy ID. Cryptology ePrint Archive, Report 2019/1366 (2019). https://eprint.iacr.org/2019/1366
12. Ling, S., Nguyen, K., Stehlé, D., Wang, H.: Improved zero-knowledge proofs of knowledge for the ISIS problem, and applications. In: Kurosawa, K., Hanaoka, G. (eds.) PKC 2013. LNCS, vol. 7778, pp. 107–124. Springer, Heidelberg (2013). https://doi.org/10.1007/978-3-642-36362-7_8

13. Lyubashevsky, V.: Towards Practical Lattice-based Cryptography. University of California, San Diego (2008)
14. Lyubashevsky, V.: Lattice signatures without trapdoors. In: Pointcheval, D., Johansson, T. (eds.) EUROCRYPT 2012. LNCS, vol. 7237, pp. 738–755. Springer, Heidelberg (2012). https://doi.org/10.1007/978-3-642-29011-4_43
15. Nejatollahi, H., Dutt, N.D., Banerjee, I., Cammarota, R.: Domain-specific accelerators for ideal lattice-based public key protocols. IACR Cryptol. ePrint Arch. **2018**, 608 (2018)
16. National Institute of Standards and Technology. Post-quantum cryptography standardization, 1 (2017). https://csrc.nist.gov/Projects/Post-Quantum-Cryptography/Post-Quantum-Cryptography-Standardization
17. Peikert, C., et al.: A decade of lattice cryptography. Found. Trends® Theor. Comput. Sci. **10**(4), 283–424 (2016)
18. Regev, O.: The learning with errors problem (invited survey). In: 2010 IEEE 25th Annual Conference on Computational Complexity, pp. 191–204. IEEE (2010)

A Generic View on the Unified Zero-Knowledge Protocol and Its Applications

Diana Maimuț[1(✉)] and George Teșeleanu[1,2]

[1] Advanced Technologies Institute, 10 Dinu Vintilă, Bucharest, Romania
{diana.maimut,tgeorge}@dcti.ro
[2] Simion Stoilow Institute of Mathematics of the Romanian Academy,
21 Calea Grivitei, Bucharest, Romania

Abstract. We present a generalization of Maurer's unified zero-knowledge (UZK) protocol, namely a unified generic zero-knowledge (UGZK) construction. We prove the security of our UGZK protocol and discuss special cases. Compared to UZK, the new protocol allows to prove knowledge of a vector of secrets instead of only one secret. We also provide the reader with a hash variant of UGZK and the corresponding security analysis. Last but not least, we extend Cogliani *et al.*'s lightweight authentication protocol by describing a new distributed unified authentication scheme suitable for wireless sensor networks and, more generally, the Internet of Things.

1 Introduction

Zero knowledge proofs (ZKPs) are closely related with one of the main cryptographic goals, entity authentication. Applying ZKPs, researchers are able to propose clever solutions to a variety of practical problems mainly in the fields of digital cash, auctioning, Internet of Things (IoT), password authentication and so on.

A standard zero knowledge protocol involves a prover *Peggy* possessing a piece of secret information x associated with her identity and a verifier *Victor* which has to check that *Peggy* indeed owns x. Two classical examples of such constructions are the Schnorr [18] and the Guillou-Quisquater [11] protocols. Raising the level of abstraction, Maurer shows in [13] that the previously mentioned protocols are actually instantiations of the same one.

Building on Maurer's result, we considered of great interest providing the reader with a generalized perspective of the Unified Zero-Knowledge (UZK) protocol as well as a hash variant of it. An important consequence of our generic approach is the unification of Maurer's [13], Feige-Fiat-Shamir's [3] and Chaum-Everste-Van De Graaf's [1] protocols. Moreover, a special case of our protocol's hash version is the *h-variant* of the Fiat-Shamir scheme [7,9].

© IFIP International Federation for Information Processing 2020
Published by Springer Nature Switzerland AG 2020
M. Laurent and T. Giannetsos (Eds.): WISTP 2019, LNCS 12024, pp. 32–46, 2020.
https://doi.org/10.1007/978-3-030-41702-4_3

Practical Implications Which Motivated Our Research. As the IoT paradigm arised, lightweight devices[1] became more and more popular. Due to the open and distributed nature of the IoT, proper security is needed for the entire network to operate accordingly. Now let us consider the case of online wireless sensor networks (WSNs). The lightweight nature of sensor nodes heavily restricts cryptographic operations. Thus, the need for specific cryptographic solutions becomes obvious. The Fiat-Shamir-like distributed authentication protocol presented in [2] represents such an example. Based on this previous construction we propose a unified generic zero-knowledge protocol. Just as the result described in [2], our protocol can be applied for securing WSNs and, more generally, IoT-related solutions. Nonetheless, our construction offers flexibility when choosing the assumptions on which its security relies. A secondary feature of our scheme is the possibility of reusing existing certificates when implementing the distributed authentication protocol.

Structure of the Paper. We establish notations and recall zero-knowledge concepts in Sect. 2. Inspired by Maurer's UZK construction, in Sect. 3 we present our main result, a Unified Generic Zero-Knowledge (UGZK) protocol, and prove it secure. We provide the reader with various special cases of UGZK in Sect. 4. A hash variant of our core protocol is tackled in Sect. 5 together with its security analysis. Following Cogliani *et al.*'s lightweight authentication protocol ideas, in Sect. 6 we describe a distributed unified Fiat-Shamir-based protocol, discuss security and complexity aspects and present implementation trade-offs which arise from small variations of the proposed result. We conclude in Sect. 7 and underline future work proposals.

2 Preliminaries

Notations. Throughout the paper, the notation $|S|$ denotes the cardinality of a set S. The subset $\{0, \ldots, s\} \in \mathbb{N}$ is denoted by $[0, s]$. The action of selecting a random element x from a sample space X is represented by $x \xleftarrow{\$} X$, while $x \leftarrow y$ indicates the assignment of value y to variable x.

2.1 Groups

Let $(\mathbb{G}, \star)$ and $(\mathbb{H}, \otimes)$ be two groups. We assume that the group operations $\star$ and $\otimes$ are efficiently computable.

Let $f : \mathbb{G} \to \mathbb{H}$ be a function (not necessarily one-to-one). We say that f is a homomorphism if $f(x \star y) = f(x) \otimes f(y)$. Throughout the paper we consider f to be a one-way function, *i.e.* it is infeasible to compute x from $f(x)$. To be consistent with [13], we denote by $[x]$ the value $f(x)$. Note that given $[x]$ and $[y]$ we can efficiently compute $[x \star y] = [x] \otimes [y]$, due to the fact that f is a homomorphism.

---

[1] Low-cost devices with limited resources, be it computational or physical.

2.2   Zero-Knowledge Protocols

Let $Q : \{0,1\}^* \times \{0,1\}^* \rightarrow \{\texttt{true}, \texttt{false}\}$ be a predicate. Given a value z, Peggy will try to convince Victor that she knows a value x such that $Q(z,x) = \texttt{true}$.

We further base our reasoning on both a definition from [3,13] and a definition from [10,13] which we recall next.

Definition 1 (Proof of Knowledge Protocol). *An interactive protocol* (P,V) *is a proof of knowledge protocol for predicate* Q *if the following properties hold*

- **Completeness**: *V accepts the proof when P has as input a value x with* $Q(z,x) = \texttt{true}$;
- **Soundness**: *there exists an efficient program K (called knowledge extractor) such that for any* $\bar{P}$ *(possibly dishonest) with non-negligible probability of making V accept the proof, K can interact with* $\bar{P}$ *and output (with overwhelming probability) an x such that* $Q(z,x) = \texttt{true}$.

Definition 2 (Zero Knowledge Protocol). *A protocol* (P,V) *is zero-knowledge if for every efficient program* $\bar{V}$ *there exists an efficient program S, the simulator, such that the output of S is indistinguishable from a transcript of the protocol execution between P and* $\bar{V}$. *If the indistinguishability is perfect*[2], *then the protocol is called perfect zero-knowledge.*

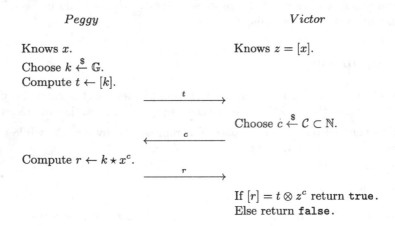

Fig. 1. Maurer's Unified Zero-Knowledge (UZK) Protocol.

According to [13], the UZK protocol presented in Fig. 1 is a zero-knowledge protocol if the conditions mentioned in Theorem 1 are satisfied.

---

[2] i.e. the probability distribution of the simulated and the actual transcript are identical.

Theorem 1. *Let $\mathcal{C}$ be the challenge space. If values $\ell \in \mathbb{Z}$ and $u \in \mathbb{G}$ are known such that*

- *$\gcd(c_0 - c_1, \ell) = 1$ for all $c_0, c_1 \in \mathcal{C}$ with $c_0 \neq c_1$,*
- *$[u] = z^\ell$,*

then by running the protocol described in Fig. 1 for m rounds we obtain a proof of knowledge protocol if $1/|\mathcal{C}|^m$ is negligible, and a zero-knowledge protocol if $|\mathcal{C}|$ is polynomially bounded.

Remark 1. If $\mathcal{C}$ is small, then several 3-move rounds are needed to make the soundness error negligible.

2.3 Hash Functions

In the following, we consider the definitions from [9]. These concepts are further applied in Sect. 5 within the security proof of our proposed generalization of the *h-variant* protocol [7].

Definition 3. *Let $\lambda \geq 2$ be an integer. An λ-collision for a hash function h is an λ-tuple $\{m_i\}_{i \in [1,\lambda]}$ such that $h(m_1) = h(m_2) = \ldots = h(m_\lambda)$.*

Definition 4. *Let $\lambda \geq 2$ be an integer. A hash function is λ-collision resistant if it is computationally infeasible to find an λ-collision.*

3 The Main Protocol

Inspired by Maurer's UZK protocol [13], we describe a UGZK protocol (Fig. 2). Note that the UZK scheme is a special case of the UGZK construction. We also prove the security of our proposed construction in a Feige-Fiat-Shamir manner [3].

3.1 Description

Let n be a positive integer. The protocol in Fig. 2 is a proof of knowledge of a vector $\{[x_i]\}_{i \in [1,n]}$ such that $z_i = [x_i]$, for all $i \in [1, n]$, where the vector $\{z_i\}_{i \in [1,n]}$ is given, provided that the conditions of Theorem 2 are satisfied. The challenge spaces $\mathcal{C}_i$ for the elements c_i are chosen as arbitrary subsets of $\mathbb{N}$, for all $i \in [1, n]$. For the sake of uniformity, we assume that all the challenge spaces $\mathcal{C}_i$ are equal and we denote them by $\mathcal{C}$. If $|\mathcal{C}|$ is chosen to be small, then several rounds are needed in order to reduce the soundness error up to the point of being negligible.

When $n = 1$ we obtain the UZK protocol introduced in [13]. Note that in this case $\mathbb{G}$ and $\mathbb{H}$ need not be commutative.

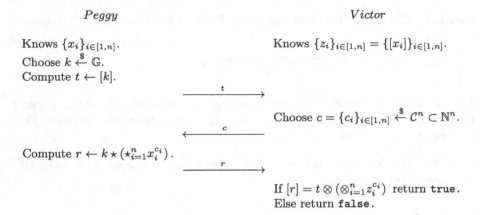

Fig. 2. A Unified Generic Zero-Knowledge (UGZK) Protocol.

3.2   Security Analysis

Theorem 2. *Let $\mathbb{H}$ be a commutative group. If for all j values $\ell_j \in \mathbb{Z}$ and $u_j \in \mathbb{G}$ are known such that*

- *$\gcd(c_j'' - c_j', \ell_j) = 1$ for all $c_j', c_j'' \in \mathcal{C}$ with $c_j' \neq c_j''$,*
- *$[u_j] = z_j^{\ell_j}$,*

then by running the protocol described in Fig. 2 for m rounds we obtain a proof of knowledge protocol if $1/|\mathcal{C}|^{nm}$ is negligible, and a zero-knowledge protocol if $|\mathcal{C}|^n$ is polynomially bounded.

Proof. Let $s = |\mathcal{C}|$. To prove that P's proof always convinces V, we evaluate the verification condition:

$$[r] = [k \star (\star_{i=1}^n x_i^{c_i})] = [k] \otimes (\otimes_{i=1}^n [x_i]^{c_i}) = t \otimes (\otimes_{i=1}^n z_i^{c_i}).$$

Note that a corrupt $\bar{P}$ can cheat V with a negligible probability s^{-nm} per iteration by guessing the $\{c_i\}_{i\in[1,n]}$ vector, preparing $t = [k] \otimes (\otimes_{i=1}^n z_i^{-c_i})$ in the first step, and providing $r = k$ in the last step.

Next, we show that whenever V accepts $\bar{P}$'s proof with non-negligible probability, there exists a knowledge extractor K that can print out all the x_is with overwhelming probability. Let T be the truncated execution tree of $(\bar{P}, V)$ for input I and random tape RA. As in [3, Theorem 3], the algorithm we construct explores this tree by repeatedly resetting $\bar{P}$ to the root, providing the necessary steering requests and verifying which one of the s sons of each explored vertex corresponds to a correct answer. V may ask s^n possible questions at each stage and, thus, the vertices in T may have polynomially many sons in terms of $|I|$. A vertex is called *heavy* if its degree is larger than s^{n-1} (i.e. if more than s^{n-1} executions of $(\bar{P}, V)$ at this state are successful). Our goal in this part of the proof is to show that all the x_is can be computed from the sons of a heavy vertex and that a PPT K can find a heavy vertex in T with overwhelming probability.

Let H be any heavy vertex in T and let Q be the set of queries in the form of vectors $\{c_i\}_{i\in[1,n]}$ which are properly answered by $\bar{P}$. It is easy to show that for any $1 \le j \le n$ a set Q of more than s^{n-1} vectors (having the length n) must contain two vectors $\{c'_i\}_{i\in[1,n]}$ and $\{c''_i\}_{i\in[1,n]}$ in which $c'_j \ne c''_j$ and $c'_i = c''_i$ for all $i \ne j$. Since both queries were properly answered, the two verification conditions imply

$$[r'_j] = t'_j \otimes \left(\otimes_{i=1}^{n} z_i^{c'_i}\right) \text{ and } [r''_j] = t''_j \otimes \left(\otimes_{i=1}^{n} z_i^{c''_i}\right).$$

However, $\bar{P}$ must choose t before he obtains V's query and, thus, $t'_j = t''_j$. From r'_j and r''_j we can obtain $\tilde{x}_j$ such that $[\tilde{x}_j] = z_j$, as

$$\tilde{x}_j = u_j^{a_j} \star (r_j''^{-1} \star r'_j)^{b_j},$$

where a_j and b_j are computed using Euclid's extended gcd algorithm such that $\ell_j a_j + (c''_j - c'_j)b_j = 1$.

By rewriting the equations we get

$$\begin{aligned}
[r_j''^{-1} \star r'_j] &= [r_j''^{-1}] \otimes [r'_j] \\
&= \left(\otimes_{i=n}^{1} z_i^{-c''_i}\right) \otimes t_j''^{-1} \otimes t'_j \otimes \left(\otimes_{i=1}^{n} z_i^{c'_i}\right) \\
&= \left(\otimes_{i=n}^{j} z_i^{-c''_i}\right) \otimes \left(\otimes_{i=j}^{n} z_i^{c'_i}\right) \\
&= z_j^{c'_j - c''_j},
\end{aligned}$$

where for obtaining the last equality we used the commutative property of $\mathbb{H}$. Thus,

$$\begin{aligned}
[\tilde{x}_j] &= [u_j^{a_j} \star (r_j''^{-1} \star r'_j)^{b_j}] \\
&= [u_j]^{a_j} \otimes ([r_j''^{-1} \star r'_j])^{b_j} \\
&= (z_j^{\ell_j})^{a_j} \otimes (z_j^{c'_j - c''_j})^{b_j} \\
&= z_j^{\ell_j a_j + (c'_j - c''_j)b_j} \\
&= z_j.
\end{aligned}$$

Now we show that at least half the vertices in at least one of the levels in T must be heavy. Let α_i be the ratio between the number of vertices at level $i+1$ and the number of vertices at level i in T. If $\alpha_i \le (1/2s)s^n$ for all $1 \le i \le m$, then the total number of leaves in T (which is the product of all these α_i) is bounded by $(1/2s)^m s^{nm}$, which is a negligible fraction of the s^{nm} possible leaves. Since we assume that this fraction is polynomial, $\alpha_i > (1/2s)s^n$ for at least one i, and thus at least half the vertices at this level must contain more than s^n/s sons.

To find a heavy vertex in T, K chooses polynomially many random vertices at each level, and determines their degrees by repeated resets and executions of $\bar{P}$. To ensure a uniform probability distribution in spite of the uneven degrees of the vertices, M should explore random paths in the untruncated tree, and restart from the root whenever the path encounters an improperly answered query. Since a non-negligible fraction of the leaves is assumed to survive the truncation, this blind exploration of T can be carried out in polynomial time.

The last part of the proof deals with the zero-knowledge aspect of the protocol. By using resettable simulation in the sense of [10], the simulator S described in Algorithm 1 can mimic the communication in $(P, \bar{V})$ with an indistinguishable probability distribution in $O(ms^n)$ expected time, which is polynomial by our assumptions on s^n.

Algorithm 1. The simulator S.

Input: The public key $\{z_i\}_{i \in [1,n]}$
Output: A transcript $\mathcal{L}$

1 **foreach** $j \in [1, m]$ **do**
2 | Choose $c = \{c_i\}_{i \in [1,n]}$ at random from C^n
3 | Select a random number $r \xleftarrow{\$} \mathbb{G}$
4 | Compute $t \leftarrow [r] \otimes \left(\otimes_{i=n}^{1} z_i^{-c_i} \right)$
5 | Call $\bar{V}$ with input t and obtain a challenge c'
6 | **if** $c = c'$ **then**
7 | | $L \leftarrow L \cup \{(t, c, r)\}$
8 | **end**
9 | **else**
10 | | Reset $\bar{V}$'s state and repeat this round with new random choices
11 | **end**
12 **end**
13 **return** $\mathcal{L}$

$\square$

4   Special Cases of the UGZK Protocol

In this section we describe a number of protocols as instantiations of our main UGZK construction. Note that when $n = 1$ we obtain the UZK protocol from [13]. Thus, some schemes described in [13] are further reconsidered, while some examples are specific to our UGZK protocol. Although in the original paper [13] Maurer shows how to use UZK to prove the knowledge of a vector of secrets, our protocol UGZK is better in terms of transcript size.

4.1   Proofs of Knowledge of a Multiple Discrete Logarithm

Let $p = 2q + 1$ be a prime number such that q is also prime. Select an element $h \in \mathbb{H}_p$ of order q in some multiplicative group of order p. The multiple discrete logarithm of a vector $\{z_i\}_{i \in [1,n]} \in \mathbb{H}_p^n$ is a vector of exponents $\{x_i\}_{i \in [1,n]}$ such that $z_i = h^{x_i}$, for all $i \in [1, n]$. We further describe a protocol for proving the knowledge of a multiple discrete logarithm.

A protocol for proving knowledge of a multiple discrete logarithm can be obtained as a special case of UGZK where $(\mathbb{G}, \star) = (\mathbb{Z}_q, +)$ and $\mathbb{H} = \langle h \rangle$. The one-way group homomorphism is defined by $[x] = h^x$, while the challenge space $\mathcal{C}$ can be any arbitrary subset of $[0, q - 1]$. The conditions of Theorem 2 are satisfied for $\ell_j = q$ and $u_j = 0$, where $j \in [1, n]$. When $n = 1$ we obtain the Schnorr protocol [18][3]. In the case $n \geq 1$ and $\mathcal{C} = \{0,1\}$ we obtain the multiple logarithm protocol described in [1].

Next we discuss a variation[5] of the previously presented protocol. Let $p = 2fp' + 1$ and $q = 2fq' + 1$ be prime numbers such that f, p' and q' are distinct primes. Select an element $h \in \mathbb{Z}_N^*$ of order f, where $N = pq$. Note that p and q are secret.

Using the UGZK notations we have $(\mathbb{G}, \star) = (\mathbb{Z}_f, +)$ and $\mathbb{H} = \langle h \rangle$. The one-way group homomorphism is defined by $[x] = h^x$ and the challenge space $\mathcal{C}$ can be any arbitrary subset of $[0, f - 1]$. We can observe that the conditions of Theorem 2 are satisfied for $\ell_j = f$ and $u_j = 0$, where $j \in [1, n]$. When $n = 1$ we obtain the Girault protocol [8].

4.2   Proofs of Knowledge of a Multiple e^{th}-root

Let p and q be two large prime numbers. Compute $N = pq$ and choose a prime e such that $\gcd(e, \varphi(N)) = 1$. A multiple e^{th}-root of a vector $\{z_i\}_{i \in [1,n]} \in (\mathbb{Z}_N^*)^n$ is a base vector $\{x_i\}_{i \in [1,n]}$ such that $z_i = x_i^e$. Note that the multiple e^{th}-root is not unique. We further describe a protocol for proving the knowledge of a multiple e^{th}-root.

Such a protocol can be obtained from UGZK with $(\mathbb{G}, \star) = (\mathbb{H}, \otimes) = (\mathbb{Z}_N^*, \cdot)$. The one-way group homomorphism is defined by $[x] = x^e$ and the challenge space $\mathcal{C}$ can be any arbitrary subset of $[0, e - 1]$. The conditions of Theorem 2 are satisfied for $\ell_j = e$ and $u_j = z$, where $j \in [1, n]$. We stress that when $e = 2$ we obtain the protocol introduced by Feige, Fiat and Shamir [3]. In the case $n = 1$ we obtain the Guillou-Quisquater protocol [11][4].

4.3   Proofs of Knowledge of a Multiple Discrete Logarithm Representation

Let $p = 2q + 1$ be a prime number such that q is also prime. Select α elements $\{h_j\}_{j \in [1,\alpha]} \in \mathbb{H}_p^\alpha$ of order q in some multiplicative group of order p. A multiple discrete logarithm representation of a vector $\{z_i\}_{i \in [1,n]} \in (\langle h_1, \ldots, h_\alpha \rangle)^n$

---

[3] This proof can be seen as a more efficient version of a proposal made by Chaum et al. [1].

[4] This proof is a generalization of a protocol introduced by Fiat and Shamir [7].

is a vector of exponent vectors $(\{x_{1,j}\}_{j\in[1,\alpha]},\ldots,\{x_{n,j}\}_{j\in[1,\alpha]})$ such that $z_i = h_1^{x_{i,1}}\ldots h_\alpha^{x_{i,\alpha}}$, for all $i \in [1,n]$. Note that multiple discrete logarithm representations are not unique. We further describe a protocol for proving the knowledge of a multiple discrete logarithm representation.

A protocol for proving the knowledge of a multiple representation can be instantiated from UGZK by setting $\mathbb{G} = \mathbb{Z}_q^\alpha$ with $\star$ defined as a component-wise addition operation and $\mathbb{H} = \langle h_1,\ldots,h_\alpha\rangle$. The one-way group homomorphism is defined by $[(x_1,\ldots,x_\alpha)] = h_1^{x_1}\ldots h_\alpha^{x_\alpha}$ and the challenge space $\mathcal{C}$ can be any arbitrary subset of $[0,q-1]$. The conditions of Theorem 2 are satisfied for $\ell_j = q$ and $u_j = (0,\ldots,0)$, where $j \in [1,n]$. When $n = 1$ we obtain a protocol proposed by Maurer in [13] which is a generalization of the protocols presented by Okamoto in [15] and Chaum et al. in [1].

Chaum et al. [1] also provide a protocol variant for a composite n. Thus, by adapting the protocol presented in Sect. 4.1 and tweaking the previously described one, we can obtain a similar version for composite numbers. Using the notations from the protocol in Sect. 4.1, we set $\mathbb{G} = \mathbb{Z}_f^\alpha$ and $\mathbb{H} = \langle h_1,\ldots,h_m\rangle$, where $h_1,\ldots,h_\alpha \in \mathbb{Z}_n^*$ are elements of order f. The one-way group homomorphism is defined by $[(x_1,\ldots,x_\alpha)] = h_1^{x_1}\ldots h_\alpha^{x_\alpha}$ and the challenge space $\mathcal{C}$ can be any arbitrary subset of $\mathbb{Z}_f$. It is easy to see that $\ell_j = f$ and $u_j = (0,\ldots,0)$, where $j \in [1,n]$.

4.4 Proofs of Knowledge of a Multiple e^{th}-root Representation

Let p and q be two large prime numbers. Compute $N = pq$ and choose primes $e_1,\ldots,e_\alpha$ such that $\gcd(e_i,\varphi(N)) = 1$, for $i \in [1,\alpha]$. A multiple e^{th}-root representation of a vector $\{z_i\}_{i\in[1,n]} \in (Z_N^*)^n$ is a vector of bases vector $(\{x_{1,j}\}_{j\in[1,\alpha]},\ldots,\{x_{n,j}\}_{j\in[1,\alpha]})$ such that $z_i = x_{i,1}^{e_1}\ldots x_{i,\alpha}^{e_\alpha}$, for all $i \in [1,n]$. Note that multiple e^{th}-root representations are not unique. We further describe a protocol for proving the knowledge of a multiple e^{th}-root representation.

A protocol for proving the knowledge of a multiple e^{th}-root representation can be obtained from UGZK if we set $\mathbb{G} = (\mathbb{Z}_N^*)^\alpha$ with $\star$ defined as multiplication applied component-wise and $(\mathbb{H},\otimes) = (\mathbb{Z}_N^*,\cdot)$. The one-way group homomorphism is defined by $[(x_1,\ldots,x_\alpha)] = x_1^{e_1}\ldots x_\alpha^{e_\alpha}$ and the challenge space $\mathcal{C}$ can be any arbitrary subset of $[0,e-1]$, where e is a prime such that $\gcd(e,\phi(N)) = 1$. It is easy to see that $\ell_j = e$ and $u_j = (x_1^e,\ldots,x_\alpha^e)$, where $j \in [1,n]$. When $n = 1$ we obtain a protocol introduced in [19].

5 Hash Protocol Variant

In order to decrease the number of communication bits, *Peggy* can hash t and send *Victor* the result. This method was proposed by Fiat and Shamir [7] and later analyzed in [9]. We employ the same technique for the protocol presented in Fig. 2 and analyze its security.

5.1   Description

Let H be a hash function that maps elements from $\mathbb{H}$ into bit streams. The hash variant of the protocol works as follows: in the first step *Peggy* sends $H(t)$ to *Victor* (instead of t) and the last step becomes

$$\text{If } H(t) = H\left([r] \otimes \left(\otimes_{i=1}^{n} z_i^{-c_i}\right)\right) \text{ return true.}$$

Else return false.

5.2   Security Analysis

Theorem 3. *Let $s = |\mathcal{C}|$. If there exists a PPT algorithm $\bar{P}$ such that the probability that $\bar{P}$ is accepted by an honest verifier is greater than $(\lambda - 1)|\mathcal{C}|^{-n} + \varepsilon$, where $\varepsilon > 0$, then there exists a PPT algorithm $\tilde{P}$ which, with overwhelming probability, either inverts $[\cdot]$ or finds a λ-collision for h.*

Proof. Let Ω be the set of $\tilde{p}$ elements in which $\tilde{P}$ picks its random values and E be the set C^n, both of them characterized by the uniform distribution. For each value $(\omega, e) \in \Omega \times E$, $\tilde{P}$ passes the protocol (and we say it is a success) or not. Let S be the subset $\Omega \times E$ composed of all possible successes. Our assumption is that

$$\frac{|S|}{|\Omega \times E|} > (r-1)|\mathcal{C}|^{-n} + \varepsilon$$

with $\varepsilon > 0$ and $|\Omega \times E| = \tilde{p} \cdot s^n$.

Let $E_r = \{e \in E \mid (\omega, e) \text{ is a success}\}$ and $\Omega_r = \{\omega \in \Omega \mid |E_r| \geq r\}$. We have that

$$|S| \leq |\Omega_r| \cdot s^n + (r-1) \cdot (\tilde{p} - |\Omega_r|).$$

Thus,

$$\frac{|S|}{|\Omega \times E|} \leq \left[\frac{|\Omega_r|}{|\Omega|} + (r-1) \cdot \left(s^{-n} - \frac{|\Omega_r|}{|\Omega \times E|}\right)\right] \leq \frac{|\Omega_r|}{|\Omega|} + (r-1) \cdot s^{-n}$$

which implies

$$\frac{|\Omega_r|}{|\Omega|} \geq \varepsilon.$$

Let $\hat{P}$ be the PPT algorithm obtained by resetting $\tilde{P}$ ε^{-1} times. With constant probability, $\hat{P}$ picks ω in Ω_r and the probability can be made close to 1 by repeating the execution of $\hat{P}$. At the end, λ values $\{r_i\}_{i\in[1,\lambda]}$ are found such that, for distinct challenges $\{c_i\}_{i\in[1,\lambda]} \in (C^n)^\lambda$

$$H\left([r_1] \otimes \left(\otimes_{i=1}^{n} z_i^{-c_{i,1}}\right)\right) = H\left([r_2] \otimes \left(\otimes_{i=1}^{n} z_i^{-c_{i,2}}\right)\right)$$

$$= \ldots$$

$$= H\left([r_\lambda] \otimes \left(\otimes_{i=1}^{n} z_i^{-c_{i,\lambda}}\right)\right).$$

Now, we have two possibilities. In the first case, two of the values, say $[r_1] \otimes \left(\otimes_{i=1}^n z_i^{-c_{i,1}}\right)$ and $[r_2] \otimes \left(\otimes_{i=1}^n z_i^{-c_{i,2}}\right)$, are equal before hashing. Let $\mathcal{C}^- = \{-c \mid c \in \mathcal{C}\}$. Then, $[r_1 r_2^{-1}] = \left(\otimes_{i=1}^n z_i^{c_i'}\right)$, where $c' \in \mathcal{C}^- \cup \mathcal{C}$. This contradicts the intractability of $[\cdot]$. In the second case, all these values are pairwise distinct and a λ-collision for H has been found. This contradicts our assumption regarding H.   □

Remark 2. This result suggests the use of hash-functions which are only resistant to λ-collisions (with $\lambda > 2$), such that the hash values computed in the first pass can be made much shorter. Indeed, the decrease of the security level can be balanced by sending a slightly larger value of c in the second pass. More precisely, if $\lambda = s^{n'}$, we choose $c \in \mathcal{C}^{n+n'}$ instead of $c \in \mathcal{C}^n$.

6   A Distributed Unified Protocol

A Fiat-Shamir-like distributed authentication protocol was proposed in [2]. Given our UGZK construction, we describe a generic collective authentication protocol which can be seen as a natural follow up of the main result in [2].

6.1   Description

Let us consider an n-node network consisting of $\mathcal{N}_1, ..., \mathcal{N}_n$. The nodes $\mathcal{N}_i$ can be seen as users and the base station $\mathcal{T}$ as a trusted center. To achieve the authentication of the entire network, we propose a unified Fiat-Shamir-like construction which we detail next.

1. Let x_i be a secret piece of information given to node $\mathcal{N}_i$. First, the network topology has to converge and a spanning tree needs to be constructed (*e.g.* with an algorithm similar with the one presented in [14]). Then, $\mathcal{T}$ sends an authentication request message to all the $\mathcal{N}_i$ directly connected to it, a message which contains a commitment to c (see 3.) to ensure the protocol's zero-knowledge property even against dishonest verifiers.

2. After receiving an authentication request message:
   - Each $\mathcal{N}_i$ generates a private k_i and computes $t_i \leftarrow [k_i]$;
   - The $\mathcal{N}_i$s send authentication messages to all their (existing) children;
   - After the children respond, nodes $\mathcal{N}_i$ compute $t_i \leftarrow t_i \otimes (\otimes_j t_j)$ and send the result up to their parents. Note that the t_js are sent by the nodes' children.

Such a construction permits the network to compute the $\otimes$ operation of all the t_is and send the result t_c to the top of the tree in d steps, where d represents the degree of the spanning tree. We refer the reader to Fig. 3 for a toy example of this step.

3. $\mathcal{T}$ sends a random $c \in \mathcal{C}^n$ as an authentication challenge to the $\mathcal{N}_i$ directly connected to it.

4. After receiving an authentication challenge c:
   - Each $\mathcal{N}_i$ computes $r_i \leftarrow k_i \star x_i^{c_i}$;
   - The $\mathcal{N}_i$s then send the authentication challenge to all their (existing) children;
   - After the children respond, the $\mathcal{N}_i$s compute $r_i \leftarrow r_i \star (\star_j r_j)$ and send the result to their parents. Note that the r_js are sent by the nodes' children.

   The network therefore computes collectively the $\star$ operation of all the r_i's and transmits the result r_c to $\mathcal{T}$. Again, we refer the reader to Fig. 3 for a toy example of this step.

5. After receiving r_c, $\mathcal{T}$ checks that $[r_c] = t_c \otimes (\otimes_{i=1}^{n} z_i^{c_i})$, where $z_1, \ldots, z_n$ are the public keys corresponding to $x_1, \ldots, x_n$ respectively.

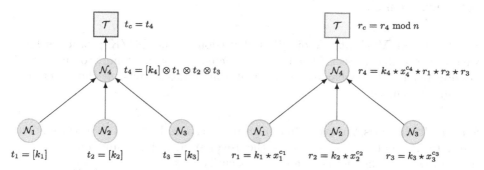

Fig. 3. The proposed algorithm running on a network consisting of 4 nodes: computation of t_c (left) and of r_c (right).

Remark 3. The protocol we have just described may be interrupted at any step and such an action results in a failed authentication.

6.2 Security Analysis

Theorem 4. *Let $\mathbb{H}$ be a commutative group. If an adversary corrupts $n' < n$ nodes and if for all j values $\ell_j \in \mathbb{Z}$ and $u_j \in \mathbb{G}$ are known such that*

- $\gcd(c''_j - c'_j, \ell_j) = 1$ *for all* $c'_j, c''_j \in \mathcal{C}$ *with* $c'_j \neq c''_j$,
- $[u_j] = z_j^{\ell_j}$,

then by running the protocol described in Sect. 6.1 for m rounds we obtain a proof of knowledge protocol if $1/|\mathcal{C}|^{(n-n')m}$ is negligible, and a zero-knowledge protocol if $|\mathcal{C}|^{(n-n')}$ is polynomially bounded.

Proof. If an adversary corrupts n' nodes, then n' secret keys x_i are known to him. Thus, the protocol is equivalent with a UGZK protocol with $n - n'$ secrets. Hence, using Theorem 2 we obtain our statement. $\square$

6.3   Complexity Analysis

The number of operations necessary for authenticating the whole network depends on the topology. Precise complexity evaluations are given in Table 1. Note that each node performs in average only a few operations (a constant number).

Let d be the degree of the minimum spanning tree of the network. Then, only $O(d)$ messages are sent and, if we do not consider atypical cases, $d = O(\log n)$. Put differently, throughout the authentication process only a logarithmic number of messages is sent.

6.4   Variations

When implementing the distributed zero knowledge protocol several trade-offs are possible. Note that when doing so any combination of the trade-offs described below may be used.

Hash Based Variant. A distributed version of the UGZK protocol's hash variant (presented in Sect. 5) can be constructed. Using this "short commitment" version reduces somewhat the number of communicated bits, at the expense of a reduced security.

Short Challenges Variant. In our protocol, the challenge c is sent throughout the network to all nodes. Assuming the use of an ideal hash function h, we may use shorter challenge without affecting security.

- A short c is sent to the nodes $\mathcal{N}_i$;
- Each $\mathcal{N}_i$ computes $c_i \leftarrow h(c\|i)$, and uses c_i as a challenge;
- The base station $\mathcal{T}$ computes c_i and uses it to check authentication.

Multiple-Secret Variant. Each node $\mathcal{N}_i$ could use a set of secret values $\{x_{i,j}\}_{j\in[1,\ell]}$ instead of only one x_i. For the algorithm to be as efficient as possible the supplementary secrets can be expanded from a concealed seed. For clarity purposes we describe the multiple secret variant for a single node.

When receiving a challenge c_i, each node computes a response

$$r_i \leftarrow k_i \star \left(\star_{j=1}^{\ell} x_{i,j}^{c_{i,j}} \right).$$

Table 1. Complexity computations.

Operation	Number of computations
$[\cdot]$	$(n+1)m$
Exponentiation	nm
$\otimes$	$\leq 2nm$
$\star$	$\leq nm$

This result be checked by the verifier by applying the next formula:

$$[r_i] = t_i \otimes \left(\otimes_{i=1}^{\ell} z_{i,j}^{c_{i,j}} \right).$$

In the case of multiple nodes, the modified protocol we obtain is a proof of knowledge if $1/|\mathcal{C}|^{(n-n')\ell m}$ is negligible and a zero-knowledge protocol if $|\mathcal{C}|^{(n-n')\ell}$ is polynomially bounded.

Practical aspects. Applying the multiple-secret variant, the trade-off between memory and communication can be adjusted, as the security level is ℓm (single-node compromission). Let μ be an integer. Therefore, if $\ell = \mu$ it suffices to authenticate once to get the same security as $t = \mu$ authentications with $\ell = 1$[5]. It is obvious that such an approach significantly reduces bandwidth usage, a clearly desirable fact in the IoT context.

7   Conclusions and Further Development

We proposed a UGZK protocol and analyzed its security. We provided various special cases of our core protocol, described a hash variant of UGZK and discussed security details. We also presented a distributed unified Fiat-Shamir-based protocol, tackled security and complexity aspects and presented implementation trade-offs.

Future work. In order to take advantage of our main protocol's characteristics, we suggest applying it for obtaining generic versions of digital signature schemes [12,16,17] and legally fair contract signing protocols [4,12]. More generally, our proposal could be useful for future works on cryptographic protocol design. In the case of failed network authentication an interesting research direction would be to devise new batch verification algorithms or adapt the ones constructed for digital signatures [5,6] for finding compromised nodes.

References

1. Chaum, D., Evertse, J.-H., van de Graaf, J.: An improved protocol for demonstrating possession of discrete logarithms and some generalizations. In: Chaum, D., Price, W.L. (eds.) EUROCRYPT 1987. LNCS, vol. 304, pp. 127–141. Springer, Heidelberg (1988). https://doi.org/10.1007/3-540-39118-5_13
2. Cogliani, S., et al.: Public key-based lightweight swarm authentication. In: Koç, Ç.K. (ed.) Cyber-Physical Systems Security, pp. 255–267. Springer, Cham (2018). https://doi.org/10.1007/978-3-319-98935-8_12
3. Feige, U., Fiat, A., Shamir, A.: Zero-knowledge proofs of identity. J. Cryptol. 1(2), 77–94 (1988)
4. Ferradi, H., Géraud, R., Maimuţ, D., Naccache, D., Pointcheval, D.: Legally fair contract signing without keystones. In: Manulis, M., Sadeghi, A.-R., Schneider, S. (eds.) ACNS 2016. LNCS, vol. 9696, pp. 175–190. Springer, Cham (2016). https://doi.org/10.1007/978-3-319-39555-5_10

---

[5] This corresponds to the protocol presented in Sect. 6.1.

5. Fiat, A.: Batch RSA. In: Brassard, G. (ed.) CRYPTO 1989. LNCS, vol. 435, pp. 175–185. Springer, New York (1990). https://doi.org/10.1007/0-387-34805-0_17
6. Fiat, A.: Batch RSA. J. Cryptol. **10**(2), 75–88 (1997)
7. Fiat, A., Shamir, A.: How to prove yourself: practical solutions to identification and signature problems. In: Odlyzko, A.M. (ed.) CRYPTO 1986. LNCS, vol. 263, pp. 186–194. Springer, Heidelberg (1987). https://doi.org/10.1007/3-540-47721-7_12
8. Girault, M.: An identity-based identification scheme based on discrete logarithms modulo a composite number. In: Damgård, I.B. (ed.) EUROCRYPT 1990. LNCS, vol. 473, pp. 481–486. Springer, Heidelberg (1991). https://doi.org/10.1007/3-540-46877-3_44
9. Girault, M., Stern, J.: On the length of cryptographic hash-values used in identification schemes. In: Desmedt, Y.G. (ed.) CRYPTO 1994. LNCS, vol. 839, pp. 202–215. Springer, Heidelberg (1994). https://doi.org/10.1007/3-540-48658-5_21
10. Goldwasser, S., Micali, S., Rackoff, C.: The knowledge complexity of interactive proof systems. SIAM J. Comput. **18**(1), 186–208 (1989)
11. Guillou, L.C., Quisquater, J.-J.: A practical zero-knowledge protocol fitted to security microprocessor minimizing both transmission and memory. In: Barstow, D., et al. (eds.) EUROCRYPT 1988. LNCS, vol. 330, pp. 123–128. Springer, Heidelberg (1988). https://doi.org/10.1007/3-540-45961-8_11
12. Maimuţ, D., Teşeleanu, G.: A unified security perspective on legally fair contract signing protocols. In: Lanet, J.-L., Toma, C. (eds.) SECITC 2018. LNCS, vol. 11359, pp. 477–491. Springer, Cham (2019). https://doi.org/10.1007/978-3-030-12942-2_35
13. Maurer, U.: Zero-knowledge proofs of knowledge for group homomorphisms. Designs Codes Cryptogr. **77**(2–3), 663–676 (2015)
14. Mooij, A.J., Goga, N., Wesselink, J.W.: A distributed spanning tree algorithm for topology-aware networks. Technische Universiteit Eindhoven, Department of Mathematics and Computer Science (2003)
15. Okamoto, T.: Provably secure and practical identification schemes and corresponding signature schemes. In: Brickell, E.F. (ed.) CRYPTO 1992. LNCS, vol. 740, pp. 31–53. Springer, Heidelberg (1993). https://doi.org/10.1007/3-540-48071-4_3
16. Pointcheval, D., Stern, J.: Security proofs for signature schemes. In: Maurer, U. (ed.) EUROCRYPT 1996. LNCS, vol. 1070, pp. 387–398. Springer, Heidelberg (1996). https://doi.org/10.1007/3-540-68339-9_33
17. Pointcheval, D., Stern, J.: Security arguments for digital signatures and blind signatures. J. Cryptol. **13**(3), 361–396 (2000)
18. Schnorr, C.P.: Efficient identification and signatures for smart cards. In: Brassard, G. (ed.) CRYPTO 1989. LNCS, vol. 435, pp. 239–252. Springer, New York (1990). https://doi.org/10.1007/0-387-34805-0_22
19. Teşeleanu, G.: Unifying kleptographic attacks. In: Gruschka, N. (ed.) NordSec 2018. LNCS, vol. 11252, pp. 73–87. Springer, Cham (2018). https://doi.org/10.1007/978-3-030-03638-6_5

Cryptography

Verifiable and Private Oblivious Polynomial Evaluation

Hardik Gajera[1]($\boxtimes$), Matthieu Giraud[2], David Gérault[2], Manik Lal Das[1], and Pascal Lafourcade[2]

[1] DA-IICT, Gandhinagar, India
{hardik_gajera,maniklal_das}@daiict.ac.in
[2] Université Clermont Auvergne, LIMOS UMR 6158, Aubière, France
{matthieu.giraud,david.gerault,pascal.lafourcade}@uca.fr

Abstract. It is a challenging problem to delegate the computation of a polynomial on encrypted data to a server in an oblivious and verifiable way. In this paper, we formally define *Verifiable and Private Oblivious Polynomial Evaluation* (VPOPE) scheme. We design a scheme called Verifiable **IND-CFA** Paillier based Private Oblivious Polynomial Evaluation (VIP-POPE). Using security properties of Private Polynomial Evaluation (PPE) schemes and Oblivious Polynomial Evaluation (OPE) schemes, we prove that our scheme is *proof unforgeability, indistinguishability against chosen function attack*, and *client privacy*-secure under the Decisional Composite Residuosity assumption in the random oracle model.

Keywords: Delegation of computation · Verifiable computation · Private Polynomial Evaluation · Oblivious evaluation · Privacy

1 Introduction

From harmless smart gardening [19] to critical applications such as forest fire detection [17], data monitoring through sensors is becoming pervasive. In particular, sensors for monitoring health-related data are more and more widely adopted, be it through smartwatches that track the heart rate, or sensors implemented in the patient's body [2]. This medical data can sometimes be used to assess the health status of an individual, by applying a single variable polynomial prediction function on it [7]. However, when it comes to medical data, extreme care must be taken to avoid any leakage. Recently, the leak of medical data of 1.5 million SingHealth users in Singapore strongly incentivized to improve the security and privacy surrounding medical data [1]. In this context, we consider the following problem:

How can a company use medical data recorded by clients to give them predictions about their health status in a private way?

For instance, this company may collect Fitbit data from its customers, and use it to predict things such as a risk factor for certain diseases. For economic reasons, this company keeps the polynomial secret: it invested time to build it and required

M. Laurent and T. Giannetsos (Eds.): WISTP 2019, LNCS 12024, pp. 49–65, 2020.
https://doi.org/10.1007/978-3-030-41702-4_4

to collect lots of data. Its economic model is based on the secrecy of the polynomial: the clients pay the company to obtain the polynomial's output on their medical data. If the polynomial was public, then the clients would directly compute it, and the company would cease to exist. However, as the company grows, it becomes difficult to treat all the computation requests, so that the company needs to delegate this computation to a cloud service. The company trusts the cloud service provider and gives the secret polynomial; however, the clients may not trust the server to produce correct results, so that the company would like the server to be able to prove the correctness of each prediction to the client, i.e., prove that its output is correct with regards to the secret prediction function.

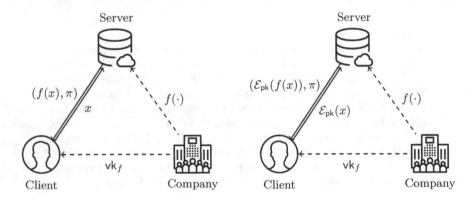

Fig. 1. Illustration of a PPE scheme.   **Fig. 2.** Illustration of a VPOPE scheme.

In this scenario, the problem is how to delegate computations on a secret polynomial function to an external server in a verifiable way. This problem is solved by *Private Polynomial Evaluation* (PPE) schemes [4,12,14,25] illustrated in Fig. 1. In a PPE scheme, the company outsources the secret polynomial function $f(\cdot)$ to an external server. Moreover, the company provides some public information vk_f called *verification key*. This verification key is used with the proof π generated by the server during the delegated computation of $f(x)$ to allow clients to verify the correctness of the result returned by the server.

However, PPE schemes do not protect the privacy of the clients: their data is handled in clear by the server. After the SingHealth hack, the company wants to be sure that even if an intruder hacks the server, he will not be able to steal the medical data of its clients. To solve this problem, we propose a new primitive called *Verifiable and Private Oblivious Polynomial Evaluation* (VPOPE). A VPOPE scheme is a private polynomial evaluation scheme, in which the data of the client cannot be read by the cloud server. More precisely, the client sends his encrypted data to the server, and the server never learns anything about x. We illustrate this new primitive in Fig. 2.

1.1   Related Works

VPOPE schemes are related to several research domains. The first one is the *Verifiable Computation* (VC) introduced by Gennaro *et al.* [13]. VC aims to delegate a costly computation to an untrusted third party. This third party returns the result of the computation and proof of correctness, which is easier to verify. Primitives, where everyone can check the correctness of the computation, are said to be *publicly verifiable* [23]. VC has given rise to a bunch of protocols [5,6,9,21,22]. Although VC is related to our paper; the difference is that in these works, the polynomial used by the server is not secret.

Another similar primitive is *Oblivious Polynomial Evaluation* (OPE) introduced by Naor and Pinkas [18]. OPE protocols are constituted of two parties. The first party, A, knows a secret function $f(\cdot)$ and the other one, B, has a secret element x. The aim of OPE is that B receives $f(x)$ in such a way A learns nothing about the value x sent by B, and that B learns nothing about the function $f(\cdot)$. OPE are used to solve different cryptographic problems as set membership, oblivious keyword search, and set intersection [10,11,16]. Although OPE and VPOPE are very similar; their difference lies in the fact that OPE do not consider the verifiability of the computation of $f(x)$, whereas it is a crucial point in VPOPE since the client does not trust the server.

Finally, the nature of VPOPE is very close to those of *Private Polynomial Evaluation* (PPE). To the best of our knowledge, only five papers [4,12,14,15,25] propose to hide a polynomial used by the server and allow a client to verify the returned results. Kate *et al.* [15] formally define a primitive called *commitments to polynomials* that can be used as a PPE scheme and propose the PolyCommit$_{Ped}$ scheme. In this primitive, the committer publishes some points (x, y) of the secret polynomial together with a proof that $y = f(x)$. Then, she can open the commitment *a posteriori* to reveal the secret polynomial. This primitive is close to PPE and VPOPE schemes since the verification key used in PPE and VPOPE can be viewed as a commitment. However, this verification key is computed by a trusted party (the company) and computations are performed by an untrusted party (the server). Although the verification cost is in constant-time, it uses three pairing computations, and we show that, in practice, the verification cost of our VPOPE scheme is more efficient (see Sect. 5.2).

Independently of Kate *et al.* [15], Guo *et al.* [14] propose a scheme with similar security properties to delegate the computation of a secret health-related function on the users' health record. The polynomials are explicitly assumed to have low coefficients and degree, which significantly reduces their randomness. However, the authors give neither security models nor proofs. Later, Gajera *et al.* [12] show that any user can guess the polynomial using the Lagrange's interpolation on several points. They propose a scheme where the degree k is hidden and claim that it does not suffer from this kind of attack.

Following this work, Bultel *et al.* [4] show that hiding the degree k is useless and that no scheme can be secure when the user query more than k points to the server. Moreover, they give cryptanalysis of Guo *et al.* [14] PPE scheme and of Gajera *et al.* [12] PPE scheme which requires only one query to the server and present the first security model for PPE schemes. A PPE scheme must satisfy the following properties: (i) *proof unforgeability* (UNF) requires that the server cannot provide a valid proof to the client for a point that is not a point of the secret polynomial; (ii) *indistinguishability against chosen function attack* (IND-CFA) requires that the client cannot distinguish which of two polynomials of her choice has been evaluated by the server. Bultel *et al.* show that PolyCommit$_{Ped}$ scheme from Kate *et al.* [15] satisfies these security properties. Moreover, Bultel *et al.* design a PPE scheme called PIPE that is IND-CFA secure and solves an open problem described by Kate *et al.* concerning the design of a scheme with a weaker assumption than t-SDH. Despite having the additional property that it protects the privacy of the client, we show that the verification of our VPOPE scheme is more efficient than for PIPE.

More recently, Xia *et al.* [25] proposed a new efficient PPE scheme. As PIPE, their scheme satisfies the required security properties defined in [4]. Their scheme is based on the Pedersen's Verifiable Secret Sharing [24] and does not depend on NIZKP to allow the client to verify the correctness of the result contrary to Bultel *et al.* [4]. Besides, to have computational advantages over previous PPE schemes, Xia *et al.*'s scheme relies only on the *Discrete Logarithm* assumption. However, the verification cost of Xia *et al.*'s scheme also requires k exponentiations where k is the degree of the secret polynomial, which makes it costlier than our scheme that needs only three exponentiations, one Paillier decryption, and k.

1.2 Contributions

The contributions of this paper are summarized as follows:

- We formally define the VPOPE schemes and give a security framework based on those of PPE and *Oblivious Polynomial Evaluation* (OPE) schemes.
- We design VIP-POPE (for *Verifiable* IND-CFA *Paillier based Private Oblivious Polynomial Evaluation*), an efficient and secure VPOPE scheme. This scheme uses the homomorphic properties of Paillier's encryption scheme [20] to achieve encrypted polynomial evaluation.
- We also formally prove its security in the random oracle model and compare its efficiency for the verification cost with the existing PPE schemes. We show that VIP-POPE is more efficient for the verification part than PPE schemes presented in [4,15,25].

1.3 Outline

In the next section, we recall the cryptographic notions used in this paper. In Sect. 3, we give the PPE and OPE security model for VPOPE schemes. Then, we present in Sect. 4, our VPOPE scheme called VIP-POPE. Before to conclude, we prove in Sect. 5 that VIP-POPE satisfies the security properties for VPOPE schemes and compares its verification cost with other PPE schemes of the literature.

2 Preliminaries

We start by recalling the definition of the cryptographic tools used in this paper. In the rest of the paper, we denote by POLY(η) the set of probabilistic polynomial-time algorithms with respect to the security parameter η.

2.1 Paillier Cryptosystem

We now recall the generation, the encryption and decryption algorithms of the Paillier's public key encryption scheme [20] used in our scheme.

Key Generation. We denote by $\mathbb{Z}_n$, the ring of integers modulo n and by $\mathbb{Z}_n^\star$ the set of invertible elements of $\mathbb{Z}_n$. The public key pk of Paillier's encryption scheme is (n, g), where $g \in \mathbb{Z}_{n^2}^\star$ and $n = pq$ is the product of two prime numbers.
    The corresponding secret key sk is (λ, μ), where λ is the least common multiple of $p - 1$ and $q - 1$ and $\mu = (L(g^\lambda \mod n^2))^{-1} \mod n$, where $L(x) = \frac{x-1}{n}$.

Encryption Algorithm. Let m be a message such that $m \in \mathbb{Z}_n$. Let r be a random element of $\mathbb{Z}_n^\star$. We denote by $\mathcal{E}_{pk}$ the encryption algorithm that produces the ciphertext c from a given plaintext m with the public key pk $= (n, g)$ as follows: $c = \mathcal{E}_{pk}(m) = g^m r^n \mod n^2$.

Decryption Algorithm. Let c be the ciphertext such that $c \in \mathbb{Z}_{n^2}$. We denote by $\mathcal{D}_{sk}$ the decryption function of the plaintext c with the secret key sk $= (\lambda, \mu)$ defined as follows: $m = \mathcal{D}_{sk}(c) = L(c^\lambda \mod n^2) \cdot \mu \mod n$.
    Paillier's cryptosystem is a partial homomorphic encryption scheme. Let m_1 and m_2 be two plaintexts in $\mathbb{Z}_n$. The product of the two associated ciphertexts with the public key pk $= (n, g)$, denoted $c_1 = \mathcal{E}_{pk}(m_1) = g^{m_1} r_1^n \mod n^2$ and $c_2 = \mathcal{E}_{pk}(m_2) = g^{m_2} r_2^n \mod n^2$, is the encryption of the sum of m_1 and m_2. We also remark that: $\mathcal{E}_{pk}(m_1) \cdot \mathcal{E}_{pk}(m_2)^{-1} = \mathcal{E}_{pk}(m_1 - m_2)$ and $\mathcal{E}_{pk}(m_1)^{m_2} = \mathcal{E}_{pk}(m_1 m_2)$.

Theorem 1. *Paillier's cryptosystem is IND-CPA-secure if and only if the Decisional Composite Residuosity (DCR) Assumption holds [20].*

To present our scheme, we first claim the following property on Paillier ciphertexts.

Property 1. Let n be the product of two prime numbers, $x \in \mathbb{Z}_n$, and $g \in \mathbb{Z}_{n^2}^\star$. We set pk $= (n, g)$ a Paillier public key. Let $\{t_i\}_{i=1}^k$ such that for all $i \in \{1, \ldots, k\}$, we have $t_i = t_{i-1}^x \cdot r_i^n$ with $t_0 = g$, and $r_i \in \mathbb{Z}_{n^2}^\star$. Then for all $i \in \{1, \ldots, k\}$, $t_i = \mathcal{E}_{pk}(x^i)$.

2.2 Zero-Knowledge Proof

We use the ZKP given by Baudron *et al.* [3] to prove the plaintexts equality of $k \in \mathbb{N}$ Paillier ciphertexts. Let $\mathbb{Z}_{n^2}^\star$ be a multiplicative group where n is the product of two prime numbers p and q. The language is the set of all statements

$(t_1, \ldots, t_k) \in (\mathbb{Z}_{n^2}^\star)^k$ for $k \in \mathbb{Z}_{\geq 2}$ such that for all $i \in \{1, \ldots, k\}$, $t_i = t_{i-1}^x \cdot r_i^n$ mod n^2 where $t_0 \in \mathbb{Z}_{n^2}^\star$ and $r_i \in \mathbb{Z}_{n^2}^\star$.

Since the ZKP given by Baudron *et al.* [3] is a sigma protocol, we can use the *Fiat-Shamir Transformation* [8] to obtain a NIZKP. We formally define this NIZKP called DecPaillierEq.

Definition 1 (DecPaillierEq [3]). *Let n be the product of two prime numbers p and q and H be a hash function, $\mathcal{L}$ be the set of all $(t_1, \ldots, t_k) \in (\mathbb{Z}_{n^2}^\star)^k$ such that for all $i \in \{1, \ldots, k\}$, $t_i = t_{i-1}^x \cdot r_i^n$ mod n^2 where $t_0 \in \mathbb{Z}_{n^2}^\star$ and $r_i \in \mathbb{Z}_{n^2}^\star$. We define the NIZKP DecPaillierEq = (Prove, Verify) for $\mathcal{L}$ as follow:*

- Prove$((t_1, \ldots, t_k), \omega)$: *Using the witness $\omega = (x, t_0, \{r_i\}_{i=1}^k)$, it picks $\rho \xleftarrow{\$} [0, 2^{\log(n)}]$ and $s_i \in \mathbb{Z}_n^\star$ for $1 \leq i \leq k$, and computes $u_i = t_{i-1}^\rho \cdot s_i^n$ mod n^2 for $1 \leq i \leq k$. Moreover, it computes $w = \rho + x \cdot H(t)$ and sets $v_i = s_i \cdot r_i^{H(t)}$ mod n for $1 \leq i \leq k$. Finally, it outputs $\pi_t = (w, \{u_i\}_{i=1}^k, \{v_i\}_{i=1}^k)$.*
- Verify$((t_1, \ldots, t_k), \pi_t)$: *Using $\pi_t = (w, \{u_i\}_{i=1}^k, \{v_i\}_{i=1}^k)$, it verifies if $w \in [0, 2^{\log(n)}]$, and if $t_{i-1}^w \cdot v_i^n = u_i \cdot t_i^{H(t)}$ mod n^2 for $1 \leq i \leq k$. Then it outputs 1, else 0.*

Moreover, Baudron *et al.* [3] prove the following theorem.

Theorem 2. DecPaillierEq *is unconditionally complete, sound and zero-knowledge in the random oracle model.*

3   Definition and Security Model

Before we present our security model, we first formally define a Private Oblivious Polynomial Evaluation scheme.

Definition 2. *A* Verifiable and Private Oblivious Polynomial Evaluation *(VPOPE) scheme is composed of eight algorithms* (setup, init, keyGen, queryGen, queryDec, compute, decrypt, verif) *defined as follows:*

- setup(η) : *Using the security parameter η, this algorithm generates a ring F, public parameters* pub *and secret parameters* sec. *It returns* (pub, F, sec).
- init(F, f, sec) : *Using F, the secret polynomial f, and parameters* sec, *this algorithm returns a verification key* vk_f *and a server key* sk_f *associated to the secret polynomial f.*
- keyGen(η, pub, k) : *Using the security parameter η and public parameters* pub, *this algorithm generates and returns a client's key pair* $(\text{pk}_c, \text{sk}_c)$.
- queryGen(pk_c, x) : *Using a public key* pk_c *and an input x, this algorithm generates an encrypted query t associated to x, a proof π_t proving that t is a valid encrypted query, and returns* (t, π_t).

- queryDec(sk_c, t) : *Using a secret key* sk_c *and an encrypted request* t, *this algorithm outputs* x *if* t *is a valid request of* x, $\perp$ *otherwise.*
- compute($t, \pi_t, f, \mathsf{sk}_f, F$) : *Using* t, π_t, f, sk_f, *and* F, *this algorithm returns an encrypted value* d *along with a proof* π_d *proving that* d *is an encryption of* $f(x)$ *if the proof* π_t *is "accepted". Else it returns* $\perp$.
- decrypt(sk_c, d) : *Using a secret key* sk_c *and the encrypted value* d, *this algorithm returns* y, *the decryption of* d.
- verif($x, \mathsf{sk}_c, \mathsf{pub}, y, \pi_d, \mathsf{vk}_f$) : *This algorithm returns* 1 *if the proof* π_d *is "accepted", 0 otherwise.*

3.1 Security Models

We use security notions of *PPE* schemes formalized by Bultel *et al.* [4], namely *Unforgeability* (UNF), and *Indistinguishability against Chosen Function Attack* (IND-CFA), and adapt them to VPOPE schemes. The security model IND-CFA ensure secrecy of the polynomial, the security model UNF ensures the validity of the verification process. Since VPOPE schemes consider encrypted data on the client-side, we recall the *Client's Privacy - Indistinguishability* (CPI) security property defined by Naor and Pinkas [18] to include the privacy of the client's data. Moreover, we define the *Query Soundness* (QS) notion to prove that a client cannot have other information than points that she queried. In all the security models, we denote by $F[x]^k$, the set of all polynomials of degree k over a finite field F.

$\mathbf{Exp}_{\Pi, \mathcal{A}}^{\mathsf{CPI}}(\eta)$:
$b \xleftarrow{\$} \{0, 1\}$;
$(\mathsf{pub}, F, \mathsf{sec}) \leftarrow \mathsf{setup}(\eta)$;
$f \xleftarrow{\$} F[X]^k$;
$(\mathsf{vk}_f, \mathsf{sk}_f) \leftarrow \mathsf{init}(F, f, \mathsf{sec})$;
$(\mathsf{pk}_c, \mathsf{sk}_c) \leftarrow \mathsf{keyGen}(\eta, \mathsf{pub}, k)$;
$(x_0, x_1, \mathsf{st}) \leftarrow \mathcal{A}_1(\mathsf{pk}_c, \mathsf{pub}, F)$;
$(t, \pi_t) \leftarrow \mathsf{queryGen}(\mathsf{pk}_c, x_b)$;
$b_* \leftarrow \mathcal{A}_2^{\mathsf{CO}_{\mathsf{CPI}}(\cdot)}(t, f, \mathsf{sk}_f, F, \mathsf{st})$;
return $(b = b_*)$.
$\mathsf{CO}_{\mathsf{CPI}}(x)$:
$(t, \pi_t) \leftarrow \mathsf{queryGen}(\mathsf{pk}_c, x)$;
return t .

Fig. 3. CPI experiment.

Client's Privacy - Indistinguishability

We first recall the *Client's Privacy - Indistinguishability* (CPI) security for VPOPE schemes introduced by Naor and Pinkas [18]. In this model, the adversary chooses two queries (x_0, x_1) and tries to guess the evaluation x_b asked by the client. The adversary has access to the ciphertext oracle $\mathsf{CO}_{\mathsf{CPI}}(\cdot)$ taking x as input and returns the encrypted query t. A VPOPE scheme is CPI-secure if no adversary can output the query chosen by the client with a better probability than by guessing.

Definition 3 (Client's privacy - indistinguishability.). *Let* Π *be a VPOPE,* $\mathcal{A} = (\mathcal{A}_1, \mathcal{A}_2) \in \mathrm{POLY}(\eta)^2$ *be a two-party adversary. The* client's privacy - indistinguishability *(CPI) experiment for* $\mathcal{A}$ *against* Π *is defined in Fig. 3,* where $\mathcal{A}$ has access to the oracle $\mathsf{CO}_{CPI}(\cdot)$. The advantage of the adversary $\mathcal{A}$ against the CPI experiment is given by:

$$\mathsf{Adv}_{\Pi,\mathcal{A}}^{CPI}(\eta) = \left| \frac{1}{2} - \Pr\left[1 \leftarrow \mathsf{Exp}_{\Pi,\mathcal{A}}^{CPI}(\eta) \right] \right| .$$

A scheme Π is CPI-secure if this advantage is negligible for any $\mathcal{A} \in \mathrm{POLY}(\eta)^2$.

Chosen Function Attack

We recall the model for k-Indistinguishability against Chosen Function Attack (k- IND-CFA). In this model, the adversary chooses two polynomials (f_0, f_1) and tries to guess the polynomial f_b used by the server, where $b \in \{0,1\}$. The adversary has access to a server oracle $\mathsf{CO}_{CFA}(\cdot)$ and sends to her an encrypted query t associated to her data x along with a proof π_t. The oracle decrypts the query t and obtains x if t is valid. If $f_0(x) = f_1(x)$,

$$
\begin{array}{l}
\mathbf{Exp}_{\Pi,\mathcal{A}}^{k\text{-}\mathbf{IND}\text{-}\mathbf{CFA}}(\eta): \\[4pt]
b \xleftarrow{\$} \{0,1\} ; \\
(\mathsf{pub}, F, \mathsf{sec}) \leftarrow \mathsf{setup}(\eta) ; \\
(\mathsf{pk}_c, \mathsf{sk}_c) \leftarrow \mathsf{keyGen}(\eta, \mathsf{pub}, k) ; \\
(f_0, f_1, \mathsf{st}_2) \leftarrow \mathcal{A}_1(\mathsf{pk}_c, \mathsf{pub}, F, k) ; \\
(\mathsf{vk}_f, \mathsf{sk}_f) \leftarrow \mathsf{init}(F, f_b, \mathsf{sec}) ; \\
b_* \leftarrow \mathcal{A}_2^{\mathsf{CO}_{CFA}(\cdot)}(\mathsf{pk}_c, \mathsf{sk}_c\mathsf{pub}, F, \mathsf{vk}_f, k, \mathsf{st}) ; \\
\text{if } f_0 \notin F[X]^k \text{ or } f_1 \notin F[X]^k: \\
\text{then return } \bot ; \\
\text{else return } (b = b_*) .
\end{array}
$$

Fig. 4. IND-CFA experiment.

the oracle returns d i.e. the encrypted value of $f_b(x)$, along with a proof π_d.

If $f_0(x) \neq f_1(x)$, then the server returns nothing. In practice, an adversary chooses (f_0, f_1) such that $f_0 \neq f_1$, but with k points (x_i, y_i) such that $f_0(x_i) = f_1(x_i)$. It allows the adversary to maximize his oracle calls in order to increase his chances of success.

Definition 4. (k-IND-CFA). Let Π be a VPOPE, $\mathcal{A} = (\mathcal{A}_1, \mathcal{A}_2) \in \mathrm{POLY}(\eta)$ be a two-party adversary and k be an integer. The k-IND-CFA experiment for $\mathcal{A}$ against Π is defined in Fig. 4, where $\mathcal{A}$ has access to the server oracle $\mathsf{CO}_{CFA}(\cdot)$. The advantage of the adversary $\mathcal{A}$ against the k-IND-CFA experiment is given by:

$$
\begin{array}{l}
\mathsf{CO}_{\mathbf{CFA}}(t, \pi_t): \\[4pt]
(d, \pi_d) \leftarrow \mathsf{compute}(t, \pi_t, f_b, \mathsf{sk}_f, F) ; \\
\text{if } x \leftarrow \mathsf{queryDec}(t, \mathsf{sk}_c) \text{ and } x \neq \bot \text{ and} \\
f_0(x) = f_1(x): \\
\text{then return } (d, \pi_d) ; \\
\text{else return } \bot .
\end{array}
$$

Fig. 5. Server oracle for IND-CFA.

$$\mathsf{Adv}_{\Pi,\mathcal{A}}^{k\text{-}IND\text{-}CFA}(\eta) = \left| \frac{1}{2} - \Pr\left[1 \leftarrow \mathsf{Exp}_{\Pi,\mathcal{A}}^{k\text{-}IND\text{-}CFA}(\eta) \right] \right| .$$

A scheme Π is k-IND-CFA-secure if this advantage is negligible for any $\mathcal{A} \in \mathrm{POLY}(\eta)^2$.

Query Soundness

We now define a model for *Query Soundness* (QS). In this model, the adversary tries to learn other information than points of the secret polynomial that she queried by sending a particular query t along with a proof π_t to the server.

$$
\begin{array}{l}
\textbf{Exp}^{\text{QS}}_{\Pi,\mathcal{A}}(\eta): \\
(\text{pub}, F, \text{sec}) \leftarrow \text{setup}(\eta) ; \\
f \xleftarrow{\$} F[X]^k ; \\
(\text{vk}_f, \text{sk}_f) \leftarrow \text{init}(F, f, \text{sec}) ; \\
(\text{pk}_c, \text{sk}_c) \leftarrow \text{keyGen}(\eta, \text{pub}, k) ; \\
(t, \pi_t) \leftarrow \mathcal{A}((\text{pk}_c, \text{sk}_c), \text{pub}, F, \text{vk}_f) ; \\
\text{if queryDec}(t) \neq \bot \text{ and compute}(t, \pi_t, f, \text{sk}_f, F) \neq \bot \\
\quad \text{and } f(\text{queryDec}(\text{sk}_c, t)) \neq \text{decrypt}(\text{sk}_c, d) \text{ such that} \\
\quad (d, \pi_d) \leftarrow \text{compute}(t, \pi_t, f, \text{sk}_f, F): \\
\text{then return } 1 ; \\
\text{else return } 0 .
\end{array}
$$

Fig. 6. QS experiment.

Definition 5 (Query Soundness). *Let Π be a VPOPE, and $\mathcal{A} \in \text{POLY}(\eta)$ be an adversary. The* Query Soundness *(QS) experiment for $\mathcal{A}$ against Π is defined in Fig. 6. The advantage of the adversary $\mathcal{A}$ against the QS experiment is given by:*

$$
\text{Adv}^{\text{QS}}_{\Pi,\mathcal{A}}(\eta) = \Pr\left[1 \leftarrow \text{Exp}^{\text{QS}}_{\Pi,\mathcal{A}}(\eta)\right] .
$$

A scheme Π is QS-secure if this advantage is negligible for any $\mathcal{A} \in \text{POLY}(\eta)$.

Unforgeability

Finally, we recall the unforgeability property. A VPOPE is unforgeable when a dishonest server cannot produce a valid proof for a point (x, y) such that $y \neq f(x)$. In this model, the secret polynomial f is chosen by the server.

Definition 6. (Unforgeability). *Let Π be a VPOPE, $\mathcal{A} = (\mathcal{A}_1, \mathcal{A}_2) \in \text{POLY}(\eta)$ be a two-party adversary. The* unforgeability *(UNF) experiment for $\mathcal{A}$ against Π is defined in Fig. 7. We define the advantage of the adversary $\mathcal{A}$ against the UNF experiment by:*

$$
\begin{array}{l}
\textbf{Exp}^{\text{UNF}}_{\Pi,\mathcal{A}}(\eta): \\
(\text{pub}, F, \text{sec}) \leftarrow \text{setup}(\eta) ; \\
(\text{pk}_c, \text{sk}_c) \leftarrow \text{keyGen}(\eta, \text{pub}, k) ; \\
(f, \text{st}) \leftarrow \mathcal{A}_1(\text{pk}_c, \text{sec}) ; \\
(\text{vk}_f, \text{sk}_f) \leftarrow \text{init}(F, f, \text{sec}) ; \\
(x_*, y_*, \pi_*) \leftarrow \mathcal{A}_2(\text{pub}, \text{sk}_f, \text{vk}_f, F, f, \text{st}) ; \\
\text{if} \quad f(x_*) \quad \neq \quad y_* \quad \text{and} \\
\text{verif}(x_*, \text{sk}_c, \text{pub}, y_*, \pi_*, \text{vk}_f) = 1: \\
\text{then return } 1 ; \\
\text{else return } 0 .
\end{array}
$$

Fig. 7. UNF experiment.

$$
\text{Adv}^{UNF}_{\Pi,\mathcal{A}}(\eta) = \Pr\left[1 \leftarrow \text{Exp}^{UNF}_{\Pi,\mathcal{A}}(\eta)\right] .
$$

A scheme Π is UNF-secure if this advantage is negligible for any $\mathcal{A} \in \text{POLY}(\eta)^2$.

3.2 Security Against Collusion Attacks

There are two possible collusion scenarios: the collusion of a client and the server, and collusion of two or more clients.

Scenario 1: In a collusion of a client and the server, the server can provide the secret polynomial to the client. This is an inherent problem and cannot be prevented. The client can share public parameters and verification keys with the server but these parameters are already public and known to the server. The collusion does not give any advantage to the server to forge fake proof of computation.

Scenario 2: In a collusion of two or more clients, sharing Paillier secret keys with each other does not provide any information about the secret polynomial. All the verification keys and public parameters are the same for each client. The inherent limitation is that the collusion of clients can share their evaluated points and if the total number of points is more than k, where k is the degree of the secret polynomial, then clients can derive the polynomial. This problem exists in any polynomial computation and cannot be prevented.

4 VIP-POPE Description

In our scheme, we assume that the server is not trusted with the computation result and clients are curious to learn about the secret polynomial. A client may forge an encrypted query to gain more information about the secret polynomial. We first give the intuition of our scheme VIP-POPE and then give its formal definition.

We use the homomorphic properties of Paillier's cryptosystem to design our scheme called VIP-POPE. The key idea is to use the fact that a client can generate an encrypted query $t = \{t_i\}_{i=1}^k$ where $t_i = \mathcal{E}_{\mathsf{pk}}(x^i)$ and k is the degree of the secret polynomial $f(\cdot)$ to allow the server to compute $\mathcal{E}_{\mathsf{pk}}(f(x))$. Since the server knows coefficients $\{a_i\}_{i=0}^k$ of $f(\cdot)$, it computes $\mathcal{E}_{\mathsf{pk}}(f(x))$ as follows:

$$\mathcal{E}_{\mathsf{pk}}(a_0) \cdot \prod_{i=1}^{i=k} \mathcal{E}_{\mathsf{pk}}(x^i)^{a_i} = \prod_{i=0}^{i=k} \mathcal{E}_{\mathsf{pk}}(a_i x^i) = \mathcal{E}_{\mathsf{pk}}\left(\sum_{i=0}^{i=k} a_i x^i\right) = \mathcal{E}_{\mathsf{pk}}(f(x)) .$$

The client may forges an untrustworthy encrypted query to learn more than a point on the polynomial. To avoid this kind of attack, the client must provide a proof of validity π_t for each query $t = \{t_i\}_{i=1}^k$ that she sends to the server, i.e., a proof that $t_i = \mathcal{E}_{\mathsf{pk}}(x^i)$ for all $i \in \{1, \ldots, k\}$. Based on Property 1, such a proof can be built using the NIZKP DecPaillierEq presented in Definition 1.

4.1 Formal Definition of VIP-POPE

We now give the formal definition of our scheme VIP-POPE. The algorithms setup and init are run by the company, the algorithm compute is run by the server and the algorithms keyGen, queryGen, decrypt and verif are run by a client.

Definition 7. *Let VIP-POPE = (setup, init, keyGen, queryGen, queryDec, compute, decrypt, verif) be a scheme defined by:*

- setup(η) : *Using the security parameter η, this algorithm first generates a prime number q. It selects a multiplicative group G of order q and generated by h. It picks $(s_1, s_2) \leftarrow (\mathbb{Z}_q^\star)^2$ and sets $\mathsf{pub} = (h^{s_1}, h^{s_2}, h, q)$, $\mathsf{sec} = (s_1, s_2)$, and $F = \mathbb{Z}_q$. Finally, it outputs pub, F, and sec.*
- init(F, f, sec) : *We set $f(x) = \sum_{i=0}^{i=k} a_i \cdot x^i$ where $a_i \in \mathbb{Z}_q$. For all $i \in \{0, \ldots, k\}$, it picks $r_i \in \mathbb{Z}_q^\star$ and computes $\alpha_i = (a_i + r_i) \cdot s_1$ and $\gamma_i = s_1 \cdot s_2^{-1} \cdot r_i$. Finally, it sets $\mathsf{vk}_f = \{\gamma_i\}_{i=0}^k$, $\mathsf{sk}_f = \{\alpha_i\}_{i=0}^k$, and returns $(\mathsf{vk}_f, \mathsf{sk}_f)$.*
- keyGen(η, pub, k) : *For a client c, it picks two primes p_c and q_c such that $(k+1)q^2 < p_c q_c$ and $p_c \approx q_c$. It sets $n_c = p_c q_c$. According to n_c, it generates a Paillier key pair such that $\mathsf{pk}_c = (n_c, g_c)$ and $\mathsf{sk}_c = (\lambda_c, \mu_c)$ as described in Sect. 2. It outputs $(\mathsf{pk}_c, \mathsf{sk}_c)$.*
- queryGen(pk_c, x) : *Using x and the Paillier public key pk_c, this algorithm computes, for all $i \in \{1, \ldots, k\}$, $t_i = \mathcal{E}_{\mathsf{pk}}(x^i)$ and returns the encrypted query $t = (\mathsf{pk}_c, \{t_i\}_{i=1}^k)$ along with a proof π_t of equality of plaintexts using proof^{PaillierEq}.*
- queryDec(sk_c, t) : *First this algorithm parses t as $(\mathsf{pk}_c, \{t_i\}_{i=1}^k)$. Using the Paillier secret key sk_c, this algorithm sets $x = \mathcal{D}_{\mathsf{sk}_c}(t_1)$. If $\mathcal{D}_{\mathsf{sk}_c}(t_i) = x^i$ for $2 \le i \le k$, it outputs x, $\bot$ otherwise.*
- compute($t, \pi_t, f, \mathsf{sk}_f, F$) : *If π_t is accepted by* verify^{PaillierEq}, *this algorithm uses $\{t_i\}_{i=1}^k$ from t, coefficients $\{a_i\}_{i=0}^k$ of the polynomial function $f(\cdot)$, and $\{\alpha_i\}_{i=0}^k$ from the server secret key sk_f to compute:*

$$d = \mathcal{E}_{\mathsf{pk}_c}(a_0) \cdot \prod_{i=1}^{i=k} t_i^{a_i} \quad and \quad \pi_d = \mathcal{E}_{\mathsf{pk}_c}(\alpha_0) \cdot \prod_{i=1}^{i=k} t_i^{\alpha_i} ,$$

and returns (d, π_d), else it returns $\bot$.
- decrypt(sk_c, d) : *Using the Paillier secret key sk_c which is equal to (λ_c, μ_c), this algorithm returns $y = \mathcal{D}_{\mathsf{sk}_c}(d) \bmod q$.*
- verif($x, \mathsf{sk}_c, \mathsf{pub}, y, \pi_d, \mathsf{vk}_f$) : *Using x, sk_c, vk_f, and the proof π_d, this algorithm computes:*

$$y' = \mathcal{D}_{\mathsf{sk}_c}(\pi_d) \bmod q \quad and \quad z = \sum_{i=0}^{i=k} \gamma_i \cdot x^i .$$

If $(h^{s_1})^y \cdot (h^{s_2})^z = h^{y'}$, then the algorithm returns 1, else it returns 0.

Parameter Selection. We need to have $\sum_{i=0}^{i=k} a_i \cdot x^i < n_c = p_c \cdot q_c$ for successful decryption due to Paillier cryptosystem properties. Since $0 \le a_i < q$ and $0 \le x^i < q$, we have $a_i \cdot x^i < q^2$ for each $i \in \{0, \ldots, k\}$ that gives us $a_0 + a_1 \cdot x + \cdots + a_k \cdot x^k < (k+1) \cdot q^2$. Hence, we need to have $(k+1) \cdot q^2 < n_c$ to always have successful decryption. Moreover, we recommend the size of each prime p_c and q_c to be at least 1024 bits to make the factorization of n_c hard.

5   Security and Performance Analysis

We first give a theorem on the security of VIP-POPE. Then we provide some comparisons with PPE schemes of the literature [4, 15, 25].

5.1   Security Proofs

We present the security proofs of VIP-POPE in our security model.

Theorem 3. *VIP-POPE is a CPI-secure scheme under the DCR assumption.*

Proof. We assume there exists $\mathcal{A} \in \text{POLY}(\eta)^2$ such that $\text{Adv}^{\text{CPI}}_{\text{VIP-POPE}, \mathcal{A}}(\eta)$ is non-negligible and we show there exists an algorithm $\mathcal{B} \in \text{POLY}(\eta)$ such that $\text{Adv}^{\text{IND-CPA}}_{\text{Paillier}, \mathcal{B}}(\eta)$ is non-negligible. We build $\mathcal{B}$ as follows:

- $\mathcal{B}$ receives $\mathbb{Z}_q, \text{sec}$ from $\text{setup}(\eta)$ and pk_c from $\text{keyGen}(\eta, \text{pub}, k)$.
- $\mathcal{B}$ runs $(x_0, x_1, \text{st}) \leftarrow \mathcal{A}_1(\text{pk}_c)$.
- $\mathcal{B}$ picks $f \xleftarrow{\$} \mathbb{Z}_q[X]^k$ and runs $\text{init}(\mathbb{Z}_q, f, \text{sec})$ to obtain vk_f and sk_f.
- $\mathcal{B}$ runs the oracle $\mathcal{E}_{\text{pk}}(\text{LR}_b(\cdot, \cdot))$ on (x_0^i, x_1^i) for $i \in \{1, \ldots, k\}$ and obtains $t = \{t_i\}_{i=1}^k$, Paillier ciphertexts of x_b^i.
- $\mathcal{B}$ runs $b_* \leftarrow \mathcal{A}_2(t, f, \text{sk}_f, \mathbb{Z}_q, \text{st})$. To simulate the oracle $\text{CO}_{\text{CPI}}(\cdot)$ on x to $\mathcal{A}$, $\mathcal{B}$ computes $t = \{\mathcal{E}_{\text{pk}_c}(x^i)\}_{i=1}^k$.
- Finally, $\mathcal{B}$ outputs b_*.

We remark that:

1. The experiment CPI is perfectly simulated for $\mathcal{A}$.
2. $\mathcal{B}$ wins the IND-CPA experiment if and only if $\mathcal{A}$ wins the CPI experiment.

Since $\text{Adv}^{\text{CPI}}_{\text{VIP-POPE}, \mathcal{A}}(\eta)$ is non-negligible, then $\text{Adv}^{\text{IND-CPA}}_{\text{Paillier}, \mathcal{B}}(\eta)$ is non-negligible. However, Paillier cryptosystem is IND-CPA under the DCR assumption, then $\mathcal{B}$ can be used to break the DCR assumption, which contradicts our hypothesis and concludes the proof.   □

Theorem 4. *For any $k \in \mathbb{N}$, VIP-POPE is a k-IND-CFA-secure scheme.*

Proof. Let $\mathcal{A} \in \text{POLY}(\eta)$ be an algorithm. We show that there exists an algorithm $\mathcal{B} \in \text{POLY}(\eta)$ simulating the experiment $\text{Exp}^{k\text{-IND-CFA}}_{\text{VIP-POPE}, \mathcal{A}}(\eta)$ to $\mathcal{A}$. We build $\mathcal{B}$ as follows:

- $\mathcal{B}$ picks $b \xleftarrow{\$} \{0, 1\}$.
- $\mathcal{B}$ generates $(\text{pub}, \mathbb{Z}_q, \text{sec}) \leftarrow \text{setup}(\eta)$, where $\text{pub} = (h^{s_1}, h^{s_2}, h)$, and $\text{sec} = (s_1, s_2) \in \mathbb{Z}_q^\star$.
- $\mathcal{B}$ runs $(f_0, f_1, \text{st}) \leftarrow \mathcal{A}_1(\mathbb{Z}_q, k)$, and it sets $f_0(x) = \sum_{i=0}^{i=k} a_{0,i} \cdot x^i$ and $f_1(x) = \sum_{i=0}^{i=k} a_{1,i} \cdot x^i$.
- $\mathcal{B}$ picks $r \xleftarrow{\$} \mathbb{Z}_q^\star$. For all $i \in \{0, \ldots, k\}$, it picks $r_i \xleftarrow{\$} \mathbb{Z}_q^\star$, and sets $\alpha_i = (a_{b,i} + r_i) \cdot s_1$, and $\gamma_i = s_1 \cdot s_2^{-1} \cdot r_i$. Finally, it sets $f'(x) = \sum_{i=0}^{i=k} \alpha_i \cdot x^i$, and returns $\text{vk}_f = \{\gamma_i\}_{i=0}^k$.

- $\mathcal{B}$ generates $(\mathsf{pk}_c, sk_c) \leftarrow \mathsf{keyGen}(\eta, \mathsf{pub}, k)$.
- $\mathcal{B}$ runs $b_* \leftarrow \mathcal{A}_2((\mathsf{pk}_c, \mathsf{sk}_c), \mathsf{pub}, \mathbb{Z}_q^*, \mathsf{vk}_f, k, \mathsf{st})$. To simulate the oracle $\mathsf{CO}_{\mathsf{CFA}}(\cdot)$ to $\mathcal{A}$ on $t = \{\mathcal{E}_{\mathsf{pk}}(x^i)\}_{i=1}^k$, $\mathcal{B}$ first verifies if $f_0(\mathcal{D}_{\mathsf{sk}_c}(\mathcal{E}_{\mathsf{pk}_c}(x))) = f_1(\mathcal{D}_{\mathsf{sk}_c}(\mathcal{E}_{\mathsf{pk}_c}(x)))$ then computes:

$$d = \mathcal{E}_{\mathsf{pk}_c}(a_{b,0}) \cdot \prod_{i=1}^{i=k} \mathcal{E}_{\mathsf{pk}}(x_j^i)^{a_{b,i}}, \qquad \pi_d = \mathcal{E}_{\mathsf{pk}_c}(\alpha_0) \cdot \prod_{i=1}^{i=k} \mathcal{E}_{\mathsf{pk}}(x_j^i)^{\alpha_i},$$

and returns (d, π_d). Else, it returns $\bot$.
- Finally, $\mathcal{B}$ outputs b_*.

We remark that r and r_i (for $0 \leq i \leq k$) are chosen in the uniform distribution of $\mathbb{Z}_q^*$, then each element of vk_f comes from the uniform distribution on $\mathbb{Z}_q^*$. Finally, we have:

$$(h^{s_1})^{f(x)} \cdot (h^{s_2})^{Z(x)} = h^{f'(x)}.$$

We deduce that the experiment k-IND-CFA is perfectly simulated for $\mathcal{A}$. Then $\mathcal{A}$ cannot do better than the random to guess the value of the chosen b. Hence, $\mathsf{Adv}_{\mathsf{VIP\text{-}POPE}, \mathcal{A}}^{k\text{-IND-CFA}}(\eta)$ is negligible which concludes the proof. $\qquad\square$

Theorem 5. *For any $k \in \mathbb{N}$, VIP-POPE is QS-secure in the random oracle model.*

Proof. The proof π_t is computed as in $\mathsf{DecPaillierEq}$ (Definition 1). This NIZKP is unconditionally *sound*, then there exists no probabilistic polynomial time algorithm that forges a valid proof on a false statement with non-negligible probability, i.e., a statement $(t_1, \ldots, t_k)$ where there exists $1 \leq i \leq k$ such that $t_i \neq t_{i-1}^x \cdot r_i^n$ where $n = p \cdot q$ and p, q are two prime numbers, $t_0 \in \mathbb{Z}_{n^2}^*$ $r_i \in \mathbb{Z}_{n^2}^*$, and $x \in \mathbb{Z}_{n^2}^*$.

We show that if there exists $\mathcal{A} \in \mathrm{POLY}(\eta)^2$ such that $\mathsf{Adv}_{\mathsf{VIP\text{-}POPE}, \mathcal{A}}^{\mathsf{QS}}(\eta)$ is non-negligible, then there exists $\mathcal{B} \in \mathrm{POLY}(\eta)$ that forges a valid proof of an instance where $t_i \neq t_{i-1}^x \cdot r_i^n$. It contradicts the soundness of $\mathsf{DecPaillierEq}$ which concludes the proof. $\mathcal{B}$ works as follows:

- $\mathcal{B}$ runs $(\mathsf{pub}, F, \mathsf{sec}) \leftarrow \mathsf{setup}(\eta)$, $(\mathsf{pk}_c, sk_c) \leftarrow \mathsf{keyGen}(\eta, \mathsf{pub}, k)$, $f \xleftarrow{\$} F[x]^k$, $(\mathsf{vk}_f, \mathsf{sk}_f) \leftarrow \mathsf{init}(F, f, \mathsf{sec})$, and $(t, \pi_t) \leftarrow \mathcal{A}((\mathsf{pk}_c, \mathsf{sk}_c), \mathsf{pub}, F, \mathsf{vk}_f)$ where $\pi_t = (w, \{u_i\}_{i=1}^k, \{v_i\}_{i=1}^k)$.
- $\mathcal{B}$ returns t as a statement together with the proof π_t.

We observe that since $\mathsf{Adv}_{\mathsf{VIP\text{-}POPE}, \mathcal{A}}^{\mathsf{QS}}(\eta)$ is non-negligible, then the probability that $f(\mathsf{queryDec}(\mathsf{sk}_c, t)) \neq \mathsf{decrypt}(\mathsf{sk}_c, d)$ and $\mathsf{compute}(t, \pi_t, f, \mathsf{sk}_f, F) \neq \bot$ is non-negligible. Moreover:

- $f(\mathsf{queryDec}(\mathsf{sk}_c, t)) \neq \mathsf{decrypt}(\mathsf{sk}_c, d) \Rightarrow f(x) \neq y$, that means there exists $1 \leq i_0 \leq k$ such that $\mathcal{D}_{\mathsf{sk}_c}(t_i) \neq x^i$.
- $\mathsf{compute}(t, \pi_t, f, \mathsf{sk}_f, F) \neq \bot \Rightarrow t_{i-1}^w \cdot v_i^n = u_i \cdot t_i^{H(t)} \mod n^2$ for $1 \leq i \leq k$. Then π_t is a valid proof.

$\mathcal{B}$ returns a valid proof of a false instance with non-negligible probability.   □

Theorem 6. *For any $k \in \mathbb{N}$, VIP-POPE is UNF-secure under the DL assumption.*

Proof. We assume there exists $\mathcal{A} \in \text{POLY}(\eta)^2$ such that $\text{Adv}_{\text{VIP-POPE},\mathcal{A}}^{\text{UNF}}(\eta)$ is non-negligible. We show that $\mathcal{A}$ can be used to construct an algorithm $\mathcal{B}$ that computes $\log_h(h^{s_1})$.

First, we note that if $y_* \neq f(x_*)$, then we also have $y'_* \neq y'$ where we denote $y'_* = \mathcal{D}_{\text{sk}_c}(\pi_*)$ and $y' = \sum_{i=0}^{i=k} \alpha_i \cdot x_*^i$. It is easy to check this condition. Therefore, we must have both inequalities $y_* \neq f(x_*)$ and $y'_* \neq y'$ hold. We show that there exists an algorithm $\mathcal{B} \in \text{POLY}(\eta)$ that breaks the DL assumption by computing $\log_h(h^{s_1})$ using $\mathcal{A}$. $\mathcal{B}$ works as follows:

- $\mathcal{B}$ obtains $(\text{pub}, F, \text{sec}) \leftarrow \text{setup}(\eta)$ and $(\text{pk}_c, sk_c) \leftarrow \text{keyGen}(\eta, \text{pub}, k)$.
- $\mathcal{B}$ receives $(f, \text{st}) \leftarrow \mathcal{A}_1(\text{pk}_c, \text{pub}, F)$.
- $\mathcal{B}$ runs $(\text{vk}_f, \text{sk}_f) \leftarrow \text{init}(F, f, \text{sec})$ where $\text{sk}_f = \{\alpha_i\}_{i=0}^k$, then obtains $(x_*, y_*, \pi_*) \leftarrow \mathcal{A}_2(\text{pub}_c, \text{sk}_f, \text{vk}_f, F, f, \text{st})$.
- $\mathcal{B}$ computes:

$$\log_h(h^{s_1}) = \frac{\mathcal{D}_{\text{sk}_c}(\pi_*) - \sum_{i=0}^{i=k} \alpha_i \cdot x_*^i}{y_* - f(x_*)} .$$

Since we have proved that $y_* \neq f(x_*)$, the discrete logarithm $\log_h(h^{s_1})$ can be computed with the same probability as $\mathcal{A}$ wins the UNF experiment. Therefore, based on the DL assumption, there cannot exist an adversary $\mathcal{A}$ such that $\text{Adv}_{\text{VIP-POPE},\mathcal{A}}^{\text{UNF}}(\eta)$ is non-negligible.   □

5.2   Comparison with Other PPE Schemes

Table 1. Comparison of VIP-POPE with other *PPE* schemes. We denote by D the constant cost of one Paillier decryption.

Schemes	Setup size	Key size	Verif. cost	Pairing	Assumption	Model	Privacy
PolyCommit$_{\text{Ped}}$ [15]	$\mathcal{O}(k)$	$\mathcal{O}(1)$	$\mathcal{O}(1)$	Yes	t-SDH	Standard	No
PIPE [4]	$\mathcal{O}(1)$	$\mathcal{O}(k)$	$\mathcal{O}(k \cdot \log(q))$	No	DDH	ROM	No
Xia *et al.*'s [25]	$\mathcal{O}(1)$	$\mathcal{O}(k)$	$\mathcal{O}(k \cdot \log(q))$	No	DL	Standard	No
VIP-POPE	$\mathcal{O}(1)$	$\mathcal{O}(k)$	$\mathcal{O}(3 \cdot \log(q) + k) + D$	No	DL/DCR	ROM	Yes

In Table 1, we provide comparison of our scheme with PolyCommit$_{\text{Ped}}$ [15], PIPE [4] and Xia *et al.*'s scheme [25]. We observe that the verification key size and verification cost are constant in PolyCommit$_{\text{Ped}}$ while in all other schemes it depends on the degree k. The verification equation in PolyCommit$_{\text{Ped}}$ involves several bilinear pairing which is costly compared to other operations. The verification key size and verification cost are not constant in our scheme but our scheme is pairing free and efficient as compared to other pairing free schemes.

Moreover, our scheme VIP-POPE provides the client's data privacy while the other three schemes do not provide any privacy. To support our claim about efficiency, we implement all these schemes for different values of degrees with realistic parameters.

In our scheme, the verification of the result obtained from the server is done by a client. In such a case, the verification cost becomes an important aspect of the scheme. We claim that our scheme is most efficient so far in terms of verification cost. We implement VIP-POPE, PIPE and Xia's scheme in SageMath 8.1 on 64-bit PC with Intel Core i5 - 6500 CPU @ 3.2 GHz and 4 GiB RAM.

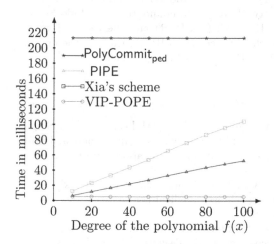

Fig. 8. Verification cost comparison.

The new scheme, VIP-POPE, provides privacy of the client's data while the other two schemes, PIPE, and Xia's scheme, do not provide privacy of the client's data. To keep the comparison as fair as possible, we implement all three schemes with the same realistic parameters. For our scheme, we choose a 1024 bit prime q and 160 bit prime q_1 such that $q' = 2q_1q + 1$ is a prime. We choose another 1024 bit prime p and set $n = pq'$. The coefficients of the polynomial $f(x)$, the secret values (s_1, s_2) and $\{r_i\}_{i=0}^k$ are all selected uniformly at random from $\mathbb{Z}_q^\star$. For Xia's scheme and PIPE, we keep the value of q, the polynomial $f(x)$ and $\{r_i\}_{i=0}^k$ same as in VIP-POPE. We compare the cost of only the verification equation in all three schemes.

For different values of the degree of the polynomial $f(x)$, we ran each scheme for 100 new instances and each instance for 10 times. We then averaged out the total time for the verification equation in each scheme. In Fig. 8, we observe that VIP-POPE takes almost constant time while the cost of verification equation in PIPE and Xia's scheme increases linearly with respect to the degree k. Moreover, our scheme takes only around 5–6 ms for verification equation even for $k = 100$ which makes it practically feasible for real applications.

6 Conclusion

In this paper, we gave a formal definition of new primitive called VPOPE (for Verifiable and Private Oblivious Polynomial Evaluation). This primitive allows a company to delegate the computation of a secret polynomial $f(\cdot)$ to an external server on the client's encrypted data in a verifiable way. In other terms, a client sends an encrypted query to a server associated with her secret data x using her public key pk. Then, the client receives d with proof that $d = \mathcal{E}_{pk}(f(x))$. We design the first VPOPE scheme called VIP-POPE (for Verifiable IND-CFA Paillier based Private Oblivious IND-CFA Polynomial Evaluation) and prove that it satisfies the required security properties, i.e., VIP-POPE is CPI-, IND-CFA-, QS-, UNF-secure in the random oracle model. Moreover, we compare our scheme to other existing PPE schemes of the literature and show that its computational verification cost is less as compared to others.

Acknowledgements. This research was conducted with the support of the FEDER program of 2014–2020, the region council of Auvergne-Rhône-Alpes, the support of the "Digital Trust" Chair from the University of Auvergne Foundation, the Indo-French Centre for the Promotion of Advanced Research (IFCPAR) and the Center Franco-Indien Pour La Promotion De La Recherche Avancée (CEFIPRA) through the project DST/CNRS 2015-03 under DST-INRIA-CNRS Targeted Programme.

References

1. Personal info of 1.5m SingHealth patients, including PM Lee, stolen in Singapore's worst cyber attack. https://www.straitstimes.com/singapore/personal-info-of-15m-singhealth-patients-including-pm-lee-stolen-in-singapores-most. Accessed 20 Agu 2019
2. Amin, R., Islam, S.H., Biswas, G., Khan, M.K., Kumar, N.: A robust and anonymous patient monitoring system using wireless medical sensor networks. Future Gener. Comput. Syst. **80**, 483–495 (2018)
3. Baudron, O., Fouque, P., Pointcheval, D., Stern, J., Poupard, G.: Practical multi-candidate election system. In: Proceedings of the Twentieth Annual ACM Symposium on Principles of Distributed Computing, PODC 2001, Newport, Rhode Island, USA, pp. 274–283 (2001)
4. Bultel, X., Das, M.L., Gajera, H., Gérault, D., Giraud, M., Lafourcade, P.: Verifiable private polynomial evaluation. In: Okamoto, T., Yu, Y., Au, M.H., Li, Y. (eds.) ProvSec 2017. LNCS, vol. 10592, pp. 487–506. Springer, Cham (2017). https://doi.org/10.1007/978-3-319-68637-0_29
5. Canetti, R., Riva, B., Rothblum, G.N.: Two protocols for delegation of computation. In: Proceedings of Information Theoretic Security - 6th International Conference, ICITS, Montreal, QC, Canada, pp. 37–61 (2012)
6. Choi, S.G., Katz, J., Kumaresan, R., Cid, C.: Multi-client non-interactive verifiable computation. In: Sahai, A. (ed.) TCC 2013. LNCS, vol. 7785, pp. 499–518. Springer, Heidelberg (2013). https://doi.org/10.1007/978-3-642-36594-2_28
7. De Muth, J.E.: Basic Statistics and Pharmaceutical Statistical Applications. Chapman and Hall/CRC, Danvers (2014)
8. Fiat, A., Shamir, A.: How to prove yourself: practical solutions to identification and signature problems. In: Odlyzko, A.M. (ed.) CRYPTO 1986. LNCS, vol. 263, pp. 186–194. Springer, Heidelberg (1987). https://doi.org/10.1007/3-540-47721-7_12
9. Fiore, D., Gennaro, R.: Publicly verifiable delegation of large polynomials and matrix computations, with applications. In: Proceedings of the ACM Conference on Computer and Communications Security, Raleigh, NC, USA, pp. 501–512 (2012)
10. Freedman, M.J., Ishai, Y., Pinkas, B., Reingold, O.: Keyword search and oblivious pseudorandom functions. In: Kilian, J. (ed.) TCC 2005. LNCS, vol. 3378, pp. 303–324. Springer, Heidelberg (2005). https://doi.org/10.1007/978-3-540-30576-7_17

11. Freedman, M.J., Nissim, K., Pinkas, B.: Efficient private matching and set intersection. In: Cachin, C., Camenisch, J.L. (eds.) EUROCRYPT 2004. LNCS, vol. 3027, pp. 1–19. Springer, Heidelberg (2004). https://doi.org/10.1007/978-3-540-24676-3_1

12. Gajera, H., Naik, S., Das, M.L.: On the security of "verifiable privacy-preserving monitoring for cloud-assisted mHealth systems". In: Ray, I., Gaur, M.S., Conti, M., Sanghi, D., Kamakoti, V. (eds.) ICISS 2016. LNCS, vol. 10063, pp. 324–335. Springer, Cham (2016). https://doi.org/10.1007/978-3-319-49806-5_17

13. Gennaro, R., Gentry, C., Parno, B.: Non-interactive verifiable computing: outsourcing computation to untrusted workers. In: Rabin, T. (ed.) CRYPTO 2010. LNCS, vol. 6223, pp. 465–482. Springer, Heidelberg (2010). https://doi.org/10.1007/978-3-642-14623-7_25

14. Guo, L., Fang, Y., Li, M., Li, P.: Verifiable privacy-preserving monitoring for cloud-assisted mHealth systems. In: Proceedings of IEEE Conference on Computer Communications, INFOCOM, Kowloon, Hong Kong, pp. 1026–1034 (2015)

15. Kate, A., Zaverucha, G.M., Goldberg, I.: Constant-size commitments to polynomials and their applications. In: Abe, M. (ed.) ASIACRYPT 2010. LNCS, vol. 6477, pp. 177–194. Springer, Heidelberg (2010). https://doi.org/10.1007/978-3-642-17373-8_11

16. Lindell, Y., Pinkas, B.: Privacy preserving data mining. J. Cryptol. 15(3), 177–206 (2002)

17. Lloret, J., Garcia, M., Bri, D., Sendra, S.: A wireless sensor network deployment for rural and forest fire detection and verification. Sensors 9(11), 8722–8747 (2009)

18. Naor, M., Pinkas, B.: Oblivious transfer and polynomial evaluation. In: Proceedings of the Thirty-First Annual ACM Symposium on Theory of Computing, Atlanta, Georgia, USA, pp. 245–254 (1999)

19. Okayama, T.: Future gardening system-smart garden. J. Dev. Sustain. Agric. 9(1), 47–50 (2014)

20. Paillier, P.: Public-key cryptosystems based on composite degree residuosity classes. In: Stern, J. (ed.) EUROCRYPT 1999. LNCS, vol. 1592, pp. 223–238. Springer, Heidelberg (1999). https://doi.org/10.1007/3-540-48910-X_16

21. Papamanthou, C., Shi, E., Tamassia, R.: Signatures of correct computation. In: Sahai, A. (ed.) TCC 2013. LNCS, vol. 7785, pp. 222–242. Springer, Heidelberg (2013). https://doi.org/10.1007/978-3-642-36594-2_13

22. Parno, B., Howell, J., Gentry, C., Raykova, M.: Pinocchio: nearly practical verifiable computation. In: Proceedings of IEEE Symposium on Security and Privacy, SP 2013, Berkeley, CA, USA, pp. 238–252 (2013)

23. Parno, B., Raykova, M., Vaikuntanathan, V.: How to delegate and verify in public: verifiable computation from attribute-based encryption. In: Cramer, R. (ed.) TCC 2012. LNCS, vol. 7194, pp. 422–439. Springer, Heidelberg (2012). https://doi.org/10.1007/978-3-642-28914-9_24

24. Pedersen, T.P.: Non-interactive and information-theoretic secure verifiable secret sharing. In: Feigenbaum, J. (ed.) CRYPTO 1991. LNCS, vol. 576, pp. 129–140. Springer, Heidelberg (1992). https://doi.org/10.1007/3-540-46766-1_9

25. Xia, Z., Yang, B., Zhang, M., Mu, Y.: An efficient and provably secure private polynomial evaluation scheme. In: Su, C., Kikuchi, H. (eds.) ISPEC 2018. LNCS, vol. 11125, pp. 595–609. Springer, Cham (2018). https://doi.org/10.1007/978-3-319-99807-7_38

Monomial Evaluation of Polynomial Functions Protected by Threshold Implementations
With an Illustration on AES

Simon Landry[1,2]([✉]) [iD], Yanis Linge[1] [iD], and Emmanuel Prouff[2,3] [iD]

[1] STMicroelectronics, Zone Industrielle, 190 Avenue Coq, 13106 Rousset, France
{simon.landry,yanis.linge}@st.com
[2] Sorbonne Universités, UPMC Univ Paris 06, POLSYS, UMR 7606, LIP6, 75005 Paris, France
emmanuel.prouff@ssi.gouv.fr
[3] ANSSI, Paris, France

Abstract. In the context of side-channel countermeasures, threshold implementations (TI) have been introduced in 2006 by Nikova *et al.* to defeat attacks in presence of hardware effects called *glitches*. On several aspects, TI may be seen as an extension of another classical side-channel countermeasure, called *masking*, which is essentially based on the sharing of any internal state of the processing into independent parts (or shares). Among the properties of TI, uniform distribution of input and output shares is generally the most complicated to satisfy. Usually, this property is achieved by generating fresh randomness throughout the execution of the protected algorithm (*e.g.* the AES block cipher). In this paper, we combine the *changing of the guards* technique published by Daemen at CHES 2017 (which reduces the need for fresh randomness) with the work of Genelle *et al.* at CHES 2011 (which combines Boolean masking and multiplicative one) to propose a new TI without fresh randomness well suited to Substitution-Permutation Networks. As an illustration, we develop our proposal for the AES block cipher, and more specifically its non-linear part implemented thanks to a field inversion. In this particular context, we argue that our proposal is a valuable alternative to the state of the art solutions. More generally, it has the advantage of being easily applicable to the evaluation of any polynomial function, which was usually not the case of previous solutions.

Keywords: SCA · Threshold implementations · AES · Masking · Sharing · Secure polynomial evaluation

M. Laurent and T. Giannetsos (Eds.): WISTP 2019, LNCS 12024, pp. 66–84, 2020.
https://doi.org/10.1007/978-3-030-41702-4_5

1 Introduction

1.1 Problematic and State of the Art

Introduced by Kocher [23] in the late nineties, *Side Channel Analysis (SCA)* is a serious threat in our connected world. Cryptography indeed evolves in a hostile environment, where an attacker can obtain information that leak from algorithms running on embedded devices. This information relate to *intermediate variables* and some of them are *sensitive* in the sense that they are linked to the secret key and can be exploited to mount a key-recovery attack [5].

The SCA threat [23] led to the increasing need for countermeasures. A solution is provided by the so-called *secret sharing* [9,20,34]. In the context of SCA, we talk about *masking* [23]. The idea is to randomly split the sensitive variable into $(d + 1)$ shares. The number d is refered as the *masking order*. A dth-order masking can be broken by a $(d + 1)^{th}$-order SCA, namely an adversary that targets $d + 1$ intermediate variables at the same time [27,30,36]. However, masking countermeasure is vulnerable to *glitches* when the algorithm is embedded on a device. Glitches refer here switching variations of logic gates that are caused by interconnection delays between two consecutive register updates. Due to glitches, it has been shown in [26] that an attack can be mounted by exploiting side-channel information leakage at the output of some logic gates. In 2006, Nikova *et al.* [29] proposed a special case of masking, called *threshold implementations (TI)* such that the security holds even in the presence of glitches. This countermeasure combines *secret sharing* and *multi-party computation (MPC)*. MPC creates methods for parties to jointly compute a public function over their inputs while keeping those inputs private (see [40] and [2] for more details).

By property of threshold implementations, it is known that at least 3 shares per internal state element are required to achieve security against first-order attacks in the presence of glitches [29]. The construction of such an implementation (with 3 shares only) for the AES algorithm has been an important research topic [3,10,21,28]. The first difficulty is to achieve uniformity efficiently. The common technique to fix this issue is called *remasking*. It consists in adding fresh randomness to the implementation during the execution. However, remasking is very time and space consuming since the random bits have to be generated and stored in registers. To fix this constraint, Daemen proposed in [12] a technique called *changing of the guards* to assure uniformity of a function without fresh randomness (see its description in the extended version of this paper [24]). Based on this technique, Sugawara presented in [37] a provably 3-sharing uniform TI of the Canright's AES Sbox [6] without remasking. Then, the second challenge is the efficiency, and more precisely the number of cycles that are required to implement a threshold implementation of the AES Sbox resistant against first-order SCA attacks.

1.2 Our Contributions

In this paper, we propose a 3-sharing TI scheme that can be applied to secure the processing of any monomial. Our technique can be extended to secure the evaluation of polynomial functions in a generic manner and the proposed scheme is proved to be resistant against first-order SCA in the presence of glitches. In the latter case, the number of cycles taken by the secure evaluation is independent of the support of the polynomial while the number of gates and registers essentially increases linearly. Eventually, the design principles can be extended to higher-order security. As an illustration, we apply our method on the AES algorithm to design a 3-sharing TI of the AES Sbox without fresh randomness. It is an alternative to Sugawara's work [37].[1]

1.3   Overview of the Paper

In Sect. 2 we first introduce notations related to the masking schemes in finite fields that we use in our paper. We present then the threshold implementations, the related security models and their properties. Based on [12], we also describe in the extended version of this paper [24] another technique than remasking to get uniformity in a construction. In Sect. 3 we present our generic TI for secure evaluation of polynomial functions in $GF(2^n)$ and we argue that it is resistant against first-order SCA in the presence of glitches. Our proposal is built upon a primitive that must securely process the function mapping $x \in GF(2^n)$ into 1 if $x = 0$ and into 0 otherwise. In Sect. 4, we describe a 3-TI implementation of this primitive called here *Dirac function*. We argue that it is secure against first-order SCA in presence of glitches. For completeness, we present in the extended version of this paper [24] another original TI construction of the Dirac function, based on Sugawara's work [37] and on Ishaï *et al.* multiplications [22]. The proofs of our lemmas and properties are given in the extended version of this paper [24]. We give an application of our technique to the AES algorithm in Sect. 5. Our first-order TI-masked 3-sharing implementation of the AES SBox is argued to be secure against SCA attacks in the presence of glitches. Finally, in Sect. 6, we discuss the performances of our construction compared to the prior state of the art.

2   Preliminaries

2.1   Basics on Sharing

In this paper, we discuss on the sharing of both field elements defined in $GF(2^n)$ for some n and (n, m)-functions defined from $GF(2^n)$ into $GF(2^m)$ for some n and m.

---

[1] In the extended version of this paper [24], we give a second possible scheme of a 3-sharing TI of the AES Sbox without fresh randomness. It takes two more cycles than our main proposal but it does not require pre-processing and additionnal memory space.

Sharing of Internal Variables. When masking is applied to secure block cipher implementations, each sensitive variable x occurring during the computation is split into d random shares following a chosen group operation. We define the tuple $\mathbf{x} = (x_1, \ldots, x_d)$ as the d-sharing of x while the x_i's are called the masks. Also, the value of d plays the role of a secure parameter. We also introduce the function $s()$ that recovers x from its d-sharing $\mathbf{x}$ and will be refered as the *reconstruction function*. It is defined by $s(\mathbf{x}) = x$. For example, if the group operation is the addition $\oplus$ in $GF(2^n)$, we have:

$$x = x_1 \oplus x_2 \oplus \ldots \oplus x_d \qquad and \qquad s(\mathbf{x}) = \bigoplus_{i=1}^{d} x_i = x.$$

In this paper, we shall work with three types of masking for $d = 3$. We shall refer to the above example as a 3-*Boolean sharing*. If the group operation is the multiplication $\otimes$ in $GF(2^n)^*$, we shall refer to it as a 3-*multiplicative sharing* [1,4]. To mask additive functions we usually use a Boolean masking. Since the propagation of Boolean masks through a multiplication is tricky to deal with, the multiplicative masking is more suitable to mask multiplicative functions (as *e.g.* power functions). Eventually, by combining a Boolean with a multiplicative one, we obtain a 3-*affine sharing* that we describe in the following definition.

Definition 1 *(3-affine sharing)* [15]. *Let $x, \tilde{x}, \beta \in GF(2^n)$ and $\alpha \in GF(2^n)^*$ be four elements such that $x = (\tilde{x} \otimes \alpha^{-1}) \oplus \beta$. Then, $\mathbf{x} = (\tilde{x}, \alpha, \beta)$ is called 3-affine sharing of x, and β (resp. α) is called the Boolean mask (resp. multiplicative mask).*

Sharing of Functions. In the sequel, we shall express the input of a function F by a small letter x and its corresponding output by a large letter X. A mapping from x to X can be defined by $F(x) = X$.

A mask realization of an (n, m)-function F is a vector $\mathbf{F} = (F_1, \ldots, F_d)$ of (dn, m)-functions. The notion of reconstruction function can then be extended to mask realizations by setting:

$$s(\mathbf{F}(\mathbf{x})) = F(x) = X$$

2.2   Basic Notions

To formally describe the security notions involved in this paper and to explain the different countermeasures, it is classical to use an abstraction of the implementation called *circuit*. We recall hereafter the definition of circuit given in [35].

Definition 2 [35] *(Circuit C_F & wire).* *Let F be a function and let $\mathcal{O}$ be a set of elementary operations. An ideal circuit C_F implementing F thanks to operations in $\mathcal{O}$ is an oriented graph where each cell c_i defines an element of $\mathcal{O}$ and each edge corresponds to an intermediate value V_i that is called a wire. V_i corresponds to an output to the operation c_i and an input of the operation c_j.*

The performance of a circuit can be measured in terms of *registers* and *clock cycles* that we define as follows.

Definition 3 *(Register & clock cycle).* *A register is a circuit component which can store one wire V_i. A set of more than one register is called a registers layer. A clock cycle corresponds to the longest path between a state register A to the next state register B.*

In our context, the set $\mathcal{O}$ contains field operations $\oplus, \otimes$ and the inverse multiplication $\otimes^{-1}$ in field of characteristic 2, and more generally any power function. The capabilities of a SCA attacker against a circuit C_F are usually defined by adversary models. Among them, the *Probing Adversary Model* [22] is the most popular one. We give its formal definition as follows.

Definition 4 *(t^{th}-order Probing Adversary Model).* *[35] Let C_F be a circuit composed with $(V_i)_{i \in I}$ wires and let t be a positive integer. Let $\mathcal{L}$ be a set of noisy leakage functions. A tth-order Probing Adversary against C_F is an adversary that can choose a subset J of I with $\#J = t$ and can observe the random variable $(\mathcal{L}(V_j))_{j \in J}$ where $(\mathcal{L}_j(.))_j$ is a t-tuple of functions in $\mathcal{L}$.*

An attack performed by the adversary in Definition 4 conducts to the notion of tth-*order probing security* of a circuit. We give formal definition hereafter.

Definition 5 *(t^{th}-order probing security).* *[8] A circuit C_F is said to be t^{th}-order probing secure if for a d-sharing $(x_1, x_2, ..., x_d)$ of some variable x in input, a tth-order Probing Adversary against C_F does not observe a dependence between t (or less) wires and x.*

An algorithm achieving t-probing security is resistant to the class of tth-order side-channel attacks. Some masking schemes have been proposed with formal security proof in the Probing Adversary Model [22,32,33]. However, Mangard *et al.* [25] showed the vulnerability of this model when the circuit evolves in the presence of glitches. Glitches occur because the signals of a combinational circuit can switch more than once per clock cycle if an input changes. The reason why most masking schemes can be attacked is that they process on the same wire masks and masked values. Since there is a link between them, the power consumption is not independent of the masks and masked values. Then the tth-Probing Adversary Model is no longer suffisant for security.

The first provably secure masking scheme with resistance to glitches was the threshold implementation scheme of Nikova *et al.* [29]. Then, based on the work in [38], Roche and Prouff [35] introduced the tth-order Glitches Adversary Model to formalize the security of masked hardware implementations in the presence of glitches. We call this new adversary model the tth-*order TI Adversary Model* and describe it in Definition 6.

In the presence of glitches, the ideal circuit without signal propagation delay (Definition 2) can be extended to a more realistic circuit wherein a transient hazard is generated due to the delay ΔT between two elementary operations (*i.e.* logic gate transitions during a cycle between two registers updates).

For a circuit C_F the internal state at *a time T* for a circuit C_F refers to all the values taken by the V_i's at time T. It is denoted by $C_F(T)$.

Definition 6 (*t^{th}-order TI Adversary Model*). *[35] Let C_F be a circuit and let t be a positive integer. Let $\mathcal{L}$ be a set of leakage functions. A tth-order TI Adversary against C_F is an adversary that can choose t times $T_1, T_2, ..., T_t$ and can observe the internal state transition at the t selected times $(L_i(C_F(T_i)))_{i \leq t}$ where, for each $i \leq t, L_i(.)$ is a function in $\mathcal{L}$.*

For example, in Fig. 1, let C_F be a circuit implementing a function F from a state register A to a state register B, and let β, β' be two Boolean masks. We hereafter focus on the capabilities of an adversary looking at the wire V_3 and we denote by br a Gaussian independent noise. For the 1st-order Probing Adversary Model of Definition 4, the attacker can observe noisy leakage functions $L_3(V_3) = x \oplus \beta' + br$ that gives no information on x. In comparison, for the 1st-order TI Adversary Model of Definition 6, due to glitches between the two previous gates $\oplus$, it might exist a time T such that $L_3(V_3(T)) = x + br$. This can happen if the first Xor gate is transiently evaluated with $x \oplus \beta$ at first input and nothing at second input (for instance because the signal on β' takes more time to be delivered).

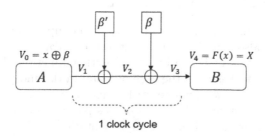

Fig. 1. Example of circuit for a 1st-order Probing (or TI) Adversary Model

Finally, an attack performed by the adversary in Definition 6 leads to the notion of tth-*order TI security* of a circuit. We give a formal definition hereafter.

Definition 7 (*t^{th}-order TI security*). *A circuit C_F is said to be t^{th}-order TI secure in the presence of glitches if for a d-sharing $(x_1, x_2, ..., x_d)$ of some variable x in input, a tth-order TI Adversary against C_F does not observe a dependence between any set t wires and x.*

An algorithm achieving t-TI security implies a t-probing security (the converse is false). In the presence of glitches, a circuit C_F implementing a function F is split into several parts C_{F_i} such that the observation of t or fewer parts gives no information on the original circuit input. Nikova *et al.* [29] achieved this goal by combining secret sharing technique and secure MPC protocols. Their countermeasure, wich can be applied to any F, is called *threshold implementations* and was originally secure in the first-order TI Adversary Model.

To be first-order TI-secure, a TI must satisfy the three following properties.

Property 1 (**Correctness**). Let a masked function $F : GF(2^{dn}) \mapsto GF(2^{dm})$ be a TI $\mathbf{F} = (F_1, ..., F_d)$. The TI $\mathbf{F}$ is correct if and only if $x = s(\mathbf{x})$ implies that $X = F(x) = s(\mathbf{F}(\mathbf{x}))$.

This property ensures that the obtained output $\mathbf{F}(\mathbf{x})$ effectively corresponds to the sharing of the output of the initial input x by the function F. The reconstruction function s of the output X does not need to be necessarily the same than for the input x.

Property 2 (**Non-completeness**). A TI $\mathbf{F} = (F_1, ..., F_d)$ mapping a sharing $(x_1, ..., x_d)$ into a new sharing $(y_1, ..., y_d)$ is *non-complete* if for every $j \leqslant d$, there exists $i \neq j$ such that F_j is functionally independent of x_i (*i.e.* $F(x_1, ..., x_i, ..., x_d) = F(x_1, ..., x_{i-1}, x_{i+1}, ..., x_d)$).

Since we have insufficient knowledge from each F_j to reconstruct the secret x, this property guarantees security in the first-order TI Adversary Model.

Property 3 (**Uniformity**). [7] For every $\mathbf{b} = (b_1, b_2, ..., b_d)$ in $GF(2^{dm})$, the number of $\mathbf{x}$ in $GF(2^{dn})$ for which $\mathbf{F}(\mathbf{x}) = \mathbf{b}$ is equal to $2^{(d-1)(n-m)}$ times the number of x in $GF(2^n)$ for which $F(x) = s(\mathbf{b})$.

This property ensures that, if the masking of the input to $\mathbf{F}$ is uniform, then the output of $\mathbf{F}$ is also a uniform masking of the output of F. It is important when the output of the TI is the input of another function. The design of TI achieving this property has been the core of many works and most of them were based on the idea of *remasking* where fresh randomness is used to uniformize the output sharing. In the extended version of this paper [24], we describe another technique to get uniformity within an implementation.

3   Our TI Generic Evaluation Technique

We describe in this section our main contribution, that is a TI-masked generic evaluation method that can be applied to any polynomial function $f(x) = \sum_{i=0}^{2^n-2} a_i x^i$ in $GF(2^n)$, contrary to the state of the art. According to our security model (see Definition 6), it is assumed that an attacker cannot see more than one intermediate result during the processing, but glitches are possible. Our construction is inspired from the ideas of affine masking and multiplicative masking, developed in [18] and [15]. However, to gain in execution time compared with [18], we try to minimize the number of conversions from Boolean masking to multiplicative masking and *vice-versa*. Through each cycle, the sensitive value is either masked thanks to a Boolean mask or a multiplicative mask, or both. Our construction is first-order TI-secure (*i.e.* resistant against first-order SCA in the presence of glitches). All the following lemmas and properties are proved in the extended version of this paper [24].

3.1   Our First-Order TI-secure Monomial Evaluation

To construct a first-order TI for any polynomial function defined in $GF(2^n)$, our generic proposal is essentially built upon a same masking scheme which will be separately applied to the evaluation of each monomial of f with non-zero coefficient. Let Q_{power} denotes one of those monomials and let us assume that is defined by $Q_{power}(x) = x^q$. In our proposed-scheme, the processing of Q_{power} is multiplicatively masked. Multiplicative masking needs to be implemented carefully not to be vulnerable to first-order SCA with a zero value power model, namely the *zero-problem* [16,19]. In the litterature [14], it has been proposed to map the zero value in $GF(2^n)$ to a non-zero value in $GF(2^n)^\star$ using the *Dirac* function in order to take care of the zero-problem.

Definition 8 *(Dirac function)*. *The Dirac function is defined such that* $\delta(x) = 1$ *if* $x = 0$ *and* $\delta(x) = 0$ *otherwise.*

In order to compute $Q_{power}(x)$, we use the following property:

Property 4. For every integer q, we have:

$$(x \oplus \delta(x))^q = x^q \oplus \delta(x).$$

If we consider an input x of 8 bits, the Dirac function can be calculated by processing 7 AND gates on the bit-wise complemented bits of x such that:

$$\delta(x) = \overline{x_1} \otimes \overline{x_2} \otimes \ldots \otimes \overline{x_8}. \tag{1}$$

We propose another secure implementations of the Dirac function based on a lookup-table (LUT) in Sect. 4. We obtain a 3-Boolean sharing $(\delta_1, \delta_2, \delta_3)$ of $\delta(x)$. The advantage of this second implementation is that it can be executed in a single cycle (see Definition 3).

The full processing of our first-order TI-secure monomial evaluation can be done in 4 cycles. At input, the value x is assumed to be split into three parts following Definition 1. We denote the 3-affine sharing of x by $\mathbf{x} = ((x \oplus \beta) \otimes \alpha, \alpha, \beta)$ such that $s(\mathbf{x}) = (x \oplus \beta) \otimes \alpha \otimes \alpha^{-1} \oplus \beta = x$. Then, to get a multiplicative masking of $Q_{power}(x) = x^q$ we first remove the Boolean mask β of x and replace it by $\delta(x)$, while satisfying all the properties of TI. It can be achieved in two cycles. Due to Property 4, we obtain a new 2-multiplicative TI sharing of $x^q \oplus \delta(x)$: $((x^q \oplus \delta(x)) \otimes \alpha^q, \alpha^q)$. We extend this sharing by adding a third share $(\beta \otimes \alpha^q)$ that will be used later. Finally, we obtain $\mathbf{x}_\delta = ((x^q \oplus \delta(x)) \otimes \alpha^q, \alpha^q, \beta \otimes \alpha^q)$.

Lemma 1. *The implementation of* $\mathbf{x}_\delta$ *is correct, non-complete and uniform. It is first-order TI-secure against SCA.*

Finally, the last two cycles allow us to replace in a secure way the Boolean mask $\delta(x)$ of x^q by a new one β'. We obtain at the end a new TI 3-affine sharing $\mathbf{xq} = ((x^q \oplus \beta') \otimes \alpha^q, \alpha^q, \beta')$ of x^q.

Lemma 2. *The implementation of* $\mathbf{xq}$ *is correct, non-complete and uniform. It is first-order TI-secure against SCA.*

The generalized scheme of our monomial evaluation is illustrated in Fig. 2.

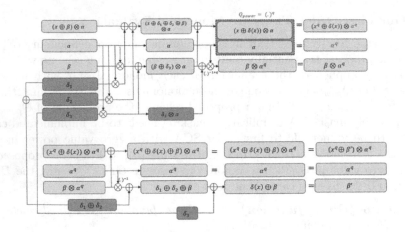

Fig. 2. First-order TI-masked monomial evaluation of x^q in 4 cycles

3.2 Extension of Our Technique for Any Polynomial Function

The concurrent application of the secure monomial evaluation described in previous section straightforwardly leads to a first-order secure TI for any polynomial function f. We describe hereafter the main steps of our proposal which, from a 3-sharing $(\tilde{x}, \alpha, \beta)$ of x, outputs a 3-sharing $(f(x), \alpha_f, \beta_f)$ of $f(x)$ in 6 cycles:

- Step 1: firstly, a 3-Boolean sharing of the Dirac $\delta(x)$ is computed in 1 cycle from the 3-affine sharing of x (for details on the construction see Sect. 4). Note that this computation is done only once to secure the whole polynomial function evaluation.
- Step 2: secondly, each monomial of f can be evaluated thanks to our TI depicted in Fig. 2. This step takes 4 cycles.
- Step 3: finally, the last step consists in combining the 3-affine sharings of all the monomial evaluations to get the 3-affine sharing $((f(x) \oplus \beta_f) \otimes \alpha_f, \alpha_f, \beta_f)$ of $f(x)$. It takes 1 cycle.

For example, let us assume that we want to securely process the 3-affine sharing of the function $f(x) = x^5 \oplus x^{33}$ from the 3-affine sharing $(\tilde{x}, \alpha, \beta)$ of x. With the method described in Sect. 4, we first securely compute a 3-Boolean sharing of $\delta(x)$ in 1 cycle. Then we apply our scheme in Fig. 2 to the monomials x^5 and x^{33}. These two computations can be done in parallel in 4 cycles and give two new 3-affine sharings of **x5** and **x33**. Finally, the last step takes 1 cycle and is split as follows:

- the multiplication of the second shares of both **x5** and **x33** to construct a new multiplicative mask $\alpha_f = \alpha^5 \otimes \alpha^{33}$.
- the xor between the third shares of **x5** and **x33** to get $\beta_f = \beta_{x^5} \oplus \beta_{x^{33}}$.
- the xor between the first share of **x5** multiplied by α^{33} and the first share of **x33** multiplied by α^5 to get $(x^5 \oplus x^{33} \oplus \beta_{x^5} \oplus \beta_{x^{33}}) \otimes (\alpha^5 \otimes \alpha^{33})$ and thus the new 3-affine sharing $\mathbf{f} = ((f(x) \oplus \beta_f) \otimes \alpha_f, \alpha_f, \beta_f)$ of f.

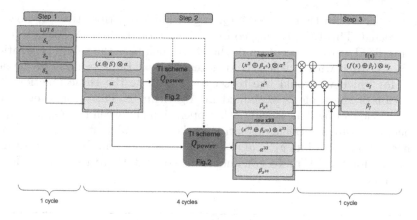

Fig. 3. First-order TI-masked evaluation of $f(x) = x^5 \oplus x^{33}$

The whole example is depicted in Fig. 3.

Remark. The secure monomials' evaluation is done in parallel, leading to an increase of the implementation area which is roughly linear in the number of monomials to evaluate. Using the ideas developed in [11], it is possible to improve the area complexity by using cyclotomic classes and the fact that some powers are linear (those in the form $x \mapsto x^{2^j}$).

The next section explains the implementation of the Dirac function used in step 1 of Fig. 3.

4   Construction of the Dirac Function as a Lookup Table (LUT)

In our first-order TI-secure evaluation of polynomial functions of the form $f(x) = \sum_{i=0}^{2^n-2} a_i x^i$, we need to securely compute a 3-Boolean sharing of the Dirac of x from the 3-affine sharing of x (see Step 1 in Fig. 3 in Sect. 3). For such a purpose, we propose below to represent the Dirac function as a lookup table. We also propose an alternative secure construction in the extended version of this paper [24].

We recall that, for each 3-affine sharing **x** of x, we know the value of its corresponding multiplicative and Boolean masks α and β, respectively. A possible implementation for the 3-Boolean sharing $(\delta_1, \delta_2, \delta_3)$ of the Dirac $\delta(x)$ is to precompute a table T of 256 bits from a 3-affine sharing $(\tilde{x}, \alpha, \beta)$ of x. We first have to know the value of the mask β and the masked value $(x \oplus \beta)$, which is given by processing $\tilde{x} \otimes \alpha^{-1}$. Then, thanks to a random bit $r \in GF(2)$, the table is constructed such that $T[x \oplus \beta]$ takes the value $r + 1$ if $x = 0$ and r otherwise. During the execution of the AES algorithm, the mask r stays unchanged while the mask β evolves. In order to be in coherence with our second construction of the Dirac function in the extended version of this paper [24], we choose to split

r into two parts such that $r = r_1 \oplus r_2$. Algorithm 1 describes the way how the LUT is created. This LUT is fully computed once for the first Dirac request and is then modified at each execution of the Dirac such that the values at positions β and β' are xored with 1, where β' denotes the next Boolean mask of the next value x' for which we would like to securely evaluate the Dirac function. The modification of the table is explained in Algorithm 2. This processing, which takes one cycle can be done during other operations between two Q_{power} layers.

Hence, to obtain a 3-Boolean sharing of the Dirac value of x, we will store in our construction three bits $\delta_1 = \delta(x) \oplus r_1 \oplus r_2, \delta_2 = r_2$ and $\delta_3 = r_1$ (see Fig. 2) and 256 bits for the LUT. To conclude, this computation takes one cycle and store 259 bits.

Algorithm 1. Compute once a 3-Boolean sharing of $\delta(x)$

Require: $r = r_1 \oplus r_2 \in GF(2), (x) \oplus \beta, \beta$
Ensure: $(\delta_1, \delta_2, \delta_3)$ s.t. $\delta_1 \oplus \delta_2 \oplus \delta_3 = \delta(x)$
$\quad T \leftarrow [0] * 256$
$\quad T[\beta] \leftarrow T[\beta] \oplus 1$
$\quad T \leftarrow T \oplus [r, ..., r]$
$\quad$**return** $T[(x) \oplus \beta], r_1, r_2$

Algorithm 2. Updating of the LUT T

Require: T, β, β'
Ensure: modified table T
$\quad T[\beta] \leftarrow T[\beta] \oplus 1$
$\quad T[\beta'] \leftarrow T[\beta'] \oplus 1$
$\quad$**return** T

To conclude, Sects. 3 and 4 describe our generic first-order TI-secure polynomial evaluation. To be able to compare this proposal with the TI of the state of the art, we give an illustration of it on the well-studied AES algorithm in the next section.

5 An Illustration on the AES Algorithm

5.1 AES Algorithm

The AES block cipher [13] operates on an 4×4 array of 16 bytes called a *state*. An AES plaintext value is modified thanks to additive and multiplicative operations in order to obtain the corresponding ciphertext at the end of the encryption. Each round of the AES is composed of four stages: *AddRoundKey*, *SubBytes*, *ShiftRows* and *MixColumns*. The AES SBox is defined as the composition of an affine transformation called AT over $GF(2^8)$ and the multiplicative inverse Inv

over the field $GF(2)[x]/(x^8 + x^4 + x^3 + x + 1)$. The *SubBytes* operation consists in applying the SBox on each byte of the state. Moreover, the last round ommits the MixColumns operation and add a final AddRoundKey stage. The processus is composed of either 10, 12 or 14 rounds, depending on the key size. Based on the secret key, a key expansion process defines all the round keys that are involved in the different rounds.

5.2   Strategy

Substitutions-Permutation Network (SPN) based block ciphers (as AES) design involve additive and multiplicative operations defined on a finite field. To efficiently mask the sensitive value through each operation, Genelle *et al.* proposed a scheme to securely transform an additive sharing into a multiplicative one [18] (Boolean masking being dedicated to Boolean operations while multiplicative masking being dedicated to multiplicative operation). In order to reduce the number of cycles for our implementation, we improved their work by using a 3-affine sharing which is constructed such that it contains both Boolean and multiplicative masks. As the existing papers [3, 10, 21, 28] proposed a masked design of the AES Sbox processing, we describe in the followed sections a TI-masked implementation of this SPN algorithm.

Through each AES operation, we denote the different 3-affine sharings S_i as in Fig. 4. All of them are obtained by the meaning of one or more intermediate 3-sharing $S_{i,j}$. Each $S_{i,j}$ represents a computation done in one cycle as defined in Definition 3. Moreover, our scheme is first-order TI-secure. The demonstration of this security is based on lemmas that are proved in the extended version of this paper [24].

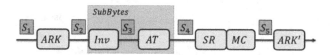

Fig. 4. 3-sharings S_i of our TI-masked AES

We first show how to apply our TI-masked monomial evaluation on the AES SBox. Then, we complete our presentation with a TI of all other steps of the AES.

5.3   Application of Our Monomial Evaluation Technique on the AES SBox

In this section we highlight our generic method by adapting it to the AES SBox processing. This step comes after the *AddRoundKey* operation and so takes the 3-affine sharing of $x \oplus k$, where x is the plaintext byte and k the round-key byte.

As discuss before, the SBox operation can be decomposed such that $SB(x) = AT(Inv(x))$, where AT represents the affine transformation and Inv the multiplicative inversion in $GF(2^8)$. In this case, this inversion is equivalent to our operation $Q_{power}(x)$ with $q = 254$ meaning $x^{254} = x^{-1}$ in $GF(2)[x]/(x^8 + x^4 + x^3 + x + 1)$.

To mask the *SubBytes* step, AT is masked additively whereas Inv denotes is multiplicatively protected. By implementing the Dirac function as a LUT, the masking processing of an AES SBox takes five cycles.[2] The scheme is illustrated in Fig. 5. It gives the new following 3-multiplicative sharing S_3 of $(x \oplus k)^{-1} \oplus \delta(x \oplus k)$ and the new 3-Boolean sharing S_4 of $SB(x \oplus k)$:

$$S_3 = ([[(x \oplus k)^{-1} \oplus \delta(x \oplus k)] \otimes \alpha^{-1}, \alpha^{-1}, \beta \otimes \alpha^{-1}),$$
$$S_4 = (SB(x \oplus k) \oplus \beta', \alpha, \beta'),$$

with $\beta' = AT(\beta) \oplus AT(\delta(x \oplus k)) \oplus 0x63$.

Lemma 3. *The implementations of S_3 and S_4 are correct, non-complete and uniform. It is first-order TI-secure against SCA.*

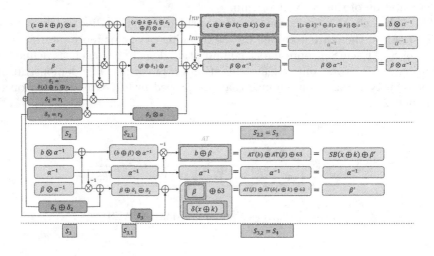

Fig. 5. First-order TI-masked SubBytes operation in 4 cycles

Remark. We made the choice to obtain a 3-Boolean sharing of $SB(x \oplus k)$ instead of a 3-affine sharing (as in our generic method in Fig. 2) because it is more suitable for the input of the next AES operation, namely the *MixColumns* operation. This last is detailed in the next section with other AES steps.

---

[2] As an observation, the scheme can also be implemented in seven cycles if the Dirac function δ is computed in three cycles with TI ISW multiplications (see in the extended version of this paper [24].

5.4   Presentation of the Other TI-masked AES Operations

Step 1: AddRoundKey (ARK). At the beginning of the computation, the sixteen plaintext bytes x and the sixteen round keys k are splitted into three parts following Definition 1. Let α be a multiplicative non-zero mask and let β_x and β_k be two Boolean masks for the plaintext and the round key, respectively. Without loss of generality, we define the first 3-affine sharing S_1 of one plaintext byte as:

$$(\tilde{x}, \alpha, \beta) = ((x \oplus \beta_x) \otimes \alpha, \alpha, \beta_x)$$

In the same way, the 3-affine sharing of one round key k is:

$$(\tilde{k}, \alpha, \beta) = ((k \oplus \beta_k) \otimes \alpha, \alpha, \beta_k)$$

Note that we choose the same multiplicative mask. Then, the ARK operation can be performed by xoring the first shares $\tilde{x}$ and $\tilde{k}$ in one hand and the third shares β_x and β_k on the other hand. We obtain in one cycle a new 3-sharing $S_2 = ((x \oplus k \oplus \beta) \otimes \alpha, \alpha, \beta = \beta_x \oplus \beta_k)$. This computation can be performed on all of the sixteen bytes in parallel.

Lemma 4. *The implementation of S_2 is correct, non-complete and uniform. It is first-order TI-secure against SCA.*

Step 2: SubBytes. This operation is detailled in Sect. 5.3.

Step 3: ShiftRows (SR). This operation is here combines with MixColumns operation and consists a shift on the left of $1, 2, 3$ bytes of the AES state. It is a reindexing of the state and it does not require any cycle.

Step 4: MixColumns (MC). Then, the MixColumns operation consit in a multiplication of each column of the AES state by the matrix MC (see $c(x)$ in Eq. 3.12 in [13]). This step takes one cycle. The jth line of MC is denoted by MC_j. Each byte x_i at input of the MC processing is represented as a 3-sharing $S_4 = (SB(x_i \oplus k) \oplus \beta_i', \alpha^{-1}, \beta_i')$. MixColumns operation will give new values y_i. Without loss of generality, we obtain the following new 3-sharing for the byte y_1: $S_5 = ((y_1 \oplus \beta'') \otimes \alpha', \alpha', \beta'')$, with $y_1 = MC_1 \otimes (SB(x_i \oplus k)_{1 \leq i \leq 4}), \alpha' = \alpha^{-1}$ and $\beta'' = MC_1 \otimes (\beta_i')_{1 \leq i \leq 4}$.

Lemma 5. *The implementation of S_5 is correct, non-complete and uniform. It is first-order TI-secure against SCA.*

In this section, we obtain a first-order TI-secure version of the whole AES. In the next section, we compare performances of our SBox TI AES proposal regarding other TI propositions of the state of the art.

6   Performances of Our Proposition

6.1   Comparison of Our Proposal for AES SBox Regarding the Prior State of the Art

In order to compare our work with the state of the art regarding the number of cycle and the number of random bits per SBox, we will use [37]. Table 1 shows theses performances evaluation. Our proposal is better or equivalent in terms of number of cycles than [3,10,21,28], and does not require fresh randomness. Compare to [37], our proposal takes one more cycle but it can be easily extended to evaluate any polynomial function as shown in Sect. 3. Moreover, our scheme is applicable to any cryptographic algorithm based on a power computation.

6.2   Performances of Our Proposal for the Complete AES

As an illustration, our first-order TI-secure implementation can be adapted to the AES algorithm as shown in Sect. 5. In this case, the construction takes 70 cycles for each byte of the AES state. Table 2 gives the number of required cycles for each AES operation in bold characters in the last column. It also gives the number of cycles that are needed to compute a byte of the AES state through all the 10 rounds. Note that the *ShiftRows* operation is missing in the table because it is combined with the *MixColumns* operation. This number of cycles could be optimized by parallelizing some computation with respect to the non-completeness property.

Table 1. Comparison of our proposal for AES SBox regarding the prior state of the art

Design	Random bits/Sbox	Nb cycles	Generalizable
[28]	44	7	No
[3]	16	5	No
[10]	54	5	No
[21]	18	6	No
[37]	0	4	No
This work	0	5	Yes

Table 2. Number of cycles for a byte of an AES state during the whole TI-masked processing

Operations	9 first rounds	Last round	Nb cycles
ARK	✓	✓(×2)	1×11
SB	✓	✓	5×10
MC	✓	×	1×9
Total			70

7   Conclusion

In this paper, we have introduced a new threshold implementation allowing to evaluate any power function in 6 cycles (while the area increases linearly with the number of powers which must be processed for the polynomial evaluation). It is provably first-order TI-secure against SCA in the presence of glitches. We have argued that this technique can be straightforwardly extended to securely process any polynomial function. Finally, we gave an illustration of our method to the AES SBox. In this case, we got a TI running in 5 cycles without fresh randomness. Our proposal is better or equivalent in terms of number of cycles than [3,10,21,28], but does not require fresh randomness. Regarding [37], our proposal takes one more cycle but it can be easily extended to evaluate any polynomial function in a generic manner. For completeness, we also proposed a full TI-masked AES. This scheme is inspired by [17] and is based on affine masking. Our construction takes 1120 cycles for the whole AES computation and does not require fresh randomness.

As a future work, it will be interesting to see how our technique can be applied to secure other algorithms. For instance, we could evaluate our method on a sponge construction-based algorithm. Moreover, it will be also interesting to compare the area required to implement our technique and to experimentally validate our theoretical performance estimations. We could improve the AES scheme by parallelizing some computations with respect to the non-completeness TI property.

References

1. Akkar, M.-L., Giraud, C.: An implementation of DES and AES, secure against some attacks. In: Koç, Ç.K., Naccache, D., Paar, C. (eds.) CHES 2001. LNCS, vol. 2162, pp. 309–318. Springer, Heidelberg (2001). https://doi.org/10.1007/3-540-44709-1_26
2. Ben-Or, M., Goldwasser, S., Wigderson, A.: Completeness theorems for non-cryptographic fault-tolerant distributed computation (extended abstract). In: Simon, J. (ed.) Proceedings of the 20th Annual ACM Symposium on Theory of Computing, Chicago, Illinois, USA, 2–4 May 1988, pp. 1–10. ACM (1988). https://doi.org/10.1145/62212.62213
3. Bilgin, B., Gierlichs, B., Nikova, S., Nikov, V., Rijmen, V.: Trade-offs for threshold implementations illustrated on AES. IEEE Trans. CAD Integr. Circ. Syst. 34(7), 1188–1200 (2015). https://doi.org/10.1109/TCAD.2015.2419623
4. Blömer, J., Guajardo, J., Krummel, V.: Provably secure masking of AES. In: Handschuh, H., Hasan, M.A. (eds.) SAC 2004. LNCS, vol. 3357, pp. 69–83. Springer, Heidelberg (2004). https://doi.org/10.1007/978-3-540-30564-4_5
5. Brier, E., Clavier, C., Olivier, F.: Correlation power analysis with a leakage model. In: Joye, M., Quisquater, J.-J. (eds.) CHES 2004. LNCS, vol. 3156, pp. 16–29. Springer, Heidelberg (2004). https://doi.org/10.1007/978-3-540-28632-5_2
6. Canright, D.: A very compact s-box for AES. In: Rao and Sunar [31], pp. 441–455. https://doi.org/10.1007/11545262_32

7. Carlet, C.: Boolean functions for cryptography and error-correcting codes. In: Encyclopedia of Mathematics and Its Applications, pp. 257–397. Cambridge University Press, Cambridge (2010). https://doi.org/10.1017/CBO9780511780448.011

8. Carlet, C., Prouff, E., Rivain, M., Roche, T.: Algebraic decomposition for probing security. IACR Cryptology ePrint Archive 2016, 321 (2016). http://eprint.iacr.org/2016/321

9. Chari, S., Jutla, C.S., Rao, J.R., Rohatgi, P.: Towards sound approaches to counteract power-analysis attacks. In: Wiener [39], pp. 398–412. https://doi.org/10.1007/3-540-48405-1_26. https://link.springer.com/content/pdf/10.1007%2F3-540-48405-1_26.pdf

10. Cnudde, T.D., Reparaz, O., Bilgin, B., Nikova, S., Nikov, V., Rijmen, V.: Masking AES with d+1 shares in hardware. In: Bilgin, B., Nikova, S., Rijmen, V. (eds.) Proceedings of the ACM Workshop on Theory of Implementation Security, TIS@CCS 2016, Vienna, Austria, October 2016, p. 43. ACM (2016). https://doi.org/10.1145/2996366.2996428

11. Coron, J., Roy, A., Vivek, S.: Fast evaluation of polynomials over binary finite fields and application to side-channel countermeasures. J. Cryptogr. Eng. 5(2), 73–83 (2015). https://doi.org/10.1007/s13389-015-0099-9

12. Daemen, J.: Changing of the guards: a simple and efficient method for achieving uniformity in threshold sharing. In: Fischer, W., Homma, N. (eds.) CHES 2017. LNCS, vol. 10529, pp. 137–153. Springer, Cham (2017). https://doi.org/10.1007/978-3-319-66787-4_7

13. Daemen, J., Rijmen, V.: The Design of Rijndael: AES - The Advanced Encryption Standard. Springer, Heidelberg (2002). https://doi.org/10.1007/978-3-662-04722-4

14. Damgård, I., Keller, M.: Secure multiparty AES. In: Sion, R. (ed.) FC 2010. LNCS, vol. 6052, pp. 367–374. Springer, Heidelberg (2010). https://doi.org/10.1007/978-3-642-14577-3_31

15. Fumaroli, G., Martinelli, A., Prouff, E., Rivain, M.: Affine masking against higher-order side channel analysis. In: Biryukov, A., Gong, G., Stinson, D.R. (eds.) SAC 2010. LNCS, vol. 6544, pp. 262–280. Springer, Heidelberg (2011). https://doi.org/10.1007/978-3-642-19574-7_18

16. Fumaroli, G., Mayer, E., Dubois, R.: First-order differential power analysis on the duplication method. In: Srinathan, K., Rangan, C.P., Yung, M. (eds.) INDOCRYPT 2007. LNCS, vol. 4859, pp. 210–223. Springer, Heidelberg (2007). https://doi.org/10.1007/978-3-540-77026-8_16

17. Genelle, L., Prouff, E., Quisquater, M.: Montgomery's trick and fast implementation of masked AES. In: Nitaj, A., Pointcheval, D. (eds.) AFRICACRYPT 2011. LNCS, vol. 6737, pp. 153–169. Springer, Heidelberg (2011). https://doi.org/10.1007/978-3-642-21969-6_10

18. Genelle, L., Prouff, E., Quisquater, M.: Thwarting higher-order side channel analysis with additive and multiplicative maskings. In: Preneel, B., Takagi, T. (eds.) CHES 2011. LNCS, vol. 6917, pp. 240–255. Springer, Heidelberg (2011). https://doi.org/10.1007/978-3-642-23951-9_16

19. Golić, J.D., Tymen, C.: Multiplicative masking and power analysis of AES. In: Kaliski, B.S., Koç, K., Paar, C. (eds.) CHES 2002. LNCS, vol. 2523, pp. 198–212. Springer, Heidelberg (2003). https://doi.org/10.1007/3-540-36400-5_16

20. Goubin, L., Patarin, J.: DES and differential power analysis the "Duplication" method. In: Koç, Ç.K., Paar, C. (eds.) CHES 1999. LNCS, vol. 1717, pp. 158–172. Springer, Heidelberg (1999). https://doi.org/10.1007/3-540-48059-5_15

21. Gross, H., Mangard, S., Korak, T.: An efficient side-channel protected AES implementation with arbitrary protection order. In: Handschuh, H. (ed.) CT-RSA 2017. LNCS, vol. 10159, pp. 95–112. Springer, Cham (2017). https://doi.org/10.1007/978-3-319-52153-4_6

22. Ishai, Y., Sahai, A., Wagner, D.: Private circuits: securing hardware against probing attacks. In: Boneh, D. (ed.) CRYPTO 2003. LNCS, vol. 2729, pp. 463–481. Springer, Heidelberg (2003). https://doi.org/10.1007/978-3-540-45146-4_27

23. Kocher, P.C., Jaffe, J., Jun, B.: Differential power analysis. In: Wiener [39], pp. 388–397. https://doi.org/10.1007/3-540-48405-1_25

24. Landry, S., Linge, Y., Prouff, E.: Monomial Evaluation of Polynomial Functions Protected by Threshold Implementations – With an Illustration on AES. Extended Version (to appear)

25. Mangard, S., Popp, T., Gammel, B.M.: Side-channel leakage of masked CMOS gates. In: Menezes, A. (ed.) CT-RSA 2005. LNCS, vol. 3376, pp. 351–365. Springer, Heidelberg (2005). https://doi.org/10.1007/978-3-540-30574-3_24

26. Mangard, S., Pramstaller, N., Oswald, E.: Successfully attacking masked AES hardware implementations. In: Rao and Sunar [31], pp. 157–171. https://doi.org/10.1007/11545262_12

27. Messerges, T.S.: Using second-order power analysis to attack DPA resistant software. In: Koç, Ç.K., Paar, C. (eds.) CHES 2000. LNCS, vol. 1965, pp. 238–251. Springer, Heidelberg (2000). https://doi.org/10.1007/3-540-44499-8_19

28. Moradi, A., Poschmann, A., Ling, S., Paar, C., Wang, H.: Pushing the limits: a very compact and a threshold implementation of AES. In: Paterson, K.G. (ed.) EUROCRYPT 2011. LNCS, vol. 6632, pp. 69–88. Springer, Heidelberg (2011). https://doi.org/10.1007/978-3-642-20465-4_6

29. Nikova, S., Rijmen, V., Schläffer, M.: Secure hardware implementation of nonlinear functions in the presence of glitches. J. Cryptol. 24(2), 292–321 (2011). https://doi.org/10.1007/s00145-010-9085-7

30. Prouff, E., Rivain, M., Bevan, R.: Statistical analysis of second order differential power analysis. IEEE Trans. Comput. 58(6), 799–811 (2009). https://doi.org/10.1109/TC.2009.15

31. Rao, J.R., Sunar, B. (eds.): CHES 2005. LNCS, vol. 3659. Springer, Heidelberg (2005). https://doi.org/10.1007/11545262

32. Rivain, M., Dottax, E., Prouff, E.: Block ciphers implementations provably secure against second order side channel analysis. In: Nyberg, K. (ed.) FSE 2008. LNCS, vol. 5086, pp. 127–143. Springer, Heidelberg (2008). https://doi.org/10.1007/978-3-540-71039-4_8

33. Rivain, M., Prouff, E.: Provably secure higher-order masking of AES. In: Mangard, S., Standaert, F.-X. (eds.) CHES 2010. LNCS, vol. 6225, pp. 413–427. Springer, Heidelberg (2010). https://doi.org/10.1007/978-3-642-15031-9_28

34. Rivest, R.L., Shamir, A., Tauman, Y.: How to leak a secret. In: Boyd, C. (ed.) ASIACRYPT 2001. LNCS, vol. 2248, pp. 552–565. Springer, Heidelberg (2001). https://doi.org/10.1007/3-540-45682-1_32

35. Roche, T., Prouff, E.: Higher-order glitch free implementation of the AES using secure multi-party computation protocols - extended version. J. Cryptogr. Eng. 2(2), 111–127 (2012). https://doi.org/10.1007/s13389-012-0033-3

36. Schramm, K., Paar, C.: Higher order masking of the AES. In: Pointcheval, D. (ed.) CT-RSA 2006. LNCS, vol. 3860, pp. 208–225. Springer, Heidelberg (2006). https://doi.org/10.1007/11605805_14

37. Sugawara, T.: 3-share threshold implementation of AES s-box without fresh randomness. IACR Trans. Cryptogr. Hardw. Embed. Syst. **2019**(1), 123–145 (2019). https://doi.org/10.13154/tches.v2019.i1.123-145
38. Suzuki, D., Saeki, M., Ichikawa, T.: DPA leakage models for CMOS logic circuits. In: Rao and Sunar [31], pp. 366–382. https://doi.org/10.1007/11545262_27
39. Wiener, M. (ed.): CRYPTO 1999. LNCS, vol. 1666. Springer, Heidelberg (1999). https://doi.org/10.1007/3-540-48405-1
40. Yao, A.C.: How to generate and exchange secrets (extended abstract). In: 27th Annual Symposium on Foundations of Computer Science, Toronto, Canada, 27–29 October 1986, pp. 162–167. IEEE Computer Society (1986). https://doi.org/10.1109/SFCS.1986.25

Strong Designated Verifier Signature Based on the Rank Metric

Hafsa Assidi$^{(\boxtimes)}$ and El Mamoun Souidi

Faculty of Sciences, Laboratory of Mathematics, Computer Science,
Applications and Information Security, Mohammed V University in Rabat,
BP 1014 RP, 10000 Rabat, Morocco
assidihafsa@gmail.com, emsouidi@gmail.com

Abstract. Strong designated verifier signatures (SDVS) allows users to produce signatures that are not publicly verifiable, such that no one other than the signer and the designated verifier can check the validity of a given signature, which preserves the privacy of the signer. This cryptographic primitive is very useful in different real life scenarios such as e-voting and e-bidding. In this paper, we propose a strong designated verifier signature scheme (SDVS) based on rank metric error correcting codes. Our construction makes a trade-off between efficiency and security requirements, for instance we achieve a signature of size 3510 bits and a public key of size equal to 23088 bits for the 80 security level. Furthermore, our proposal is quantum computer resistant since it is based on coding theory.

Keywords: Strong designated verifier signature · Digital signature · Code-based cryptography · LRPC codes · Rank metric · Post-quantum

1 Introduction

A classical digital signature scheme is publicly verifiable where everyone can check the validity of a given signature. In some applications, such as e-voting and e-bidding, the signer wants to prove the validity of his signature to a specific user but not for others. As a consequence, the public verifiability of the signature is considered as an undesired feature.

To overcome this problem, Chaum and Antwerpen proposed the concept of undeniable signature [8] where the signer has a control over his signatures. In such a signature scheme, the verification is done in an interactive way between the signer and the verifier. However, the signer is able to decide when to prove but not whom verifying. Thereafter, Jakobsson *et al.* in [13] introduced the designated verifier signature (DVS). In a DVS scheme, the designated verifier is convinced by the validity of a signature but cannot transfer this conviction to others. Due to the non-transferability of DVS, the signature generated by the signer himself is indistinguishable from one simulated by the designated verifier.

© IFIP International Federation for Information Processing 2020
Published by Springer Nature Switzerland AG 2020
M. Laurent and T. Giannetsos (Eds.): WISTP 2019, LNCS 12024, pp. 85–102, 2020.
https://doi.org/10.1007/978-3-030-41702-4_6

Jacobsson *et al.* [13] proposed a variant of DVS called strong designated verifier signature (SDVS). SDVS differs from DVS in the fact that the private key of a designated verifier is involved in the verification process and consequently there is no requirement for a third part to prove the validity of the designated verifier signature. The first formalisation of SDVS was presented by Saeednia *et al.* in [21] where an efficient construction of SDVS based on discrete logarithm problem is proposed. The authors in [21] introduced also the notion of signer ambiguity where it is infeasible to guess if a signature is produced by the signer or simulated by the designated verifier. Thereafter, the work in [21] was extended by Laguillaumie *et al.* in [16] using a number theory construction of SDVS.

Later, many proposals of SDVS have been presented and are based on bilinear pairing like [11, 14, 15, 17], these schemes are identity based strong designated verifier signature where the private keys of both the signer and the designated verifier are generated trough a key generator center. In 2013 Yang *et al.* [25] proposed a novel construction of SDVS with secure disavowability. In addition, Tian *et al.* [24] presented a systematic method to design strong designated verifier signature but without random oracles. The schemes in [24, 25] are both based on computational Diffie-Hellman Problem. A recent work by Hu *et al.* in [12] has consisted of an SDVS scheme that supports the undeniability property besides the classical security requirements. In 2018, Lin *et al.* [18] proposed a new certificateless strong designated verifier signature scheme that is non-delegatable and verifies SSA-KCA security. Furthermore, Pereira de Almeida *et al.* presented in [1] a novel Dos defense mechanism based on strong designated verifier signatures.

The first provably secure code based SDVS was presented by Shooshtari *et al.* [22] presented. Then Asaar *et al.* proved in [2] that the scheme in [22] presents some weakness in the sense that it does not verify the signer ambiguity or non-transferability that is the main feature of strong designated verifier signatures. The authors of [2] showed also that the scheme in [22] is not strongly unforgeable if it does not preserve the non-transferability and they proposed in [2] a novel construction to overcome the aforementioned weakness. In the literature, we recognise also some constructions of SDVS that are derived from lattice assumptions such as [20].

Given that the number theoretic cryptography will not resist to the quantum computer as shown by Shor in his paper [23], the research for alternative solutions is very active. Code based cryptography, lattice based cryptography, multivariate cryptography and isogeny based cryptography are considered as an attractive and prominent alternative to classical cryptography in the era of quantum computers. In the literature, many cryptographic primitives are derived from coding theory assumptions such as group signature [3, 5], ring and threshold ring signature [7, 19] and also for authentication in RFID systems such as [4] where the authors proposed two mutual Zero-Knowledge authentication protocols based on error correcting code assumptions.

In the present paper, we propose a code based strong designated verifier signature using the LRPC codes. We use the signature scheme of Gaborit *et al.* [9] as the cryptographic primitive in our SDVS scheme. Our construction is resistant to quantum computer and fulfills the security requirements of an SDVS scheme. Namely, the correctness, the unforgeability, the non-transferability and the privacy of signer's identity. The practical results show that our proposal is practical, for instance, we achieve a signature of size equal to 3510 bits and a public key of size equal to 23088 bits for an 80 bits security level.

The organisation of the current paper is as follows: In Sect. 2, we recall some definitions from error correcting codes in rank metric, we recall also the algorithms that define a strong designated verifier signature and we give formal definitions of the security requirements. In Sect. 3, we present our proposed strong designated verifier signature. Section 4 is devoted to the security analysis of our SDVS proposal. In Sect. 5, we analyse the performance of the proposed SDVS scheme in terms of public key and signature sizes. We also analyse the results and we make a comparison with some recent related works. We conclude in Sect. 6.

2   Backgrounds and Definitions

In this section, we define some general notations and we recall definitions related to error correcting codes with rank metric as well as the hard problems on codes that are used for cryptographic constructions.

- By $a \xleftarrow{\$} A$ we note an element a chosen uniformly at random from the set A.
- $Adv_{B,A}^{C}$: the advantage (the probability) that an adversary A breaks the property C of the scheme B.
- $Exp_{B,\mathcal{A}}^{C}$: is the experiment (the game) that describes how an adversary $\mathcal{A}$ can break the security property C of the scheme B.
- $a|b$: refers to the concatenation of two matrices or vectors a and b.
- ε: a value that is considered as negligible.
- x^T: refers to the transpose of the vector x.

2.1   Error Correcting Codes in Hamming Metric

Linear Codes. Let $GF(q)$ be the finite field of $q = p^s$ elements (p prime, and $s > 0$), n and k be non-negative integers with $k \leq n$. A linear code C of length n and dimension k over $GF(q)$ is a subspace of dimension k of the full space $GF(q)^n$.

A linear $[n, k]$ code can be defined either by its generator matrix or parity check matrix defined as follows:

Let C be an $[n, k]$ linear code over $GF(q)$. A matrix $G \in \mathcal{M}_{k,n}(GF(q))$ is a generator matrix of C if its rows form a basis of C. That is to say $C = \{mG, m \in GF(q)^k\}$.

A parity-check matrix $H \in \mathcal{M}_{n-k,n}(F_q)$ of a linear $[n, k]$-code C is defined as: $C = \{Hc^T = 0 | c \in GF(q)^n\}$.

Let H be a parity check matrix of an $[n,k]$ code C on $GF(q)$ and y belonging to $GF(q)^n$. The syndrome $s \in GF(q)^{n-k}$ of y associated to C is given by $s^T = Hy^T$ (Where w is an integer that represent a small Hamming weight).

Code-based cryptography relies on the assumption of the hardness of syndrome decoding problem, this problem is proved to be NP-complete by Berlekamp in [6]:

Problem 1 (Syndrome Decoding problem (SD)). *The $SD(n,k,\omega)$ problem is formulated as follows: let n, k and ω be integers, given uniformly a random matrix $H \in \mathcal{M}_{k \times n}(GF(2))$ and an uniformly random syndrome $y \in GF(2)^k$, find a vector $s \in GF(2)^n$ such that $wt(s) \leq \omega$ and $H \cdot s^T = y^T$.*

2.2   Error Correcting Codes in the Rank Metric

Let q be a power of a prime p and $GF(q)$ be the finite field with q elements. For an integer m, we define $GF(q^m)$ as a finite field of cardinality q^m. We consider $GF(q^m)$ as an m-dimensional vector space over $GF(q)$ and we denote by $\beta = (\beta_1, \cdots, \beta_m)$ an arbitrary basis of $GF(q^m)$ over $GF(q)$. Let $x = (x_1, \cdots, x_n) \in GF(q^m)^n$ where each x_j can be decomposed in the basis β as $x_j = \sum_{i=1}^m a_{ij}\beta_i$. We associate to the vector x the $m \times n$ matrix $A(x) = (a_{ij})_{1 \leq i \leq m, 1 \leq j \leq n}$. We denote by $rank(x)$ the rank weight of x which is the rank of the associated matrix $A(x)$.

$$rank(x) = Rank A(x)$$

We define the distance between two vectors $(x,y) \in (GF(q^m))^2$ by

$$d_r(x,y) = rank(x-y)$$

A rank code C of length n and dimension k over $GF(q^m)$ is a subspace of dimension k of $GF(q^m)^n$ with the rank metric d_r.

By analogy to Hamming metric, the minimum rank distance of a code C can be defined as the minimum rank of non-zero vectors of the code C.

Definition 1. *Let $x = (x_1, \cdots, x_n) \in GF(q^m)^n$ be a vector of rank r. We denote by $E = <x_1, x_2, \cdots, x_n>$ the $GF(q)$-linear subspace of $GF(q^m)$ generated by $x_1, x_2, \cdots, x_n$. The vector space E is called the support of x.*

Definition 2. *Let e be an error vector of rank r and error support E. We denote by the erasure of dimension t of an error e a subspace T of dimension t of its error support E.*

Low Rank Parity Check (LRPC) Codes

Definition 3 ([9]). *A Low Rank Parity Check (LRPC) code of rank d, length n and dimension k over $GF(q^m)$ is a code defined by an $(n-k) \times n$ parity check matrix $H = (h_{ij})$ (where $1 \leq i \leq n-k, 1 \leq j \leq n$), such that all its coordinates h_{ij} belong to the same $GF(q)$-subspace F of dimension d of $GF(q^m)$.*

The definition of syndrome decoding problem for the Hamming metric is extended to the rank metric which gives rise to the following hard problems [9].

Problem 2 (Approximate - Rank Syndrome Decoding problem). Let H be an $(n - k) \times n$ matrix over $GF(q^m)$ with $k \leq n$, $s \in GF(q^m)^{n-k}$ and $r \in \mathbb{N}^*$. The problem is to find $x \in GF(q^m)^n$ such that $Hx^t = s$ and $rank(x) = r$.

The Approximate RSD problem has been proven to be hard in [10] by Gaborit *et al.* where the proof is based on probabilistic reduction.

Problem 3 Approximate - Rank Syndrome Decoding problem for augmented LRPC codes).] Given a masked parity-check matrix $H' = A(R|H)P$ of an augmented LRPC codes and a random syndrome s, find a vector x of rank d such that $H'x^T = s$ (where P and A are invertible matrices in $GF(q)$ and $GF(q^m)$ respectively. The matrix R is chosen randomly in $GF(q^m)$ and H is a parity check matrix of an LRPC code).

The Approximate RSD for LRPC codes is a particular case of the Approximate RSD. The problem on itself is not proved to be hard, however it is difficult to resolve such problem under the assumption that is difficult to distinguish between the augmented LRPC codes and random codes [9]. On one hand, it is obvious that the family augmented LRPC codes is not a family of random codes, but they are weakly structured codes: the main point being that they have a parity-check matrix one part of which consists only in low rank coordinates the other part consisting in random entries. The attacker never has direct access to the LRPC matrix H, which is hidden by the augmented part. On the other hand, the minimum weight of augmented LRPC codes is smaller than the Gilbert Varshamov bound, hence natural attacks consist in trying to use their special structure to attack them. There exist general attacks for recovering the minimum weight of a code but these attacks have a fast increasing complexity especially when the size of the base field $GF(q)$ increases. More details on this attacks are discussed in [9].

2.3   Strong Designated Verifier Signature

In this subsection, we recall from [2] the building blocks that compose an SDVS scheme with their corresponding security properties.

Definition 4 *(Strong Designated Verifier Signature).* *A Strong Designated Verifier Signature is a sequence of five algorithms $SDVS = (Setup, KeyGen, Sign, Verify, Sim)$ such that:*

- *$Setup(1^\lambda)$ is a probabilistic algorithm that takes as input a security parameter λ and outputs U the set of users, M the message space and the public parameters of the scheme pp.*
- *$KeyGen(pp)$ is a deterministic algorithm that outputs (sk_s, pk_s) a secret and a public key of the signer S and (sk_v, pk_v) a private and a public key of the designated verifier $\mathcal{V}$.*

- $Sign(pp, sk_s, pk_s, pk_v, M)$ *is a probabilistic algorithm. Given the public parameters pp, the secret and public keys of the sign* (sk_s, pk_s), *the public key of the designated verifier* pk_v *and the message M, this algorithm outputs a signature* $\sigma = Sign(pp, sk_s, pk_s, pk_v, M)$.
- $Verify(pp, pk_s, sk_v, pk_v, M, \sigma)$ *is a deterministic algorithm. It takes as input the public parameters pp, the secret key of the signer* sk_s *the secret and public key of the designated verifier* (sk_v, pk_v), *the message M and a signature* σ *on M. It outputs* $b = 1$ *if* σ *is a valid signature on M and* $b = 0$ *otherwise.*
- $Sim(pp, sk_v, pk_v, pk_s, M)$: *is a probabilistic algorithm. Given the public parameters pp, the secret and public keys of the signer* (sk_v, pk_v), *the public key of the designated verifier* pk_s *and the message M, this algorithm outputs a signature* $\sigma = Sign(pp, sk_v, pk_v, pk_s, M)$ *indistinguishable from one produced by the Sign algorithm.*

2.4   Security Model of SDVS

There are four security requirements that must be verified by a strong designated verifier signature namely: correctness, unforgeability, non-transferability and privacy of signer's identity [2].

Correctness: An SDVS is correct if for every valid secret key and public key of the signer and the designated verifier (sk_s, pk_s), (sk_v, pk_v) generated by $KeyGen$ algorithm and every message M we have:

$$Verify(pp, pk_s, sk_v, pk_v, M, \sigma) = 1$$

and

$$Verify(pp, pk_s, sk_v, pk_v, M, \sigma') = 1$$

Where $\sigma = Sign(pp, sk_s, pk_s, pk_v, M)$ and $\sigma' = Sim(pp, sk_v, pk_v, pk_s, M)$.

Unforgeability (UF): means that it is infeasible for an adversary $\mathcal{A}$ to produce a valid strong designated verifier signature without possessing the signer secret key sk_s or the designated verifier secret key sk_v. We consider the experiment between an adversary $\mathcal{A}$ and a challenger $\mathcal{C}$ as described in Algorithm 1. An SDVS scheme is existentially unforgeable if the advantage $Adv_{SDVS,\mathcal{A}}^{UF}(\lambda)$ (which is the probability that the adversary $\mathcal{A}$ breaks the existential unforgeability for the SDVS scheme) of the experiment in Algorithm 1 is negligible. A formal description of the unforgeability is given as it follows.

Algorithm 1. Unforgeability: Experiment $Exp_{SDVS,\mathcal{A}}^{UF}(\lambda)$

1. A challenger $\mathcal{C}$ runs the *Setup* algorithm to get the public parameters pp, runs the *KeyGen* algorithm to get the signer's key pair (sk_s, pk_s) and the verifier's key pair (sk_v, pk_v). The triple (pp, pk_s, pk_v) are given to $\mathcal{A}$.
2. An adversary $\mathcal{A}$ is given access to the following oracles:
   - $\mathcal{O}_{sign}$: This oracle uses sk_s to produce a signature σ on a given message M, that is valid with regard to pk_s, pk_v and sends it to $\mathcal{A}$.
   - $\mathcal{O}_{sim}$: This oracle uses sk_v to produce a signature σ on a given message M, that is valid with regard to pk_s, pk_v and sends it to $\mathcal{A}$.
   - $\mathcal{O}_{ver}$: This oracle takes (m, σ) as a query and gives a bit that is 1 when σ is valid with regard to pk_s and pk_v, and 0 otherwise.
3. The adversary $\mathcal{A}$ returns a forged signature σ^* on a message M^* where the two conditions hold:
   - a) $Verify(pp, pk_s, sk_v, pk_v, M^*, \sigma^*) = 1$ and
   - b) The adversary $\mathcal{A}$ did not query the sign oracle $\mathcal{O}_{sign}$ and the sim oracle $\mathcal{O}_{sim}$ on the message M^*.

$$Adv_{SDVS,\mathcal{A}}^{UF}(\lambda) = Pr[a \text{ and } b \text{ occur}]$$

Definition 5. *An SDVS scheme is unforgeable if adversary $\mathcal{A}$ with at most q_v queries to $\mathcal{O}_{ver}$, q_s queries to $\mathcal{O}_{sign}$, q_{sim} to $\mathcal{O}_{sim}$ and q_{ro} random oracle queries has negligible success probability, that is, $Adv_{SDVS,\mathcal{A}}^{UF}(\lambda) \leq \varepsilon$ (Where ε is negligible).*

Non-transferability: it means that the signature σ_0 generated by a signer $\mathcal{S}$ is indistinguishable from σ_1 the signature simulated by the designated verifier $\mathcal{V}$. We present forward a formal definition of non-transferability.

Definition 6. *An SDVS scheme is non-transferable if for all (sk_s, pk_s), (sk_v, pk_v), distinguisher $\mathcal{A}$ and message M we have:*

$$\left| pr\left[b' = b\right] - \frac{1}{2} \right| < \varepsilon$$

where $\sigma_0 = Sign(pp, sk_s, pk_s, pk_v, M)$, $\sigma_1 = Sim(pp, sk_v, pk_v, pk_s, M)$, $b \in \{0, 1\}$, $b' = \mathcal{A}(pk_s, pk_v, sk_s, sk_v, \sigma_b)$ and ε is negligible.

Privacy of Signer's Identity (PSI): An SDVS scheme preserves the privacy of signer identity (PSI) if it is infeasible for an adversary $\mathcal{A}$ to guess the signer behind a given signature in the case when we have two or more potential signers. Formally, we define this property between a challenger $\mathcal{C}$ and an adversary $\mathcal{A}$ as in the experiment bellow in Algorithm 2.

Algorithm 2. Privacy of Signer Identity $Exp_{SDVS,\mathcal{A}}^{PSI}(\lambda)$

---

1. A challenger $\mathcal{C}$ runs the *Setup* algorithm to get a public parameters pp, runs the *KeyGen* algorithm to get tow signer's key pair (sk_{s0}, pk_{s0}), (sk_{s1}, pk_{s1}) and the verifier's key pair (sk_v, pk_v). Then $(pp, pk_{s0}, pk_{s1}, pk_v)$ are given to an adversary $\mathcal{A}$.
2. The adversary $\mathcal{A}$ is given access to the same oracles as in the unforgeability game (Algorithm 1).
3. The challenger $\mathcal{C}$ chooses randomly $b \in \{0, 1\}$ and returns a signature $\sigma_b = Sign(pp, sk_{sb}, pk_{sb}, pk_v, M)$ to $\mathcal{A}$ where M is the signed message.
4. The adversary $\mathcal{A}$ outputs a bit $b' \in \{0, 1\}$ and wins the experiment if $b = b'$ and $\mathcal{A}$ has not made $\mathcal{O}_{ver}$ query on input (b, σ_b, pk_v, M).

Definition 7. *An SDVS scheme preserves the privacy of signer's identity if the advantage of an adversary $\mathcal{A}$ to win the experiment in Algorithm 2 is negligible i.e.*

$$Adv_{SDVS,\mathcal{A}}^{PSI}(\lambda) = \left| Pr[b = b'] - \frac{1}{2} \right| \leq \varepsilon$$

where ε is negligible.

3   The Proposed Strong Designated Verifier Signature

In this section, we present our proposal according to SDVS scheme based on error correcting codes. We explain in details the components used in our construction namely Algorithms 3, 4, 5, 6 and 7.

Setup: Given the security parameter λ, this algorithm outputs the public parameters pp, the secret and public keys of signer and designated verifier respectively (sk_s, pk_s) and (sk_v, pk_v) as described in Algorithm 3.

Algorithm 3. $Setup(1^\lambda)$

Input: a security parameter λ
Output: a public parameters pp

- The public parameters are $pp = \{n, k, m, q, f, \Psi, h\}$ where $h : \{0, 1\}^* \rightarrow \{0, 1\}^{n-k}$, $f : GF(q^m)^* \rightarrow GF(q^m)^{n-k}$ are random oracles, $\Psi_{h(M),i} : GF(q^m)^{n-k} \rightarrow GF(q^m)^{n-k}$ is a random permutation with keys $h(M)$ for $i \in \{signer, verifier\}$ and $(n, k, m, q,)$ are the parameters of the code.

KeyGen: Given the security parameter λ and public parameters pp, it outputs the secret and public keys of signer and designated verifier respectively (sk_s, pk_s) and (sk_v, pk_v) as described in Algorithm 4.

Algorithm 4. $KeyGen(1^\lambda, pp)$

Input: λ a security parameter, pp the public parameters produced by Algorithm 3
Output: (sk_s, pk_s) and (sk_v, pk_v)

- The public key of the signer is $pk_s = H_s' = (A_s(R_s|H_s)P_s, l_s)$ where P_s is an $(n+t) \times (n+t)$ invertible matrix in $GF(q)$, A_s is $(n-k) \times (n-k)$ invertible matrix in $GF(q^m)$, R_s is an $(n-k) \times t$ random matrix in $GF(q^m)$, H_s is a parity check matrix of an LRPC code and l_s is an integer.
- The secret key of the user is $sk_s = ((R_s|H_s), P_s, A_s)$.
- The designated verifier public key is $pk_v = H_v' = (A_v(R_v|H_v)P_v, l_v)$ where P_v is an $(n+t) \times (n+t)$ invertible matrix in $GF(q)$, A_v is an $(n-k) \times (n-k)$ invertible matrix in $GF(q^m)$, R_v is an $(n-k) \times t$ random matrix in $GF(q^m)$, l_v is an integer and H_v is a parity check matrix of an LRPC code.
- The secret key of the user is $sk_v = ((R_v|H_v), P_v, A_v)$.

Sign: The signature algorithm takes as input the public parameters pp, the secret and public keys of the signer (sk_s, pk_s), the verifier's public key pk_v generated in the Setup and the KeyGen Algorithms and a message M. The signature process is explained in Algorithm 5. We denote by Ω the general errors/erasures decoding algorithm for LRPC codes used in [9].

Algorithm 5. $Sign(pp, sk_s, pk_s, pk_v, M)$

Input: pp, sk_s, pk_s, pk_v, M
Output: σ

1. The signer chooses $\alpha \xleftarrow{\$} GF(q^m)^{n+t}$ and pick t random elements $(e_1, \cdots, e_t)$ in $GF(q^m)$ and $x_v \xleftarrow{\$} GF(q^m)^{n+t}$ such that $rank(\alpha) \le d$, $rank(x_v) \le d$ and computes $y = H_v' \alpha^T$.
2. The signer computes $s = \Psi_{h(M),s}^{-1}(f(\alpha, y, H_s', H_v', M) - \Psi_{h(M),v}(H_v' x_v^T))$.
3. Decodes by the LRPC matrix H_s the syndrome $s' = A_s^{-1} s^T - R_s(e_1, \cdots, e_t)^T$ with erasure space $T = <e_1, \cdots, e_t>$ and r' errors by the decoding algorithm Ω.
4. If the decoding algorithm returns a word $(e_{t+1}, \cdots, e_{n+t})$ of weight $r = t + r'$, the signature is $\sigma = [x_s = (e_1, \cdots, e_{n+t})(P_s^T)^{-1}, x_v, y]$ else return to step 1.

Verify: The verification step consists of checking the validity of a given signature, it returns $True$ if the verification succeed and $False$ otherwise.

Algorithm 6. $Verify(pp, pk_s, sk_v, pk_v, M, \sigma)$

Input: $pp, pk_s, sk_v, pk_v, M, \sigma$
Output: *True* or *False*

- The designated verifier receives a signature $\sigma = [x_s = (e_1, \cdots, e_{n+t})(P_s^T)^{-1}, x_v, y]$.
- He/she uses the decoding algorithm Ω to recover α from y using $(R_v|H_v), P_v, A_v$.
- He/she computes $a = f(\alpha, y, H_s', H_v', M)$,

if $\Psi_{h(M),s}(H_s' x_s^T) + \Psi_{h(M),v}(H_v' x_v^T) = a$, $rank(e) = r = t + r'$, $rank(\alpha) \leq d$ and $rank(x_v) \leq d$ then
  return *True*
else
  return *False*
end if

Sim: The simulation algorithm takes as input the public parameters pp, the secret and public keys of the designated verifier (sk_v, pk_v), the signer's public key pk_s generated in the Setup Algorithm 3 and a message M. The simulated signature is explained in Algorithm 7.

Algorithm 7. $Sim(pp, sk_v, pk_v, pk_s, M)$

Input: pp, sk_v, pk_v, pk_s, M
Output: σ'.
To simulate a signature on the message M, the designated verifier proceeds as follow:

1. Chooses randomly $\alpha' \xleftarrow{\$} GF(q^m)^{n+t}$ and pick t random elements $(e_1', \cdots, e_t')$ of $GF(q^m)$ and $x_s' \xleftarrow{\$} GF(q^m)^{n+t}$ such that $rank(\alpha') \leq d$, $rank(x_s') \leq d$ and computes $y' = H_v' \alpha'^T$.
2. The designated verifier computes

$$s = \Psi_{h(M),v}^{-1}(f(\alpha', y', H_s', H_v', M) - \Psi_{h(M),s}(H_s' x_s'^T)).$$

3. The designated verifier, decodes by the LRPC matrix H_v the syndrome $s' = A_v^{-1} s^T - R_v(e_1', \cdots, e_t')^T$ with errasure space $T = \langle e_1', \cdots, e_t' \rangle$ and r' errors by the decoding algorithm Ω.
4. If the decoding algorithm returns a word $(e_{t+1}', \cdots, e_{n+t}')$ of weight $r = t + r'$, the signature is $\sigma' = [x_s', x_v' = (e_1', \cdots, e_{n+t}')(P_v^T)^{-1}, y']$ else return to step 1.

---

4 Security Analysis

In this section, we analyse the security properties using the Random Oracle model of the proposed strong designated verifier signature scheme by proving, respectively, the correctness, the unforgeability, the non-transferability and the privacy of signer's identity.

Correctness: Let $\sigma = Sign(pp, sk_s, pk_s, pk_v, M)$ be a signature generated by the signer on a message M and $\sigma' = Sim(pp, sk_v, pk_v, pk_s, M)$ be a simulated signature produced by the designated verifier, the scheme is correct if

$$Verify(pp, pk_s, sk_v, pk_v, M, \sigma) = 1$$

and

$$Verify(pp, pk_s, sk_v, pk_v, M, \sigma') = 1$$

We prove only the correctness for signature generated by the signer because the proof for simulated signature is similar.

Let $\sigma = [x_s = (e_1, \cdots, e_{n+t})(P_s^T)^{-1}, x_v, y]$ be a signature generated as described in Algorithm 5, we have to prove the following: $\Psi_{h(M),s}(H_s' x_s^T) + \Psi_{h(M),v}(H_v' x_v^T) = a$, $rank(e) = r = t + r'$, $rank(\alpha) \leq d$ and $rank(x_v) \leq d$ where $a = f(\alpha, y, H_s', H_v', M)$ (Ψ, H_s' and H_v' are defined in Algorithms 3 and 4). We have on one hand:

$$\begin{aligned}
H_s' x_s^T &= H_s'(P_s^T)^{-1T}(e_1, \cdots, e_{n+t})^T \\
&= A_s(R_s|H_s)P_s(P_s^T)^{-1T}(e_1, \cdots, e_{n+t})^T \\
&= A_s(R_s|H_s)(e_1, \cdots, e_{n+t})^T \\
&= s
\end{aligned}$$

And on the other hand:

$$\begin{aligned}
\Psi_{h(M),s}(H_s' x_s^T) + \Psi_{h(M),v}(H_v' x_v^T) &= \Psi_{h(M),s}(s) + \Psi_{h(M),v}(H_v' x_v^T) \\
&= f(\alpha, y, H_s', H_v', M) - \Psi_{h(M),v}(H_v' x_v^T) \\
&\quad + \Psi_{h(M),v}(H_v' x_v^T) \\
&= f(\alpha, y, H_s', H_v', M) \\
&= a
\end{aligned}$$

The verifier can check easily that $rank(e) = r = t + r'$, $rank(\alpha) \leq d$ and $rank(x_v) \leq d$.

Unforgeability: We recall that this property means that it is infeasible for an adversary $\mathcal{A}$ to produce a valid SDVS without the knowledge of the signer secret key sk_s or the designated verifier secret key sk_v.

Theorem 1. *If there is an adversary $\mathcal{A}$ against the unforgeability of the scheme with non negligible probability then, there exists an adversary $\mathcal{C}$ that can solve the Problem 3 with non negligible probability.*

Proof. We assume that there exists an adversary $\mathcal{A}$ who can produce a forged signature with success probability at most ε_1. Let $\mathcal{C}$ be an adversary who can solve an instance of the Problem 3 with probability equal to ε_2 *i.e.* the adversary $\mathcal{C}$ returns a vector x^* of rank less or equal to d such that $H'^* x^* = s^*$ where $H'^* = A^*(R^*|H^*)P^*$, $A^* \in GL_{n-k}(GF(q^m))$, $P^* \in GL_{n+t}(GF(q))$, R^* is a random $(n-k) \times t$ matrix in $GF(q^m)$ and H^* is a parity check matrix of an LRPC code. The challenger $\mathcal{C}$ runs the *Setup* algorithm to get the public parameters, runs the *KeyGen* algorithm to get signer's and designated verifier's key pair (sk_s, pk_s) and (sk_v, pk_v) respectively. The adversary $\mathcal{C}$ provides $\mathcal{A}$ with public parameters pp, signer's public key $pk_s = H'_s$ and designated verifier public key $pk_v = H'_v$. The adversary $\mathcal{A}$ asks q_f, q_Ψ, q_{sign}, q_{sim} and q_v queries for the following oracles $f(.)$, $\Psi(.)$, $\mathcal{O}_{sign}$, $\mathcal{O}_{sim}$ and $\mathcal{O}_{ver}$ respectively.

- $f(.)$ queries: if $T_f[.]$ is defined for query $(\alpha, y, H'_s, H'_v, M)$, then $\mathcal{C}$ returns its value else, $\mathcal{C}$ returns a random value $T_f[\alpha, y, H'_s, H'_v, M] \overset{\$}{\leftarrow} GF(q^m)^{n-k}$.
- $\Psi(.)$ or $\Psi^{-1}(.)$ queries: for a query under the form $\Psi^{-1}_{h(M),i} = H'_i x_i^T$ or under the form $\Psi_{h(M),i} = (f(\alpha, y, H'_s, H'_v, M) - \Psi_{h(M),\bar{i}}(H'_{\bar{i}} x_{\bar{i}}^T)$ (where $i \in \{signer, verifier\}$), the adversary $\mathcal{C}$ searches in $T_\Psi[.]$ and returns its value if it exists otherwise, it returns a random value from $GF(q^m)^{n-k}$ and send it to the adversary $\mathcal{A}$.
- $\mathcal{O}_{sign}$: for query (H'_s, H'_v, M), $\mathcal{C}$ chooses randomly $\alpha \overset{\$}{\leftarrow} GF(q^m)^{(n+t)}$, $x_v \overset{\$}{\leftarrow} GF(q^m)^{(n+t)}$ and $x_s \overset{\$}{\leftarrow} GF(q^m)^{n+t}$ such that $rank(\alpha) \leq d$ and $rank(x_v) \leq d$. The challenger $\mathcal{C}$ computes $y = H'_v \alpha^T$ and $a = \Psi^{-1}_{h(M),s}(H'_s x_s^T) + \Psi_{h(M),s}(H'_v x_v^T)$. If $T_f[\alpha, y, H'_s, H'_v, M]$ have been already defined, then $\mathcal{C}$ aborts, otherwise we make $T_f[\alpha, y, H'_s, H'_v, M] \leftarrow a$ and an SDVS signature on the message M under H'_s, H'_v is equal to $\sigma = (x_s, x_v, y)$. The adversary $\mathcal{C}$ sends σ to $\mathcal{A}$.
- $\mathcal{O}_{sim}$: for query (H'_v, H'_s, M), this oracle is programmed as the $\mathcal{O}_{sign}$ oracle.
- $\mathcal{O}_{ver}$ queries: for a query $(x_s, x_v, y, H'_v, H'_s, M)$, the challenger $\mathcal{C}$ searches in table $T_f[.]$ for the tuple $(\alpha, y, H'_v, H'_s, M)$ such that $y = H'_v \alpha^T$ and $rank(\alpha) \leq d$ and also in table $T_\Psi[.]$ for queries in form of $H'_s x_s^T$ and $H'_v x_v^T$ in order to have $\Psi_{h(M),s} = \Psi_{h(M),s}(H'_s x_s^T)$ and $\Psi_{h(M),v} = \Psi_{h(M),v}(H'_v x_v^T)$ and verifies if $\Psi_{h(M),s}(H'_s x_s^T) + \Psi_{h(M),v}(H'_v x_v^T) = f(\alpha, y, H'_v, H'_s, M)$ and $rank(x_x) \leq d$.
- Finally, the adversary $\mathcal{A}$ outputs a forged signature $\sigma^* = (x_s^*, x_v^*, y^*)$ on a message M^* under signer's and designated verifier's public keys pk_s, pk_v such that $Verify(pp, pk_s, pk_v, sk_v, \sigma^*, M^*) = 1$ and $\mathcal{A}$ has never questioned the Sign Algorithm for input (pk_v, pk_s, M^*).

The adversary $\mathcal{A}$ wins the unforgeability game with probability equal to

$$Pr[Event1] \times Pr[Event2|Event1]$$

where Event1 and Event2 are defined as follows:

- Event 1: The adversary $\mathcal{C}$ does not abort in Sign and Sim oracles.
- Event 2: The adversary $\mathcal{A}$ breaks the unforgeability of the scheme.

In order to compute the probability of the Event1, we distinguish two cases:

- Case 1: if $(\alpha y, H'_s, H'_v, M)$ produced in one Sign or Sim oracles has occurred by chance in a previous query to the oracle $f(.)$, then $bad \leftarrow True$ (The event *bad* refers to the adversary $\mathcal{C}$ aborts in *Sign* and *Sim* algorithms). Given that there exist at most $(q_f + q_{sign} + q_{sim})$ entries in table $T_f[.]$ and the number of elements α chosen randomly in $GF(q^m)^{n+t}$ such that $rank(\alpha) \leq d$ is equal to ξ. As a consequence, the probability of this event for $(q_{sign} + q_{sim})$ queries is at most

$$\frac{(q_{sign} + q_{sim})(q_f + q_{sign} + q_{sim})}{\xi} \tag{1}$$

– Case 2: if the adversary $\mathcal{C}$ used the same random elements $\alpha \in GF(q^m)^n$ such that $rank(\alpha) \leq d$ in one $\mathcal{O}_{sign}$ or $\mathcal{O}_{sim}$ oracles, we have *bad* = *true* and $\mathcal{C}$ makes at most $(q_{sign} + q_{sim})$ queries to Sign and Sim oracles. Therefore, the probability is at most $\frac{(q_{sign}+q_{sim})^2}{\xi}$ Consequently,

$$Pr[Event1] = 1 - Pr[bad] \geq 1 - \frac{(q_{sign} + q_{sim})(q_f + 2(q_{sign} + q_{sim}))}{\xi}$$

However, we have $Pr[Event2|Event1] \geq \varepsilon_1$.

As a consequence, the adversary $\mathcal{A}$ outputs a tuple $(x_s^*, x_v^*, y^*, f, \Psi_{h(M),s}^{-1}, \Psi_{h(M),v})$ with probability at least

$$\varepsilon_1 - \frac{(q_{sign} + q_{sim})(q_f + 2(q_{sign} + q_{sim}))}{\xi}$$

The challenger $\mathcal{C}$ employs $\mathcal{A}$, guesses an index $1 \leq \gamma \leq q_\Psi$ and wishes that γ is the index of the query $\Psi_{h(M),s} = (f(\alpha^*, y^*, H_s', H_v', M) - \Psi_{h(M),v}(H_v' x_v^*)$ to the oracle $\Psi_{h(M),i}^{-1}$. The algorithm $\mathcal{C}$ outputs s^* as a response to this query with probability $\frac{1}{q_\Psi}$. The tuple $(x_s^*,, x_v^*, y^*, f, \Psi_{h(M),s}^{-1}, \Psi_{h(M),v})$ is a valid SDVS signature and as a consequence we have: $rank(x_s^*) \leq d$, $rank(x_v^*) \leq d$ and

$$H_s' x_s^{*T} = \Psi_{h(M^*),s}^*(\Psi_{h(M^*),v}(H_v x_v^{*T}) - f(\alpha^*, y^*, H_s'^*, H_v'^*))$$

We take $s^* = \Psi_{h(M^*),s}^*(\Psi_{h(M^*),v}(H_v x_v^{*T}) - f(\alpha^*, y^*, H_s'^*, H_v'^*))$ and then $\mathcal{C}$ solves the following instance of Problem 3 $H_s' x_s^{*T} = s^*$ with probability at least

$$\frac{\varepsilon_1}{q_\Psi} - \frac{(q_{sign} + q_{sim})(q_f + 2(q_{sign} + q_{sim}))}{\xi \cdot q_\Psi}$$

Thus, we conclude the proof.   ■

Non-transferability. Hereafter we discuss about the non transferability of the proposed SDVS scheme.

Theorem 2. *The proposed SDVS scheme is non-transferable.*

Proof. We keep the same notations as before, then, we have to prove that the signature produced by the signer and the one simulated by the designated verifier are indistinguishable. For this reason, we prove that the following distributions are the same

$$\sigma_{signer} = (x_s, x_v, y) : \begin{cases} \alpha \xleftarrow{\$} GF(q^m)^{n+t}, rank(\alpha) \leq d \\ x_v \xleftarrow{\$} GF(q^m)^{n+t}, rank(x_v) \leq d \\ y = H'_v \alpha^T \\ s_1 = \Psi_{h(M),s}^{-1}(f(\alpha, y, H'_s, H'_v, M) - \Psi_{h(M),v}(H'_v x_v^T)) \\ x_s = (e_1, \cdots, e_{n+t})(P_s^T)^{-1} \end{cases}$$

$$\sigma_{sim} = (x'_s, x'_v, y') : \begin{cases} \alpha' \xleftarrow{\$} GF(q^m)^{n+t}, rank(\alpha') \leq d \\ x'_s \xleftarrow{\$} GF(q^m)^{n+t}, rank(x'_v) \leq d \\ y' = H'_v \alpha'^T \\ s_2 = \Psi_{h(M),s}^{-1}(f(\alpha', y', H'_s, H'_v, M) - \Psi_{h(M),v}(H'_v x'^T_v)) \\ x'_v = (e'_1, \cdots, e'_{n+t})(P_v^T)^{-1} \end{cases}$$

We suppose that $\overline{\sigma}$ is a valid signature selected from the set of all the valid signature of the signer and we compute the following probabilities:

$$Pr_{\sigma_{signer}} = Pr_{\alpha, x_v}[\overline{\sigma} = \sigma_{signer}] = (Pr\{\alpha \xleftarrow{\$} GF(q^m)^{n+t}, rank(\alpha) \leq d\})^2$$

and

$$Pr_{\sigma_{sim}} = Pr_{\alpha', x'_v}[\overline{\sigma} = \sigma_{sim}] = (Pr\{\alpha' \xleftarrow{\$} GF(q^m)^{n+t}, rank(\alpha') \leq d\})^2$$

As a consequence, we have $Pr_{\sigma_{signer}} = Pr_{\sigma_{sim}}$ ∎

Privacy of Signer Identity (PSI)

Theorem 3. *If there exist an adversary $\mathcal{A}$ who can break the PSI property of the scheme with non-negligible probability, then there exists an adversary $\mathcal{C}$ that can solve Problem 3 with non negligible probability.*

Proof. We suppose that there exists an adversary $\mathcal{A}$ who can break the PSI of the scheme with success probability at most ε_1. We consider $\mathcal{C}$ as an adversary who can solve an instance of Problem 3 with probability equal to ε_2 *i.e.* the adversary $\mathcal{C}$ returns a vector x^* of rank less or equal to d such that $H'^* x^* = s^*$ where $H'^* = A^*(R^*|H^*)P^*$, $A^* \in GL_{n-k}(GF(q^m))$, $P^* \in GL_{n+t}(GF(q))$ and R^* is a random $(n-k) \times t$ matrix in $GF(q^m)$. The adversary $\mathcal{C}$ runs the Setup algorithm in order to get the public parameters pp, runs the $KeyGen$ algorithm (Algorithm 4) to get the public keys of the two signers H'_{s_0} and H'_{s_1} with their corresponding secret keys. The adversary $\mathcal{C}$ sets the designated verifier's public key $H'_v = H'^*$ and the adversary $\mathcal{A}$ makes q_f query to the $f(.)$ oracle, q_Ψ query to $\Psi_{h(M),i}$ oracle, q_{sign} query to the sign oracle $\mathcal{O}_{sign}$, q_{sim} query to the sim oracle $\mathcal{O}_{sim}$ and q_v query to the verification oracle $\mathcal{O}_{ver}$. The oracles $f(.)$ and $\Psi_{h(M),i}(.)$ are programmed as in the proof of Theorem 1 [unforgeability], at the beginning we take empty tables $T_f[.]$, $T_\Psi[.]$ and $T_s[.]$ (in which we store the issued signatures). The oracle queries are as follows:

- Sign query $\mathcal{O}_{sign}$: for a query (b, H'_{s_b}, H_v, M) where $b \in \{0,1\}$, the adversary $\mathcal{C}$ returns a signature $\sigma_b = (x_{s_b}, x_v, y)$ on a message M by running the sign algorithm since $\mathcal{C}$ has the signer's secret key and then transfers σ_b to $\mathcal{A}$.
- Verify queries $\mathcal{O}_{ver}$: for a query $(b, \sigma_b, H'_v, H'_{s_b}, M)$ where $b \in \{0,1\}$. This oracle returns 1 if σ_b is in $T_s[.]$ and σ_b was never returned by $\mathcal{C}$ and 0 otherwise.
- The adversary $\mathcal{C}$ chooses randomly $b \in \{0,1\}$, $x_v \in GF(q^m)^{(n+t)}$ with $rank(x_v) \leq d$, puts $y = s^*$, makes query to the oracle $f(.)$ on the tuple $(T, s^*, H'_{s_b}, H'^*, M)$, computes x_s as in Algorithm 5 (Step 2, 3 and 4) and returns to the adversary $\mathcal{A}$ the signature σ_b, the public keys H'_{s_0}, H'_{s_1} and the designated verifier public key H'_v.
- After making a number of queries to the aforementioned oracles, the adversary $\mathcal{C}$ changes the answers of the oracles adequately. In the case of queries of the form (x^*, y, H'_s, H'_v, M) where $y \neq s^*$, it returns a random value from $GF(q^m)^{n-k}$. If $y = s^*$ and $rank(x^*) \leq d$ it returns a random value from $GF(q^m)^{n-k}$ and changes T by x.
- The adversary $\mathcal{A}$ returns $b' = b$.

To succeed in the PSI attack, the adversary $\mathcal{A}$ has to make query to the $f(.)$ oracle on the tuple $(x^*, s^*, H'_{s_b}, H'^*, M)$ where $s^* = H'^* x^{*T}$. Since $f(.)$ is a random oracle, $\mathcal{A}$ can guess its value with probability $\frac{1}{(q^m)^{n-k}}$. In addition, the probability that $\Psi_{h(M),s_b} = \Psi_{h(M),s_b}(H'_{s_b} x^T_{s_b})$ and $\Psi_{h(M),v} = \Psi_{h(M),v}(H'_v x^T_v)$ is less than $\frac{2}{(q^m)^{n-k}}$. Consequently, x^* is a solution to the following instance $H'^* x^{*T} = s^*$ where $rank(x^*) \leq d$ of Problem 3 with probability ε_2 such that:

$$\varepsilon_2 \geq \varepsilon_1 - \frac{3}{(q^m)^{n-k}}$$

■

5   Parameters and Results

In this section, we give parameters for the proposed strong designated verifier signature scheme in Table 1 for different security levels. We also compare our results with some related works in Tables 2 and 3, in particular with the post-quantum constructions of SDVS namely [2,22]. The comparison is done in terms of security properties, public key and signature sizes.

- The signer's and designated verifier's public key size:

$$size_{(pk_s)} = size_{(pk_v)}$$
$$= (n-k)(n+t)m log_2(q) - bits$$

– The signature size is computed as follows:

$$size_{(sig)} = size(x_s) + size(x_v) + size(y)$$
$$= [2(n+t) + (n-k)]mlog_2(q) - bits$$

Table 1. Parameters for different security levels.

Security level	n	k	t	m	q	Public key size (bits)	Signature size (bits)
80 bits	32	16	5	39	2	23088	3510
110 bit	40	20	5	45	2	40000	4950
120 bit	16	8	2	18	2^8	16000	6336
130 bit	16	8	2	18	2^{40}	96000	31680

Table 2. Comparison in terms of security properties with some related works.

Scheme	Correctness	Non-transferability	Unforgeability	Privacy of signer identity
Scheme of [22]	Yes	No	No	Yes
Scheme of [2]	Yes	Yes	Yes	Yes
Our scheme	Yes	Yes	Yes	Yes

Table 3. Comparison in terms of public key and signature sizes.

Scheme	Hard problem	Security model	Signature size (bit)	Public key size (bit)
Scheme of [22]	Syndrome Decoding	Random oracle	624	57.75
Scheme of [2]	Syndrome Decoding	Random oracle	530	99
Our scheme	Rank Syndrome Decoding	Random oracle	3510	0.003

6   Conclusion

In this paper, we have proposed an efficient strong designated verifier signature scheme from coding theory assumptions that is supposed to be resistant to quantum computers. Our approach relies on using rank metric codes rather than classical Hamming codes; indeed we proposed to use LRPC codes. Our construction combines efficiency and security requirements, as we have achieved a reasonable size for the public key length and for the signature size. In addition, the security properties required for an SDVS scheme are fulfilled. As a perspective to the present paper, we consider to propose in a future work an SDVS scheme that combines between efficiency and security especially in the era of post quantum cryptography.

References

1. de Almeida, M.P., de Sousa Júnior, R.T., García-Villalba, L.J., Kim, T.: New dos defense method based on strong designated verifier signatures. Sensors **18**(9), 2813 (2018). https://doi.org/10.3390/s18092813
2. Asaar, M.R., Salmasizadeh, M., Aref, M.R.: Code-based strong designated verifier signatures: security analysis and a new construction. IACR Cryptology ePrint Archive **2016**, 779 (2016)
3. Assidi, H., Ayebie, E.B., Souidi, E.M.: A code-based group signature scheme with shorter public key length. In: Proceedings of the 13th International Joint Conference on e-Business and Telecommunications (ICETE 2016) - Volume 4: SECRYPT, Lisbon, Portugal, 26–28 July 2016, pp. 432–439 (2016). https://doi.org/10.5220/0005969204320439
4. Assidi, H., Ayebie, E.B., Souidi, E.M.: Two mutual authentication protocols based on zero-knowledge proofs for RFID systems. In: Kim, H., Kim, D.-C. (eds.) ICISC 2017. LNCS, vol. 10779, pp. 267–283. Springer, Cham (2018). https://doi.org/10.1007/978-3-319-78556-1_15
5. Ayebie, B.E., Assidi, H., Souidi, E.M.: A new dynamic code-based group signature scheme. In: El Hajji, S., Nitaj, A., Souidi, E.M. (eds.) C2SI 2017. LNCS, vol. 10194, pp. 346–364. Springer, Cham (2017). https://doi.org/10.1007/978-3-319-55589-8_23
6. Berlekamp, E.R., McEliece, R.J., van Tilborg, H.: On the inherent intractability of certaincoding problems (Coresp.). IEEE Trans. Inf. Theory **24**(3), 384–386 (1978). https://doi.org/10.1109/TIT.1978.1055873
7. Cayrel, P.-L., El Yousfi Alaoui, S.M., Hoffmann, G., Véron, P.: An improved threshold ring signature scheme based on error correcting codes. In: Özbudak, F., Rodríguez-Henríquez, F. (eds.) WAIFI 2012. LNCS, vol. 7369, pp. 45–63. Springer, Heidelberg (2012). https://doi.org/10.1007/978-3-642-31662-3_4
8. Chaum, D., van Antwerpen, H.: Undeniable signatures. In: Brassard, G. (ed.) CRYPTO 1989. LNCS, vol. 435, pp. 212–216. Springer, New York (1990). https://doi.org/10.1007/0-387-34805-0_20
9. Gaborit, P., Ruatta, O., Schrek, J., Zémor, G.: RankSign: an efficient signature algorithm based on the rank metric. In: Mosca, M. (ed.) PQCrypto 2014. LNCS, vol. 8772, pp. 88–107. Springer, Cham (2014). https://doi.org/10.1007/978-3-319-11659-4_6
10. Gaborit, P., Zémor, G.: On the hardness of the decoding and the minimum distance problems for rank codes. IEEE Trans. Inf. Theory **62**(12), 7245–7252 (2016). https://doi.org/10.1109/TIT.2016.2616127
11. Gorantla, M.C., Boyd, C., Nieto, J.M.G.: Strong designated verifier signature in a multi-user setting. In: Seventh Australasian Information Security Conference, AISC 2009, Wellington, New Zealand, January 2009, pp. 21–31 (2009)
12. Hu, X., Tan, W., Xu, H., Wang, J., Ma, C.: Strong designated verifier signature schemes with undeniable property and their applications. Secur. Commun. Netw. **2017**, 7921782:1–7921782:9 (2017). https://doi.org/10.1155/2017/7921782
13. Jakobsson, M., Sako, K., Impagliazzo, R.: Designated verifier proofs and their applications. In: Maurer, U. (ed.) EUROCRYPT 1996. LNCS, vol. 1070, pp. 143–154. Springer, Heidelberg (1996). https://doi.org/10.1007/3-540-68339-9_13
14. Kancharla, P.K., Gummadidala, S., Saxena, A.: Identity based strong designated verifier signature scheme. Informatica Lith. Acad. Sci. **18**(2), 239–252 (2007)

15. Kang, B., Boyd, C., Dawson, E.: A novel identity-based strong designated verifier signature scheme. J. Syst. Softw. **82**(2), 270–273 (2009). https://doi.org/10.1016/j.jss.2008.06.014

16. Laguillaumie, F., Vergnaud, D.: Designated verifier signatures: anonymity and efficient construction from *Any* bilinear map. In: Blundo, C., Cimato, S. (eds.) SCN 2004. LNCS, vol. 3352, pp. 105–119. Springer, Heidelberg (2005). https://doi.org/10.1007/978-3-540-30598-9_8

17. Lal, S., Verma, V.: Identity based strong designated verifier proxy signature schemes. IACR Cryptology ePrint Archive **2006**, 394 (2006)

18. Lin, H.: A new certificateless strong designated verifier signature scheme: non-delegatable and SSA-KCA secure. IEEE Access **6**, 50765–50775 (2018). https://doi.org/10.1109/ACCESS.2018.2809437

19. Melchor, C.A., Cayrel, P., Gaborit, P.: A new efficient threshold ring signature scheme based on coding theory. In: Post-Quantum Cryptography, Second International Workshop, PQCrypto 2008, Cincinnati, OH, USA, 17–19 October 2008, Proceedings, pp. 1–16 (2008). https://doi.org/10.1007/978-3-540-88403-3_1

20. Noh, G., Jeong, I.R.: Strong designated verifier signature scheme from lattices in the standard model. Secur. Commun. Netw. **9**(18), 6202–6214 (2016). https://doi.org/10.1002/sec.1766

21. Saeednia, S., Kremer, S., Markowitch, O.: An efficient strong designated verifier signature scheme. In: Lim, J.-I., Lee, D.-H. (eds.) ICISC 2003. LNCS, vol. 2971, pp. 40–54. Springer, Heidelberg (2004). https://doi.org/10.1007/978-3-540-24691-6_4

22. Shooshtari, M.K., Ahmadian-Attari, M., Aref, M.R.: Provably secure strong designated verifier signature scheme based on coding theory. Int. J. Commun. Syst. **30**(7), e3162 (2017). https://doi.org/10.1002/dac.3162

23. Shor, P.W.: Algorithms for quantum computation: discrete logarithms and factoring. In: 35th Annual Symposium on Foundations of Computer Science, Santa Fe, New Mexico, USA, 20–22 November 1994, pp. 124–134 (1994). https://doi.org/10.1109/SFCS.1994.365700

24. Tian, H., Jiang, Z., Liu, Y., Wei, B.: A systematic method to design strong designated verifier signature without random oracles. Cluster Comput. **16**(4), 817–827 (2013). https://doi.org/10.1007/s10586-013-0255-x

25. Yang, B., Yu, Y., Sun, Y.: A novel construction of SDVS with secure disavowability. Cluster Comput. **16**(4), 807–815 (2013). https://doi.org/10.1007/s10586-013-0254-y

A Lightweight Implementation of NTRU Prime for the Post-quantum Internet of Things

Hao Cheng[1(✉)], Daniel Dinu[2], Johann Großschädl[1], Peter B. Rønne[1], and Peter Y. A. Ryan[1]

[1] SnT and CSC, University of Luxembourg, 6, Avenue de la Fonte, 4364 Esch-sur-Alzette, Luxembourg
{hao.cheng,johann.groszschaedl,peter.roenne,peter.ryan}@uni.lu
[2] IPAS, Intel, Chandler, AZ 85226, USA
daniel.dinu@intel.com

Abstract. The dawning era of quantum computing has initiated various initiatives for the standardization of post-quantum cryptosystems with the goal of (eventually) replacing RSA and ECC. NTRU Prime is a variant of the classical NTRU cryptosystem that comes with a couple of tweaks to minimize the attack surface; most notably, it avoids rings with "worrisome" structure. This paper presents, to our knowledge, the first assembler-optimized implementation of Streamlined NTRU Prime for an 8-bit AVR microcontroller and shows that high-security lattice-based cryptography is feasible for small IoT devices. An encapsulation operation using parameters for 128-bit post-quantum security requires 8.2 million clock cycles when executed on an 8-bit ATmega1284 microcontroller. The decapsulation is approximately twice as costly and has an execution time of 15.6 million cycles. We achieved this performance through (i) new low-level software optimization techniques to accelerate Karatsuba-based polynomial multiplication on the 8-bit AVR platform and (ii) an efficient implementation of the coefficient modular reduction written in assembly language. The execution time of encapsulation and decapsulation is independent of secret data, which makes our software resistant against timing attacks. Finally, we assess the performance one could theoretically gain by using a so-called product-form polynomial as part of the secret key and discuss potential security implications.

Keywords: Lightweight cryptography · Post-Quantum Cryptography · Key Encapsulation Mechanism · NTRU Prime · Efficient implementation

1 Introduction

The advent of quantum computing is a technological revolution that will soon have a massive impact on our daily life and may even disrupt whole

© IFIP International Federation for Information Processing 2020
Published by Springer Nature Switzerland AG 2020
M. Laurent and T. Giannetsos (Eds.): WISTP 2019, LNCS 12024, pp. 103–119, 2020.
https://doi.org/10.1007/978-3-030-41702-4_7

industries [19]. In short, a quantum computer operates on so-called qubits (the "quantum analog" of bits), which can not only take the two states 0 and 1, but also be in a superposition of both states. A quantum computer with n qubits can be in an arbitrary superposition of up to 2^n states simultaneously, enabling it to process 2^n values in parallel or to store 2^n values in one step. For example, a quantum computer with about 50 logical qubits could solve certain complex optimization problems a lot faster than the most advanced classical supercomputer today. In the not-so-distant future, our daily life will start to get affected by large-scale quantum computers that are powerful enough to aid the discovery of new drugs or materials, organize the routes of millions of self-driving cars in metropolitan areas without introducing traffic jams, and improve the efficiency of national power grids [19]. Unfortunately, quantum computing has also a destructive side because a large-scale quantum computer with a few thousand qubits would be able to break essentially every public-key cryptosystem in use today. This was discovered in the mid-90s by Peter Shor, who also developed a polynomial-time quantum algorithm to factor large integers, which could break the widely-used RSA cryptosystem [25]. Later, it was also found that a generalization of Shor's algorithm would enable one to take discrete logarithms in a large elliptic curve groups, thereby breaking Elliptic Curve Cryptography (ECC).

Estimates as to when the first large-scale quantum computer might become available vary significantly, but optimistic predictions suggest it could happen before the end of the 2020s [21]. Given the real-world threat posed by quantum computing, it is little surprising that research in the domain of *Post-Quantum Cryptography (PQC)*, i.e. cryptography that is able to withstand cryptanalytic attacks carried out using a large quantum computer [3], has gained momentum over the past few years. In 2016, the U.S. National Institute of Standards and Technology (NIST) announced a process to "solicit, evaluate, and standardize quantum-resistant public-key cryptographic algorithms" and published a call to submit proposals [22]. This call, whose submission deadline passed at the end of November 2017, covered the complete spectrum of public-key functionalities considered by the NIST, i.e. public-key encryption, key agreement, and digital signatures. A total of 72 candidates were submitted, of which 69 satisfied the minimum requirements for acceptability and entered the first round of a multi-year evaluation process. In early 2019, the NIST selected 26 of the submissions as candidates for the second round; among these are 17 public-key encryption or key-establishment algorithms and nine signature schemes. The 17 algorithms for encryption (resp. key establishment) include nine that are based on certain hard problems in lattices, seven whose security rests upon classical problems in coding theory, and one that claims security from the presumed hardness of the (supersingular) isogeny walk problem on elliptic curves [22].

NTRU Prime is a family of lattice-based cryptosystems developed by Bernstein, Chuengsatiansup, Lange, and van Vredendaal [4], who drew inspiration from the 20-year old classical NTRU cryptosystem [12]. There are two variants of NTRU Prime; one is the so-called *Streamlined NTRU Prime*, which uses the quotient $h = g/(3f)$ of two secret polynomials g, f as public key (similar to the classical NTRU), while the other, *NTRU LPRime*, has public keys of the form $h = e + Af$, where e, f are secret and A is public (like in cryptosystems based on the Ring Learning With Errors (RLWE) problem [20], e.g. NewHope [1]). In essence, NTRU Prime can be seen as an attempt to improve the security of the classical NTRU encryption algorithm (and other lattice-based cryptosystems) by avoiding rings with "worrisome" structure and using extension fields of the form $\mathcal{R}/q = (\mathbb{Z}/q)[x]/(x^p - x - 1)$ instead, where p is prime. Multiplication in such fields can be efficiently implemented through several layers of Karatsuba's technique [17], which makes NTRU Prime relatively fast on 64-bit processors with vector instructions. Concretely, the designers of NTRU Prime describe in [4] a highly-optimized implementation of the field multiplication using Intel's AVX2 vector instructions that executes 16 separate multiplications of integers modulo 2^{16} in a SIMD-parallel way. NTRU Prime is among the 26 candidates in the second round of NIST's evaluation process. This second round will focus on evaluating the candidates' performance across a wide variety of systems and platforms, which includes "not only big computers and smart phones, but also devices that have limited processor power" [22].

Research on software optimization techniques that enable fast implementations of (Streamlined) NTRU Prime has, until now, been limited to 64-bit Intel processors with AVX2 vector engine. When using a parameter set for 128 bits of post-quantum security, the AVX2 implementation introduced in [4] requires 59,600 clock cycles for encryption (i.e. "encapsulation" of a 256-bit key) on an Intel Haswell processor, while the decryption ("decapsulation") is 63.5% more costly and takes 97,452 cycles. The only performance figures for NTRU Prime on small platforms (e.g. 8, 16, or 32-bit microcontrollers) we are aware of were reported in a recent paper on pqm4 [16], a testing and benchmarking toolsuite for NIST PQC candidates on ARM Cortex-M4 devices. Due to the lack of an optimized ARM implementation, the authors of [16] resorted to the reference C code provided by the designers of NTRU Prime, which requires 54.9 million clock cycles for encapsulation and 166.5 million cycles for decapsulation (these cycle counts were determined with Streamlined NTRU Prime and parameters for 128-bit post-quantum security). However, both results do not allow one to reason about the actual performance of NTRU Prime on microcontrollers since the aim of a reference C implementation is to promote the understanding of an algorithm rather than achieving high speed. Therefore, not much is known on how to optimize NTRU Prime for a small microcontroller and what execution time a carefully-tuned assembler implementation could achieve.

In this paper we present a highly-optimized implementation of Streamlined NTRU Prime for 8-bit AVR microcontrollers that we developed from scratch to reach high speed and resistance against timing attacks. We chose 8-bit AVR as evaluation platform for two reasons. First, the 8-bit AVR architecture remains very popular in devices with increased security requirements, e.g. smart cards and (wireless) sensor nodes. Second, 8-bit AVR microcontrollers are among the most resource-limited of all currently used computing platforms, which implies that if NTRU Prime can be implemented to run with acceptable speed on an AVR device, it can also be implemented to run satisfactorily on more powerful 16 and 32-bit microcontrollers (e.g. an ARM Cortex-M), whereas the opposite is not necessarily true. The implementation we describe in the next sections is not purely optimized for speed, but strives for a balance between performance and other metrics of interest for low-end devices used in the Internet of Things (IoT), in particular binary code size. Therefore, we decided to refrain from full loop unrolling and other optimization techniques that are likely to increase the code size significantly (especially on an 8-bit device) for marginal performance benefits. We also restrict our arsenal of polynomial multiplication algorithms to the basic (i.e. recursive) Karatsuba variant and the schoolbook method for the same reason. Recent results by Kannwischer et al. [15] show that a combination of Karatsuba's technique with the asymptotically faster Toom-Cook algorithm [27] can slightly reduce the multiplication time, e.g. by 17.4% for polynomials of degree 701 (excluding the reduction of coefficients), but only at the expense of almost doubled stack usage and significantly increased implementation complexity. On the other hand, our Karatsuba/schoolbook multiplication is simple to implement and has the further advantage of enabling compact code size (see Sect. 4) while remaining competitive in terms of performance.

Instead of potential speed-ups due to the Toom-Cook algorithm, we analyze the performance benefits one could achieve by utilizing so-called *product-form polynomials*, which were first proposed in [13,14] to reduce the computational cost of the classical NTRU scheme. We show that representing the secret key in product form would cut the decapsulation time by 30%, but we also emphasize that the security implications of product-form secret keys in NTRU Prime are yet to be carefully analyzed. Furthermore, we present efficient implementations of the fast reduction of coefficient products of a length of up to 29 bits modulo a 13-bit prime q. Finally, we demonstrate that, for some 8-bit AVR models like the ATtiny45, the modulo-3 reduction code generated by optimizing compilers may have operand-dependent execution time and enable timing attacks.

2   A Brief Overview of NTRU Prime

NTRU Prime is introduced in [4] as a high-security *prime-degree large-Galois-group inert-modulus* ideal-lattice-based cryptosystem. A distinguishing feature of NTRU Prime is the use of an irreducible non-cyclotomic polynomial P; the designers recommend to choose a polynomial P of prime degree p with a large Galois group. More specifically, they suggest $P = x^p - x - 1$ and recommend to take a prime modulus q such that P is irreducible modulo q, which means q is inert in the ring $\mathcal{R} = \mathbb{Z}[x]/P$ and $\mathcal{R}/q = (\mathbb{Z}/q)[x]/P$ is actually a field. Due to the prime degree of P, the only subfields of $(\mathbb{Z}/q)[x]/P$ are $\mathbb{Z}/q$ and the entire field $(\mathbb{Z}/q)[x]/P$. Furthermore, the requirement of a large Galois group implies that P has, at most, a few roots in any field of reasonable degree, which makes automorphism computations hard. Finally, since q is an inert prime, there are no ring homomorphisms from $(\mathbb{Z}/q)[x]/P$ to any smaller non-0 ring.

The NTRU Prime family of Key Encapsulation Mechanisms (KEMs) specified in [4,5] consists of Streamlined NTRU Prime and NTRU LPrime, but we only consider the former since it is more implementation-friendly. Streamlined

NTRU Prime is similar to classical NTRU, but adopts a rounding technique in the encapsulation and, as explained above, uses a field instead of a ring.

Notation and Parameters. A parameter set for Streamlined NTRU Prime consists of the triple (p, q, w), which defines the main algebraic structures. The parameter p is the degree of the irreducible polynomial $P = x^p - x - 1$ and is prime; the parameter sets given in [5] use 653, 761, and 857. Also the modulus q, which represents the characteristic of the field $\mathcal{R}/q = (\mathbb{Z}/q)[x]/P$, is a prime with typical values of 4621, 4591, and 5167, respectively, for the three degrees considered in [5]. The weight parameter w is a positive integer that defines the number of non-0 coefficients of certain polynomials. A valid parameter set has to satisfy $2p \geq 3w$ and $q \geq 16w + 1$. Reusing the notation of [5], we abbreviate the ring $\mathbb{Z}[x]/P$, the ring $(\mathbb{Z}/3)[x]/P$, and the field $(\mathbb{Z}/q)[x]/P$ as $\mathcal{R}$, $\mathcal{R}/3$, and $\mathcal{R}/q$, respectively. An element of the ring $\mathcal{R}$ is *small* if all its coefficients are in $\{-1, 0, 1\}$. Short is defined as the set of small weight-w elements of $\mathcal{R}$, while Rounded is the set of polynomials $r(x) \in \mathcal{R}$ where each coefficient r_i lies is the range $[-(q-1)/2, (q-1)/2]$ and is rounded to the nearest multiple of 3.

Key Generation. To generate a key pair for Streamlined NTRU Prime, the following operations have to be performed (note that, for brevity, we skip some operations such as the encoding of polynomials to strings).

1. Generate a uniform random *small* polynomial $g(x) \in \mathcal{R}$. Repeat this step until $g(x)$ is invertible in $\mathcal{R}/3$.
2. Compute $v(x) = 1/g(x)$ in $\mathcal{R}/3$.
3. Generate a uniform random polynomial $f(x) \in$ Short.
4. Compute $h(x) = g(x)/(3f(x))$ in $\mathcal{R}/q$.
5. Generate a uniform random polynomial $\rho(x) \in$ Short.
6. Output $h(x)$ as *public key* and $(f(x), v(x), h(x), \rho(x))$ as *private key*.

Encapsulation. The encapsulation operation gets a public key as input and produces a ciphertext and session key as output (again, for brevity, we skip all encoding and decoding operations).

1. Generate a uniform random polynomial $r(x) \in$ Short.
2. Compute $c(x) = h(x)r(x) \in$ Rounded.
3. Compute $C = (c(x), \text{HASH}(r(x), h(x)))$.
4. Output C as *ciphertext* and $\text{HASH}(1, r(x), C)$ as *session key*.

Decapsulation. The decapsulation gets a key pair and a ciphertext as input and produces a session key as output (encodings and decodings are skipped).

1. Compute $e(x) = 3f(x)c(x) \in \mathcal{R}/q$ and represent each coefficient e_i of $e(x)$ as an integer between $-(q-1)/2$ and $(q-1)/2$.
2. Compute $e(x) = e(x) \bmod 3 \in \mathcal{R}/3$ (i.e. reduce each e_i modulo 3).
3. Compute $r'(x) = e(x)v(x) \in \mathcal{R}/3$.
4. Lift $r'(x) \in \mathcal{R}/3$ to a small polynomial $r'(x) \in \mathcal{R}$.

5. If the weight of $r'(x)$ is not w then set $r'(x) = (1, 1, \ldots, 1, 0, 0, \ldots, 0)$.
6. Compute $c'(x) = h(x)r'(x) \in$ Rounded.
7. Compute $C' = (c'(x), \text{HASH}(r'(x), h(x)))$.
8. If C' equals C then output $\text{HASH}(1, r'(x), C)$ else output $\text{HASH}(0, \rho(x), C)$ as *session key*.

3   Polynomial Multiplication

Since Streamlined NTRU Prime is closely related to the classical NTRU scheme (i.e. NTRUEncrypt), it is not surprising that they share many implementation aspects; in particular, they have in common that their performance depends to a large extent on the polynomial arithmetic. However, the underlying algebraic structures are (slightly) different: NTRUEncrypt is based on the residue class ring $\mathcal{R} = (\mathbb{Z}/q)[x]/(x^N - 1)$ where q is a power of two, while NTRU Prime uses the extension field $(\mathbb{Z}/q)[x]/(x^p - x - 1)$ where q is a prime, e.g. $q = 4621$. The reduction modulo q is basically free in the former case, but relatively expensive for NTRU Prime, especially when constant execution time is required so as to foil timing attacks. Furthermore, the irreducible polynomial P of NTRU Prime contains an additional non-0 coefficient, which makes the reduction operation more costly. Finally, most performance-optimized implementations of classical NTRU for constrained IoT devices use a parameter set with so-called product-form polynomials [14] to minimize the execution time of the ring multiplication (see e.g. [2,7]). However, product-form parameter sets were not included in the NTRU Prime specification. For all these reasons, one can expect the arithmetic part of NTRU Prime, when implemented for an 8-bit AVR microcontroller, to be significantly slower than that of the classical NTRU cryptosystem.

The encapsulation operation of NTRU Prime includes a single polynomial multiplication where one operand is an element of $\mathcal{R}/q$ (i.e. its coefficients are bounded by q) and the other operand is an element of Short, which means it is a ternary polynomial with exactly w non-0 coefficients. Hence, the polynomial multiplication carried out in NTRU Prime encapsulation is very similar to the ring multiplication in the encryption operation of classical NTRU [12]. On the other hand, the decapsulation of NTRU Prime involves three polynomial multiplications, which is one more than the number of multiplications that have to be executed in classical NTRU decryption. The first polynomial multiplication in the decapsulation gets an element of Rounded (i.e. an element of $\mathcal{R}/q$) and an element of Short as input. In contrast, the second polynomial multiplication (Step 3 of the decapsulation as presented in the previous section) is performed on two elements of $\mathcal{R}/3$, i.e. two ternary polynomials. The third multiplication of the decapsulation is exactly the same as the polynomial multiplication in the encapsulation, which means the operands are elements of $\mathcal{R}/q$ and Short.

3.1   Karatsuba-Based Polynomial Multiplication

Most algorithms for high-speed polynomial multiplication have their origins in well-known algorithms for multiple-precision multiplication of integers, such as needed for common public-key cryptosystems like RSA and ECC [8,11]. From a high-level perspective, polynomial multiplication algorithms can be split into two main categories, namely basic techniques that require n^2 coefficient multiplications to obtain the product of two polynomials consisting of n coefficients each, and advanced techniques with sub-quadratic complexity, e.g. Karatsuba's algorithm [17]. Examples of the former category are the *operand-scanning* and *product-scanning* method, which produce the coefficient-products in a row-wise or column-wise fashion and differ with respect of the number of load and store instructions they need to execute [11]. The so-called *hybrid technique* proposed in [10] is beneficial on microcontrollers with a large number of general-purpose registers (e.g. AVR ATmega) and combines the individual strengths of operand scanning and product scanning. It has a "nested loop" structure and computes $d \geq 2$ coefficient-products in each iteration of the inner loop, which reduces the number of load instructions by a factor of d compared to product scanning.

Multiplication algorithms with sub-quadratic complexity have been known since the 1960s when Karatsuba published his seminal paper [17]. Karatsuba's method reduces a multiplication of two operands consisting of n coefficients to three multiplications of $(n/2)$-coefficient polynomials and a few additions. The half-size multiplications, in turn, can be implemented using any multiplication technique, including conventional operand and product scanning, as well as the hybrid method. Alternatively, it is possible to apply the Karatsuba algorithm recursively until the operands consist of just a single coefficient, in which case the asymptotic complexity becomes $\Theta(n^{\log_2(3)})$. Yet another option is the so-called Arbitrary Degree Karatsuba (ADK) variant described and analyzed in detail in [24]. Also a few multiplication algorithms with even better asymptotic complexity have been studied; an example is the Toom-Cook multiplication we mentioned in Sect. 1 in the context of Kannwischer et al.'s work on polynomial multiplication for ARM Cortex-M4 processors [15]. An efficient implementation of a 4-way Toom-Cook algorithm for multiplication of degree-256 polynomials on a Cortex-M4 device is described in [18].

Finding the optimal multiplication strategy for the two forms of polynomial multiplication mentioned at the beginning of this section (i.e. $\mathcal{R}/q \times$ Short and $\mathcal{R}/3 \times \mathcal{R}/3$) is a difficult task. Intuitively, one may assume that a combination of multiplication techniques with sub-quadratic and quadratic complexity will yield peak performance. Yet, the concrete implementation of such a combined strategy raises a few non-trivial questions. Asymptotic complexity bounds are not always meaningful in the real world, especially when the involved operands are relatively short. Therefore, it is necessary to find out which sub-quadratic algorithms are most efficient ones for the multiplications in NTRU Prime (this depends besides the lengths of the polynomials also on certain characteristics of the target architecture). For constrained platforms like 8-bit AVR, it makes sense to base this decision not solely on speed but also on RAM requirements and code size. A second important question is how many recursions of Karatsuba's and/or Toom-Cook's algorithm should be performed before switching to a multiplication method with quadratic complexity, i.e. what operand length is the "crossover" point? Finally, a third question is which of the basic algorithms should be used: operand scanning, product scanning, or the hybrid method? In order to answer all these questions, we conducted a multitude of experiments with different sub-quadratic algorithms[1], different numbers of recursions of the sub-quadratic algorithms (i.e. different "crossover" points), and different basic multiplication techniques with quadratic complexity.

The results of these experiments show that for a polynomial multiplication of the form $\mathcal{R}/q \times$ Short (carried out in Step 2 of encapsulation as well as Step 1 and 6 of decapsulation), five recursions of Karatsuba's algorithm provide the best performance across all parameter sets specified in [5]. Below the five levels of Karatsuba, the normal product-scanning technique is used since, due to the bitlength of the coefficient-products and the limited register space, the hybrid multiplication is not efficient. Also alternative Karatsuba variants, such as the ADK algorithm from [24], did not yield superior performance. The situation is different for the polynomial multiplication of the form $\mathcal{R}/3 \times \mathcal{R}/3$, which has to be carried out in Step 3 of the decapsulation. For this multiplication, a combination of the (recursive) Karatsuba algorithm and hybrid method achieves the best results. To be precise, we reached peak performance with four recursions of Karatsuba and using the hybrid method with $d = 4$ at the "lower level" (this is possible because the coefficient-products are relatively small and, thus, more free registers are available). We implemented Karatsuba's algorithm in C and the hybrid multiplication method in both C and AVR assembler, whereby the latter is very similar to the implementations described in [8,10].

A multiplication of two polynomials of degree $p - 1$ through a combination of Karatsuba's algorithm and the hybrid method (or any other multiplication technique) yields a product-polynomial $r(x)$ of degree $2p - 2$, which has to be reduced modulo the irreducible polynomial $P = x^p - x - 1$ to get a polynomial of degree $p - 1$. Thanks to the relation $x^p \equiv x + 1 \bmod P$, this reduction can be performed by simply substituting each term $r_i x^i$ with $i \geq p$ in $r(x)$ by the sum $r_i x^{i-p+1} + r_i x^{i-p}$ [5]. These substitutions are nothing else than additions of the $p - 1$ higher coefficients r_i to r_{i-p+1} and r_{i-p}, which reduces the degree of $r(x)$ to (at most) p so that two further coefficient additions suffice to obtain a result of degree $p - 1$. Thus, the cost of the reduction modulo P amounts to $2p$ additions of (unreduced) coefficients. The final step of the multiplication is the reduction of the $p - 1$ remaining coefficients modulo q or modulo 3.

Coefficient-Reduction Modulo q. As explained above, we implemented the multiplication of the form $\mathcal{R}/q \times$ Short using five recursions of Karatsuba as "higher level" algorithm and product scanning at the "lower level." Taking the parameter set `sntrup653` as example, we have $p = 653$, which means the hybrid method is executed with operands of degree $\lceil 653/2^5 \rceil = 21$. Furthermore, since $q = 4621$ and we represent the -1 coefficients of a ternary polynomial (i.e. an element of Short) as $q - 1 = 4620$, a single coefficient-product has a maximum

---

[1] As stated in Sect. 1, we do not consider the Toom-Cook multiplication algorithm due to its high RAM consumption. The AVR device we use for benchmarking, an ATmega1284 microcontroller, has only 16 kB SRAM, which makes a strong case to take memory requirements into account in the algorithm exploration.

Algorithm 1. Table-based constant-time modular reduction

Input: Integer s of a length of (up to) 29 bits, modulus q of a fixed length of 13 bits
Output: $r = s \bmod q$

1: $b \leftarrow (s_{28}, \ldots, s_{24})$ $\triangleright$ extract the five bits $b = (s_{28}, \ldots, s_{24})$ from s
2: $r \leftarrow \mathrm{RT1}[b]$ $\triangleright$ reduce $b2^{24}$ modulo q via look-up table RT1
3: $b \leftarrow (s_{23}, \ldots, s_{16})$ $\triangleright$ extract the eight bits $b = (s_{23}, \ldots, s_{16})$ from s
4: $r \leftarrow r + \mathrm{RT2}[b]$ $\triangleright$ reduce $b2^{16}$ modulo q via look-up table RT2
5: $r \leftarrow r + s \,\&\, \mathrm{0xffff}$ $\triangleright$ add 16 least-significant bits of s to r
6: $b \leftarrow (r_{16}, \ldots, r_{12})$ $\triangleright$ extract the five bits $b = (r_{16}, \ldots, r_{12})$ from r
7: $r \leftarrow (r \,\&\, \mathrm{0xfff}) + \mathrm{RT3}[b]$ $\triangleright$ reduce $b2^{12}$ modulo q via look-up table RT3
8: $r \leftarrow r - q \cdot (r \geqslant q)$ $\triangleright$ conditionally subtract q from r
9: **return** r

---

length of 24 bits. The column sum to which the 24-bit coefficient-products are accumulated can become up to 29 bits long, i.e. we need an efficient algorithm for reducing a 29-bit integer modulo a 13-bit integer.

Algorithm 1 shows a generic technique for reducing a 29-bit integer modulo an arbitrary 13-bit integer q using three look-up tables, which we call reduction tables. It is assumed that the input s (representing a column sum of the hybrid method described above) is held in four 8-bit registers, i.e. the individual bytes of s can be conveniently accessed. At first, the five most-significant bits of s are assigned to b and then $b2^{24} \bmod q$ is computed with the help of reduction table RT1, which contains 32 entries. Next, the second-most significant byte of s is processed in a similar way, whereby the 256-entry table RT2 is used to obtain its residue modulo q. The two residues are added up and form the intermediate result r. Then, we extract the 16 least-significant bits from s and add them to r, which has now a length of at most 17 bits. Similar as before, we assign the five most-significant bits of r to b, reduce it using RT3, and add the residue to the 12 least-significant bits of r. Because r is now always less than $2q$, a single subtraction of q is sufficient to have a fully reduced result. However, to ensure constant execution time, we first compare r with the modulus q, which returns 1 if $r \geq q$ and 0 otherwise. This comparison-result is multiplied by q and the product (either q or 0) is then subtracted from r. Note that Algorithm 1 works for any 13-bit modulus q, though each q requires its own set of tables.

Coefficient-Reduction Modulo 3. The reduction modulo 3 can exploit the fact that some multiples of 3 (e.g. 15, 255) have the form $2^k \pm 1$, which allows for a particularly efficient implementation. Thus, the reduction modulo 3 is less costly (in terms of look-up tables) than the modulo-q case, but requires special attention regarding timing attacks. Namely, as described in Sect. 2, one of the operands of the $\mathcal{R}/3 \times \mathcal{R}/3$ multiplication in the decapsulation is $v(x)$, which is a part of the private key. Therefore, an implementer has to take care that this multiplication, including the reduction of all coefficient-products modulo 3, has constant execution time. When using C or C++, a modulo-3 reduction can be implemented by an operation of the form y = x % 3, whereby in our case x is a 16-bit integer. However, in the course of our work we found out that one can

Table 1. Execution time (in cycles) of the __udivmodhi4 function for all 2^{16} possible 16-bit unsigned integers. Columns labeled with "Frequ" and "%" give the frequency (in absolute numbers) and probability (in per cent) of the occurrence of the cycle count.

Cycles	Frequ.	%	Cycles	Frequ.	%	Cycles	Frequ.	%
193	3	0.005	198	7956	12.140	203	3825	5.836
194	45	0.069	199	12243	18.681	204	1323	2.019
195	312	0.476	200	14121	21.547	205	312	0.476
196	1323	2.019	201	12244	18.683	206	45	0.069
197	3825	5.836	202	7956	12.140	207	3	0.005

not take it for granted that a C compiler generates constant-time code for this operation. Concretely, we discovered that certain versions of avr-gcc generate code with operand-dependent execution time for some AVR models, which can leak information about the secret polynomial $v(x)$.

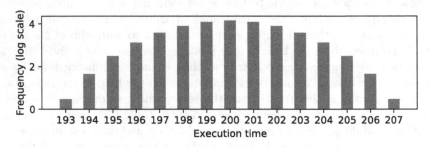

Fig. 1. Frequency of the occurrence (in absolute numbers) of a certain execution time (in cycles) of the __udivmodhi4 function for all 2^{16} possible 16-bit unsigned integers.

For example, we determined the execution time of the modulo-3 reduction compiled with avr-gcc 4.8.2 for an ATtiny45 microcontroller with help of the cycle-accurate simulator Avrora [26]. For target devices that have no hardware multiplier, e.g. ATtiny microcontrollers, avr-gcc uses the __udivmodhi4 function from the runtime library libgcc to perform the reduction modulo 3. The same function was also used for devices with hardware multiplier, including the ATmega1284 (our benchmarking device, see Sect. 4), until version 4.7.0 of the avr-gcc compiler; thereafter it was replaced with __umulhisi3 [9]. While the latter function has a constant execution time (i.e. 54 cycles) for all 2^{16} possible inputs, the time required by the former depends on the value of the operand to be reduced. Concretely, the execution time of __udivmodhi4 varies between 193 clock cycles (for input values 0, 1, and 2) and 207 cycles (for 49149, 49150, and 49151). Thus, the time difference between the longest and shortest execution is 14 cycles. Further details are provided in Table 1 and Fig. 1.

In order to ensure that the resistance against timing attacks does not depend on the compiler, we implemented the modulo-3 reduction in assembly language following the approach described in [7].

3.2 Product-Form Polynomial Multiplication

A well-known way to improve the execution time of the original NTRU scheme (i.e. NTRUEncrypt) is to use ternary polynomials in product form, which was originally proposed some 20 years ago [13,14]. In essence, a ternary polynomial $f(x)$ in product form can be expressed as $f(x) = f_1(x) \star f_2(x) + f_3(x)$, where $f_1(x)$, $f_2(x)$, $f_3(x)$ are three extremely sparsely populated ternary polynomials and $\star$ symbolizes a "convolution," i.e. a polynomial multiplication modulo the irreducible polynomial $P = x^N - 1$ of NTRUEncrypt [12]. For example, when using parameters for 128-bit security (based on a ring of degree $N = 443$), the given number of $+1$ and -1 coefficients of $f_1(x)$, $f_2(x)$, and $f_3(x)$ is 9, 8, and 5, respectively, which means that a convolution requires just a bit over 15,000 coefficient additions or subtractions. Despite the extremely low weight of these "sub-polynomials," it is possible to maintain security against all known attacks since the terms of $f_1(x)$ and $f_2(x)$ cross-multiply and the polynomial $f(x)$ has a weight of about $2N/3$. However, product-form parameters are rarely used in practice because the necessary index-based sparse polynomial multiplication is difficult to implement in a timing-attack-resistant fashion. Only recently it was shown that on AVR (and other microcontrollers without cache), product-form convolution can be fast *and* have constant execution time [7].

The designers of NTRU Prime decided not to support product-form parameters, claiming that product-form arithmetic "saves time for non-constant-time sparse-polynomial-multiplication algorithms, but loses time for constant-time algorithms" [4, Sect. T.3]. However, as recently demonstrated in [7], this claim is not necessarily true for microcontrollers without data cache. The advantages and disadvantages of the product form for NTRU Prime were also discussed on the official mailing list of NIST's PQC standardization project[2]. In light of the interest in product-form polynomials, we decided to assess how much they can accelerate NTRU Prime. Concretely, we evaluated the performance gain for the decapsulation when the ternary polynomial $f(x) \in$ Short, which is a part of the private key, is represented in product form. However, our work should not be seen as a recommendation to use the product form in practice.

A product-form parameter set for the classical NTRU cryptosystem includes the parameters d_1, d_2, d_3 specifying the number of $+1$ coefficients of the sub-polynomials $f_1(x)$, $f_2(x)$, $f_3(x)$, whereby the number of $+1$ coefficients equals the number of -1 coefficients (i.e. polynomial $f_i(x)$ has weight $w_i = 2d_i$). On the other hand, a set of parameters for NTRU Prime comes with just a single weight parameter w that specifies the number of non-0 coefficients of elements of Short. Hence, in order to use the product form for NTRU Prime, we have to

---

[2] https://groups.google.com/a/list.nist.gov/d/msg/pqc-forum/fh2xGahC4LE/ NycdEhTHAgAJ.

determine the weights w_1, w_2, w_3 of the sub-polynomials a ternary polynomial $f(x) \in$ Short is composed of. The parameter generation approach we follow in this paper is derived from [23, Sect. 3.4.2] and assumes an equal split between $+1$ and -1 coefficients, though this requirement was dropped in NTRU Prime to allow for more choices of polynomials [4, Sect. 3.6]. Hoffstein and Silverman observed in one of the first papers about product-form polynomials that, when $f_1(x)$ and $f_2(x)$ are binary polynomials with d_1 and d_2 ones, respectively, the number of ones in the product $f_1(x)f_2(x)$ is essentially d_1d_2 [13]. Based on this observation, the weight of $f(x) = f_1(x) \star f_2(x) + f_3(x)$ can be estimated to be roughly $4d_1d_2 + 2d_3$ (see [23] for details). However, the weight of $f(x)$ depends not only on d_1, d_2, and d_3, but also on the irreducible polynomial used in the convolution. Since the irreducible polynomial P of NTRU Prime has the form $x^p - x - 1$, the reduction of the product $f_1(x)f_2(x)$ modulo P introduces more non-0 coefficients than a reduction modulo $x^p - 1$, the irreducible polynomial of NTRU. For example, any term of the form $a_n x^n$ with $n \geq p$ gets reduced to $a_n x^{n-p+1} + a_n x^{n-p}$ in NTRU Prime, but to just $a_n x^{n-p}$ in classical NTRU.

Our approach to calculate (d_1, d_2, d_3) for the NTRU Prime parameter sets (which require $f(x)$ to have a weight of $w = 288$, 286, and 322, respectively) is based on [23, Sect. 3.4.2], but takes the difference in the irreducible polynomial into account. For example, for the parameter set sntrup653 (i.e. $w = 288$) we obtained $(d_1, d_2, d_3) = (9, 8, 4)$, i.e. the three sub-polynomials $f_1(x)$, $f_2(x)$, and $f_3(x)$ should have a weight of 18, 16, and 8, respectively. We conducted a large number of experiments for all three parameter sets of NTRU Prime to ensure that our approach to generate product-form polynomials is correct. In the case of sntrup653, the weight of $f(x)$ was always between 280 and 300.

While the security implications of using the product form have been studied in detail for classical NTRU [14], we are not aware of a similar security analysis for NTRU Prime. In the course of our work we discovered that the polynomial $f(x) = f_1(x) \star f_2(x) + f_3(x)$ has a linear distribution of non-0 terms (instead of a uniform distribution like in classical NTRU) if the non-0 coefficients of the sparse polynomials $f_1(x)$, $f_2(x)$, $f_3(x)$ are uniformly distributed. However, this effect can be compensated by choosing the distribution of the non-0 coefficients of $f_3(x)$ accordingly. We leave a full-fledged security analysis of product-form polynomials in NTRU Prime as part of our future work.

We implemented a product-form variant of NTRU Prime by re-using parts of the NTRU software for 8-bit AVR microcontrollers from [7], in particular the ring arithmetic. This software contains a ring multiplication function where one operand is an element of $\mathcal{R}/q$ (i.e. a polynomial with coefficients in the range $[0, q - 1])$ and the second operand is a ternary polynomial in product form. We adapted this function to suit the requirements of NTRU Prime, which uses the field $\mathbb{Z}[x]/P$ with $P = x^p - x - 1$ as underlying algebraic structure. In concrete terms, this means we modified the reduction modulo the irreducible polynomial and the reduction of coefficient-sums modulo the prime q. The latter reduction can be performed in a similar way as described in Subsect. 3.1, except that the maximum length of a coefficient sum before modulo-q reduction is

Table 2. Execution time (in clock cycles) and code size (in bytes) of the main arithmetic operations and full encapsulation and decapsulation of NTRU Prime using the parameter set sntrup653 on an ATmega1284 microcontroller. Operations annotated with "PF" use the product-form technique described in Subsect. 3.2.

Operation	Time	Size
$\mathcal{R}/q \times$ Short multiplication	5,604,929	2,230
$\mathcal{R}/q \times$ Short multiplication (PF)	740,980	2,812
$\mathcal{R}/3 \times \mathcal{R}/3$ multiplication	1,277,675	1,510
Full encapsulation	8,160,665	8,694
Full decapsulation	15,602,748	11,478
Full decapsulation (PF)	10,754,219	14,370

only 17 bits (for all three parameter sets of Streamlined NTRU Prime), i.e. Algorithm 1 can be slightly optimized. We refer to [7] for an in-depth description of the original product-form multiplication for 8-bit AVR. As explained in Sect. 2, the decapsulation of NTRU Prime includes as first step a multiplication of a polynomial that is an element of $\mathcal{R}/q$ by a ternary polynomial of fixed weight, namely the polynomial $f(x) \in$ Short. This multiplication can be accelerated by using the product-form technique described above when $f(x)$ is generated accordingly.

4   Results and Comparison

The 8-bit AVR device we used to test and benchmark our NTRU Prime implementation is an ATmega1284 microcontroller, which features 16 kB SRAM and 128 kB flash memory for storing program code. Our software consists of a mix of C and assembly language; we implement the main arithmetic operations in assembly to achieve fast and operand-independent execution time, whereas all functions that are neither performance-critical nor security-critical are written in C to maximize portability. We use the optimized Assembler implementation of the SHA-512 hash function introduced in [6] to minimize the execution time of certain auxiliary functions that are performance-critical. When executed on our target device, the compression function of SHA-512 takes slightly less than 60 k clock cycles, which corresponds to a compression rate of about 467 cycles per byte. Our implementation of (Streamlined) NTRU Prime can be compiled with Atmel Studio v7.0 under the -O2 optimization option, which produces an executable that, according to our experiments, does not leak secret information through execution time and can, therefore, withstand timing attacks.

Table 2 summarizes the execution time and code size of the core arithmetic operations (i.e. polynomial multiplications) as well as a full encapsulation and decapsulation of our NTRU Prime software. The table shows the results of two implementations of the polynomial multiplication of the form $\mathcal{R}/q \times$ Short; the first uses a combination of Karatsuba's algorithm and product scanning at the

Table 3. Comparison of our NTRU Prime implementation with other post-quantum key-establishment algorithms and ECC (all of which target 128 bits of security).

Implementation	Algorithm	Platform	Encaps.	Decaps.
This work	NTRU Prime	ATmega1284	8,160,665	15,602,748
Cheng et al. [7]	NTRU (PF)	ATmega1281	847,973	1,051,871
Düll et al. [8]	ECC-255	ATmega2560	13,900,397	13,900,397
Kannwischer et al. [16]	NTRU Prime	Cortex M4	54,942,173	166, 481, 625
Kannwischer et al. [16]	Frodo	Cortex M4	45,883,334	45,366,065
Kannwischer et al. [16]	NewHope	Cortex M4	1,903,231	1,927,505
Kannwischer et al. [16]	Kyber	Cortex M4	652,769	621,245
Kannwischer et al. [16]	NTRU	Cortex M4	645,329	542,439

lower level (see Subsect. 3.1), whereas the second is based on the product-form approach (see Subsect. 3.2). The results in Table 2 show that the product-form multiplication is significantly faster; it outperforms the Karatsuba-based multiplication by a factor of 7.56. On the other hand, these two implementations differ only marginally in terms of binary code size. The implementation of the $\mathcal{R}/3 \times \mathcal{R}/3$ polynomial multiplication combines Karatsuba's method with the hybrid technique and is much faster than the polynomial multiplication of the form $\mathcal{R}/q \times$ Short. This reduced running time is due to the smaller coefficients (enabling faster coefficient multiplication), smaller intermediate results (requiring fewer registers) and faster reduction (modulo 3 vs. modulo q). Also given in Table 2 are the execution times of encapsulation and decapsulation, which are primarily dominated by the polynomial arithmetic. The encapsulation includes just a single multiplication, namely a multiplication of an element of $\mathcal{R}/q$ by an element of Short (i.e. $\mathcal{R}/q \times$ Short) that accounts for roughly two thirds of the overall execution time. On the other hand, the decapsulation operation has to perform three polynomial multiplications (two of the form $\mathcal{R}/q \times$ Short and one of the form $\mathcal{R}/3 \times \mathcal{R}/3$); together they contribute 80% to the overall execution time. The first $\mathcal{R}/q \times$ Short multiplication, i.e. the multiplication of $c(x)$ by the ternary polynomial $f(x) \in$ Short, can be accelerated through the product-form technique, which reduces the execution time from 15.6 to 10.8 million cycles. In other words, product-form multiplication makes a decapsulation 31% faster.

Our software is, to the best of our knowledge, the first optimized implementation of Streamlined NTRU Prime for constrained devices. The only previous implementation of NTRU Prime for microcontrollers published in the literature is the implementation from pqm4 [16], which is essentially the reference C code without any assembler optimizations. Compared with the pqm4 timings on an ARM Cortex-M4, our implementation is 6.7 times faster for encapsulation and 10.7 times faster for decapsulation (see Table 3). However, it needs to be taken into account that a 32-bit ARM Cortex-M4 is significantly more powerful than an 8-bit AVR microcontroller. The AVR assembler implementation of classical

NTRU (i.e. NTRUEncrypt with `ees443ep1` parameters) introduced in [7] uses a highly efficient product-form convolution and outperforms our NTRU Prime software by roughly an order of magnitude. On the other hand, when compared with ECC, our NTRU Prime encapsulation is much faster than a variable-base scalar multiplication on Curve25519, while the decapsulation is a bit slower. Due to the limited number of state-of-the-art implementations of other NIST PQC candidates for 8-bit AVR, we give in Table 3 also a few recent results from the `pqm4` library for 32-bit ARM Cortex-M4 microcontrollers.

5   Conclusions

We presented the first highly-optimized implementation of NTRU Prime for an 8-bit microcontroller that is capable to resist timing attacks. When executed on an ATmega1284 device, the encapsulation takes about 8.2 million cycles, while the decapsulation has an execution time of 15.6 million cycles (both results are based on the parameter set `sntrup653`). For comparison, the reference C code from the designers requires 54.9 and 166.5 million cycles for encapsulation and decapsulation, respectively, on a much more powerful 32-bit Cortex-M4 microcontroller. To achieve these results, we implemented all expensive operations in AVR assembly language, most notably the polynomial arithmetic, whereby we strived for a balance between execution time and code size. We also discussed how the concept of product-form polynomials to speed up classical NTRU can be applied to NTRU Prime and demonstrated that product-form multiplication would make the decapsulation 30% faster. However, since a thorough analysis of the security implications of the product form in NTRU Prime is lacking, we do (currently) not recommend to use product-form polynomials in a real-world application. Furthermore, we showed that one cannot count on a C compiler to generate constant-time code for the modulo-3 reduction, which generally raises concerns about the security (i.e. resistance against timing attacks) of C implementations of NTRU Prime. In summary, our results show that NTRU Prime can be well optimized to run efficiently on small microcontrollers, which makes it an interesting candidate for securing the post-quantum IoT.

Acknowledgements. This work was supported by the European Union's Horizon 2020 research and innovation program under grant agreement No. 779391 (FutureTPM). The authors thank John Schanck for answering questions on the generation of product-form parameters for NTRU Prime. The research described in this paper was conducted before Daniel Dinu joined Intel and may not reflect the views of his current or previous employers.

References

1. Alkim, E., Ducas, L., Pöppelmann, T., Schwabe, P.: Post-quantum key exchange - a new hope. In: Holz, T., Savage, S. (eds.) Proceedings of the 25th USENIX Security Symposium (USS 2016), pp. 327–343. USENIX Association (2016)

2. Bailey, D.V., Coffin, D., Elbirt, A., Silverman, J.H., Woodbury, A.D.: NTRU in constrained devices. In: Koç, Ç.K., Naccache, D., Paar, C. (eds.) CHES 2001. LNCS, vol. 2162, pp. 262–272. Springer, Heidelberg (2001). https://doi.org/10.1007/3-540-44709-1_22

3. Bernstein, D.J., Buchmann, J., Dahmen, E. (eds.): Post-Quantum Cryptography. Springer, Heidelberg (2009). https://doi.org/10.1007/978-3-540-88702-7

4. Bernstein, D.J., Chuengsatiansup, C., Lange, T., van Vredendaal, C.: NTRU prime: reducing attack surface at low cost. In: Adams, C., Camenisch, J. (eds.) SAC 2017. LNCS, vol. 10719, pp. 235–260. Springer, Cham (2018). https://doi.org/10.1007/978-3-319-72565-9_12

5. Bernstein, D.J., Chuengsatiansup, C., Lange, T., van Vredendaal, C.: NTRU Prime: Round 2 specification (2019). http://csrc.nist.gov/projects/post-quantum-cryptography/round-2-submissions

6. Cheng, H., Dinu, D., Großschädl, J.: Efficient implementation of the SHA-512 hash function for 8-Bit AVR microcontrollers. In: Lanet, J.-L., Toma, C. (eds.) SECITC 2018. LNCS, vol. 11359, pp. 273–287. Springer, Cham (2019). https://doi.org/10.1007/978-3-030-12942-2_21

7. Cheng, H., Großschädl, J., Rønne, P.B., Ryan, P.Y.: A lightweight implementation of NTRUEncrypt for 8-bit AVR microcontrollers. In: Proceedings of the 2nd NIST PQC Standardization Conference (2019). http://csrc.nist.gov/Events/2019/second-pqc-standardization-conference

8. Düll, M., et al.: High-speed Curve25519 on 8-bit, 16-bit and 32-bit microcontrollers. Des. Codes Crypt. **77**(2–3), 493–514 (2015)

9. GCC Team: AVR-GCC Wiki (2017). http://gcc.gnu.org/wiki/avr-gcc#Exceptions_to_the_Calling_Convention

10. Gura, N., Patel, A., Wander, A., Eberle, H., Shantz, S.C.: Comparing elliptic curve cryptography and RSA on 8-bit CPUs. In: Joye, M., Quisquater, J.-J. (eds.) CHES 2004. LNCS, vol. 3156, pp. 119–132. Springer, Heidelberg (2004). https://doi.org/10.1007/978-3-540-28632-5_9

11. Hankerson, D.R., Menezes, A.J., Vanstone, S.A.: Guide to Elliptic Curve Cryptography. Springer, New York (2004). https://doi.org/10.1007/b97644

12. Hoffstein, J., Pipher, J., Silverman, J.H.: NTRU: a ring-based public key cryptosystem. In: Buhler, J.P. (ed.) ANTS 1998. LNCS, vol. 1423, pp. 267–288. Springer, Heidelberg (1998). https://doi.org/10.1007/BFb0054868

13. Hoffstein, J., Silverman, J.H.: Optimizations for NTRU. In: Alster, K., Urbanowicz, J., Williams, H.C. (eds.) Public-Key Cryptography and Computational Number Theory, De Gruyter Proceedings in Mathematics, pp. 77–88. Walter de Gruyter (2001)

14. Hoffstein, J., Silverman, J.H.: Random small Hamming weight products with applications to cryptography. Discret. Appl. Math. **130**(1), 37–49 (2003)

15. Kannwischer, M.J., Rijneveld, J., Schwabe, P.: Faster multiplication in $\mathbb{Z}_{2^m}[x]$ on Cortex-M4 to speed up NIST PQC candidates. In: Deng, R.H., Gauthier-Umaña, V., Ochoa, M., Yung, M. (eds.) ACNS 2019. LNCS, vol. 11464, pp. 281–301. Springer, Cham (2019). https://doi.org/10.1007/978-3-030-21568-2_14

16. Kannwischer, M.J., Rijneveld, J., Schwabe, P., Stoffelen, K.: pqm4: testing and benchmarking NIST PQC on ARM Cortex-M4. Cryptology ePrint Archive, Report 2019/844 (2019). http://eprint.iacr.org

17. Karatsuba, A.A., Ofman, Y.P.: Multiplication of multidigit numbers on automata. In: Soviet Physics - Doklady, vol. 7, no. 7, pp. 595–596 (1963)

18. Karmakar, A., Bermudo Mera, J.M., Roy, S.S., Verbauwhede, I.: Saber on ARM: CCA-secure module lattice-based key encapsulation on ARM. IACR Trans. Cryptogr. Hardw. Embed. Syst. **2018**(3), 243–266 (2018)
19. Kaye, P.R., Laflamme, R., Mosca, M.: An Introduction to Quantum Computing. Oxford University Press, Oxford (2007)
20. Lyubashevsky, V., Peikert, C., Regev, O.: On ideal lattices and learning with errors over rings. Commun. ACM **60**(6), 43:1–43:35 (2013)
21. Mariantoni, M.: Building a superconducting quantum computer. Invited presentation given at the 6th International Conference on Post-Quantum Cryptography (PQCrypto 2014), Waterloo, ON, Canada, October 2014. http://www.youtube.com/watch?v=wWHAs-HA1c
22. National Institute of Standards and Technology (NIST): NIST reveals 26 algorithms advancing to the post-quantum crypto 'semifinals'. Press release (2019). http://www.nist.gov/news-events/news/2019/01/nist-reveals-26-algorithms-advancing-post-quantum-crypto-semifinals
23. Schanck, J.M.: Practical Lattice Cryptosystems: NTRUEncrypt and NTRUMLS. M.Sc. thesis, University of Waterloo, Waterloo, ON, Canada (2015)
24. Scott, M.: Missing a trick: Karatsuba variations. Cryptogr. Commun. **10**(1), 5–15 (2018)
25. Shor, P.W.: Algorithms for quantum computation: discrete logarithms and factoring. In: Proceedings of the 35th Annual Symposium on Foundations of Computer Science (FOCS 1994), pp. 124–134. IEEE Computer Society Press (1994)
26. Titzer, B.L., Lee, D.K., Palsberg, J.: Avrora: scalable sensor network simulation with precise timing. In: Proceedings of the 4th International Symposium on Information Processing in Sensor Networks (IPSN 2005), pp. 477–482. IEEE (2005)
27. Toom, A.L.: The complexity of a scheme of functional elements realizing the multiplication of integers. Soviet Math. - Doklady **4**(3), 714–716 (1963)

Threats

Fault Injection Characterization on Modern CPUs
From the ISA to the Micro-Architecture

Thomas Trouchkine[1], Guillaume Bouffard[1,2](✉) ⓘ, and Jessy Clédière[3]

[1] National Cybersecurity Agency of France (ANSSI),
51, boulevard de La Tour-Maubourg, 75700 Paris 07, SP, France
thomas.trouchkine@ssi.gouv.fr
[2] Information Security Group, École Normale Supérieure, 46 rue d'Ulm,
75230 Paris Cedex 05, France
guillaume.bouffard@ens.fr
[3] CEA, LETI, MINATEC Campus, 38054 Grenoble, France
jessy.clediere@cea.fr

Abstract. Recently, several Fault Attacks (FAs) which target modern Central Processing Units (CPUs) have emerged. These attacks are studied from a practical point of view and, due to the modern CPUs complexity, the underlying fault effect is usually unknown.

In this article, we focus on the characterization of a perturbation (the fault model) on modern CPU. For that, we introduce the first approach to characterize the fault model on modern CPU from the Instruction Set Architecture (ISA) level to the micro-architectural level. This fault model helps at determining which micro-architecture elements are disrupted and how. Our fault model aims at finding original attack paths and design efficient countermeasures. To confront our approach to real modern CPUs, we apply our approach on ARM and x86 architectures CPUs, mainly on the BCM2837 and an Intel Core i3.

1 Introduction

Nowadays, mobile devices are widely used. They are based on high performance System on Chips (SoCs) which embed performance oriented Central Processing Units (CPUs). With all their optimizations, these modern CPUs have shown flaws in their security [8,11].

Since 2015, several Fault Attacks (FAs) on modern CPUs have been presented, some are new and some others already applied on Micro-Controller Units (MCUs) CPUs [12]. These attacks are very practical and, due to the complexity of modern CPUs, the underlying fault effect is usually unknown. The fault effect knowledge is mandatory for building efficient countermeasures and evaluating the impact of an attack. Therefore, we think that fault characterization on modern CPUs is an important work for the future.

Many fault model characterizations have been done on MCUs but only few on modern CPUs. For determining the fault model on such targets and for

© IFIP International Federation for Information Processing 2020
Published by Springer Nature Switzerland AG 2020
M. Laurent and T. Giannetsos (Eds.): WISTP 2019, LNCS 12024, pp. 123–138, 2020.
https://doi.org/10.1007/978-3-030-41702-4_8

making it reproducible, we propose a characterization method and we show its applicability on modern CPUs, based on ARM or x86 cores. The proposed method is inspired by all the works done on MCUs and integrates the different approaches introduced in these different works.

This article is organized as follows. The Sect. 1 presents the background about fault model characterization, our motivations and the modern CPUs specificities. Section 2 introduces a model for CPUs on which we base our method, Sect. 3 describes our method and Sect. 4 presents its application with experimental results. The Sect. 5 concludes and opens on future works.

1.1   Related Works

Practical fault attacks emerged on 2002 with an optical fault attack [23]. Since then, several practical attacks have been applied on cryptographic implementations [20–22] or on secure softwares [4,5,29]. These attacks aim at breaking the implemented algorithm and therefore focus on obtaining a precise fault. Therefore, only few information is given about the characterization process.

The seminal work on the fault model characterization of a CPU was published in 2011 and focus on the clock glitch effects on an ATMega163 MCU [3]. During the next years, many works have been done on the fault model characterization of MCUs CPU and memory [6,9,10,13–15,19,31]. These works gave useful information about the fault effect on CPUs micro-architecture. This knowledge helped in building countermeasures. However, in 2015 and 2016, several software countermeasures have been shown to be ineffective against certain class of FAs [16,30].

Since 2015, researchers had started to focus on modern CPUs. Their works aim at breaking complex security features like secure boot [26,27], Trusted Execution Environments (TEEs) [24] or kernel security mechanisms [25,28] via fault injection. All these works focus on the mobile devices security area, where modern CPUs run a complex Operating System (OS) like Linux, Android or iOS.

These articles focus on the attacks practicality and do not present any methodology about the fault characterization. In 2019, Proy et al. [18] propose the first fault characterization work on ARM Cortex-A9 based CPU for evaluating their countermeasures against FAs. This work is a first step for fault characterization on modern CPUs. However, the applied method is not clearly described. The authors realize several classical tests to determine how the program execution is modified by the fault. They mainly focus on the Instruction Set Architecture (ISA) layer whereas we propose to determine micro-architectural effects from the ISA fault model.

1.2   Motivations

Regarding the state of the art presented in Sect. 1.1, we think that a fault characterization method on modern CPUs is needed to design efficient countermeasures. Also, these systems are widely used in mobile devices which tend to be integrated almost everywhere in the future and used for critical usage as banking, healthcare, *etc.*, enforcing their need in security and reliability.

1.3 Contribution

We propose a method that would allow us to characterize fault model on a modern CPU. This method is based on an ISA fault model determination but is oriented to also provide information about the micro-architectural fault effect. Therefore, we have two contributions, a modern CPU model and then a fault characterization method built on this model. The introduced modern CPU model is easily adaptable to match with MCU CPUs. This makes our approach adaptable to any type of CPU matching this model, even most MCU CPUs.

2 Modern CPU Modeling

2.1 Modern CPUs Specificities

The previous works on fault characterization on MCUs give information about what we can expect from a characterization and how to do it. Unfortunately, modern CPUs are different from MCU CPUs as shown on Fig. 1. Indeed, they are more complex and embed several cores with optimizations like out-of-order execution, speculative execution, branch prediction, *etc.* They also have multiple levels of caches and a Memory Management Unit (MMU) abstracting their memory.

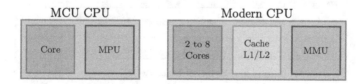

Fig. 1. Micro-controller and modern architectures

Even if their specification is public, another issue with CPUs is that their implementation is not available. Moreover, most of the time, debug tools for these platforms are either only partially open or not available. Therefore, the only way to retrieve information is through the ISA layer. In other words, as we do not have access to the physical layout, we aim at characterizing the fault model at the program level. This is a real issue as for building efficient countermeasures, a software knowledge is not enough, but a micro-architectural fault effect knowledge is also necessary. Therefore, a method that enables to retrieve information on the micro-architectural CPU behavior, based on the ISA fault model, is required.

2.2 Modern CPU Model

This section aims at offering a complete and comprehensive description of modern CPUs. We start from the observation that any CPUs can be modeled with three functional elements.

- A pipeline which fetches, decodes and executes instructions.
- The registers where the manipulated data are stored.
- A memory storing the instructions and some data.

Actually, the memory is external to the CPU. However, there is an internal one, called *cache*, where a part of the external memory is copied. The three functional elements are based on Micro-Architectural Blocks (MABs) as introduced in Fig. 2.

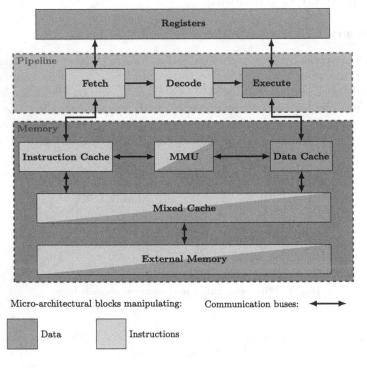

Fig. 2. CPU model

The *pipeline* fetches and decodes the instructions then the *execute stage* realizes the operation. In modern CPUs, these blocks have several optimizations that we do not consider in our model. The memory relies on several cache level and a MMU. Usually, CPUs have a mixed architecture where the data path and the instruction path are separated only at the lowest cache level. The instructions and the data are not differentiated in the high cache level (L2/L3) and the external memory, this is a *Von Neumann* architecture. But, in the lowest level of cache (L1) the instructions and data are separated, this is an *Harvard* architecture. As modern CPUs have both organizations, they are said to have a mixed architecture.

Physically, a core corresponds to the registers, the pipeline, the MMU and the cache. The CPU is composed of one or more cores, but in the end, its behavior corresponds to this model.

This model is usually used for fault characterization on MCUs as all fault models are explained by a MAB perturbation presented in Fig. 2. As most of the MCUs have only one core in their CPU, this model fits them well. The question is to know whether this model is still relevant for a multi-core optimized CPU. We will show that, on average, it is enough for determining more than 80% of the fault effects.

3 Fault Effect Analysis on CPU

During a Fault Injection (FI), one or several CPU MABs are disturbed. As they can all be perturbed during a fault injection, the full fault effect characterization can be a complicated process. However, according to the previous works, in most cases, the fault affects only a single MAB [9,19]. We actually verified this assumption on modern CPUs. Under this simplified paradigm, the fault characterization problem aims at determining which MAB is faulted and how.

To reach our objective, the proposed method consists in realizing a fault during the test program execution and in determining the micro-architectural fault that can explain the observed misbehavior. An underlying assumption is that the fault affects the same MABs in the same way independently of the executed program. This has been experimentally verified; depending on the processor state some new effects can appear, but a set of usual effects remains.

3.1 Determining the Faulted Element

The method general idea is to apply a top-down approach. We start by determining whether the fault affects the registers, the pipeline or the memory. Once we know which element is affected, we determine which of its MABs is faulted.

To achieve this, we rely on the available registers observation and the executed instructions knowledge. The way they are faulted gives information about the faulted element. To discriminate which element is faulted, we repeatedly execute the same instruction as introduced in Listing 1.1 (for ARM) and Listing 1.2 (for x86) on a known state CPU.

Listing 1.1. mov r0, r0 (ARM)

```
mov r0, r0 // Several times
```

Listing 1.2. mov rax, rax (x86)

```
mov rax, rax // Several times
```

These instructions are given as examples but have two important properties. First, they do not fetch any data from the memory, which means that a fault in the memory can only affect the instructions, which simplifies the analysis. Secondly, the instructions do nothing and are therefore semantically equivalent to nop. This is helpful since a modification of the registers state can only be caused by a fault[1] and its effect is not drowned within a complex program.

Disturbing the program execution will give a distribution of faulted values in the registers. The next step consists in determining whether these faulted values come from a fault on the manipulated data or on the instructions. Indeed, the execution of the nth program instruction by the CPU can be modeled such as in (1):

$$s_{n+1} = ins_n(s_n), \tag{1}$$

where s_{n+1} is the CPU state after the execution of the nth instruction ins_n. The CPU state corresponds to all its registers and is usually named the data. An instruction is composed of three elements: an opcode encoding the operation to do, a reference to the destination register and reference(s) to the operand(s). These operands can be registers or immediate values. Depending on the architecture, the encoding of this information may vary but they are always present.

When there is a fault during an instruction execution, we assume here that it either applies on the data or on the instruction. We experimentally verified this assumption. Therefore, the faulted instruction execution can be modeled such as in (2).

$$s_{\widetilde{n+1}} = \widetilde{ins}(\widetilde{s_n}), \tag{2}$$

where $\tilde{x}$ denotes the faulted representation of x. From this representation, we can define the fault model f_{data} on the data as introduced in (3), and the fault model f_{ins} on the instruction as presented in (4).

$$\widetilde{s_n} = f_{data}(s_n), \tag{3}$$

$$\widetilde{ins} = f_{ins}(ins). \tag{4}$$

These fault models can have different descriptions to match with the different underlying fault causes. The data fault types and their corresponding MABs are presented in Table 1.

Based on the Fig. 2 and Table 1, it is possible, from these fault types, to determine which MABs have been faulted. In the case of a register corruption, it is straightforward that the registers are faulted. If there is a memory corruption,

Table 1. Data fault models

Faulted element	Data				
Fault type	Register corruption	Memory corruption		Bad fetch	
Faulted MAB	Registers	Cache	Data bus	Cache	MMU

---

[1] This assumption must be carefully studied as some registers like the Program Counter (PC) are always modified independently of the executed instruction.

the cache storing the data or the data bus is faulted. In the *bad fetch* case, either the cache has loaded the wrong data or the MMU has failed the address translation.

For the instructions, the fault types, presented in Table 2, are corruption and bad fetch.

Table 2. Instruction fault models

Faulted element	Instruction				
Fault type	Corruption			Bad fetch	
Faulted MAB	Pipeline	Cache	Bus	Cache	MMU

If an instruction corruption is observed, the fault affects either one of the pipeline MABs or the cache or the instruction bus. In the case of a bad fetch, either the instruction cache has loaded the wrong instruction or the address translation has failed.

Regarding the test code presented in Listings 1.1 and 1.2, the data fault models *memory corruption* and *bad fetch* cannot appear as there is no data fetched from the memory. Therefore, we can focus on the remaining fault models and this is enough for determining which element among the registers, the pipeline or the memory has been faulted.

4   Experimental Analysis

This section aims at applying the approach introduced in Sect. 2. We present the experimental protocol and the corresponding results on two targets, a BCM2837 from a Raspberry Pi 3 model B board and an Intel Core i3 from a classical computer.

4.1   BCM2837

Now that we introduced a method which determines the affected element, we decide to apply our approach on an experimental work. The presented work comes from an attack campaign realized on a BCM2837 SoC from a Raspberry Pi 3 model B board. The tested code is the repetition of the `orr r3, r3` instruction and the observed registers initial values are presented in Table 3. These values are chosen to be identifiable and hard to compute from each others with simple operations (`or`, `xor`, *etc.*).

This setup has been disturbed using ElectroMagnetic Pulse (EMP). The obtained faulted values are presented with their probability of appearance in Fig. 3.

Several values appear with different probabilities, however there are always some outstanding values that are frequently obtained. Here, these values are

Table 3. Observed registers initial values

Register	Initial value	Register	Initial value
r0	0x80000001	r5	0x04000020
r1	0x40000002	r6	0x02000040
r2	0x20000004	r7	0x01000080
r3	0x10000008	r8	0x00800100
r4	0x08000010	r9	0x00400200

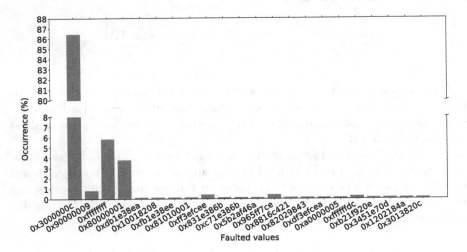

Fig. 3. Faulted values distribution with their occurrence probability obtained from an ElectroMagnetic Fault Injection (EMFI) campaign on a BCM2837.

0x3000000c (86.45%), 0xffffffff (5.83%) and 0x80000001 (3.79%). We ignore the other values as the latter ones are sufficient for demonstrating the method relevance.

Register Corruption Analysis. According to the method presented in Sect. 2, we want to check if the perturbation corrupted the registers. To do so, we need to know the registers initial content. In our experiment, the only faulted registers are r0, r1 and r3.

Giving the faulted and the initial values, it is possible to determine the fault model on the registers. The fault model we consider for register corruption is the masking fault model, this defines the fault as a logical mask applied to the initial value. In other words, the random variable f_{data} is one of the following functions[2]:

$$f_{\text{xor},e} : x \rightarrow x \text{ xor } e,$$

---

[2] It is possible to consider f_{data} as the combination of these functions with different errors, but this do not change the way to apply our methodology.

$$f_{\text{and},e} : x \rightarrow x \text{ and } e,$$

$$f_{\text{or},e} : x \rightarrow x \text{ or } e,$$

with e the error viewed as a logical word with the same size as x.

As several fault models can explain the obtained faulted value, we consider that a fault model is relevant if it explains the obtained faulted value for at least two different experiments. In our context, the only observed *register corruption* fault model is when the faulted value is 0xffffffff and the corresponding function is $f_{\text{or},\text{0xffffffff}}$. This fault model appears in around 5% of the cases.

Instruction Corruption Analysis. As the register corruption analysis was inconsistent for some faulted values, the next step consisted in checking if a faulted instruction can explain them. The idea here is to first determine the instructions that, from the registers initial state, explain the faulted value.

Regarding the faulted values and the registers initial state we observe that 0x3000000c can be obtained with the or between r2 and r3 and that 0x80000001 can be obtained by moving the value in r1 into the faulted register. The corresponding faulted instructions are orr r3, r2 and mov r3, r1.

Because the initial instruction is known, we can determine the fault model f_{ins}. We decided to consider a fault model that modifies the elements (opcode, operands, *etc.*) constituting the instruction. The faulted instruction $\tilde{ins}$ is derived from the initial instruction ins. Determining the fault model consists in determining which part of the instruction was corrupted and how.

In this experiment, the fault model corresponding to the 0x3000000c faulted value is that the instruction second operand is set to r2 and correspond to the orr r3, r2 faulted instruction. This happens in around 85% of the cases and was tested with other instructions. The fault model corresponding to the 0x80000001 faulted value is that the opcode is set to a mov and the second operand to r1, it happens in around 3.5% of the cases.

Conclusion. During this experiment, the faults may affect the pipeline or the registers. We have determined the faulted element with their corresponding fault model for the three main cases (*i.e.* those with greatest occurrence probability in Fig. 3). This covers 96.07% of the observed faults and it experimentally validates that the model is relevant for this CPU.

4.2 Intel Core I3

After having tested our method on an ARM architecture, we want to test it on an x86 architecture. Therefore, we realized an attack campaign on an Intel Core i3 CPU using the repetition of the mov rbx, rbx instruction as a test code.

As the x86 architecture is different from the ARM architecture, the available registers for observation are not the same. Also, the tested architecture is a 64 bits architecture. It appears that these differences do not impact our methodology and we were able to determine the fault model for almost 80% of the cases. The faulted values distribution is presented in Fig. 4.

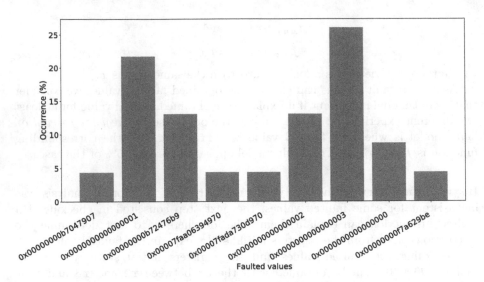

Fig. 4. Faulted values distribution with their occurrence probability obtained from an EMFI campaign on an Intel Core i3.

Using our method, we are able to determine that the faulted register is always `rbx`. There is a register corruption which sets the register to 0x0 in 8.7% of the cases corresponding to the fault model $f_{and,0x0000000000000000}$. In 56.53% of the cases, the faulted value comes from another register, these faulted values are 0x1 (register `rax`), 0x3 (register `rdi`) and 0x00007fXXXXXXXXXX (register `rci` with a different value for every execution of the tested program). The corresponding fault model is to set the instruction second operand to either 0x0, 0x2 or 0x5.

The last identified fault model is for the faulted value 0x2 and corresponds to the logical AND between `rbx` and `r11`. This happens in 13% of the cases and corresponds to set the opcode to 0x21 and the second operand to 0xb.

The remaining faults (21.78%) could not be determined with our method. However, the observed faulted values seems to correspond to values manipulated by the Linux OS layer. However, this investigation is out of the scope of this work and therefore not further explained.

Conclusion. With these results, we demonstrated that our method is reliable independently of the target architecture. However, on targets implementing optimizations (like the Intel Core i3), this approach is not exhaustive.

The analysis presented in Sects. 4.1 and 4.2 enable to model the fault at the Instruction Set Architecture (ISA) level. In other words, we can use this model to explain how the program execution is affected by our faults. With this knowledge it is possible to build some software countermeasures. But, as explained in Sect. 1.1, software countermeasures may become irrelevant because the faulted MAB is not clearly identified.

4.3   Determining the Faulted MAB

After having determined which CPU element (*cf.* Tables 1 and 2) is faulted, it is interesting to check which of its MAB is affected. Usually, this determination is done using debug tools. However, as we mentioned, these tools are, most of the time, not available on our targets. In this section, we then present how we can determine which MAB is faulted using different test programs.

Pipeline Characterization. As presented in Fig. 2 the pipeline has three main functions. The fetch function is mainly linked to the memory system. Then, for the pipeline characterization, it is more relevant to consider only the instruction decoding and its execution.

The first step consists in determining whether the fault affects the instruction before it was decoded or not. If the fault appears before the decoding, then either the instruction bus or the decoding are faulted. In the other case, the fault targets the execute stage. To determine if the instruction is faulted before its decoding, we check if the fault perturbs similarly instructions with different encoding. The proposed method can be applied on every encoded part of the instruction.

As this is instruction targeted part dependent, we present an example with the fault campaign realized on the BCM2837 where we were able to fault the instruction second operand. To determine if the fault appears before the instruction decoding, we aim at faulting an instruction which encodes a different information where the second operand is usually encoded.

The determined fault model is that the instruction second operand is set to r2. According to the ARM instruction encoding, this corresponds to set the eleven instruction Least Significant Bits (LSBs) to 0x002. If the fault corrupts the instruction before its decoding, then the fault effect must be independent of the information encoded on these bits. In the tested case (mov r3, r3), these bits encode a register. Therefore, we can fault another instruction which uses the same bits to encode another information, an immediate value for example. If the fault corrupts the instruction and the obtained immediate value is 0x02, then we conclude that the instruction has been perturbed before its decoding. Otherwise, we conclude that the instruction is faulted during its execution. Listing 1.3 introduces a code example for realizing this test.

This test code is a bit different from the previous ones as it uses several types of instructions. However, thanks to our own analysis reported in Sect. 4.1 (or Sect. 4.2), the ISA fault model is here assumed to be known and it can hence be applied to anticipate the fault effects at this level. As we intent to fault the mov r3, #0x03 instruction, we will repeat the first three instructions to be sure to fault only one of them. These instructions are needed as the program must terminate as soon as a fault is detected. Otherwise, the next mov r3, #0x03 will overwrite the fault.

Listing 1.3: Immediate value test code (ARM)

```
         mov  r3, #0x03 // −+
         cmp  r3, #0x02 //  | Several times
         be  fault      // −+
         mov  r9, #0x55
         b  end
fault:   mov  r9, 0xaa
end:     nop
```

The ISA fault model determined in Sect. 4.1 (or Sect. 4.2) implies that if the first instruction second operand is set to 0x02, then a fault is obtained. If it occurs on the second instruction, then there is no error since the second operand is already set to 0x02. Eventually, if it occurs on the third instruction, then we observe a modification of the instruction offset. Moreover, this offset can be manipulated using nop[3] instructions to have its eleven LSBs set to 0x002. In this case, the fault has no impact.

This example was done with a fault model that modifies the second operand. However, some other instructions parts may be affected, such as the opcode. In this case, the demonstrated test can still be done but with different instructions. This requires the Instruction Set Format (ISF) knowledge implemented by the target. For instance, the ARM ISF is available on their website[4].

Memory Characterization. The memory relies on three main elements: the buses, the MMU and the cache. If an instruction corruption is detected and has occurred before the decoding stage, two MABs can have been faulted: the buses or the cache. Distinguishing between these two cases is difficult but it is possible to determine if it happens on the mixed cache and buses or on the dedicated one. Indeed, as the highest level of cache memory is both dedicated to the data and the instructions, a fault targeting this part of the memory subsystem corrupts the instruction and the data similarly. If not, then the dedicated part of the memory subsystem is corrupted. For this characterization step, we propose a method we applied on the BCM2837.

The method consists in (1) initializing a page of memory (4 kB), then (2) setting the observed registers values to addresses in this page and fault a code such as introduced in Listing 1.4.

This code realizes memory loads and stores at/from the address stored in r9 to/from the register r8. As the memory page is initialized with known values, the expected value in r8 are known. The ISA fault model built in Sect. 4.1 (or Sect. 4.2) implies that the perturbation should set the second operand to 0x2 and the faulted instructions should become str r8, [r2] or ldr r8, [r2].

---

[3] Using mov r2, r2 to be fault resistant for instance.
[4] http://infocenter.arm.com/help/index.jsp?topic=/com.arm.doc.ddi0210c/CACCCHGF.html.

Listing 1.4. Memory test code (ARM)

```
str r8, [r9] // Several
ldr r8, [r9] //     times
```

An unanticipated fault is that with probability 25%, the faulted value is the `ldr r8, [r9]` instruction encoded value. In this case, the faulted instruction is `ldr r8, [PC]` which corresponds to set the first operand to `0xff`.

For the other faults (74.4% exactly), the observed faulted value is always $b_{ad} + 50$ where b_{ad} the page memory base address. This is the value stored in `r2`. In this case, the faulted instruction is `mov r8, r2`. This is consistent with the previously determined fault model (see Sects. 4.1 and 4.2). Moreover, the fault does not only modify the second operand but also the opcode, forcing the instruction into a data processing instruction instead of memory loading instruction. As we already tested data processing instructions, we did not see this fault effect. This shows the importance of testing different types of instructions for determining the complete fault effect.

During this experiment, we did not observe faults on the fetched data. Therefore, we conclude that the fault targets the dedicated to the instruction part of the memory subsystems. In Fig. 2, it corresponds to the instruction cache, its connected buses and the fetch MAB.

Regarding the tested codes presented in Listing 1.1, in the case the fault does not fit neither a fault model on the registers nor a fault model on the instructions we conclude that the fault provokes an instruction *bad fetch*. Usually, the corresponding fault models are either instruction skipping [9,21], instruction replay [18,19] or instruction replacement [3,14]. The literature proposes a large panel of fault models on the cache with different characterization methods but only on MCUs (except [18]). As MCUs do not embed MMU, the failed translation of the address fault does not appears simplifying the analysis.

We could characterize the fault on the MMU but only using debug tools. In order to remain in the scope of this work, we consider that if no cache fault model is consistent, the fault affects the MMU.

5   Conclusion and Future Works

In this paper, we introduced for the first time a general method for characterizing the fault model of perturbations on a CPU and demonstrated its applicability on modern CPUs embedded in a BCM2837 and an Intel Core i3 SoC. This method focuses on determining the faults effect at the ISA level and then at the microarchitectural level using only simple tests programs. As the method works for modern CPUs with many features, we strongly believe that it can been applied on MCUs CPU as well by not considering unimplemented MABs.

This approach gives us a better understanding of faults effect and therefore exploit them or mitigate them. This is a useful tool especially for evaluations where we need to determine the fault model, use it to find attack paths and build efficient countermeasures. As both a knowledge at the ISA level and micro-architectural level are determined using our method, it is possible to build both software and hardware countermeasures.

Based on this result, the future works consist in applying this method to characterize the faults effects on popular systems. Such as mobile devices, determining how these systems can be faulted will help in understanding the impact of physical attacks targeting them and build efficient countermeasures.

Another future work is to improve the CPU model and adapt the method to match with some new optimization mechanisms that are implemented in modern CPUs. Indeed, even if the presented work on the BCM2837 shows that we are able, in more than 95% of the cases, to determine the fault model, on some other targets, like an Intel Core i3, this model able to recover only 80% of the cases. We think that some complex optimization mechanisms that are not considered in our model are involved in the faulty behavior and it is interesting to work on how to model them and to characterize a fault considering them.

References

1. Workshop on Fault Diagnosis and Tolerance in Cryptography, FDTC 2016, Santa Barbara, CA, USA, 16 August 2016. IEEE Computer Society (2016)
2. Workshop on Fault Diagnosis and Tolerance in Cryptography, FDTC 2017, Taipei, Taiwan, 25 September 2017. IEEE Computer Society (2017)
3. Balasch, J., Gierlichs, B., Verbauwhede, I.: An in-depth and black-box characterization of the effects of clock glitches on 8-bit MCUs. In: Breveglieri et al. [7], pp. 105–114
4. Barbu, G., Duc, G., Hoogvorst, P.: Java card operand stack: fault attacks, combined attacks and countermeasures. In: Prouff [17], pp. 297–313
5. Bouffard, G., Iguchi-Cartigny, J., Lanet, J.: Combined software and hardware attacks on the Java card control flow. In: Prouff [17], pp. 283–296
6. Bozzato, C., Focardi, R., Palmarini, F.: Shaping the glitch: optimizing voltage fault injection attacks. IACR Trans. Cryptogr. Hardw. Embed. Syst. **2019**(2), 199–224 (2019)
7. Breveglieri, L., Guilley, S., Koren, I., Naccache, D., Takahashi, J. (eds.): Workshop on Fault Diagnosis and Tolerance in Cryptography, FDTC 2011, Tokyo, Japan, 29 September 2011. IEEE Computer Society (2011)
8. Kocher, P., et al.: Spectre attacks: exploiting speculative execution, pp. 1–19 (2019)
9. Korak, T., Hoefler, M.: On the effects of clock and power supply tampering on two microcontroller platforms. In: Tria, A., Choi, D. (eds.) Workshop on Fault Diagnosis and Tolerance in Cryptography, FDTC 2014, Busan, South Korea, 23 September 2014, pp. 8–17. IEEE Computer Society (2014)
10. Kumar, D.S.V., Beckers, A., Balasch, J., Gierlichs, B., Verbauwhede, I.: An in-depth and black-box characterization of the effects of laser pulses on ATmega328P. In: Bilgin, B., Fischer, J.-B. (eds.) CARDIS 2018. LNCS, vol. 11389, pp. 156–170. Springer, Cham (2019). https://doi.org/10.1007/978-3-030-15462-2_11
11. Lipp, M., et al.: Meltdown: reading kernel memory from user space. In: Enck, W., Felt, A.P. (eds.) 27th USENIX Security Symposium, USENIX Security 2018, Baltimore, MD, USA, 15–17 August 2018, pp. 973–990. USENIX Association (2018)

12. Majéric, F., Bourbao, E., Bossuet, L.: Electromagnetic security tests for SoC. In: 2016 IEEE International Conference on Electronics, Circuits and Systems, ICECS 2016, Monte Carlo, Monaco, 11–14 December 2016, pp. 265–268. IEEE (2016)
13. Menu, A., Bhasin, S., Dutertre, J., Rigaud, J., Danger, J.: Precise spatio-temporal electromagnetic fault injections on data transfers. In: Workshop on Fault Diagnosis and Tolerance in Cryptography, FDTC 2019, Atlanta, GA, USA, 24 August 2019, pp. 1–8. IEEE (2019)
14. Moro, N., Dehbaoui, A., Heydemann, K., Robisson, B., Encrenaz, E.: Electromagnetic fault injection: towards a fault model on a 32-bit microcontroller. In: Fischer, W., Schmidt, J. (eds.) Workshop on Fault Diagnosis and Tolerance in Cryptography, Los Alamitos, CA, USA, 20 August 2013, pp. 77–88. IEEE Computer Society (2013)
15. Obermaier, J., Tatschner, S.: Shedding too much light on a microcontroller's firmware protection. In: Enck, W., Mulliner, C. (eds.) 11th USENIX Workshop on Offensive Technologies, WOOT 2017, Vancouver, BC, Canada, 14–15 August 2017. USENIX Association (2017)
16. Patranabis, S., Chakraborty, A., Nguyen, P.H., Mukhopadhyay, D.: A biased fault attack on the time redundancy countermeasure for AES. In: Mangard, S., Poschmann, A.Y. (eds.) COSADE 2014. LNCS, vol. 9064, pp. 189–203. Springer, Cham (2015). https://doi.org/10.1007/978-3-319-21476-4_13
17. Prouff, E. (ed.): CARDIS 2011. LNCS, vol. 7079. Springer, Heidelberg (2011). https://doi.org/10.1007/978-3-642-27257-8
18. Proy, J., Heydemann, K., Berzati, A., Majéric, F., Cohen, A.: A first ISA-level characterization of EM pulse effects on superscalar microarchitectures: a secure software perspective. In: Proceedings of the 14th International Conference on Availability, Reliability and Security, ARES 2019, Canterbury, UK, 26–29 August 2019, pp. 7:1–7:10. ACM (2019)
19. Rivière, L., Najm, Z., Rauzy, P., Danger, J., Bringer, J., Sauvage, L.: High precision fault injections on the instruction cache of ARMv7-M architectures. In: IEEE International Symposium on Hardware Oriented Security and Trust, HOST 2015, Washington, DC, USA, 5–7 May, 2015, pp. 62–67. IEEE Computer Society (2015)
20. Schmidt, J.M., Hutter, M.: Optical and EM Fault-Attacks on CRT-based RSA: Concrete Results (2007)
21. Schmidt, J., Herbst, C.: A practical fault attack on square and multiply. In: Breveglieri, L., Gueron, S., Koren, I., Naccache, D., Seifert, J. (eds.) Fifth International Workshop on Fault Diagnosis and Tolerance in Cryptography, FDTC 2008, Washington, DC, USA, 10 August 2008, pp. 53–58. IEEE Computer Society (2008)
22. Schmidt, J., Hutter, M., Plos, T.: Optical fault attacks on AES: a threat in violet. In: Breveglieri, L., Koren, I., Naccache, D., Oswald, E., Seifert, J. (eds.) Sixth International Workshop on Fault Diagnosis and Tolerance in Cryptography, FDTC 2009, Lausanne, Switzerland, 6 September 2009, pp. 13–22. IEEE Computer Society (2009)
23. Skorobogatov, S.P., Anderson, R.J.: Optical fault induction attacks. In: Kaliski Jr., B.S., Koç, K., Paar, C. (eds.) CHES 2002. LNCS, vol. 2523, pp. 2–12. Springer, Heidelberg (2003). https://doi.org/10.1007/3-540-36400-5_2
24. Tang, A., Sethumadhavan, S., Stolfo, S.J.: CLKSCREW: exposing the perils of security-oblivious energy management. In: Kirda, E., Ristenpart, T. (eds.) 26th USENIX Security Symposium, USENIX Security 2017, Vancouver, BC, Canada, 16–18 August 2017, pp. 1057–1074. USENIX Association (2017)

25. Timmers, N., Mune, C.: Escalating Privileges in linux using voltage fault injection. In: Workshop on Fault Diagnosis and Tolerance in Cryptography, FDTC 2017, Taipei, Taiwan, 25 September 2017 [2], pp. 1–8
26. Timmers, N., Spruyt, A., Witteman, M.: Controlling PC on ARM using fault injection. In: 2016 Workshop on Fault Diagnosis and Tolerance in Cryptography, FDTC 2016, Santa Barbara, CA, USA, 16 August 2016 [1], pp. 25–35
27. Vasselle, A., Thiebeauld, H., Maouhoub, Q., Morisset, A., Ermeneux, S.: Laser-induced fault injection on smartphone bypassing the secure boot. In: Workshop on Fault Diagnosis and Tolerance in Cryptography, FDTC 2017, Taipei, Taiwan, 25 September 2017 [2], pp. 41–48
28. van der Veen, V., et al.: Drammer: deterministic rowhammer attacks on mobile platforms. In: Weippl, E.R., Katzenbeisser, S., Kruegel, C., Myers, A.C., Halevi, S. (eds.) Proceedings of the 2016 ACM SIGSAC Conference on Computer and Communications Security, Vienna, Austria, 24–28 October 2016, pp. 1675–1689. ACM (2016)
29. van Woudenberg, J.G.J., Witteman, M.F., Menarini, F.: Practical optical fault injection on secure microcontrollers. In: Breveglieri et al. [7], pp. 91–99
30. Yuce, B., Ghalaty, N.F., Santapuri, H., Deshpande, C., Patrick, C., Schaumont, P.: Software fault resistance is futile: effective single-glitch attacks. In: Workshop on Fault Diagnosis and Tolerance in Cryptography, FDTC 2016, Santa Barbara, CA, USA, 16 August 2016 [1], pp. 47–58
31. Yuce, B., Ghalaty, N.F., Schaumont, P.: Improving fault attacks on embedded software using RISC pipeline characterization. In: Homma, N., Lomné, V. (eds.) Workshop on Fault Diagnosis and Tolerance in Cryptography, FDTC 2015, Saint Malo, France, 13 September 2015, pp. 97–108. IEEE Computer Society (2015)

Threat Analysis of Poisoning Attack Against Ethereum Blockchain

Teppei Sato[1]($\boxtimes$), Mitsuyoshi Imamura[1], and Kazumasa Omote[1,2]

[1] University of Tsukuba, 1-1-1, Tennodai, Tsukuba 305-8573, Japan
s1820583@s.tsukuba.ac.jp, ic140tg528@gmail.com, omote@risk.tsukuba.ac.jp
[2] National Institute of Information and Communications Technology,
4-2-1, Nukui-Kitamachi, Koganei, Tokyo 184-8795, Japan

Abstract. In recent years, blockchain technology has witnessed remarkable developments in its application to crypto assets (cryptocurrency) considering not only function storing values but also extension of the smart contract and anonymity improvement. Ethereum is a blockchain that features the smart contract and there is a data space, where programs can be freely stored, on the blockchain. However, pollution of such data space can jeopardize the existence of Ethereum.

In this study, we analyze the fact that the malicious files that are stored in the data space of Ethereum and discuss "blockchain poisoning attacks" that significantly contaminate the blockchains by embedding malicious data at a relatively lower cost. We try to tackle Ethereum-specific risks which are not mentioned in previous study. In addition, we empirically examine the possibility of a poisoning attack on a private blockchain network.

Keywords: Blockchain · Crypto assets · Security · Poisoning attack

1 Introduction

Blockchain is a distributed ledger technology that is a part of Bitcoin [16]. It was introduced in 2008. While the technology is well known as the base technology of crypto assets (cryptocurrency), it also acts as not only the function to store values, extending into industrial fields. The technology has some advantages. It provides a certain degree of anonymity, ensures that the network is not shut down, and manipulation-resistance to the data on it. Some researchers proposed its applications in various fields such as IoT security [7], PKI [8], and management of medical data [4]. However, the blockchain technology faces certain security problems and challenges, including typical attacks [9,13] such as the majority attack (51% Attacks), double-spending and cryptojacking, and new types of attacks such as the "blockchain poisoning attack", which can be a critical treat to the blockchain system (Fig. 1).

Blockchains can be attacked by embedding malicious or illegal files in the flexible space of blockchain [15]. We define this type of attack as a blockchain

© IFIP International Federation for Information Processing 2020
Published by Springer Nature Switzerland AG 2020
M. Laurent and T. Giannetsos (Eds.): WISTP 2019, LNCS 12024, pp. 139–154, 2020.
https://doi.org/10.1007/978-3-030-41702-4_9

poisoning attack. Such poisoning attacks are considered to be more malicious than conventional poisoning attacks, such as DNS cache poisoning, against public databases because repairing a poisoned blockchain without hard fork is not feasible owing to the feature of blockchains where the transactions inside a blockchain cannot be modified or cancelled by anyone. In addition, because the data contained in the blockchain are synchronized by each node, attackers can force the nodes to download any malicious files by embedding them into the blockchain.

Smart contract, which was first proposed by Szabo [20], is a computer protocol designed to digitally facilitate, verify, or enforce the negotiation of a transaction without any trusted third parties. Ethereum is well known as a implementation of smart contract which is turing-complete.

Unlike Bitcoin blockchain, Ethereum has a legitimate and flexible space that contains the bytecodes of smart contracts. Anyone can officially embed any data into Ethereum blockchain. Unfortunately, this indicates that this feature also provides flexibility to attackers. Hence, the poisoning attacks against Ethereum blockchain (and blockchains that have a flexible space like Ethereum) are easier.

In this study, we analyze the Ethereum blockchain to examine blockchain poisoning, and further verify the ease of blockchain poisoning attack using our experimental blockchain environment.

The contributions of this paper are following:

- We analyzed the Ethereum blockchain to examine the actual situation of blockchain poisoning (until December 31, 2018 UTC), and found 154 files including some malicious files.
- Using experimental blockchain environments, we demonstrated that blockchain poisoning can be easily done through web browsers and one-liner shell command. This risk is specific to Ethereum, not discussed in previous study [15].
- We indicate the new C&C technique using the Ethereum blockchain, which is different from methods [1,2]. Existing malwares can easily use such technique, since the malwares using the method use HTTP/HTTPS protocol to get commands from botmaster.

2   Background

2.1   Ethereum

"Ethereum is a decentralized platform that runs smart contracts: applications that run exactly as programmed without any possibility of downtime, censorship, fraud or third-party interference."[1]

Two Types of Accounts. Ethereum has two types of accounts: Externally Owned Account (EOA) and Contract account. EOA is used to send Ether to another account, make contracts, and execute the contract. It is controlled by a

---

[1] Ethereum: https://www.ethereum.org/.

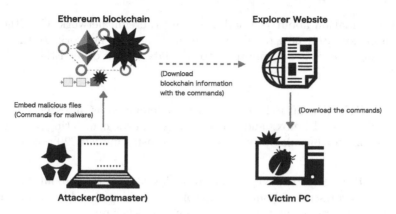

Fig. 1. Threat of blockchain poisoning attack: When performing the poisoning attack, attackers embed malicious files into the targeted blockchain. We examined the actual situation of blockchain poisoning as stated in Sect. 5. In addition, when abusing the blockchain in C&C, botmasters embed commands into the blockchain, then the Explorer website downloads blockchain information with the commands. The malware obtains the commands by accessing the Explorer. We analyzed the feasibility of C&C technique with blockchain poisoning in Sect. 6.

private key[2]. In contrast, a Contract represents an account of smart contract on Ethereum itself. In other words, EOA sends a transaction to a Contract account to execute the contract.

Smart Contract and Flexible Space on Ethereum. Smart contract on Ethereum is written in bytecode, known as EVM code, and is executed on a virtual machine called Ethereum Virtual Machine (EVM), which runs on a node in the Ethereum network. Ethereum transactions have spaces that are used for the smart contract: *init* and *data* areas. *Init* area contains EVM code and is used to deploy the smart contract. In contrast, *data* area is used to call a function of a contract and give arguments to the function. This area can be freely used irrespective of smart contract.

Because both *init* and *data* areas are arrays of unlimited bytes (according to Ethereum yellow paper [22]), there are no theoretical upper limits to the size of data. However, because a transaction fee cannot exceed the block fee limit determined by miner voting, there is a practical upper limit for the data size. In addition, Go Ethereum, which is the official Go implementation of Ethereum, has another limitation. With its comment "Heuristic limit, reject transactions over 32 KB to prevent DOS attacks", a filter was added to the application to reject transactions containing more than 32 kB data in its *init/data* area. This limitation has been added since version v1.6.6. According to ethernodes.org[3], which

---

[2] Ethereum   Development   Tutorial   https://github.com/ethereum/wiki/wiki/Ethereum-Development-Tutorial.

[3] ethernodes.org: https://www.ethernodes.org/.

contains information about the nodes in the Ethereum network, Go Ethereum runs on approximately 50% of all nodes in the Ethereum network. To the best of our knowledge, there is no limitation to the data size in other Ethereum client applications.

METAMASK. It is an Ethereum wallet implemented as an extension of web browsers: Chrome, Firefox, and Opera[4]. It supports connecting to not only Ethereum mainnet but also private net, and transferring ERC20 token.

Explorer. It is a web services that provides information about blockchain through web browsers without special software or running blockchain nodes. The services are important for transparency in blockchain.

Etherscan[5] is a well-known explorer in Ethereum. It provides information related to the Ethereum blockchain such as source code of contract, data in *init* and *data* areas, block hash, and transaction hash.

2.2 How to Use Smart Contract on Ethereum

We can use smart contract on Ethereum by the following two steps.

Deploy a Contract. We define a contract using high-level programming languages. A well-known language to define contracts on Ethereum is Solidity[6], which looks like JavaScript. The contract is compiled into byte-code called EVM code.

Next, the EVM code is deployed on the Ethereum network to use the contract. The input EVM code is returned by the compiler as output to *init* of a new transaction, without an Integrated Development Environment (IDE), the recipient address of the transaction is set to *null*. At this time, a contract account associated with the contract has not been generated yet. After the transaction is sent using the Ethereum wallet, it is broadcasted in the network and miners in the Ethereum network put the transactions into the new block to generate the next block. In the mining process, the Contract account is generated.

Execute the Contract. To execute a contract, a transaction must be made. You input byte-array to specify which function is called and give arguments to the function to *data* area for new transaction.

The transaction is then sent from EOA to the Contract account. In the mining process, the result of the contract execution is reflected in the blockchain.

Furthermore, in order to send a transaction containing EVM code, certain Ethereum wallet applications have functions that receive data in hex string and write it into a transaction.

---

[4] METAMASK: https://metamask.io.
[5] Etherscan: https://etherscan.io.
[6] Solidity: https://github.com/ethereum/solidity.

3   Related Work

Smart contract extends the function of blockchain and provides a programmable logic platform for all users on the blockchain network. However, when considering the security risks, it is reasonable to not allow programmable operations to untrusted users. So far, researchers have studied security and attacks regarding blockchain, crypto assets, and smart contract [9,13,21]. In this section, we introduce the attacks in programs and stored data related to smart contract and poisoning attacks related to crypto assets.

3.1   Data Stored Space Attack

Matzutt et al. studied the data inserted into the Bitcoin blockchain [15] and proposed countermeasures for undesirable data [14]. They discussed the benefits and risks of arbitrary blockchain contents and summarized some methods for data insertion into the Bitcoin blockchain. In addition, they found several types of undesirable content, including child pornography and violate another individual's privacy on the Bitcoin blockchain.

However, the spaces designed for data insertion on the Bitcoin blockchain are caused by OP_RETURN and Coinbase transaction and only the miner can insert data into Coinbase transaction. Hence, usual network participants can insert only 80 bytes of data to OP_RETURN at once. In contrast, Ethereum has more flexible space than Bitcoin. If a blockchain has designed flexible spaces, the poisoning attack becomes easier. Thus, we examine the possibility of the poisoning attack in Ethereum.

3.2   Programs Attack

Atzei et al. [3] reported a series of security vulnerabilities in Ethereum smart contracts. They categorized the vulnerabilities into three levels (Solidity, EVM, Blockchain) based on the causes of vulnerability and explained them by examining the source codes written in Solidity. The attacks work against the users and administrators of the smart contracts with vulnerabilities. In contrast, the poisoning attack, explained in this paper and [14,15], affects all users of a system which contains blockchain. This indicates that poisoning attack is a direct attack against blockchain.

3.3   C&C Technique Using Blockchain Network

Ali et al. [1,2] proposed C&C mechanism that leveraged the Bitcoin network. They indicated methods to insert C&C payload to Bitcoin transactions, except our method, which are reported in Sect. 3.1. Furthermore, they explained the advantages of C&C using Bitcoin network including the difficulty of takedown without causing any harmful effects to legitimate Bitcoin users and the cost for maintaining a C&C network. They also built a botnet on the Bitcoin main network and measured *response time*, which is the time period from when the botmaster issues an instruction and it is successfully received by the bot, to evaluate the method.

If a blockchain has a designed flexible space, attacker can embed C&C payload on the blockchain and bots can access the payload on the blockchain more easily using web service called Explorer.

4   Blockchain Poisoning Attack

4.1   What Is Blockchain Poisoning Attack

Blockchain poisoning attack is an attack against blockchain by embedding malicious or illegal files in the flexible space of blockchain. Attackers can force nodes in the blockchain network to download the files. This causes DoS attacks against blockchain. The attack target can be the blockchain and its users.

Attackers perform the attack as follows:

1. An attacker prepares a malicious or illegal file.
2. The attacker embeds the file into the flexible space of transaction, and broadcasts the transaction in the blockchain network.
3. The malicious file is embedded into the blockchain through the mining process and then shared among the network participants.

Files used for blockchain poisoning attack can be privacy information, malwares, and any illegal contents. Such files are also described in [15].

4.2   Why Blockchain Poisoning Attack Is Critical/Impact of Blockchain Poisoning Attack

The reasons why the attack is critical are as follows:

– Blockchain is shared among participants of blockchain P2P network.
– Transactions contained blockchain are hard to be modified or cancelled.

In a blockchain system, each full node needs to store block data synchronized by the P2P network. It means that attackers force the nodes to download and store malicious or illegal files by embedding such files into the blockchain. Certainly, nodes which don't store full blockchain data, like SPV nodes in the network, are not damaged directly by the attack as much as full nodes. However, since blockchain network is backed mainly by full nodes, the attack affects all users of the blockchain indirectly.

Immutability is one of the important features of blockchain. Because of this feature, transactions contained blockchain are hard to be modified or cancelled. Hence, blockchain poisoning attack is considered to be more persistent than conventional poisoning attacks, such as DNS cache poisoning, against public database, because repairing a poisoned blockchain without hard fork is not feasible. In contrast, once a transaction fee is paid, it is easy to send transaction with malicious data. It means that blockchain is heavily damaged by the attack while attackers can perform the attack in a low degree of dificulty.

4.3 Application of Blockchain Poisoning

C&C Using Blockchain. In a blockchain system, each node needs to store block data synchronized by the P2P network. Anyone can access the blockchain data by connecting to the network. These features can be used for C&C.

The mechanism of C&C using blockchain has already been presented by Ali et al. [1,2]. In this technique, bots are implemented by modifying bitcoin node software (freely available), and the bots connect to the bitcoin P2P network and use the network for C&C.

The methods that malware gets commands from bot master via blockchain. These methods are different from the ones described in previous studies [1,2].

– Get commands from blockchain on victim node.
– Access Explorer website to get command.

The first one can be used only when the victim server is running as a node of the blockchain network. Because each node synchronizes blockchain and the blockchain data is stored on itself, a malware can easily access the commands by reading the blockchain data, which are embedded into blockchain by bot master, data which stored on the server. Using this technique, malwares can hide their C&C communications in P2P communications of the blockchain network. For example, a malware aims at the nodes of crypto assets to steal their private keys and then, can get commands without direct communications with bot master and C&C server.

In the second method, the malware accesses the Explorer website to receive commands. It is difficult to detect and prevent this attack technique because most companies allow HTTP/HTTPS protocols and the content of HTTPS communication is encrypted.

Note that such attack techniques, including the method presented by Ali et al. [1,2], are also disadvantageous for attackers. Data in blockchain are unchangeable and unremovable. Once the malware is found by security researchers, they can get information about C&C from the blockchain and analyze it.

Hash Rate Decreasing of Blockchain/Price Manipulation of Crypto Assets. After performing blockchain poisoning, publishing information such as "The blockchain contains illegal files!!" can produce a negative impression on the users that uses the blockchain and they might leave the system. This is a DoS attack against blockchain because the hash rate of a network is very important for security in the blockchain system.

If a crypto asset encounters the attack mentioned above, its price can be declined. Thus, the attacker can reduce the price and benefit from the price difference between before and after attacking.

5 Evaluation of Flexible Space

We investigated the programmable space on the Ethereum main network (from 0 to 6,988,614 in block height) (July 30, 2015–December 31, 2018 UTC).

5.1   Methodology

We detected the transactions embedded files using the file carving method. This method is used to recover files from the unallocated spaces of a storage, for instance, in digital forensics. It can identify files embedded in unknown binary data by techniques such as searching file headers and using file structures [12]. We used Foremost[7] in this evaluation because it is used in general and open source program.

The procedure of our investigation is as follows:

1. Convert data extracted from a transaction from a byte-array to a binary file and then save the file.
2. Input the binary file to a file carving tool.
3. If the tool detects some files in the binary file, record the information of the transaction

Eighteen file types were used in this study for detection: jpg, gif, png, bmp, avi, exe, mpg, wav, riff, wmv, mov, pdf, ole, doc, zip, rar, html, and cpp.

In this evaluation, we did not cover files divided and embedded into the blockchain separately and encoded in some way. Attackers need certain burden (e.g., management of files, gas, etc.) to hide the embedded files or data on a blockchain by dividing or encoding.

5.2   Files Embedded in Transactions

Our investigation of data extracted from the transactions showed that 154 files were embedded in the Ethereum blockchain.

Figure 2 shows the file-types of the extracted files. As evident from Fig. 2, approximately 80% of extracted files were image files (jpg, png, and gif). Most of the image content were not problematic as they were group pictures and landscape. However, some pictures consisted of undesirable content. In addition, the pictures, appearing at first glance to be normal, may be malicious because they can violate the privacy of others, and be abused by steganography techniques [5].

We found three exe files in the Ethereum blockchain. The MD5 hashes of these three exe files are shown below;

(1) c9a31ea148232b201fe7cb7db5c75f5e
(2) c1e5dae72a51a7b7219346c4a360d867
(3) c9a31ea148232b201fe7cb7db5c75f5e

The two files are evidently the same. We inputted these hashes to VirusTotal to evaluate the files and concluded that the three exe files are malware because the analysis result of file (1) and file (3) indicated that their rates of detection by anti-virus software are 56/70 and the result of file (2) indicated that its rate of detection is 58/66. Moreover, according to a report [19], a malware called W32.Duqu has the same hash value as the file (1) and file (3).

---

[7] Foremost: http://foremost.sourceforge.net/.

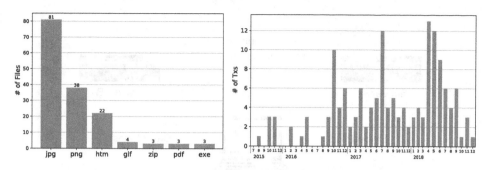

Fig. 2. The type of the embedded file

Fig. 3. Time-series histogram of file-embedded transactions

Table 1. Numbers of relation between sender and recipient accounts

(a) sender and recipient are the same	79
(b) sender and recipient are the different	70
(c) recipient is null (contract creation transaction)	5

Furthermore, we found that these three exe files were embedded by one account and the account sent three file-embedded transactions in approximately 6 min. Figure 3 shows time-series histogram of file-embedded transactions. We show when such transactions were contained by the Ethereum blockchain.

We demonstrate the relation the between sender and recipient of the transactions embedded files. The number of sender accounts was 113 and that of file-embedded transactions is 154. It indicates that some accounts embedded a file to the Ethereum blockchain several times. The maximum number of file-embedded transactions sent by one account is 10.

Table 1 presents the numbers of relation between sender and recipient accounts. There are three types of relations: (a) sender and recipient are the same, (b) sender and recipient are the different, and (c) recipient is null (i.e., contract creation transaction). Most accounts with file-embedded transactions send the transaction to any recipient except null. Some accounts embedded a file into a contract creation transaction.

6   Feasibility Experiment of Poisoning Attack

Determining the feasibility of an attack is important to assess the risk of the attack. We constructed an experimental environment, which imitates the actual environment of Ethereum blockchain, to assess the possibility of poisoning attack. In the environment, we attempted to embed files into our private Ethereum blockchain and extracted the same files from the Explorer using a web browser. We extracted and embedded the files to verify the usability of

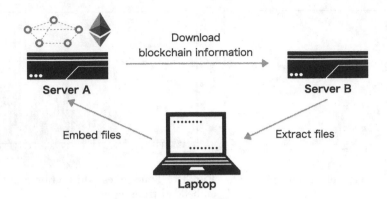

Fig. 4. Our experimental environment

blockchain poisoning as C&C infrastructure using web browsers and one-liner shell commands. This indicates ease of the attack.

6.1   Experimental Environment

Our experimental environment was constructed using two servers (Server A and Server B) and a laptop, as shown in Fig. 4. The components of the experimental environment are as follows:

Server A (Ethereum Privatenet). Go Ethereum is installed on this server that is configured to mine a private blockchain. This server plays the role of Ethereum mainnet in the actual environment.

Server B (Explorer). On this server, we set up a web server to display information about the Ethereum private blockchain on Server A using EthExplorer[8]. This web server plays the role of blockchain explorer, such as Etherscan in the actual environment.

Laptop. We used MacBook Pro to execute shell commands and Google Chrome (with METAMASK installed) for the experiment. These enabled the embedding and extracting of files in the same process as performing a poisoning attack against Ethereum main net.

6.2   Experiment

We explain the experiment procedure in three steps (preparation, embedding a file, and extracting the file). Because Go Ethereum rejects the transactions that contain data over 32 kB (as stated in Sect. 2.1), we used image files under 32 kB to embed into our private blockchain.

---

[8] EthExplorer: https://github.com/etherparty/explorer.

Preparation. This is the setting on Server A.

1. Start mining on Server A.
2. Connect METAMASK to Ethereum private net on Server A.
3. Create an account on METAMASK and send Ether to that account from the Coinbase account on Server A.
4. In the setting of METAMASK, turn on the "Show Hex Data" toggle switch.

Embed File. In this section, we describe the process to embed file on the blockchain.

1. To obtain the hexdump of a file (e.g., pic.jpg), the following command is executed and the result is copied to the clipboard.

    xxd -p pic.png | perl -pe 's/\ n//g'

2. Click "SEND" on METAMASK.
3. Select any account to send a transaction and paste the hexdump of the file to the field "Hex Data".
4. Click "NEXT" and "CONFIRM" to send transaction.
5. After the blockchain receives the transaction, we can confirm that the blockchain contains the hexdump in the web application on Server B.

Extract File. The process to extract a file from the blockchain is given below. It should be noted that the name of the extracted file is "pic_extracted.png".

1. Copy a hex string showed on the web application of Server B.
2. Replace <hex> by the following command on the hex string and execute it.

    echo <hex> | xxd -p -r > pic_extracted.png

6.3   Ease of Poisoning Attack

Section 6.2 demonstrates that files can be embedded into the Ethereum blockchain using only METAMASK and one-liner shell command. We used shell command to obtain the hexdump of files in this experiment, there is web service which provides conversion from binary file to a hex string. It is substantially possible to embed files into the Ethereum blockchain only using the web browser.

Section 6.2 demonstrates that the embedded data can be accessed using explorer website and extracted using a one-liner shell command.

In this experiment, we used a image file, which is about 28 KB, to embed. The transaction embedded the file costs 1952132 of gas.

7   Discussion

7.1   Behavior of a Suspicious Account

As stated in Sect. 5.2, we found that three exe files, judged as malware by Virus-Total, were embedded into the Ethereum blockchain by a single account.

Heuristic analysis, which detects malwares analyzing suspicious behavior, is a popular malware detection technique [11,18,23]. Considering the possibility that heuristic analysis can be implemented against blockchain poisoning, we observed the behavior of the suspicious account.

We found in our evaluation that the suspicious account sent and received ten transactions in total. These transactions are given below. Assume that "*account X*" denotes the suspicious account and *account A, B, and C* denotes the normal accounts.

(1) "An Ether transfer transaction" from *account A* to **account X**
(2) "An Ether transfer transaction" from **account X** to *account B*
(3) ~ (8) Self-sent transactions with data in their *data* area
   (3) 4.1 kB random-like data
   (4) 20.5 kB random-like data
   (5) broken PNG image
   (6) malware EXE file (1)
   (7) malware EXE file (2)
   (8) malware EXE file (3)
(9) "An Ether transfer transaction" from **account X** to *account C*
(10) Empty transaction from *account C* to **account X**

This series of transactions indicates an attempt by an attacker to check if malicious files can be embedded into the blockchain. This attempt can be interpreted as follows.

First, this suspicious account received some Ether (1) required to send transactions and embed data into transactions. To check the data size that can be embedded into the blockchain, this account sent two transactions of different sizes (3)(4). Next, the account sent a transaction embedded PNG file to check if it can be embedded into the blockchain (5). The account then sent three transactions containing malware binary file to check if malicious files can be embedded into the blockchain (6)(7)(8).

We found suspicious behavior by a single account. However, there is a clear difference between malware and such suspicious accounts. Malwares have a series of actions. In contrast, attackers can also create unlimited accounts (say, address) on a blockchain. Although a single account sent the transactions in this case, they could be divided and sent by multiple accounts. Therefore, owing to the difference between malwares and accounts on blockchains, performing heuristic analysis on each account is ineffective and countermeasures against blockchain poisoning should be made by observing each transaction instead of account.

7.2   Risk of Flexible Space of Blockchain

We discuss the risks due to the flexible space of Ethereum blockchain, considering our evaluation of programmable space and our experiments on poisoning attack. Following are the reasons for increasing the risks.

Functions for Embedding Data Are Officially Provided. Techniques to embedding arbitrary data into the Bitcoin blockchain [15] are not officially allowed except for OP_RETURN and Coinbase transaction. Therefore, when embedding any data into the blockchain that does not have flexible space, it is necessary to use difficult way like "coding Bitcoin script" because general wallets of such blockchains do not have embedding functions.

However, in the case of blockchains that have flexible space, including Ethereum, some functions for writing data to the space are officially provided. As stated in Sect. 6, attackers can use wallet apps, which can be also used by benign users, to perform a poisoning attack through the same procedure. Therefore, a flexible space in blockchain facilitate poisoning attack.

Explorer Exists. As described in Sect. 2.1, there are websites called Explorer in each blockchain, which provide information related to the blockchain. The content of these websites are different according to the structure and functions of each blockchain. If a blockchain has flexible space, the embedded data can be easily obtained in any form such as ascii and hexadecimal.

Ali et al. [1,2] proposed the C&C technique using Bitcoin blockchain. As mentioned before, Explorer websites can be used in C&C on both Bitcoin and Ethereum. We can get data embedded into blockchain via explorer using a web browser, according to the experiment in Sect. 6. It means that it is possible to get embedded data via HTTP/HTTPS, whose communication is allowed in many companies. For an attacker using C&C, blockchain with flexible space is an advantage.

In the study [1,2], they built a botnet using the Bitcoin network by Bitcoin SPV client. As mentioned above, the technique that uses Explorer website can use HTTP/HTTPS to communicate with C&C server. In the past, malwares that use blogs and social media [6] and those that use GitHub [17] for C&C have been reported. The techniques that use Explorer can be easily implemented on such malwares.

It is important for attackers to not be involved in the migration of data from the blockchain to the Explorer website. As stated in Sect. 6, attackers access the blockchain network while embedding data into the blockchain. However, when bots receive the data, they independently access the Explorer website. This implies that C&C technique using blockchain Explorer is effective for an attack because it is difficult to link a bot to an attacker.

Listing 1.1. Example of contract with hexdump of a file

```
1    pragma solidity ^0.5.0;
2
3    contract Test {
4        function testfunc() public pure returns(bytes memory){
5            bytes memory data = hex"<hexdump of a file>";
6            return data;
7        }
8    }
```

7.3 Possibility of Wrapping Arbitrary Binary in a Contract

Unfavorable data can be embedded into blockchain owing to flexibility. Hence, as a simple countermeasure for unfavorable transactions in blockchain network, we can decrease the flexibility of the space used for embedding data.

Most files found in the studies described in Sect. 5 are embedded in form of hexdump. In Ethereum, transactions that have hexdump of files in their *init* area can be rejected by allowing only valid data as EVM code.

However, the source code can be successfully compiled into an EVM code even if it is embedded hexdump, like the Solidity source code showed in Listing 1.1. This implied that we can make a valid EVM code containing arbitrary hexdump of files. Therefore, it is difficult to take measures against embedding malicious data into a blockchain.

7.4 Countermeasure Against Blockchain Poisoning

As one of the countermeasures against content insertion, *mandatory minimal fees* to penalize large transactions is proposed [14]. Certainly, economic costs are effective because Proof of Work has never been broken except for some specific situations such as the decrease of hash rate. However, the proposed method [14] has a drawback due to a lack of correlation between the size and maliciousness of the data.

The following can be considered as a new naive countermeasure against blockchain poisoning attack. The countermeasure adopt mandatory minimal fee determined by its similarity with other contracts. The fee is calculated using all contracts which are deployed on the blockchain in the past and it becomes larger when there are no similar contracts. As the number of similar contracts increases, the minimal fee decreases.

In this mechanism, the cost for sending a transaction depends on the number of similar contracts instead of the size of transactions. Because the number of such malicious transactions is small in the blockchain, the attacker can be forced to pay large costs.

Previous study [10] demonstrated that there are similar contracts that are actually used owing to some reasons such as reusing source codes of contracts. In a blockchain network, the content of blocks are determined by consensus between the network participants. However, it is generally difficult to take a consensus if a file is benign or malicious. Therefore, we demonstrated the important approach to obtain consensus using the similarity of contracts as one of the solutions to the problem.

8   Conclusions

To assess the risk of blockchain poisoning attack, we analyzed the Ethereum blockchain to examine the actual situation, verified the ease of attack using our experimental blockchain environments.

We confirmed that 154 files were embedded on the Ethereum blockchain, including some malicious files. Furthermore, we showed that blockchain poisoning can be easily performed using web browsers and one-liner shell command. We indicated the possibility of C&C technique using the Ethereum blockchain, which is different from previous methods [1,2]. The method can be easily applied to existing malwares because they use HTTP/HTTPS protocol to receive commands from botmaster.

Acknowledgement. This work was partly supported by the Grant-in-Aid for Scientific Research (B) (19H04107).

References

1. Ali, S.T., McCorry, P., Lee, P.H.-J., Hao, F.: ZombieCoin: powering next-generation botnets with bitcoin. In: Brenner, M., Christin, N., Johnson, B., Rohloff, K. (eds.) FC 2015. LNCS, vol. 8976, pp. 34–48. Springer, Heidelberg (2015). https://doi.org/10.1007/978-3-662-48051-9_3
2. Ali, S.T., McCorry, P., Lee, P.H.J., Hao, F.: ZombieCoin 2.0: managing next-generation botnets using bitcoin. Int. J. Inf. Secur. **17**(4), 411–422 (2018)
3. Atzei, N., Bartoletti, M., Cimoli, T.: A survey of attacks on ethereum smart contracts (SoK). In: Maffei, M., Ryan, M. (eds.) POST 2017. LNCS, vol. 10204, pp. 164–186. Springer, Heidelberg (2017). https://doi.org/10.1007/978-3-662-54455-6_8
4. Azaria, A., Ekblaw, A., Vieira, T., Lippman, A.: MedRec: using blockchain for medical data access and permission management. In: 2016 2nd International Conference on Open and Big Data (OBD), pp. 25–30. IEEE (2016)
5. Cheddad, A., Condell, J., Curran, K., Mc Kevitt, P.: Digital image steganography: survey and analysis of current methods. Sig. Process. **90**(3), 727–752 (2010)
6. Chen, J.: Blackgear cyberespionage campaign resurfaces, abuses social media for c&c communication (2018). https://blog.trendmicro.com/trendlabs-security-intelligence/blackgear-cyberespionage-campaign-resurfaces-abuses-social-media-for-cc-communication/. Accessed 13 Dec 2018
7. Dorri, A., Kanhere, S.S., Jurdak, R., Gauravaram, P.: Blockchain for IoT security and privacy: the case study of a smart home. In: 2017 IEEE International Conference on Pervasive Computing and Communications Workshops (PerCom Workshops), pp. 618–623. IEEE (2017)

8. Fromknecht, C., Velicanu, D.: CertCoin: a NameCoin based decentralized authentication system 6. 857 class project (2014)
9. Hasanova, H., Baek, U., Shin, M.G., Cho, K., Kim, M.S.: A survey on blockchain cybersecurity vulnerabilities and possible countermeasures. Int. J. Netw. Manage. **29**(2), 2060 (2019)
10. Kiffer, L., Levin, D., Mislove, A.: Analyzing ethereum's contract topology. In: Proceedings of the Internet Measurement Conference 2018, pp. 494–499. ACM (2018)
11. Kolbitsch, C., Comparetti, P.M., Kruegel, C., Kirda, E., Zhou, X.y., Wang, X.: Effective and efficient malware detection at the end host. In: USENIX Security Symposium, vol. 4, pp. 351–366 (2009)
12. Laurenson, T.: Performance analysis of file carving tools. In: Janczewski, L.J., Wolfe, H.B., Shenoi, S. (eds.) SEC 2013. IAICT, vol. 405, pp. 419–433. Springer, Heidelberg (2013). https://doi.org/10.1007/978-3-642-39218-4_31
13. Li, X., Jiang, P., Chen, T., Luo, X., Wen, Q.: A survey on the security of blockchain systems. Future Gener. Comput. Syst. (2017)
14. Matzutt, R., Henze, M., Ziegeldorf, J.H., Hiller, J., Wehrle, K.: Thwarting unwanted blockchain content insertion. In: 2018 IEEE International Conference on Cloud Engineering (IC2E), pp. 364–370, April 2018
15. Matzutt, R., et al.: A quantitative analysis of the impact of arbitrary blockchain content on bitcoin. In: Meiklejohn, S., Sako, K. (eds.) FC 2018. LNCS, vol. 10957, pp. 420–438. Springer, Heidelberg (2018). https://doi.org/10.1007/978-3-662-58387-6_23
16. Nakamoto, S., et al.: Bitcoin: A Peer-to-Peer Electronic Cash System (2008)
17. Pernet, C.: Winnti abuses GitHub for C&C communications (2017). https://blog.trendmicro.com/trendlabs-security-intelligence/winnti-abuses-github/. Accessed 13 Dec 2018
18. Song, D., et al.: BitBlaze: a new approach to computer security via binary analysis. In: Sekar, R., Pujari, A.K. (eds.) ICISS 2008. LNCS, vol. 5352, pp. 1–25. Springer, Heidelberg (2008). https://doi.org/10.1007/978-3-540-89862-7_1
19. Symantec: W32.duqu the precursor to the next stuxnet (2011). https://www.symantec.com/content/en/us/enterprise/media/security_response/whitepapers/w32_duqu_the_precursor_to_the_next_stuxnet.pdf
20. Szabo, N.: Smart contracts: building blocks for digital free markets. Extropy, no. 16 (1996). http://www.fon.hum.uva.nl/rob/Courses/InformationInSpeech/CDROM/Literature/LOTwinterschool2006/szabo.best.vwh.net/smart_contracts_2.html
21. Wohrer, M., Zdun, U.: Smart contracts: security patterns in the ethereum ecosystem and solidity. In: 2018 International Workshop on Blockchain Oriented Software Engineering (IWBOSE), pp. 2–8. IEEE (2018)
22. Wood, G.: Ethereum: a secure decentralised generalised transaction ledger. Byzantium version (2018). https://ethereum.github.io/yellowpaper/paper.pdf. Accessed 3 Dec 2018
23. Yin, H., Song, D., Egele, M., Kruegel, C., Kirda, E.: Panorama: capturing system-wide information flow for malware detection and analysis. In: Proceedings of the 14th ACM Conference on Computer and Communications Security, pp. 116–127. ACM (2007)

A Template-Based Method
for the Generation of Attack Trees

Jeremy Bryans[1], Lin Shen Liew[2], Hoang Nga Nguyen[1(✉)],
Giedre Sabaliauskaite[2], Siraj Shaikh[1], and Fengjun Zhou[2]

[1] Coventry University, Coventry, UK
{ac1126,ac1222,aa8135}@coventry.ac.uk
[2] Singapore University of Technology and Design, Singapore, Singapore
{linshen_liew,giedre,fengjun_zhou}@sutd.edu.sg

Abstract. Attack trees are used in cybersecurity analysis to give an
analyst a view of all the ways in which an attack can be carried out.
Attack trees can become large, and developing them by hand can be
tedious and error-prone. In this paper the automated generation of attack
trees is considered. The method proposed is based on a library of attack
templates – parameterisable patterns of attacks such as denial of service
or eavesdropping – and that also uses an abstract model of the network
architecture under attack. A pseudocode implementation of the method
is also presented. The example application given is from the automotive
domain and using an architecture consisting of linked CAN networks –
a network configuration found in virtually every current vehicle.

Keywords: Attack trees · Generation · Automotive · Cybersecurity

1 Introduction

Attack trees are a well-known graphical model for capturing and analysing
attacks on a system [12]. Their intuitive simplicity and ability to succinctly capture all attacks on a system have made them popular in many domains, including
SCADA systems [2], ATM security [4], the analysis of insider attacks [11] and
the automotive domain [1]. They give an analyst an overview of all the known
ways in which an attack can be carried out, and show how single attack steps
combine and build into complex attacks.

Attack trees are directed acyclic graphs with a single end node, which is the
goal of the attack. To construct an attack an analyst considers all the steps
which would immediately lead to the goal of the attack being realised. These
become the subgoals, or intermediate leaves of the tree. Each of these leaves is
now considered as a (sub)goal, and the steps that would lead to it's realisation
are identified. The process is recursively repeated until the branches of the tree
cannot be further expanded. This process can be time-consuming, especially
for large attack trees [4] and several researchers have therefore investigated the
automatic generation of the trees [5,6,10,13].

© IFIP International Federation for Information Processing 2020
Published by Springer Nature Switzerland AG 2020
M. Laurent and T. Giannetsos (Eds.): WISTP 2019, LNCS 12024, pp. 155–165, 2020.
https://doi.org/10.1007/978-3-030-41702-4_10

Within the literature, two main approaches to automating the generation or synthesis of attack trees have developed: (i) model transformation and (ii) semantic-based construction. In the model transformation approach, a target system and attackers are modelled using either graphical [6] or formal [13] presentations as input. The desired target of the attackers is identified, and from this the tree root from which the tree construction starts is established. In [6], system models contain actors, processes, items and locations, and connections between these elements to the desired target are utilised to develop the attack tree. Similarly, systems and attackers in [13] are modelled in a process calculus as input. They are first transformed into propositional formulae. Given a target location, these formulae are utilised to construct attack trees by means of backwards-chaining search. While techniques in the model transformation approach are automated, they suffer from lacking a basis for correctness. There is no rigorous relation between generated attack trees and the attacks implicitly implied from input models. In order to fill this gap, [10] proposed ATSyRA, an interactive tool for synthesising attack trees from attack graphs. First, ATSyRA generates all attack paths from the input graphs by model checking. Then, users are required to specify a refinement relation between a set of actions to recursively refine attack paths to eventually construct an attack tree. While ATSyRA establishes the semantic connection between the constructed tree and the input model via attack paths, it is not fully automated. To overcome this shortcoming, [8] introduced an approach to extending an existing attack tree by means of a library of attack trees. The extension is enabled by adding logical preconditions and assertions to tree nodes. Then an attack tree from the library can be attached to a node of the attack tree to be extended if certain relations between the preconditions and assertions are satisfied. To this end, logical reasoning must be employed. Similarly, [5] has proposed a different approach which is based on the formal semantics of attack trees [7]. To this end, the synthesis problem becomes that of generating attack trees from a given semantics, i.e., a set of attack traces. It is reduced to a biclique problem, which is known to be NP-complete, and a heuristic algorithm is suggested for the construction.

In this paper we propose a method for the generation of attack trees based on *templates*: abstracted and parameterizable known patterns of attack, and represent steps such as spoofing of one node by another, or eavesdropping on traffic between two nodes, which together can be built up into an attack. The method takes as input a description of the architecture of the network that is being attacked and the set of templates.

These networks are modelled by graphs consisting of nodes and connectivity information. Each node represents a component of the network. The network information required includes the *access points*. These are the nodes within the network that are exposed to attackers outside the network. We present a method that applies each element from the library of attack patterns to the graphical network model in order to form attack trees. We give as well an algorithm for our method. Given a network and a set of templates, the algorithm can generate all possible attacks conforming to the template library.

The contributions in this paper are the template-based method for the generation of attack trees and it's algorithm, and the automotive example demonstrating the method. The paper proceeds as follows: Sect. 2 begins with an introduction to automotive communication networks and attack trees. In Sect. 3 we give the description of the template-based methodology for generating attack trees, and in Sect. 4 we give the pseudo-code description of the generation algorithm and briefly present the results of our automotive example.

2   Background

2.1   Automotive Communication Network

An automotive communication network facilitates the communication between electronic control units (ECUs) within a vehicle. It is usually divided into subnetworks of related ECUs. Depending on the communication requirements of each subnetwork (such as bandwidth, time, etc.), different network types can be employed such as CAN, CANFD, FLEXRAY, LIN, ETHERNET, etc. These networks can be interconnected via Gateway ECUs which will coordinate the traffic between them.

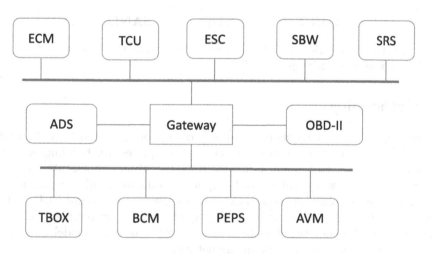

Fig. 1. An automotive internal network.

In this paper, we model an automotive communication network as a tuple (NET, ECU, AP, net) where NET is a finite set of subnetworks, ECU is a finite set of ECUs, $AP \subseteq ECU$ identifies ECUs that are accessible to attackers (such as OBD-II or TBOX), and net : NET $\rightarrow \wp(ECU)$ is a mapping to determine to which subnetwork an ECU belongs. For example, the network in Fig. 1 is modelled by $M_f = (NET_f, ECU_f, AP_f, net_f)$ where:

- $\mathrm{NET}_f = \{\mathrm{CAN}_1, \mathrm{CAN}_2, \mathrm{CAN}_3, \mathrm{CAN}_4\}$;
- $\mathrm{ECU}_f = \{\mathrm{ECM, TCU, ESC, SBW, SRS, ADS, Gateway, OBD\text{-}II, TBOX,}$ BCM, PEPS, AVM$\}$;
- $\mathrm{AP}_f = \{ \mathrm{OBD\text{-}II, TBOX}\}$;
- $\mathrm{net}_f = \{\mathrm{CAN}_1 \mapsto \{\mathrm{ECM, TCU, ESC, SBW, SRS, Gateway}\}, \mathrm{CAN}_2 \mapsto$ $\{\mathrm{TBOX, BCM, PEPS, AVM, Gateway}\}, \mathrm{CAN}_3 \mapsto \{\mathrm{ADS, Gateway}\},$ $\mathrm{CAN}_4 \mapsto \{\mathrm{OBD\text{-}II, Gateway}\}\}$.

2.2 Attack Trees

Attack trees contain a goal (the root of the tree), a set of sub-goals, structured using the operators conjunction (**AND**) and disjunction (**OR**), and leaf nodes, which represent atomic attacker actions. The **AND** nodes are complete when all child nodes are carried out and the **OR** nodes are complete when at least one child node is complete.

Extensions have been proposed using **Sequential AND** (or **SAND**) [7]. We follow the formalisation of attack trees given in [7,9]. If $\mathbb{A}$ is the set of possible atomic attacker actions, the elements of the attack tree $\mathbb{T}$ are $\mathbb{A} \cup \{\mathbf{OR}, \mathbf{AND}, \mathbf{SAND}\}$, and an attack tree is generated by the following grammar, where $a \in \mathbb{A}$:

$$t ::= a \mid \mathbf{OR}(t, \ldots, t) \mid \mathbf{AND}(t, \ldots, t) \mid \mathbf{SAND}(t, \ldots, t)$$

Attack tree semantics have been defined by interpreting the attack tree as a set of series-parallel (SP) graphs [7].

3 Methodology

We develop a method to generate attack trees from a network model and a library of attack tree templates. Attack tree templates are building-blocks to assemble an attack tree. Each template from the library represents an attack step within the network which can be applied to different subnetworks and/or ECUs. The adaptability of the attack to various subnetworks and ECUs can be captured by using variables within the template. When the templates are fully instantiated with concrete values from the sets of the network model, it provides a concrete example of an attack on the network.

For example, attacks on a communication network can be categorised into two passive or active attacks; eavesdropping and traffic analysis are two examples of passive attacks, while spoofing, replay and DoS (Denial of Service) are active attacks. This is captured in Fig. 2. Variables are used in all the leaves of this template which can be replaced by concrete values. Let us consider the leaf Eavesdrop X:NET. The variables X can be replaced by any value from the component NET of the network model. If we consider the network model M_f as depicted in Fig. 1, X can be replaced by CAN_1, CAN_2, CAN_3 or CAN_4.

The connectivity between ECUs within the network will be represented in attack tree templates using lists. When instantiated, a list of ECUs corresponds

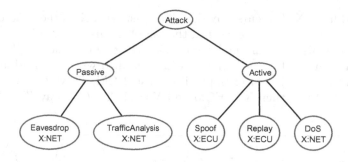

Fig. 2. An initial attack template tree.

to the ability to send data from the first ECU in the list to next one, then the next one, and so on until the data reaches the last ECU in the list. This means consecutive ECUs in the list must belong to the same subnetwork. Gateway ECUs may appear in the list to capture the connectivity between ECUs of different subnetworks. For example, if we consider the model M_f, a list of ECUs is [ECM, TCU, Gateway, TBOX] where ECM is connected to TCU and TCU to Gateway in CAN_1, and Gateway to TBOX in CAN_2.

The generation of attack trees starts with a specified template from the library. This template has no closed variables. The generation is carried out recursively. At each recursion, a leaf which may contain open variables is considered for expansion. When there are $n > 0$ assignments for the open variables, this leaf node is converted into an OR node with n children with each child corresponding to one assignment. The assignments are copies of the leaf node where the open variables are replaced by values. Each child is then replaced by a template from the library where the name of the template root matches the name of the child and the parameters of the root can be unified with the parameters of the child. The unification of the parameters will give rise to an assignment of closed variables of the template. The replacement of the child with the template will also replace all closed variables with the values from the assignment. This process is illustrated in Fig. 3. A white circle represents a node with variables while a black one states that its variables have been replaced with values by some assignment.

A special case of assignments is for unassigned lists. An assignment for an unassigned list [X .. Y] is a list of constants from NET and ECU. The start and the end of the list must satisfy any condition for X and Y. For example, consider the network M_f. An unassigned list [ECM..Y:AP] must be assigned to a list of ECUs from ECM to an ECU that is an access point, i.e, in AP_f. There are two ECUs that Y can be assigned to: OBD-II and TBOX. Then, one of the list of connected ECUs that [ECM..Y:AP] can be assigned to is [ECM, TCM, Gateway, TBOX] where they are consecutively connected and the last ECU (TBOX) is an access point. Obviously, this is not the only assignment. Two of other candidates to assign this list to are [ECM, Gateway, TBOX] and [ECM, TCM, Gateway, OBD-II].

Assigned lists [X|Y] recursively describe a list with X as the head of the list and Y as the remaining elements, i.e., the tail of the list. [] stands for an empty list. An assigned list [X|Y] normally appears at the root of some templates. When it is unified with a list of elements, X will be unified with the head and Y will be unified with the tail. For example, if the list [ECM, TCM, Gateway, TBOX] is unified with [X|Y], then X = ECM and Y = [TCM, Gateway, TBOX].

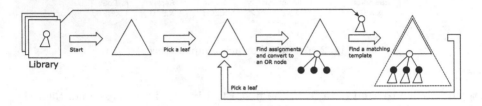

Fig. 3. Methodology.

3.1 Attack Tree Templates

More formally, nodes in an attack tree template may contain parameters which are made of variables, list terms or constants (i.e., elements of NET and ECU of a network model). Variables can be instantiated with node names. Let N be a set of names for tree nodes, V a set of variables and $C = \text{NET} \cup \text{ECU}$ a set of constants. The syntax of an attack tree template is defined below:

$$
\begin{aligned}
tree ::= \ &leaf\text{-}node \ | \\
&tree\text{-}node\mathbf{AND}(tree, \dots, tree) \ | \\
&tree\text{-}node\mathbf{SAND}(tree, \dots, tree) \ | \\
&tree\text{-}node\mathbf{OR}(tree, \dots, tree) \\
leaf\text{-}node ::= \ &n \, parameter^* \\
tree\text{-}node ::= \ &n \, parameter^* \\
parameter ::= \ &variable \ | \ list \ | \ c \\
variable ::= \ &X[\text{``}:\text{''}type][/Y[\text{``}:\text{''}\text{NET}]][\#Z[\text{``}:\text{''}\text{ECU}]] \\
type ::= \ &\text{NET} \ | \ \text{ECU} \ | \ \text{AP} \\
list ::= \ &unassigned\text{-}list \ | \ assigned\text{-}list \\
unassigned\text{-}list ::= \ &[\,variable \ \text{``..''} \ variable\,] \\
assigned\text{-}list ::= \ &[\,variable \ \text{``|''} \ variable\,]
\end{aligned}
$$

where $X, Y \in V$, $n \in N$ and $c \in C$.

Informally, an attack tree template is an attack tree in which each node contains a name and possibly a list of parameters. A parameter can be a variable, a constant (node names) or a list of variables and constants. Variables occurring in the root node of an attack tree template are called closed variables. They may reoccur in the descendants of the root. Once root variables are instantiated, their values are propagated down to the descendant nodes correspondingly. In contrast to closed variables, variables in a template that do not appear in its root are called open.

We postulate the following conditions on the occurrence of variables on an attack tree template:

- Assigned lists can only appear at the root;
- Open variables can only appear at the leaves;
- Unassigned lists can only appear at the leaves.

The assignment of values to variables can be restricted with types, by using the condition ": type". This condition restricts a variable to be instantiated with a constant of type NET, ECU or AP. For example, consider the network in Fig. 1. Given X:NET, X can only be assigned to CAN_1, CAN_2, CAN_3 or CAN_4. Given X:ECU, X can only be assigned to ECM, TCU, Gateway, OBD-II, BCM or TBOX. AP stands for access points OBD-II and TBOX, i.e., places where attackers can have cyber access to the network. Then, X:AP says that X can only be assigned to OBD-II or TBOX. A further restriction can be introduced to the assignment by "/ Y : NET". Once Y is instantiated with a constant of type NET, "X / Y:NET" states that X can only be assigned to an ECU within the subnetwork Y. For example, " X / Y:NET" where Y is CAN_1 means that X can only be assigned to ECM, TCU, or Gateway. Finally, one can require that X is not assigned to an ECU by using the restriction $\#Z$ where Z is of type ECU. Once Z is instantiated with an ECU, X cannot be assigned to that ECU.

3.2   A Simple Example

We illustrate our method on an automotive network, depicted in Fig. 4(a). It contains two CAN buses: the powertrain, consisting of three ECUs: ECM (Engine Control Module), TCU (Transmission Control Unit) and GW (the Gateway) and the telematics bus, containing two ECUs: TBox (Telematics Box) accessible to attackers and the same GW, which connects the two buses.

This network is modelled by a tuple $(NET_m, ECU_m, AP_m, net_f)$ where:

- $NET_m = \{CAN_1, CAN_2\}$;
- $ECU_m = \{ECM, TCU, GW, TBOX\}$;
- $AP_m = \{TBOX\}$; and
- $net = \{CAN_1 \mapsto \{ECM, TCU, GW\}, CAN_2 \mapsto \{GW, TBOX\}\}$.

We then consider a library of attack tree templates that focus on how to compromise ECM. The library consists of two templates, depicted in Fig. 4(b) and (c). The template (b) describes a compromise attack on ECM. Essentially, this attack can be realised by starting compromising an ECU to which attackers have access to (Z:AP). Then, the compromise attack can be propagated to the next ECU connected to a compromised one until we reach ECM. This is described by the unassigned list [Z:AP .. ECM]. The template (b) is also specified as the start tree of the generation process. The template (c) describes how compromise attack can be carried out from the first ECU to the last in the list [Z|L]. Note that Z is the head of the list and L is the tail. On Fig. 4(c) the arrow between the edges leading to the two nodes indicates that both nodes must be carried

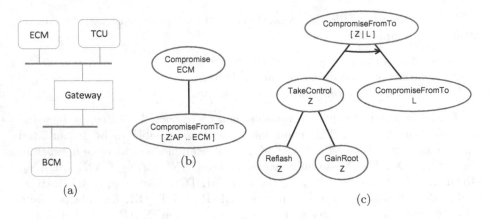

Fig. 4. The compromise attack template tree.

out in order (a **SAND** node). Not joining the edges in Fig. 4(c) signifies an **OR** node, and joining edges with a line (rather than an arrow) signifies that the root node is an **AND** node.

This is done by taking control of the ECU Z at the head of the list and then recursively taking control of the rest of the list. Taking control can be done by either re-flashing or gaining root access to Z.

Initially, the construction starts with the template (b) in Fig. 4. The leaf of this expanded tree "CompromiseFromTo [Z:AP .. ECM]" is now considered for further expansion. It has an open parameter which is an unassigned-list. There are two possible assignments for it; one is [ECM, GW, TBOX] and the other is [ECM, TCU, GW, TBOX]. However, the second list is considered redundant as ECM is directly connected and can communicate with GW without using TCU. This is derived from the nature of CAN bus communication where ECUs on the same bus are directly connected with each other. Therefore, the leaf is appended with one child corresponding to the assignment of [Z:AP .. ECM] to [ECM, GW, TBOX]. This child is then expanded by the template (c) in Fig. 4. This template is used several times depending on the length of the list. Finally, we obtain the tree[1] which has height 9 and contains 17 nodes.

4   Implementation

We now present the algorithm used to implement our generation method (Algorithm 1.) The inputs are (1) a model of the network structured as in Sect. 2 and (2) a library of attack tree templates and it produces an attack tree as the output.

The algorithm starts with the initial tree InitTree from the input library in line 2. It then loops as long as there is a leaf on the constructed tree and a

---

[1] The tree can be viewed at https://tinyurl.com/s55u7qh.

Algorithm 1. Generating attack trees

```
 1: function BUILDTREE(Model, Library)
 2:     tree ← InitTree ∈ Library
 3:     while ∃leaf ∈ tree, subtree ∈ Library: leaf matches subtree do
 4:         assignments ← GETASSIGNMENTS(leaf, Model)
 5:         Turn leaf into an "or" nodes
 6:         for each assignment of assignments do
 7:             assignedLeaf ← APPLY(assignment, leaf)
 8:             unification ← UNIFY(subtree, assignedLeaf)
 9:             add APPLY(unification, subtree) as a child of leaf
10:         end for
11:     end while
12:     return tree
13: end function
```

---

template, namely subtree, from the library that can be matched. In this loop, all assignments for the variables of the leaf are first computed in line 4. Then for each of the assignments, a unification of subtree and the application of the assignment to the leaf is calculated in line 8. Then the subtree to which the unification is applied is added as a child of the leaf in line 9. Note that the leaf is now converted into an "or" node in line 5. The loop at line 3 will continue until no more leaves and matching templates can be found.

The function APPLY replaces attack tree template variables with the corresponding values in the input assignment, from the root to the leaves recursively. UNIFY in line 8 is a standard unification procedure. It tries to unify the root of subtree with the leaf to which the considered assignment is applied. It yields a unifier which can be considered as an assignment to the whole subtree.

GETVARASSIGNMENTS generates Cartesian product of all assignments for the variables and unassigned lists in the input leaf.

Experiment

We briefly present the experimental result of our implementation on two examples, implemented in Python[2] and carried out on a PC with a processor Intel Core i5-4590 3.3 GHz with 8GB of memory.

We first rerun the mini example described in Sect. 3.2 which confirms the output tree obtained in Sect. 3.2. Using Python "cProfile" module, the run-time of this experiment is 0.025s and uses 19739 function calls. The second experiment[4] is to generate an attack tree for the automotive network M_f as depicted in Fig. 1. It consists of 4 CAN bus networks with 12 ECUs. The template library contains 21 attack tree templates, including the initial tree as depicted in Fig. 2. In total, the run-time is 0.292s, using 574133 function calls. The generated attack tree[3] has 3756 nodes and of height 19. An attack example extracted from the tree is an eavesdropping attack carried out at a compromised TCU.

---

[2] The source code can be downloaded from https://tinyurl.com/uoptgfb.
[3] The tree can be viewed at https://tinyurl.com/vzscydf.

Access was gained at the TBOX, then the gateway was compromised followed by the TCU:
GainRoot(TBOX) → Reflash(GW) → Reflash(TCU) → CollectDataFrom(TCU).

5 Conclusion

In this paper, we have proposed a practical method for identifying all the possible attacks on a known system. We use a library of templates of the atomic attack steps that can be taken against components in the system and give an algorithm for building these into a tree capturing all the attacks. Future steps will include adapting to other types of networks including wireless and ethernet, and also mixed networks which include networks running under different protocols. We also plan to integrate the automated attack tree generation work presented here into work on model-based security test-case generation which currently assumes the existence of the attack tree such as [3].

References

1. Bryans, J., Nguyen, H., Shaikh, S.: Attack defense trees with sequential conjunction. In: 19th IEEE HASE, pp. 247–252 (2019)
2. Byres, E.J., Franz, M., Miller, D.: The use of attack trees in assessing vulnerabilities in SCADA systems. In: IEEE Conference IISW (2004)
3. Cheah, M., Nguyen, H.N., Bryans, J., Shaikh, S.A.: Formalising systematic security evaluations using attack trees for automotive applications. In: Hancke, G.P., Damiani, E. (eds.) WISTP 2017. LNCS, vol. 10741, pp. 113–129. Springer, Cham (2018). https://doi.org/10.1007/978-3-319-93524-9_7
4. Fraile, M., Ford, M., Gadyatskaya, O., Kumar, R., Stoelinga, M., Trujillo-Rasua, R.: Using attack-defense trees to analyze threats and countermeasures in an ATM: a case study. In: Horkoff, J., Jeusfeld, M.A., Persson, A. (eds.) PoEM 2016. LNBIP, vol. 267, pp. 326–334. Springer, Cham (2016). https://doi.org/10.1007/978-3-319-48393-1_24
5. Gadyatskaya, O., Jhawar, R., Mauw, S., Trujillo-Rasua, R., Willemse, T.A.C.: Refinement-aware generation of attack trees. In: Livraga, G., Mitchell, C. (eds.) STM 2017. LNCS, vol. 10547, pp. 164–179. Springer, Cham (2017). https://doi.org/10.1007/978-3-319-68063-7_11
6. Ivanova, M.G., Probst, C.W., Hansen, R.R., Kammüller, F.: Transforming graphical system models to graphical attack models. In: Mauw, S., Kordy, B., Jajodia, S. (eds.) GraMSec 2015. LNCS, vol. 9390, pp. 82–96. Springer, Cham (2016). https://doi.org/10.1007/978-3-319-29968-6_6
7. Jhawar, R., Kordy, B., Mauw, S., Radomirović, S., Trujillo-Rasua, R.: Attack trees with sequential conjunction. In: Federrath, H., Gollmann, D. (eds.) SEC 2015. IAICT, vol. 455, pp. 339–353. Springer, Cham (2015). https://doi.org/10.1007/978-3-319-18467-8_23
8. Jhawar, R., Lounis, K., Mauw, S., Ramírez-Cruz, Y.: Semi-automatically augmenting attack trees using an annotated attack tree library. In: Katsikas, S.K., Alcaraz, C. (eds.) STM 2018. LNCS, vol. 11091, pp. 85–101. Springer, Cham (2018). https://doi.org/10.1007/978-3-030-01141-3_6

9. Mauw, S., Oostdijk, M.: Foundations of attack trees. In: Won, D.H., Kim, S. (eds.) ICISC 2005. LNCS, vol. 3935, pp. 186–198. Springer, Heidelberg (2006). https://doi.org/10.1007/11734727_17

10. Pinchinat, S., Acher, M., Vojtisek, D.: ATSyRa: an integrated environment for synthesizing attack trees. In: Mauw, S., Kordy, B., Jajodia, S. (eds.) GraMSec 2015. LNCS, vol. 9390, pp. 97–101. Springer, Cham (2016). https://doi.org/10.1007/978-3-319-29968-6_7

11. Ray, I., Poolsapassit, N.: Using attack trees to identify malicious attacks from authorized insiders. In: di Vimercati, S.C., Syverson, P., Gollmann, D. (eds.) ESORICS 2005. LNCS, vol. 3679, pp. 231–246. Springer, Heidelberg (2005). https://doi.org/10.1007/11555827_14

12. Schneier, B.: Attack trees. Dr Dobbs J. (1999)

13. Vigo, R., Nielson, F., Nielson, H.R.: Automated generation of attack trees. In: 2014 IEEE 27th Computer Security Foundations Symposium, pp. 337–350. IEEE (2014)

Cybersecurity

Analysis of QUIC Session Establishment and Its Implementations

Eva Gagliardi[1] and Olivier Levillain[2]([⊠])

[1] French Ministry of the Armies, Paris, France
[2] Télécom SudParis, Institut Polytechnique de Paris, Évry, France
olivier.levillain@telecom-sudparis.eu

Abstract. In the recent years, the major web companies have been working to improve the user experience and to secure the communications between their users and the services they provide. QUIC is such an initiative, and it is currently being designed by the IETF. In a nutshell, QUIC originally intended to merge features from TCP/SCTP, TLS 1.3 and HTTP/2 into one big protocol. The current specification proposes a more modular definition, where each feature (transport, cryptography, application, packet reemission) are defined in separate internet drafts.

We studied the QUIC internet drafts related to the transport and cryptographic layers, from version 18 to version 23, and focused on the connection establishment with existing implementations.

We propose a first implementation of QUIC connection establishment using Scapy, which allowed us to forge a critical opinion of the current specification, with a special focus on the induced difficulties in the implementation. With our simple stack, we also tested the behaviour of the existing implementations with regards to security-related constraints (explicit or implicit) from the internet drafts. This gives us an interesting view of the state of QUIC implementations.

Keywords: QUIC · Secure communications · Protocol implementation

1 Introduction

In the recent years, the major web companies have been working to improve the user experience and to secure the communications between their users and the services they provide. One of this effort was QUIC, proposed by Google in 2012. Another change in parallel was the standardization of TLS 1.3[1], which both achieves better performance, with a faster session establishment, and better security, since only up-to-date and secure primitives were kept in this new version of the protocol.

However, even with TLS 1.3 and HTTP/2, the TLS/HTTP combination is still considered a bottleneck by some actors. So the development of QUIC went

---

[1] Actually, TLS 1.3 borrowed several ideas from the initial QUIC design.

© IFIP International Federation for Information Processing 2020
Published by Springer Nature Switzerland AG 2020
M. Laurent and T. Giannetsos (Eds.): WISTP 2019, LNCS 12024, pp. 169–184, 2020.
https://doi.org/10.1007/978-3-030-41702-4_11

on, and Google proposed their protocol to the IETF for a standardization. A working group was formed and since 2016, 23 draft versions of the protocol have been discussed. The original protocol has since been renamed gQUIC (for Google QUIC). In the remainder of this article, QUIC refers to the IETF version of the protocol, which differs significantly from gQUIC. Indeed, the IETF version offers a more modular protocol than the original proposal. QUIC design relies on the following architecture:

- A transport layer is defined in the `quic-transport` internet draft [4] over UDP. This way, QUIC avoids the delay induced by the TCP three-way handshake, but obviously has to handle packet loss and reordering.
- During the session establishment, cryptographic parameters and keys are negotiated using TLS 1.3 Handshake message. The way QUIC embeds and interacts with TLS is described in the `quic-tls` internet draft [11].
- On top of the transport layer, a new version of the HTTP protocol is being proposed, HTTP/3, which will be designed for QUIC [2].

The working group also wrote several peripheral internet drafts to specify generic properties for QUIC [7,10] or to give details on specific features [3,6]. In this article, we focus on the establishment phase described by `quic-transport` and `quic-tls` drafts.

Section 2 describes the QUIC protocol and Sect. 3 details the protection mechanism used to encrypt QUIC packets. For our study, we implemented parts of the protocol with Scapy; Sect. 4 presents the challenges we had to face to interact with existing QUIC stacks. Using our tool, we ran some tests to study the behaviour of public servers with regards to security-related constraints (explicit or implicit) from the internet drafts; Sect. 5 describes the test bench while Sect. 6 contains the obtained results. Related work is presented in Sect. 7 before our conclusion.

2   QUIC in a Nutshell

The message flow of a typical QUIC connection is given in Fig. 1. First, the client sends an Initial packet, which includes a TLS 1.3 ClientHello. If the enclosed (QUIC and TLS) parameters are acceptable for the server, it answers with an Initial packet (including the TLS ServerHello). This message is followed by a Handshake packet including the rest of the TLS server messages (in particular the messages related to server authentication). The handshake ends with a message from the client. Then, application data can be exchanged using so-called 1-RTT packets. The three phases, corresponding to different packet types (Initial, Handshake, 1-RTT) correspond to the three cryptographic epochs used in TLS 1.3 (cleartext messages, protection using Handshake secrets, protection using Traffic secrets), with the notable exception that Initial packets are actually encrypted using publicly-available data (we explore this in Sect. 3.1).

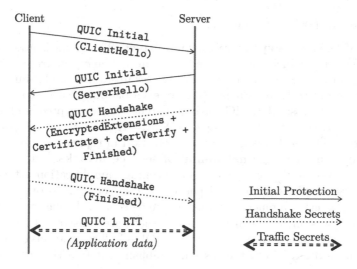

Fig. 1. A typical QUIC connection. The TLS 1.3 messages encapsulated in CRYPTO frames are given in parentheses. ACK and Padding frames have been left out for clarity.

2.1   QUIC Main Goals and Features

The QUIC protocol aims at providing an efficient and secure channel for application data. The efficiency properties include:

- **Low-latency session establishment.** As shown in Fig. 1, a typical connection allows the client to send application data to the server after only 1-RTT[2], whereas TLS 1.2 usually requires 3 (including the TCP handshake) and TLS 1.3 typically requires 2. Moreover, when connecting to a known server, a client can benefit from TLS 1.3 0-RTT feature to send application data in its first datagram (whereas TLS 1.3 still requires the RTT induced by the TCP handshake).
- **Stream multiplexing within a shared connection.** 1-RTT packets (as well as 0-RTT packets) include application data which are associated with streams. From the QUIC point of view, these streams are independant and can be multiplexed in QUIC packets using the client and server policies. This feature (also present in HTTP/2) solves the so-called Head of Line blocking issue from HTTP/1.1 pipelining where you must wait for the end of a request to emit the next one.
- **Low bandwidth usage.** The message design in QUIC was made to limit the bandwidth usage of the signaling and transport structures. For example, the draft uses several variable-length fields to limit their sizes. It also defines a padding scheme without any overhead (in case padding is not used).

---

[2] The session establishment latency is usually measured in RTTs (Round-Trip Time), that is the time required for the client to send a request and get an answer.

The security properties rely on:

- **State-of-the art cryptographic primitives**. This point is granted by the use of TLS 1.3, which was designed to clean up the cryptographic zoo accumulated for more than 20 years and only uses up-to-date and robust schemes.
- **Privacy-oriented measures**. QUIC offers a padding feature to avoid traffic analysis, and most of QUIC packet contents are encrypted and integrity-protected. However, as discussed in Sect. 3.1, even if Initial packets are encrypted, this mechanism offers no protection in typical attacker models.
- **Countermeasures against denial-of-service attacks**. Since QUIC uses UDP, it is essential not to enable or encourage amplification attacks where an attacker would send a small packet to a server with a forged source IP address, expecting a much larger answer to be sent to the victim. To this aim, before the session has been established, there are constraints on the size of the data the server can send. Moreover, QUIC allows the server to validate the client address before the session establishment (via the so-called Retry mechanism).

Another goal for the IETF working group is for QUIC to be compatible with the internet. In particular, the working group has to face so-called middleboxes, network devices that may intercept or block traffic at different places of the internet[3]. This goal led to the definition of several QUIC invariants [10], which should be taken into account by middleboxes. It also led to encrypting as much as possible, including Initial packets, to make a QUIC packet as hard as possible to grasp for a piece of equipment unaware of a particular version of QUIC.

3   QUIC Packet Protection

Almost every QUIC packet follows the steps described in Fig. 2 to encrypt both the payload and parts of the header. Moreover, since the header is fed as Associated Data to the AEAD (Authenticated Encryption with Associated Data) algorithms, both header and payload are integrity-protected.

To protect a packet, the header is first isolated from the payload. Then, the payload is encrypted using the negotiated AEAD. It takes as input the plaintext payload, a key derived from the key exchange, and a nonce (which comes from the XOR of the packet number from the header with an IV also derived from the key exchange).

Then, part of the payload is sampled and used as input to an encryption algorithm (in typical setups, the sample is 16 bit long and is encrypted with AES-ECB). The resulting ciphertext is used to mask (with a XOR) several fields of the header.

This convoluted procedure aims at protecting several fields in the header, such as the Packet Number.

---

[3] These middleboxes were a real problem during the definition of TLS 1.3 and the TLS working group actually decided to include optional dummy messages in the message flow to accomodate them.

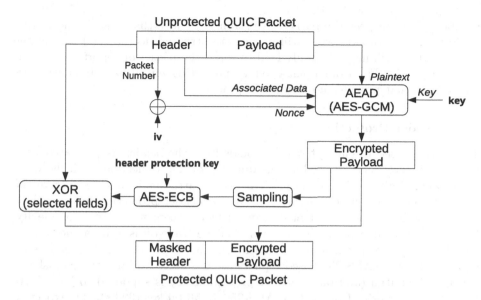

Fig. 2. QUIC packet protection mechanism. The inputs are the packet to protect, the key and the iv used to encrypt the payload, and the header protection key.

3.1 The Special Case of Initial Packets

There is however an egg-and-chicken problem with Initial packets, since they are supposed to be protected, but they contain the key exchange messages which should provide the keying material.

Actually, Initial packets must be protected, but the used parameters are defined by the RFC and one field from the client Initial packet:

- the AEAD used to protect the payload is AEAD_AES_128_GCM;
- the Initial secret (from which the key, the IV and the header protection key are derived), is derived from the so-called salt, a constant defined in the specification for a given version of the protocol, and the Destination Connection ID (DCID) embedded in the client Initial packet.

This DCID is actually only sent in the first packet, since each endpoint is responsible for the definition of its own Connection ID (which can be void). Thus, a server would typically answer with an Initial message with a freshly generated Source Connection ID and the DCID chosen by the client (in the Source Connection ID field of the first packet).

It must be clearly stated that this mechanism offers absolutely no protection from an attacker able to observe the first packet sent by the client. The draft indeed states that "[t]his provides protection against off-path attackers and robustness against QUIC version unaware middleboxes, but not against on-path attackers." The part about robustness refers to the idea that middleboxes unaware of a given QUIC version will not know the corresponding salt and will not be able to inspect the packet. We strongly believe that this is a naive reasoning, and that middleboxes will nevertheless try and decrypt and inspect the packet, which will most certainly lead to reject the packet or report an incident in typical cases. From our point of view, protecting initial packets is a useless mechanism that provides no security in practice.

3.2 Header Protection Keys

The hp key, used to encrypt selected fields from the header, is generated from the Initial secret, and "is used for the duration of the connection, with the value not changing after a key update." Thus, if an attacker is able to observe the client first packet, she can easily remove the header protection for the whole connection. Since the header protection includes a somewhat great complexity, for a very small benefit, we wonder whether the trade-off is well balanced.

Moreover, the specification is unclear on how to protect the header when a Chacha20- or an AES-256-based ciphersuite is selected during the handshake. Indeed, the initial (and only) header protection key is supposed to be 16-byte long. Yet, when using Chacha20 or AES-256, a 256-bit key (32 bytes) is expected. How should we reconcile this?

4   Implementation of the Initial Exchange

To better assess the reality of the message protection scheme, we implemented a portion of the QUIC protocol in Scapy, a Python framework used to dissect and forge packets for various network protocols [1]. Appendix A presents excerpts of our implementation.

What struck us during this work was the complexity of the mechanism, especially for the client initial packet. Indeed, protecting a packet corresponds to the following sequence (step 5 is only required for the first Initial packet):

1. build[4] the header from its fields;
2. build the payload from its fields;
3. pad the payload so the packet size is long enough;
4. report the payload length in the header to take the padding into account;
5. derive secrets from the version and the DCID;
6. derive the nonce from the IV (derived during the previous step) and the Packet Number (from the header);
7. encrypt the payload;
8. extract the sample;
9. encrypt the header.

The corresponding actions to unprotect a received packet are the following (step 2 is only needed to handle the client initial packet):

---

[4] We use the term *build* to describe the production of a byte string from the abstract structure manipulated by the rest of the application. It is the reverse operation of the binary parsing, and is sometimes called unparsing, dumping, or serializing.

1. parse the first fields of the header;
2. derive secrets from the version and the DCID;
3. extract the sample from the payload, assuming the Packet Number Length is 4 (more on this later);
4. decrypt the Packet Number Length;
5. infer the real offset/length of the Packet Number field and of the payload;
6. decrypt the Packet Number;
7. derive the nonce from the IV and the Packet Number;
8. decrypt the payload.

Even if these description are very detailed and even if some of our difficulties might be related to the way Scapy works, we strongly believe the sequence is inherently complex. Focusing on the protection procedure, it mixes classical building steps (steps 1 and 2), cryptographic operations (steps 5, 6, 7 and 9), but also raw manipulations of the binary packet (steps 3, 4 and 8[5]). Such manipulations are highly undesirable from a software engineering point of view, especially when they are intertwined with cryptographic or parsing/building steps.

Moreover, the manipulation steps are really hard to get right. For example, updating the payload length in the header requires identifying the offset of this specific field (which is not fixed) and encoding the new length using a variable length field: the precise length of the packet may be different after this update!

Another example of the complexity induced by the specification: since the Packet Number Length is encrypted, there is no way for the receiver to establish where the payload actually starts. This is why the sample required to encrypt the header is not computed from the start of the payload, but from what would be the first byte of the payload, assuming the Packet Number Length is 4 (this means a shift of 0 to 3 bytes).

Overall, the QUIC design forces developers to write so-called shotgun parsers, that is parsers which mix several kind of operations (parsing, input-validating code, processing code) [9], whereas a cleaner design would lead to a simpler and more straightforward implementation.

5   Test Description

To better understand the emerging QUIC ecosystem, we then looked at the existing implementations in the wild, as listed on the QUIC Working Group wiki[6]. During our study, which spanned over several months and followed drafts 18 to 23, we contacted around 20 public servers, corresponding to 16 different implementations. To investigate several configurations further, we also installed several implementations locally.

Table 1 describe the implementations we considered and their availability in October 2019. Out of the 16 public servers, 10 were available and up to date after the draft-23 publication.

---

[5] As a matter of fact, since header encryption (step 9) is not a straightforward XOR on a clearly delimited message, this could also be considered as a raw manipulation.
[6] https://github.com/quicwg/base-drafts/wiki/Implementations.

Table 1. List of the servers we probed during our study and their status in October 2019 when facing a draft-23 Client Initial packet. Two servers never answered to our stimuli during the whole study (`mozquic` and `QUICker`), which might be explained by the fact that their development seems to be on hold. For the results described in this article, we will only consider the 10 servers we could connect to properly during our latest tests (after draft-23 publication).

Implem.	Test server	Comments
aioqquic	quic.aiortc.org:443	**OK (draft-23)**
ats	quic.ogre.com:4443	**OK (draft-23)**
f5	204.134.187.194:4433	No answer (latest draft: -22)
lsquic	http3-test.litespeedtech.com:4433	No complete Handshake
mozquic	mozquic.ducksong.com:4433	No answer (latest draft: -12)
msquic	quic.westus.cloudapp.azure.com:4433	No complete Handshake
mvfst	fb.mvfst.net:4433	**OK (draft-23)**
ngtcp2	nghttp2.org:4433	**OK (draft-23)**
ngx_quic	cloudflare-quic.com:443	**OK (draft-23)**
Pandora	pandora.cm.in.tum.de:4433	**OK (draft-23)**
picoquic	test.privateoctopus.com:4433	**OK (draft-23)**
quant	quant.eggert.org:4433	**OK (draft-23)**
quiche	quic.tech:4433	**OK (draft-23)**
QUICker	quicker.edm.uhasselt.be:4433	No answer (latest draft: -20)
quicly	quic.example.net:4433	No complete Handshake
Quinn	ralith.com:4433	**OK (draft-23)**

Indeed, one major difficulty we faced during our tests was that public servers would randomly go down and stop answering to our stimuli. The problem was especially visible each time a new draft was published.

To test the behaviour of these implementations, we sent different stimuli. The baseline was a valid QUIC Client Initial Packet corresponding to the latest version[7]. Then, we sent variations around this first stimulus:

- packets with a future version of the protocol, some of them being partly incompatible with the current wire format;
- packets not respecting the constraints on Client Initial Packet length;
- packets missing mandatory information (QUIC transport parameters, TLS Application-Layer Protocol Negotiation extension);
- packets containing forbidden frame types;
- packets with mangled CRYPTO frames.

---

[7] To be precise, we actually sent several valid stimuli, to accomodate with minor quirks with the ALPN extension, as described in Sect. 6.3.

6   Results

For this section, we chose to use the latest results, which correspond to the 23rd version of the drafts, published in September 2019. As explained in the previous section, due to the unavailability of several servers, we could only scan 10 implementations in a reliable way before the submission.

Moreover, it is important to keep in mind that the tested implementations, as well as the specifications, are still works in progress, and that the results presented here are only a snapshot of a fast-evolving ecosystem. Our goal is thus *not* to blame a given QUIC stack for possible deviations with regards to the draft (or its spirit, in case of implicit constraints), but to draw the attention on possible issues, which are the consequence of a complex protocol.

6.1   Version Negotiation

The QUIC specification aims at describing a robust protocol able to survive future changes of the concrete representation of messages on the wire. This is why the beginning of a QUIC packet is defined in a document called "QUIC Invariants" [10]: the long header should always look like the definition in Fig. 3.

It is important to notice in particular that the payload length is *not* part of this definition. Thus, a QUIC packet advertising a new version should be able to redefine how the packet length is specified. This is why we sent three different stimuli to the test servers: a standard valid draft23-compatible Initial packet, a similar packet advertising a yet-to-be-defined version, and a similar packet advertising the same future version but with the current Length field set to a huge value. Since the length should not be parsed for unknown versions, we expect compliant implementations to answer the first stimulus with a valid handshake (an Initial packet followed by Handshake packets) and the two other stimuli with a Version Negotiation message, asking the client to re-emit its packet using a version of the protocol supported by the server.

The majority of the contacted servers actually behaved this way, but we also witnessed one implementation (see Table 2, ngtcp2 implementation) that answered correctly with a Version Negotiation message when our stimulus contained a *correct* length, while timing out when the length was *incorrect*. This is a violation of the invariants as described in the specifications.

As a side note, it is interesting that we discover this behaviour by accident after a change in the draft describing the invariants when draft-22 was published. Indeed, in July 2019, the working group decided to change the way Connection ID length was sent on the wire[8]. Since we studied both pre-draft-22 and draft-22 implementations at the time, we triggered the incorrect behaviour with recent versions choking an on old stimulus (or the other way around).

---

[8] We let the reader reflect on the introduction of a *change* in a document describing the protocol *invariants*. Even though this was a bit unsettling, let us recall that this change was a simplification in the design and that QUIC documents are still drafts.

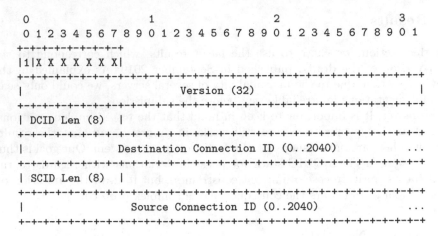

Fig. 3. Description of the first fields of any (long-header) QUIC packet, as defined in the "QUIC Invariants" Internet draft [10].

Table 2. Reaction of the servers selected in the previous section to an initial packets advertising a future version of the protocol. The first one presents a correct length field (with regards to the current specification) while the second presents a bigger length. The Time Out in the second column corresponds to a server waiting for what it interprets as missing bytes.

Implem.	Reaction to a Future version with	
	Correct length	Incorrect length
Expected	Version Negotiation	Version Negotiation
aioqquic	Version Negotiation	Version Negotiation
ats	Version Negotiation	Version Negotiation
mvfst	Version Negotiation	Version Negotiation
ngtcp2	Version Negotiation	**Time Out**
ngx_quic	Version Negotiation	Version Negotiation
Pandora	Version Negotiation	Version Negotiation
picoquic	Version Negotiation	Version Negotiation
quant	Version Negotiation	Version Negotiation
quiche	Version Negotiation	Version Negotiation
Quinn	Version Negotiation	Version Negotiation

6.2 Client Initial Packet Length

Since QUIC uses UDP, it is inherently subject to reflection attacks, where an attacker sends a packet with a forged source address, leading the server to answer to the victim. In some cases, the attacker can trigger a huge amount of data using a small packet. These so-called amplification attacks may lead to denial of service situations.

To avoid such attacks, QUIC specifies that a client should send at least a 1,200-byte long initial packet, and that a server should never answer with more than three times the amount of data the client initially sent. Moreover, a server should ignored a client Initial packet which is too small. The combination of these constraints allows the server to send up to 3,600 bytes in its first flight, which is considered sufficient.

To check how servers behaved regarding these constraints, we sent small stimuli, and observed the reaction of the public servers. Several implementations actually answered our invalid packet, as shown in Table 3. The exact implementations that were affected did vary across time, but we also always observed that the server answer was capped at three times the size of the client Initial packet, which at least limited the amplification impact, as planned.

6.3 Missing Parameters

Scattered across the specifications, several parameters of the client Initial packet are described as mandatory. In particular, the TLS 1.3 ClientHello must contain an extension dedicated to QUIC to define the initial values of several transport parameters (e.g. to define the maximum size of the exchanged packets) and the ALPN extension (which defines the nature of the protocol encapsulated in QUIC).

We found out that several implementations seemed to accept a stimulus missing these elements, and in the case of ALPN, we even found implementations that only answered when the extension was missing. The situation might not be a problem after all, since we only looked at the first messages of the connections, and what seemed to be a valid connection might then be shut down by the server when handling the application layer.

Yet, we believe errors should be triggered as soon as possible, both to avoid useless resource usage and to make debugging easier. Indeed, several implementations return an empty error packet when some parameters are missing (or do not correspond to the expected values), and the only way to understand what is happening is to have access to the server logs, or to compare the behaviour of a given server with different stimuli.

6.4 Frame Mangling

Another venue we investigated was to send forbidden frames to the servers. The specification indicates that the only frames that should be sent in an Initial packet are crypto frames (which embed TLS messages), acknowledgement (ACK) frames, Connection Close frames (which signal errors) and padding frames. However, we observed that several servers would accept a Ping frame enclosed in the first client Initial packet[9]. Again, we would expect the servers to be stricter with the messages they accept.

---

[9] As a side note, it appears that placing the Ping frame after instead of before the Crypto frame gets the stimulus accepted by one more server.

Table 3. Reaction of the selected servers to a small initial packet (300 bytes). Even if several implementations answer with the beginning of a Handshake, they respect the constraint not to send more than three times the amount of data initially received.

Implem.	Reaction to a small Initial packet
Expected	Time Out
aioqquic	Time Out
ats	**Handshake (886 bytes)**
mvfst	Time Out
ngtcp2	Time Out
ngx_quic	Time Out
Pandora	Time Out
picoquic	Time Out
quant	Time Out
quiche	**Handshake (896 bytes)**
Quinn	Time Out

Table 4. Reaction of the selected servers to a initial packets containing strange frames. Behaviours in bold are unexpected ones.

Implem.	Ping frame	Split Crypto	Overlapping Crypto frames	
			Consistent	Inconsistent
Expected	Error	Error	Error	Error
aioqquic	**Handshake**	**Handshake**	**Handshake**	**Handshake**
ats	**Handshake**	**Handshake**	Error	Error
mvfst	Error	**Handshake**	**Handshake**	**Handshake**
ngtcp2	**Handshake**	**Handshake**	**Handshake**	**Handshake**
ngx_quic	Error	**Handshake**	**Handshake**	**Handshake**
Pandora	Error	Time Out	Error	Error
picoquic	Time Out	**Handshake**	**Handshake**	**Handshake**
quant	Error	Error	Error	Error
quiche	Error	**Handshake**	**Handshake**	**Handshake**
Quinn	Error	**Handshake**	**Handshake**	**Handshake**

We also tried to split the TLS ClientHello across two Crypto frames, which should be rejected by implementations, since the specification states that "[t]he first packet sent by a client always includes a CRYPTO frame that contains the entirety of the first cryptographic handshake message.". Most of the implementations nevertheless answered our stimulus.

Finally, we sent packets with two overlapping Crypto frames (bytes 0 to 149, followed by bytes 50 to the end), first where both fragments would contain the same content, and then with a glitch introduced in the first fragment[10]. We thus observed that most of the servers tolerated overlapping frames, including when they were inconsistent. There is no obvious way to directly exploit this behaviour, but we found this a bit unsettling, and would advocate a stricter set of rules in the implementations.

Table 4 summarises these experiments on frame mangling.

7 Related Work

QUIC is a relatively new protocol, and most of the literature related to QUIC is about gQUIC. For example, Jager et al. showed how to exploit the Bleichenbacher attack against RSA Encryption to forge a signature and bypass server authentication in Google QUIC [5].

More recently, McMillan and Zuck presented a modeling of QUIC to test the state machines of existing implementations [8]. We believe our approaches are complementary since we propose a (partial) concrete test bench, whereas they validate implementations at a more abstract level. Their work showed in particular the existence of ambiguities in the specification, which our measurements seem to confirm, when we look at the diversity of behaviours in the existing implementations.

An online tool, QUIC Tracker[11], describes a test suite regarding QUIC features, and shows the reaction of existing implementations. Yet, QUIC Tracker seems to only look at features whereas we believe measuring the conformance to specific constraints from the specification would be of great help.

8 Conclusion and Perspectives

QUIC is a relatively recent protocols aiming at improving the efficiency and security of the web. As of today, it is still a work in progress, which reflects on the stability and robustness of the implementations. In our work, we focused on the initial negotiation phase of the protocol, and how to implement it.

We assessed the complexity in practice of the QUIC protection mechanisms by writing a Scapy implementation. We learned that QUIC is a complex beast and we believe it would be useful to simplify several aspects of the specification which are not justified in our mind. We already discussed with the IETF Working Group of several aspects of our findings and plan to continue this interaction.

We proposed a first framework to send stimuli to servers and observe their behaviour during the session establishment. Obviously, it would be useful to pursue this effort and propose more elaborate scenarios to test other features, e.g. address migration or 0-RTT data exchanges.

---

[10] We also tried with the glitch on the second fragment, but we mostly obtained errors from the servers.

[11] https://quic-tracker.info.ucl.ac.be.

In the end, QUIC is a very complex protocol, and this complexity will certainly lead to implementation bugs. Indeed, the current situation is far from perfect, since most of the studied implementations do not conform to the specification on several aspects, and some of these aspects could be the first step towards a complex attack.

A   Scapy Implementation

The description of a QUIC packet in Scapy can be done as shown in the following extract:

```
class QUIC(Packet):
    fields_desc = [
        # Flags
        BitEnumField("header_type", 1, 1, {0: "short", 1: "long"}),
        BitEnumField("fixed_bit", 1, 1, {0: "error", 1: "1"}),
        BitEnumField("type", 0, 2, {0: "initial", 1: "0-RTT",
                                    2: "handshake", 3: "retry"} ),
        BitField("reserved", 0, 2),
        BitFieldLenField("PNL", None, 2, length_of="PN",
                         adjust=lambda pkt,x:x-1),

        # Version
        XIntField("version", 0x0),

        # Connection IDs (DCID/SCID)
        BitFieldLenField("DCIL", None, 8, length_of="DCID"),
        StrLenField("DCID", b'', length_from=lambda pkt:pkt.DCIL),

        BitFieldLenField("SCIL", None, 8, length_of="SCID"),
        StrLenField("SCID", b'', length_from=lambda pkt:pkt.SCIL),

        # Token (only when type is initial)
        ConditionalField(QuicVarLenField("token_length", None,
                                         length_of="token"),
                         lambda pkt: pkt.version != 0 and pkt.type == 0),
        ConditionalField(StrLenField("token", b'',
                                     length_from = lambda pkt:pkt.token_length),
                         lambda pkt: pkt.version != 0 and pkt.type == 0),
        # Length (only when type is 0-RTT or initial)
        ConditionalField(QuicVarLenField("length", None),
                         lambda pkt: pkt.version != 0 and pkt.type != 3),

        # Packet Number (only when type is 0-RTT or initial)
        ConditionalField(StrLenField("PN", b'\x00',
                                     length_from = lambda pkt:pkt.PNL+1),
                         lambda pkt: pkt.version != 0 and pkt.type != 3),
    ]
```

Of course, since most fields are only valid for specific types of QUIC packets, we need to determine the presence most of the fields by the presence of certain values before in the packet.

To apply packet protection, we had to write dedicated functions. The following excerpt shows a simplified version of the protection function, which takes a QUIC packet as input and produces the byte string that can be sent on the wire.

```
def protect(material, packet):
    (key, iv, hp) = material
    header = packet.copy()
    header.payload = Raw()
    payload = packet[1]

    # Compute nonce
    nonce = int.from_bytes(iv, byteorder='big') ^
            int.from_bytes(header.PN, byteorder='big')
    nonce = nonce.to_bytes(12, byteorder = 'big')

    # Encrypt the payload
    encryptor = Cipher(algorithms.AES(key), modes.GCM(nonce),
                       backend=default_backend()).encryptor()
    encryptor.authenticate_additional_data(raw(header))
    encrypted_payload = encryptor.update(raw(payload)) +
                        encryptor.finalize() + encryptor.tag

    # Extract the sample
    PNL = header.PNL + 1
    sample_start = 4 - PNL     # The receiver will assume PNL is 4
    sample = encrypted_payload[sample_start:sample_start + 16]

    # Compute the mask
    encryptor = Cipher(algorithms.AES(hp), modes.ECB(),
                       backend=default_backend()).encryptor()
    mask = encryptor.update(sample) + encryptor.finalize()

    # Encrypt the flags and the PN
    encrypted_header = bytearray(raw(header))
    encrypted_header[0] ^= (mask[0] & 0x0f)
    for i in range(PNL):
        encrypted_header[-PNL + i] ^= mask[i+1]
    encrypted_header = bytes(encrypted_header)

    return encrypted_header + encrypted_payload
```

Our implementation could be improved by the addition of a Scapy automaton to handle the QUIC state machine and its transitions. However, we must keep in mind that our goal was to send possibly non-conformant stimuli to servers, so we might want not to follow the expected state machine all the time in our future work.

References

1. Biondi, P., The Scapy community: Scapy (2003–2016). http://www.secdev.org/projects/scapy/, http://www.secdev.org/projects/scapy/
2. Bishop, M.: Hypertext Transfer Protocol Version 3 (HTTP/3). Internet-Draft draft-ietf-quic-http-23, Internet Engineering Task Force, September 2019. https://datatracker.ietf.org/doc/html/draft-ietf-quic-http-23. Work in Progress
3. Iyengar, J., Swett, I.: QUIC Loss Detection and Congestion Control. Internet-Draft draft-ietf-quic-recovery-23, Internet Engineering Task Force, Septenber 2019. https://datatracker.ietf.org/doc/html/draft-ietf-quic-recovery-23. Work in Progress
4. Iyengar, J., Thomson, M.: QUIC: A UDP-Based Multiplexed and Secure Transport. Internet-Draft draft-ietf-quic-transport-23, Internet Engineering Task Force, September 2019. https://datatracker.ietf.org/doc/html/draft-ietf-quic-transport-23. Work in Progress

5. Jager, T., Schwenk, J., Somorovsky, J.: On the security of TLS 1.3 and QUIC against weaknesses in PKCS#1 v1.5 encryption. In: Proceedings of the 22nd ACM SIGSAC Conference on Computer and Communications Security, Denver, CO, USA, 12–16 October 2015, pp. 1185–1196 (2015)
6. Krasic, C.B., Bishop, M., Frindell, A.: QPACK: Header Compression for HTTP/3. Internet-Draft draft-ietf-quic-qpack-10, Internet Engineering Task Force, September 2019. https://datatracker.ietf.org/doc/html/draft-ietf-quic-qpack-10. work in Progress
7. Kühlewind, M., Trammell, B.: Applicability of the QUIC Transport Protocol. Internet-Draft draft-ietf-quic-applicability-05, Internet Engineering Task Force, July 2019. https://datatracker.ietf.org/doc/html/draft-ietf-quic-applicability-05. work in Progress
8. McMillan, K.L., Zuck, L.D.: Formal specification and testing of QUIC. In: Proceedings of the ACM Special Interest Group on Data Communication, SIGCOMM 2019, Beijing, China, 19–23 August 2019, pp. 227–240 (2019)
9. Momot, F., Bratus, S., Hallberg, S.M., Patterson, M.L.: The Seven turrets of babel: a taxonomy of LangSec errors and how to expunge them. In: IEEE Cybersecurity Development, SecDev 2016, Boston, MA, USA, 3–4 November 2016, pp. 45–52 (2016)
10. Thomson, M.: Version-Independent Properties of QUIC. Internet-Draft draft-ietf-quic-invariants-07, Internet Engineering Task Force, September 2019. https://datatracker.ietf.org/doc/html/draft-ietf-quic-invariants-07. Work in Progress
11. Thomson, M., Turner, S.: Using TLS to Secure QUIC. Internet-Draft draft-ietf-quic-tls-23, Internet Engineering Task Force, September 2019. https://datatracker.ietf.org/doc/html/draft-ietf-quic-tls-23. Work in Progress

CompactFlow: A Hybrid Binary Format for Network Flow Data

Michal Piskozub[✉], Riccardo Spolaor, and Ivan Martinovic

University of Oxford, Oxford, UK
{michal.piskozub,riccardo.spolaor,ivan.martinovic}@cs.ox.ac.uk

Abstract. Network traffic monitoring has become fundamental to obtaining insights about a network and its activities. This knowledge allows network administrators to detect anomalies, identify faulty hardware, and make informed decisions. The increase of the number of connected devices and the consequent volume of traffic poses a serious challenge to carrying out the task of network monitoring. Such a task requires techniques that process traffic in an efficient and timely manner. Moreover, it is crucial to be able to store network traffic for forensic purposes for as long a period of time as possible.

In this paper, we propose CompactFlow, a hybrid binary format for efficient storage and processing of network flow data. Our solution offers a trade-off between the space required and query performance via an optimized binary representation of flow records and optional indexing. We experimentally assess the efficiency of CompactFlow by comparing it to a wide range of binary flow storage formats. We show that Compact-Flow format improves the state of the art by reducing the size required to store network flows by more than 24%.

Keywords: Networks · Binary format · Cybersecurity data processing

1 Introduction

In recent years, we have witnessed an astonishing evolution of networks in terms of complexity, variety, and versatility. An increasing number of devices have started to embed networking capabilities and to require Internet connection to provide their full functionalities. Hence, guaranteeing the connectivity of such devices has become fundamental to the operation of the entire networking infrastructure. In order to carry out this task, network administrators have to be provided with reliable tools to monitor traffic flowing through a network. In addition to that, administrators have to be able to investigate past events by retrospectively analyzing the state of a network at any given point in time. For this reason, it is necessary to archive network traffic in a fast and space-efficient way.

Monitoring networks at the granularity of packets offers perfect visibility of their state but also requires overwhelming computing resources and storage

© IFIP International Federation for Information Processing 2020
Published by Springer Nature Switzerland AG 2020
M. Laurent and T. Giannetsos (Eds.): WISTP 2019, LNCS 12024, pp. 185–201, 2020.
https://doi.org/10.1007/978-3-030-41702-4_12

space to be devoted. While packet-level approach may have been possible in the early days of networking, it is infeasible in modern networks due to the increasing number of interconnected devices and the volume of data produced by them. Moreover, the ubiquitous adoption of encryption in network communication to protect user privacy has made packet-level traffic capturing obsolete since encrypted payloads do not provide any meaningful information. Due to these limitations, network monitoring has shifted toward a network flow as a more coarse-grained representation of traffic data. A network flow comprises information of a communication from a temporal perspective as a five-tuple: protocol, source and destination IP addresses and ports. Differently from packet-level data, flows capture only metadata, such as the overall number and size of exchanged packets.

Flow exporters are devices in the flow creation process that capture and assign network packets to flows based on their five-tuple and within a temporal interval. Once flows are created, they are sent to a flow collector using a given export protocol. A flow collector is a device in charge of storing flow data for future use. The most popular export protocol is Cisco's NetFlow [9], which inspired the creation of the open standard IPFIX [8].

Over the years, a number of flow collectors have been proposed by networking companies and researchers. The main goal of such devices is to rapidly collect and store flows in such a way that avoids blocking the next oncoming flows. More importantly, they have to adopt a storage format that is efficient in terms of the size required and indexing to process future queries. Network administrators are constrained by the space available to store network traffic, thus older traffic has to be periodically deleted. For this reason, a space-optimized format saves storage space, which allows for keeping network traffic of longer periods for retrospective analysis. Unfortunately, our investigation of open-source flow collectors showed that they use an inefficient flow representation in their formats, even among the ones that favor storage efficiency over processing speed.

In this paper, we present CompactFlow - a binary format to represent network flows that favors storage and processing performance while supporting indexing. In particular, the CompactFlow format relies on dynamic field sizes and is based on a linked list to store the contents of flows. This accounts for a significant reduction of storage size. In fact, experimental results show that CompactFlow files are on average almost 3 times smaller than the ones using binary formats of other flow collectors, and 24% smaller than the ones using the binary format of the state-of-the-art System for Internet-Level Knowledge (SiLK) collector [29].

CompactFlow can be considered a hybrid binary format since it allows for customization according to administrators' analysis purposes: (i) it supports additional indexing methods to increase the speed of repetitive queries, and (ii) it is possible to choose which flow fields or which specific values of a flow field to index. Unlike database-based approaches, our solution allows for high-speed saving of flows without the risk of dropping them or resorting to sampling since the indexing can be done after successful storage. The design principles of CompactFlow join two best practices of storage (binary files) and querying (indexing), to have a robust system for network monitoring and processing of cybersecurity events.

Contributions. The contribution of this paper is twofold:

- We present a binary file format to store network flows using less space than state-of-the-art approaches. Our format supports popular indexing methods to allow faster data processing in the security context.
- We perform a thorough analysis of all open-source network flow collectors and a popular data serialization library by analyzing their binary formats.

Organization. The remainder of the paper is organized as follows. In Sect. 2, we survey the state-of-the-art techniques for network traffic monitoring. We present our CompactFlow format in Sect. 3 while we evaluate and compare its performance to other formats in Sect. 4. In Sect. 5, we discuss the results. Finally, we present conclusions in Sect. 6.

2 Related Work

In the last two decades, many approaches have been proposed to monitor network traffic. This effort has been necessary to carry out management and security analyses on networks, such as identification of anomalies or failures, and detection of attacks. Most of these analyses cannot be done in real-time, hence network traffic has to be stored in persistent memory in order to make it available when needed. For this reason, it is necessary to store and query network traffic efficiently. A first important distinction between storage approaches is related to the granularity of traffic collection: packet- and flow-level.

2.1 Packet-Level Traffic Collection

Collecting network data at packet-level provides fine-grained information about traffic but it requires fast dedicated equipment. Desnoyers et al. in [12] propose Hyperion, a system that relies on a log-structured file system that is optimized for writing data streams to store packet-level network traffic. This system indexes data stream segments via distributed multi-level Signature indexes. The authors claim to be able to write and index up to 1M and 200K packets per second, respectively.

Maier et al. in [25] propose to focus only on the part of the packet stream that may be interesting for a network intrusion detection system (NIDS). Hence, they present the TimeMachine system which applies a cut-off heuristic (i.e. it only considers the first N bytes) to reduce the size of the data stream to store.

Fusco et al. in [15] present PcapIndex which extends *Libpcap* by supporting rapid packet filtering via COMPAX compressed bitmap index [14]. Doing this, PcapIndex reduces the disk overhead and the response time of queries.

Unfortunately, the aforementioned methods are not suitable for large-scale networks since they do not scale on the number of devices connected. Moreover, such fine-grained information would require an overwhelming storage capacity.

2.2   Flow-Level Traffic Collectors

In order to cope with the shortcomings of packet-level traffic collection, the networking community has moved toward the collection of traffic information by aggregating packets into flows. Compared to packet-level one, flow-level network traffic is more privacy-preserving (i.e. packets are aggregated), and more scalable over the amount of traffic and number of connected devices in modern networks. The first standard for exporting network flow information was NetFlow [9]. Initially, Netflow version 5 was released by Cisco in 1996 and then extended to version 9 in 2004. Subsequently, the Internet Engineering Task Force (IETF) in 2013 released the IP Flow Information eXport (IPFIX) Internet Standard [8] which is a further enrichment of NetFlow v9. In what follows, we present various solutions available to collect, store and access network flows.

Storage Formats. Network flow collectors adopt several solutions to store flow-level network traffic in persistent memory. Such solutions can be divided according to the way they structure and index the data [20]. A popular data structure to store flows is a database. The advantage of databases is that such data structures automatically handle the information storage and indexing via a DataBase Management System (DBMS). Traditional DataBase Management Systems, such as MySQL and PostgreSQL, store the information by rows (*row-based databases*). In our case, a row represents an entire flow (i.e. all its fields). Two examples of flow collectors that use a row-based database to store network traffic are Vermont and pmacct. Regarding the queries, row-based databases offer good flexibility but they have poor performance in terms of data retrieval and new flow insertion time. Moreover, a row-based database is not storage-efficient since it requires considerable indexing.

For this reason, column-based databases have been proposed for network flow storage. Rather than to consecutively store entire flows, column-based databases store them in columns by flow fields. Examples of column-based databases are MariaDB ColumnStore [3] and bitmap indexing methods (e.g. FastBit [31], and COMPAX [14]). Indexing by columns decreases data retrieval time for queries while maintaining good flexibility and moderate insertion time. In particular, FastBit is an order of magnitude faster than MySQL [11]. IPFIXcol is a collector that relies on FastBit. It supports IPFIX, bidirectional flows, and variable length fields. Unfortunately, the main shortcoming of column-based databases is poor performance in retrieving flows in their entirety. Moreover, such databases still have to maintain a reference to a specific flow (i.e. index) for each flow field resulting in overhead in storage size.

Another solution that aims to reduce storage space is to rely on *flat files*. A flat file typically stores data sequentially and does not embed any hierarchy nor indexing by default. For this reason, flat files do not offer query flexibility but they occupy much less space than a database [19]. Data in flat files can be represented in a text or binary format. Despite the portability of a flat file in text format, representing data in a binary format further reduces the storage

Table 1. Comparison of open-source flow collectors.

Collectors	Storage formats				Bidirectional
	Database		Flat files		
	Row-based	Column-based	Binary format	Text format	
Argus [4]	✓		✓	✓	✓
flowd [1]			✓		
IPFIXcol [30]		✓			✓
nfdump [17]			✓		
pmacct [24]	✓			✓	✓
SiLK [29]			✓		
Vermont [21]	✓				✓

size and the query response time. Examples of flow collectors that save network traffic in a binary format are Argus, flowd, nfdump, and SiLK.

In Table 1, we report several open-source network flow collectors and we compare them according to storage formats supported and whether they can represent bidirectional flows. It is worth noting that some collectors can use more than one storage format (e.g. Argus, and pmacct) and that the majority use flat file formats.

To perform a thorough comparison between our proposal and the state of the art, we analyze the binary formats used by collectors that allow storing network flows in flat files (i.e. Argus, flowd, nfdump, and SiLK). In Sect. 4, we show that our compact format outperforms all of them in terms of space efficiency.

Indexing Methods. Flat file formats are optimal for network flow storage because they save space and have a negligible computational overhead in inserting new flows. However, the limitation of this format is that it does not provide integrated indexing of the flows, thus it lacks in query performance and flexibility. To cope with this shortcoming, researchers propose solutions to build indexes which offer a low retrieval time and require little storage. Typically, storing network flows from a flow exporter consists of two aspects: writing the flows to a flat file and building indexes of those flows. For this reason, most solutions rely on the multi-processing capabilities of modern computers [13,22].

In the literature, researchers use different data structures to organize flow (or query) indexes [7]. For example, TelegraphCQ [5] stores indexes and results of queries via a modified version of PostgreSQL. Three other examples, GigaScope [10], MIND [23], and FloSiS [22] arrange indexes into trees, multi-level hashing tables, and Bloom filters, respectively. However, the most popular and best-performing approach leverages bitmap indexing. As an example, Reiss et al. in [28] and Chen et al. in [6] applied the concept of bitmap indexing (i.e. FastBit [31]) to improve the performance of TelegraphCQ [5] and TimeMachine

[25] (applied on network flows), respectively. More recently, Xie et al. in [32] present Index-trie, a novel data structure to index flows that combines trees and bitmaps. Our CompactFlow format is designed to be hybrid. This means that it is able to support a variety of flow indexing methods.

Several approaches also propose fast compression/decompression algorithms to be applied to both stored flow data and indexing data structures to further reduce the storage size. Fusco et al. propose NET-Fli [14] and RasterZip [16] systems that compress on-the-fly flow data streams via compression algorithms, e.g. Lempel--Ziv--Oberhumer (LZO) [26], and Run-Length Encoding (RLE) [18]. Unfortunately, even the fastest compression algorithms generate computational overhead which translates to increased processing time.

3   CompactFlow Format Design

Network flow data is comprised of information relating to communication between two hosts on a network. Every flow consists of core fields (traditionally called a five-tuple) and additional fields that contain volumetric and temporal information pertaining to communications. A five-tuple includes protocol, source IP address, source port, destination IP address and destination port. The basic additional fields of a flow are the timestamp of the first packet, the overall duration, the number of packets and the total size of packets.

In this section, we introduce CompactFlow, a new format specifically designed to provide more efficient storage and fast processing of network flow data. Our proposal relies on a new binary file format, which supports both unidirectional and bidirectional flows. In Fig. 1, we show the general structure of a CompactFlow file. In what follows, we describe all of its components and discuss our design choices.

3.1   CompactFlow File Header

A CompactFlow file is structurally divided into the header and body. The header stores information about the format (i.e. binary file marker, format version, and byte order) and contained flows (i.e. type, IP version, number of flows, and timestamp) that are later encoded in the body of the file. The header of a CompactFlow file contains a *Marker* as a first field by which the format can be recognized. We designed its value to be 0x00434600, where the inner bytes represent characters 'C' and 'F' and the outer bytes are non-character values to avoid being misinterpreted by applications for text files. The *Ver* value represents a version of the CompactFlow specification with the first byte being major and the second minor versions (e.g. 0.3). The *T* value stands for the type of flow in terms of its direction (unidirectional or bidirectional). Since CompactFlow supports both IPv4 and IPv6, the version of IP is given by the *IP* parameter. By design, IPv4 and IPv6 flows are stored in separate files. The *Flow Count* value stores the total number of flows contained in the file. Instead of storing complete timestamps in each flow, we only save the *Timestamp* (down to a precision of

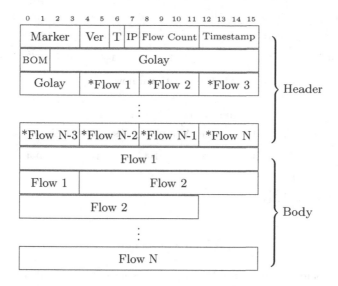

Fig. 1. CompactFlow file format (in bytes).

an hour) in the header since each file represents up to one hour of traffic. This allows for each flow record to store only the added time to that timestamp to reconstruct it fully. The *Byte Order Mark* (BOM) is used to clarify that the CompactFlow file uses big-endian encoding. This decision is justified by the fact that big-endian order is used by default in network communications, in fact to such an extent that it is often referred to as the network order.

All fields described above constitute mandatory data in the header. Since those fields carry high importance to the remainder of the file, we use the *extended binary Golay code* (G_{24}) to detect and correct errors in them in the case of corruption. Such code allows us to recover 3 bits for each 12-bit word at a cost of doubling the size of data. Fortunately, we can afford it since the header constitutes a minimal, almost negligible, percentage of the size of the whole file.

Our proposal uses dynamic field sizes to store flows, thus flow records can vary in size. This means that given a current flow it is not possible to know in advance where the next one starts. Typically this is not a problem in the context of network security analysis since the way to process flows is to sequentially traverse each one to get to the ones of interest [29], or to build more complex network behavior profiles [27]. However, if CompactFlow is used in a network administration context, the types of workflows could require running the same queries to extract flows with a fixed set of parameters (e.g. given IP addresses). One could speed up such queries by indexing data of interest and then accessing it. This is described as *random access* and to enable this, CompactFlow precomputes an array of 4-byte pointers (offsets from the beginning of a file) to each flow record. Additionally, one can opt to use one of the indexing methods

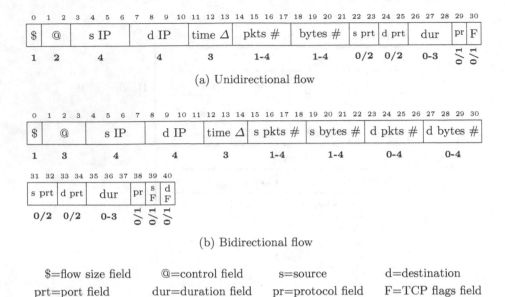

(a) Unidirectional flow

(b) Bidirectional flow

$=flow size field   @=control field   s=source   d=destination
prt=port field   dur=duration field   pr=protocol field   F=TCP flags field

Fig. 2. Binary schema of CompactFlow records (in bytes).

reported in Sect. 2.2. It is worth noting that this step is optional and such an array is not contained in the format by default. Overall, the header without an array of pointers takes 36 bytes of space.

3.2   Flow Binary Representation

Flow records feature dynamic field sizes that are adjusted to the size of data that needs to be accommodated. The use of dynamic fields makes the flow more compact in cases where field values to be stored are small. As depicted in Fig. 2a, every flow record contains the following fields: flow size (in bytes), control, source IP address, destination IP address, start time of the flow in terms of added milliseconds to the timestamp in the header, total number of packets, and total number of bytes. Optionally a flow can include a protocol, source and destination ports in the case of TCP or UDP protocols, duration and TCP flags. The length and position of variable-size fields is given by interpreting bits in the control field, described in Fig. 3.

We noticed that some values are repeatedly used in flows. Saving the full values of such fields each time would require additional bytes per flow, which quickly build up if the number of flows is in the order of billions per day. For example, according to our observations the majority of traffic uses ICMP, TCP or UDP protocols. In order to save space, we use 2 bits (bits 0 to 1) of the control field, that allow for the storage of 4 values, to encode them with the fourth value meaning that another protocol is used which implies the existence of the protocol field in the binary data.

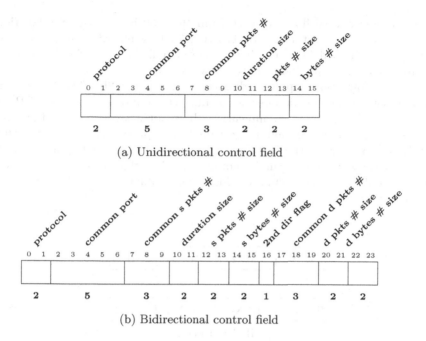

(a) Unidirectional control field

(b) Bidirectional control field

Fig. 3. CompactFlow control fields (in bits).

Port values (non-ephemeral) are encoded in a similar fashion using 5 bits (bits 2 to 6). They are only consulted if the protocol is either TCP or UDP (in other cases the port fields do not exist in the binary format). Encoded port values are specific to a given production network, hence they should be determined beforehand. Using those 5 bits, we can encode 32 values. The value of 0 means that neither source port nor destination port belong to the list of most frequently used ports. The value of 1 is not used. The remaining 15 and 15 values mean that the source or destination port respectively is in the list of common ports. Each common port list hit saves 2 bytes of space. Since we observed that a significant number of flows constitute requests without a response which translate to a small number of packets, we use the next 3 bits (bits 7 to 9) to store small packet numbers. The value of 0 has a special meaning - the number of packets if different from a list of common small packet numbers. The remaining values from 1 to 7 are used to represent packet numbers, which results in 1 byte of saved space per flow. The next 2 bits (bits 10 to 11) in the control field store the length of the duration field. The value of 0 denotes that the duration is 0 and the respective duration field does not exist in the binary representation. The duration field can support non-standard values of up to 4.5 h (with millisecond precision), even though the default active timeout value in the NetFlow 9 export protocol is only 30 min. This makes the format more robust towards changes of default values in flow exporters. The sizes of packets and bytes fields take 2 bits each (bits 12 to 13 and 14 to 15) to denote values up to 4 bytes. Summarizing, the size of a unidirectional flow can vary from 16 to 30 bytes. Each unidirectional CompactFlow file can store up to 143,165,576 flow records (unsigned integer using 4 bytes divided by a maximum size of a flow - 30), if one chooses to compute the array of pointers to each flow record.

CompactFlow also supports bidirectional flows (Fig. 2b). The bidirectional format differs by the addition of packet and byte counters as well as TCP flags for the other side of the communication. It is not always the case that those counters exist, e.g. the communication might comprise only a request with no reply. In such scenarios, the destination counter values are not captured, hence the size of those counters can be equal to 0. For that reason, the size of a bidirectional flow is larger than its unidirectional counterpart and can take from 17 to 40 bytes.

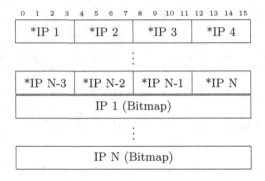

Fig. 4. Bitmap index of IP addresses.

To increase data processing performance, CompactFlow automatically places dynamic fields that could have the size of 0 at the end of the flow. If those fields were placed throughout the flow record, then one would need to query their size by calculating the corresponding flags in the control field in order to get to fields positioned after them. By using this design, we tried to minimize this behavior. Additionally, IPv6 flow records are supported and saved into separate files. The format for such files differs in the number of bytes allocated for each address - 4 bytes for IPv4 and 16 bytes for IPv6.

The second part of the CompactFlow framework considers flow processing techniques. Our proposal supports a variety of indexing methods. We present how to create the bitmap index, which is considered a state-of-the-art approach. Bitmap indexing is efficient as it uses only 1 bit per flow record to denote whether a given value of a flow field is present in a flow. Hence, each bitmap index is an array of bits with the size equal to the number of all flow records. Figure 4 reports the structure of such a bitmap index that is stored in a separate file as part of the CompactFlow format. Similarly, to the header of the unidirectional CompactFlow file, it stores the pointers to the locations of bitmap arrays for each field. In the case of this figure, these are IP addresses. In order to obtain selected flows, one needs to take the positions of bits with the value of 1 and jump to the respective flows by using the array of pointers in a binary CompactFlow file. Since the size of pointers is fixed-size (4 bytes), it is easy to jump to the correct ones with negligible overhead.

4 Evaluation

We compare our format to most popular open-source flow collectors that support binary file storage, i.e. Argus, flowd, nfdump, and SiLK. To carry out this comparison, we analyze the binary formats of such collectors to have full understanding of their flow representation. In Fig. 5, we show the same unidirectional flow represented using the aforementioned binary formats and our proposed Compact-Flow format. The flow is shown in the plaintext format (Fig. 5a) with color-coded field names (explained in Fig. 5b). In our comparison we configure flow collectors to store only the fields that we consider, whenever possible. Most binary formats use fixed-length representation of each flow record, which makes the file format more straightforward to read from. Indeed, it is possible to jump by a constant number of bytes to get to the same field in the next flow. However, this feature also makes it extremely inefficient space-wise. CompactFlow is designed to achieve a trade-off between file size and processing speed. In fact, our proposed format applies a hybrid approach, in which the always-present fields are of constant length and the fields whose values can change are of variable length. This results in a compact representation that is the smallest of all presented binary formats, as shown in Fig. 5h. It is worth noting that the protocol, destination port and number of packets are included in the control field as an optimization by our binary format (see Sect. 3.2). The sample flow in CompactFlow binary format is only 20 bytes. In what follows, we discuss and compare different flow collectors one by one.

Audit Record Generation and Utilization System (Argus) [4] is a popular, open-source flow monitoring framework. The Argus collector provides a binary file format to store flow records, which assigns a fixed-length space for fields constituting a flow. It is worth noting that such length remains fixed even when not all fields are captured. This approach leads to wasted space, which is a fundamental factor when dealing with large data sets. In total a flow record takes 116 bytes.

Another flow collector, flowd [1], offers binary storage at a reduced size of 48 bytes per flow record. It uses big-endian encoding and provides no file header. It offers an option to save protocol, TCP flags, and Type of Service without being able to selectively pick each one. Additionally, there is no option to save the timestamp from when the flow started, only the timestamp of receiving the flow by the collector. It also does not provide an option to store the duration of a flow. Both of these shortcomings limit its use in real-world settings.

A slight improvement in those regards is offered by nfdump [17]. It uses the nfcapd tool to collect flows from the exporter and to save them to binary files. It also allows for fine-grained specification of which fields to store. However, it keeps

02:59:40 8.96 TCP 192.168.1.43 58769 72.163.4.161 443 3 152

(a) Sample flow

timestamp duration proto srcIP srcPort destIP destPort packets bytes TCP flags

(b) Color legend

```
01:   3320 001d 0101 0102   c0a8 0101 0201 4105
02:   c0a8 012b 48a3 04a1   0600 e591 01bb 2020
03:   031a 1805 5c55 079c   0007 62a0 5c55 07a5
04:   0006 c660 1001 0602   0003 0098 3004 0003
05:   0000 0000 0000 0000   4800 0102 0000 0000
06:   4200 0005 0000 0000   0000 0000 0000 0000
07:   0000 0000 3200 0004   0000 0000 0000 0000
08:   0000 0000
```

(c) Argus

```
01:   600a 0000 0000 38a6   5c55 07ab 0002 d4a1
02:   1806 0000 c0a8 012b   48a3 04a1 e591 01bb
03:   0000 0000 0000 0003   0000 0000 0000 0098
```

(d) flowd

```
01:   0a00 3800 0600 0000   e401 bc01 9c07 555c
02:   a507 555c 0018 0600   91e5 bb01 0100 0000
03:   2b01 a8c0 a104 a348   0300 0000 0000 0000
04:   9800 0000 0000 0000
```

(e) nfdump

```
01:   da89 1003 2a80 2300   1840 0003 0000 0000
02:   e591 01bb c0a8 012b   48a3 04a1
```

(f) SiLK

```
01:   0000 1600 2c00 2b00   2400 2000 1400 1000
02:   0c00 0a00 0800 0400   1600 0000 0023 0000
03:   bb01 91e5 9800 0000   0300 0000 44bb 25ac
04:   6801 0000 0000 0000   a104 a348 2b01 a8c0
```

(g) FlatBuffers

```
01:   1862 e1c0 a801 2b48   a304 a136 a244 9891
02:   e523 0018
```

(h) CompactFlow

Fig. 5. Comparison of binary file formats.

Table 2. Comparison of compression methods used with a CompactFlow file of 67,257,407 unidirectional IPv4 flow records.

Compression		File size (MB)	Size gain (%)	RAM load time (s)	Processing time (s)	Total time (s)	Time loss (%)
Method	CPU cores						
Uncompressed		1,425	–	3.267	0.548	3.815	–
gzip	1	791	44	1.887	12.065	13.952	366
gzip	32	792	44	1.881	7.408	9.289	243
bzip2	1	697	51	1.609	61.638	63.247	1,658
bzip2	32	696	51	1.603	3.155	4.758	125
lzo	1	1,023	28	2.325	4.818	7.143	187

start and end timestamp from which duration field is calculated, which is not an efficient approach. It also uses little-endian encoding, which might seem strange since network order is big-endian. Moreover, the conversion between encodings might add unnecessary overhead to the collection process. The binary format of nfdump stores the header in 344 bytes, each flow record in 56 bytes and the footer in 44 bytes.

SiLK [29] is the most optimized open-source flow collector with a state-of-the-art binary format and a set of processing tools. It provides an option to specify endianness of files and provides optimizations such as storing flow duration instead of end time or storing average amount of bytes transferred per packet. This results in the smallest binary format of all open-source tools with 24–88 bytes for the header and 28 bytes per flow record. However, it does not support bidirectional flows (even though it provides tools to match flows after they are captured) and it does not provide functionality to index flows. Moreover, it relies on the file hierarchy, which divides traffic into internal to internal, external to external, incoming and outgoing Web and ICMP traffic. While the hierarchy can speed up select queries regarding one of those types, it also makes the binary format more complex and adds overhead for more analytic queries, such as the selection of all flows within a time period to train machine learning models.

Additionally to flow collectors, we examine a popular, fast data serialization library, FlatBuffers [2]. This library supports a large variety of extensions in different programming languages to interact with its binary data format. One of its advantages is the flexibility of what information to store. This is done by writing a schema with a structure of data to be stored. In the case of storing flow records, FlatBuffers does not perform better than most of flow collectors. It uses 64 bytes per flow record. This is due to the support of only regular types (e.g. uint8, uint16, uint32, uint64) and no custom types (such as uint24) which leads to wasted space. Additionally, in order to store a collection of records, one needs to specify another type that will serve as a container for those records.

Even though the comparison favors the CompactFlow format, a single flow is not representative of a larger variety of flows on networks. In fact, the uni-directional record takes from 16 to 30 bytes, which in some cases can exceed

SiLK's 28 bytes per flow record. For this reason, we evaluate the average size of a CompactFlow record by considering a variety of flows from a production network. Experimental results based on the analysis of 1,802,377,030 flows show that the average size of a flow in our proposed unidirectional binary format is 21.4 bytes - a value 24% smaller than SiLK's format.

To get a clearer view of what different binary formats mean in the real world, we used each of them to store over five months of flow data from the University of Oxford. The results are shown in Fig. 6. In total 181,315,995,252 flows are stored that come from three networks with over 64 thousand hosts. The most inefficient format takes over 21 TB to store the entirety of this data. While the state-of-the-art binary format of SiLK uses about 5 TB, our proposed format uses only 3.88 TB.

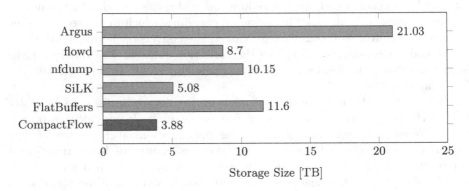

Fig. 6. 181 million flows from the University of Oxford using different flow collectors.

The final aspect of the evaluation is a comparison of an uncompressed CompactFlow file against three common compression algorithms (i.e. gzip, bzip2, and lzo). Such an analysis is meant to show which approach is the fastest in terms of loading the file into memory (RAM load time) and reading contained flow records (processing time). We observed that those two metrics are a trade-off between disk speed and a chosen compression algorithm. As it was shown in 2014 in the evaluation of SiLK [29], reading flow records was faster from a compressed binary file. This was due to the limited speed of then widely used hard disk drives (HDDs). However, we assess that this is no longer true with the rising popularity and decreasing prices of solid-state drives (SSDs). In Table 2, we show that the increase of disk speeds (from 100 MB/s in [29] to 436 MB/s in our analysis) results in faster processing of raw, uncompressed binary files. In order to reverse this trend, one can assign more CPU cores to speed up the decompression. We used 32 cores of a dual Intel Xeon CPU to determine that it takes 25% longer in total while reducing the file size by half. However, the prices and power requirements of such CPUs are high, which means that often they are not available to network administrators. As a result, compression is not suitable in the case of commodity hardware, which puts more emphasis on a small binary representation of flow data.

5   Discussion

Storing data in a binary format is more efficient than database-based methods in terms of size. In fact, the database-based methods need more space for indexing purposes, which may even take double the space required for the data [20]. They also do not allow a fine-grained control of what and when is indexed which accounts for their poor per-flow storage times. Our format provides a quicker and hybrid solution. It is also robust in case of errors. We use Golay code in the header to preserve fundamental information regarding the flows in the file, such as an hour-based timestamp, the IP version supported, or the type of flow. Secondly, the header can be optionally enriched with an array of flow pointers. In this way, it would be easy to isolate the faulty flows in case errors occur within the file body. Faulty flows can be easily detected by relying on the first two flow fields, namely *flow size* and *flow control*. As a first check, we have to verify the following condition on the *flow size* value: $flow\_size \geq \sum_{i \in C} size(i) + 2$, where C is a set of flow fields of constant size and $size(i)$ is the size of field i. The additional 2 is related to the two variable fields with a minimum size of 1 byte (i.e. number of packets and bytes). The condition does not comprise the other variable fields since their minimum size is 0. A second check on flow consistency could be made on the packet and byte flow fields. Indeed, it is known that not only is the former smaller than the latter, but that the following condition is verified: $bytes\# \geq min\_packet\_size * packets\#$, where min_packet_size is the minimum allowed packet size by the considered protocol.

Our evaluation shows that even though flow collectors use the most efficient type of data storage, binary files, they usually do so in an inefficient manner. In fact, a string representation of each flow record would take less space than in most evaluated binary formats.

We do not evaluate compressed sizes of different flow collectors' binary formats. Even if compressed sizes were similar, in order to process the data, one needs to decompress it - which brings us to the initial problem since the file sizes start to matter again. We show in Sect. 4 that compression slows down the processing of flows. Moreover, memory prices show no signs of decreasing, hence it is important for a format to have a minimal memory footprint.

6   Conclusion

In this paper, we presented a hybrid binary file format to store network flow data. It not only is compact in its representation, but also supports well-known indexing approaches to speed up flow queries. To assess the performance of the CompactFlow format, we compared it to the most popular open-source flow collectors with an in-depth analysis of their binary formats. Then, we carried out an extensive comparison in terms of storage size on a real-world traffic dataset from the University of Oxford. Finally, we evaluated the impact of compression on our format in terms of file size and processing time.

References

1. flowd. https://code.google.com/archive/p/flowd/
2. Flatbuffers (2015). https://google.github.io/flatbuffers/
3. MariaDB ColumnStore (2017). https://mariadb.com/kb/en/library/mariadb-columnstore/
4. Argus (1985). https://qosient.com/argus/
5. Chandrasekaran, S., et al.: TelegraphCQ: continuous dataflow processing for an uncertain world. In: Proceedings of of ACM SIGMOD (2003)
6. Chen, Z., et al.: TIFAflow: enhancing traffic archiving system with flow granularity for forensic analysis in network security. Tsinghua Sci. Technol. **18**, 406–417 (2013)
7. Chen, Z., et al.: A survey of bitmap index compression algorithms for big data. Tsinghua Sci. Technol. **20**, 100–115 (2015)
8. Claise, B., et al.: IPFIX protocol specifications. RFC7011 (2004)
9. Claise, B.: Cisco Systems NetFlow Services Export Version 9. The Internet Society, Technical report (2004)
10. Cranor, C., et al.: Gigascope: a stream database for network applications. In: Proceedings of ACM SIGMOD (2003)
11. Deri, L., et al.: Collection and exploration of large data monitoring sets using bitmap databases. In: Proceedings of TMA (2010)
12. Desnoyers, P.J., et al.: Hyperion: high volume stream archival for retrospective querying. In: Proceedings of USENIX ATC (2007)
13. Fusco, F., et al.: High speed network traffic analysis with commodity multi-core systems. In: Proceedings of of IMC (2010)
14. Fusco, F., et al.: NET-FLi: on-the-fly compression, archiving and indexing of streaming network traffic. In: Proceedings of the VLDB Endowment (2010)
15. Fusco, F., et al.: pcapIndex: an index for network packet traces with legacy compatibility. ACM SIGCOMM Comput. Commun. Rev. **42**, 47–53 (2012)
16. Fusco, F., et al.: RasterZip: compressing network monitoring data with support for partial decompression. In: Proceedings of IMC (2012)
17. Haag, P.: Watch your Flows with NfSen and NFDUMP (2005)
18. Held, G., Marshall, T.: Data Compression; Techniques and Applications: Hardwareand Software Considerations. Wiley, New York (1991)
19. Hofstede, R., et al.: The network data handling war: MySQL vs. NfDump. In: EUNICE (2010)
20. Hofstede, R., et al.: Flow monitoring explained: from packet capture to data analysis with NetFlow and IPFIX. IEEE COMST **16**, 2037–2064 (2014)
21. Lampertand, R.T., et al.: Vermont - a versatile monitoring toolkit for IPFIX and PSAMP. In: IEEE/IST Workshop MonAM (2006)
22. Lee, J., et al.: FloSIS: a highly scalable network flow capture system for fast retrieval and storage efficiency. In: Proceedings of USENIX ATC (2015)
23. Li, X., et al.: Advanced indexing techniques for wide-area network monitoring. In: Proceedings of ICDE (2008)
24. Lucente, P.: pmacct: steps forward interface counters (2008). http://www.pmacct.net/pmacct-stepsforward.pdf

25. Maier, G., et al.: Enriching network security analysis with time travel. ACM SIG-COMM Comput. Commun. Rev. (2008)
26. Oberhumer, M.: Lempel–Ziv–Oberhumer data compression (2013)
27. Piskozub, M., et al.: MalAlert: detecting malware in large-scale network traffic using statistical features. SIGMETRICS Perform. Eval. Rev. $46(3)$, 151–154 (2019)
28. Reiss, F., et al.: Enabling real-time querying of live and historical stream data. In: Proceedings of SSBD (2007)
29. Thomas, M., et al.: SiLK: a tool suite for unsampled network flow analysis at scale. In: Proceedings of IEEE BigData (2014)
30. Velan, P., Krejčí, R.: Flow information storage assessment using IPFIXcol. In: Sadre, R., Novotný, J., Čeleda, P., Waldburger, M., Stiller, B. (eds.) AIMS 2012. LNCS, vol. 7279, pp. 155–158. Springer, Heidelberg (2012). https://doi.org/10.1007/978-3-642-30633-4_21
31. Wu, K., et al.: FastBit: interactively searching massive data. J. Phys. 180, 012053 (2009)
32. Xie, G., et al.: Index-Trie: efficient archival and retrieval of network traffic. Comput. Netw. 124, 140–156 (2017)

SSI-AWARE: Self-sovereign Identity Authenticated Backup with Auditing by Remote Entities

Philipp Jakubeit[1,2]($\boxtimes$), Albert Dercksen[2], and Andreas Peter[1]

[1] Services and Cybersecurity Group, University of Twente,
Enschede, The Netherlands
{P.Jakubeit,A.Peter}@utwente.nl
[2] Nedap N.V., 7141 DC Groenlo, The Netherlands
Albert.Dercksen@nedap.com

Abstract. The self-sovereign identity (SSI) model entails the full responsibility and sovereignty of a user regarding his identity data. This identity data can contain private data which is solely known to the user. The user himself is therefore required to manage the whole lifecycle of his private data, including the backup and restore. We show that prior work on how to backup and restore the user's identity data does not meet the requirements of the SSI setting, and we present the first solution which does meet the requirements. Authenticated backup with auditing by remote entities (AWARE) combines SSI sustaining aspects and extends them to create a truly self-sovereign backup-and-restore protocol. In AWARE, trusted, physically met humans, called custodians, hold a secure device. Custodians with a secure device offer an offline backup possibility and a secure channel. The backup and restore are audited by commits on a publicly accessible distributed ledger. These commits are answered by auditing services which are required during restore. Only some auditing services hold relevant data for a restore. The self sovereignty of the user lies in the exclusive information which auditing services hold relevant data. AWARE is the first backup-and-restore mechanism that fully complies with the SSI model. We perform an in-depth security-risk analysis of AWARE, showing a risk rating which is comparable to the best risk rating o related non-SSI-compliant backup-and-restore mechanisms. We instantiate the AWARE protocol with cryptographic primitives providing a high security level of 256-bit. We show its implementation feasibility by providing a simulation of AWARE, and conclude with an estimated performance analysis on a microcontoller architecture based on our simulation and implementation results in the literature.

1 Introduction

The amount of digital information is ever-increasing. The International Data Corporation predicts an annual growth rate of 61% from 2018 to 2025 to the

© IFIP International Federation for Information Processing 2020
Published by Springer Nature Switzerland AG 2020
M. Laurent and T. Giannetsos (Eds.): WISTP 2019, LNCS 12024, pp. 202–219, 2020.
https://doi.org/10.1007/978-3-030-41702-4_13

global datasphere's volume of 175ZB [9]. With the majority of this data being user generated. From 2010 to 2019 the amount of internet users doubled and nearly reached 60% of the world population [23]. The user generated data consists of content and identity data. This identity data is traditionally known to the user and the service. The identity data can include private data, which is a privacy challenge for the user and an increasing challenge for the services. The General Data Protection Regulation (GDPR) [12], an EU law regarding data protection and privacy of the EU citizens, exemplifies the legislative relevance of privacy.

Several identity models have been proposed that achieve different levels of privacy protection [1]. In case of the *isolated identity model* the service, a trusted authority (TA) stores and manages the user's identity data directly. In case of the *central identity model* an identity provider, a TA, stores and manages the user's identity data and transfers it to a service. In case of the *federated identity model* the identity data is stored and managed distributed across multiple identity providers (TAs). In case of the *user-centric identity model*, a service manages the identity data, but a device is distributed to the user, a security token (ST). It empowers the user to store his identity data. It can be realized by a smart card or other dedicated hardware. The sharing of identity data requires explicit user consent, but the identity data is still managed by an identity provider. The *self-sovereign identity* (SSI) model emerged due to the rise of distributed ledger (DL) technology, it extends the user-centric identity model. In the SSI model, the user stores his own identity data and also manages his identity data over its entire lifecycle. Therefore, the user instead of a central authority, is in control of the identity data and the user decides how personal attributes and credentials are shared [4].

An essential but overlooked aspect of SSI is backup and restore of the *private data* PD_u of a user u. The user is responsible for the entire lifecycle of his private data, therefore, also for backup and restore. Private data PD_u is per assumption not known to any other entity than the user u. Therefore, the user u is the only entity capable of conducting the backup of PD_u. The process of backup is to store a copy of the data such that it is available for restore in case of lost access. The process of restore is to access the backed up copy of the data. Abilities gained by the private data are given to any entity who can access it. The access to the backed up data thus determines who is sovereign. Access control consists of three steps: authentication, authorization, and auditing [26]. Authentication describes that the authenticity of an entity trying to access the data must be verified. Authorization describes the decision whether to grant or deny access to the data for a specific entity. Auditing describes the capability of the system to trace the actions of its participants. Since sovereignty lies in the access to the data, we define:

A self-sovereign solution must require the user to conduct the step of authorization and the user must also choose who authenticates and who audits the restore.

We show that in prior works on how backup and restore can be conducted the user is not sovereign in case of lost access to his private data. We therefore present our self-sovereign backup-and-restore protocol of authenticated backup with auditing by remote entities (AWARE). The user is empowered to decide if the restore is granted. We achieve this by backing up the data to physically met custodians who are audited on a public DL. The user is just required to hold a low entropy information (about 6 digits) to restore his PD_u. The AWARE protocol further extends the STs of the user-centric model by interconnectable security tokens (IST's). An IST is an ST which has a procedure to exchange specific information with other IST's. We conduct a security-risk analysis of the AWARE protocol and compare the results to the current proposals. We show that the AWARE protocol is the only backup-and-restore mechanism providing self sovereignty while its worst risk rating is close to the best risk rating of the proposals not offering self sovereignty.

2   The Problem of Backup and Restore in the SSI Model

The problem of backup and restore in the SSI model is that the user u has private data PD_u which is solely known to him. He wants to backup PD_u such that after he lost access to PD_u he can regain access to it. A perfect requirement would be that only the user u can access PD_u while any other entity $e \neq u$ cannot. However, over an insecure channel perfect authenticity cannot be achieved [21]. Realizable requirements are:

1. The user u has a high likelihood of accessing his backed up PD_u.
2. Any other entity $e \neq u$ has a very low likelihood of accessing the backed up PD_u.

Two systems realizing SSI management explicitly offer a suggestion on how to conduct backup and restore: Sovrin [30] and uPort [7]. Sovrin proposes the use of distributed storage devices or social backup, backing up at entities the user trusts (custodians). uPort proposes a smart contract based solution in which the private key can be swapped to another key, based on the rules specified in a smart contract and promotions of earlier specified online entities the user trusts.

By definition, a backup-and-restore mechanism is self sovereign if the user performs the authorization during restore and chooses who authenticates and who audits the restore process. The authentication must be performed by some other entity than the user. Since the user is not capable of authenticating himself after data loss. Neither the user nor the authenticating entity can audit themselves. Therefore, the auditing must be conducted by another entity than the user or the authenticating entity. The audit trail must be accessible to the unauthenticated user as he is not capable of accessing his private data. Next to the steps of access control, the accessibility itself must be minimized. Therefore, the backed up private data should be stored offline.

In the literature we identified four backup-and-restore mechanisms: *Trusted authorities*, one identity service knows all the private data; *Local backup*, a user backs up his private data on several devices, which the user distributes (e.g. at home, deposit box, at work); *Social backup*, a user distributes his private data across several personally trusted entities (custodians); *Smart contract* based, the user allows trusted online entities to promote a new key into his controlling smart contract. A smart contract is a protocol executed on a DL. It empowers its participants to conduct credible transactions without the need for third parties. In Table 1 we show per backup-and-restore mechanism which entity conducts which step of access control and whether the backup is accessible online or offline.

Table 1. Per backup-and-restore mechanism the table presents which step of access control is conducted by which entity as well as the accessibility of the private data.

B-and-R mech.	Authentication	Authorization	Audit	Accessibility
Trusted authority	TA	TA	Not defined	Online
Local backup	Not defined	Not defined	Not defined	Not defined
Social backup	Custodians	Custodians	Not defined	Offline
Smart contract	Trusted online entities	Smart contract	DL	Online

In case of the *TA*s every step of access control is managed by a TA. Authentication is only possible via a public channel (the Internet) and the data is stored online. It is thus not self sovereign. In case of the *local backup* the steps of access control and the accessibility are not clearly defined. It is therefore not self sovereign. In case of *social backup* authentication is conducted by custodians via a secure channel. The authorization, however, is also conducted by the custodians without any defined procedure of audit. It is thus not self sovereign. In case of the *smart contract* based backup-and-restore mechanism the authentication is conducted by trusted entities via a public channel which can trigger the authorization of the smart contract by promoting a new key. It is not self sovereign and the private data is stored online. However, it offers a publicly accessible auditing trail by writing the promotions on the DL. In conclusion, none of the backup-and-restore mechanisms in the literature is self sovereign. The aspect of a secure channel between the user and his custodians and a publicly accessible auditing trail on the DL, however, form a starting point for us to build a self sovereign solution.

3   AWARE

The self sovereignty of the user, even under data loss, is the aim of our protocol on authenticated backup with auditing by remote entities (AWARE). We have the following participants: *The user* performs the authorization and decides who conducts the authentication and who conducts the auditing. *Custodians* are entities the user trusts and meets physically, they conduct the authentication. Likely candidates are family and friends for personal data backup and colleagues for company related data backup. *Auditing services* conduct the auditing, logging on a DL. The accessibility of the backed up PD_u is offline to decrease the attack surface. The physically met custodians in combination with their IST's allow for offline data storage and a secure channel. In our AWARE protocol only auditing requires online communication.

Notation. All participants of the protocol are modeled as elements of the set of entities E. We abbreviate a specific entity by a small letter (e.g. the user $u \in E$). We indicate the relation to a specific entity by placing this entity in the index (e.g. the user u's private data is abbreviated as PD_u). If an entity belongs to a subgroup of known size we denote it with a numbering in the index. The i'th user of the subgroup of n users U is denoted with $u_i \in U$ for $i \in \{1, \ldots, n\}$.

Regarding functionality, we use the following notation: We denote the symmetric-key encryption of data D by a symmetric-key k with $Enc_k(D)$ and respectively the decryption such that $Dec_k(Enc_k(D)) = D$. Asymmetric-key encryption of data D by an asymmetric-key pek with $Enc_{pek}(D)$ and respectively the decryption such that $Dec_{sek}(Enc_{pek}(D)) = D$. We denote the splitting of data D into n shares by secret sharing $D \xrightarrow{ss(t,n)} \{s_1(D), \ldots, s_n(D)\}$ such that t of these shares can be used to reconstruct the data D. Regarding some set B we denote a uniformly random pick with $a \xleftarrow{\$} B$ for $a \in B$.

Parameters. In Table 2 the parameters of the AWARE protocol description are presented in their contexts.

Assumptions. A user u of our system,

- holds private data PD_u,
- is capable of memorizing the low entropy information ρ (q numbers less than p),
- possesses an interconnectable security token (IST_u).

The concept of an interconnectable security token (IST) is an extension on the ST used in the user-centric identity model. It stores PD_u securely, just accessible to the user u. The extension lies in the connectivity of the IST. While a smartcard or ordinary ST device can just connect to a smartphone or computer the ISTs are capable to interconnect. An IST_u of a user u guarantees that

- private data PD_u stored on IST_u is only accessible to the user u,
- it is offline by default and the user needs to specifically enable communication,
- it is interconnectable with other IST_e for $e \neq u$ via a short range channel (e.g. Infrared [3], Near Field Communication [16]),
- it is connectable via another channel to an internet capable device (e.g. smartphone, computer, etc.).

Table 2. Parameters of the AWARE protocol.

Variable	Context
u	The user
C_u	The custodians of user u
$\mathcal{AS}_u$	The auditing service list of user u
$\mathcal{ASS}_u$	The auditing services shares from the user u
π_u	The policy of user u
$l \in \mathbb{N}$	The key length
k	The key $k \xleftarrow{\$} \{0,1\}^l$
n,t	n-out-of-t shares of $\mathrm{Enc}_k(PD_u)$ (using secret sharing)
r,q	r-out-of-q shares of k (using secret sharing)
x,y	x-out-of-y key promotions required in policy π_u
$p \geq q$	The total amount of auditing services
h	The maximum of publishable restore releases
ρ	Memorizable, low entropy information of q services holding a key share

The participants of the AWARE protocol are the user u who has n custodians ($\mathcal{C}_u$) and p auditing services ($\mathcal{AS}_u$). The user u and his custodians $\mathcal{C}_u$ posses an interconnectable security token (IST). All participants hold two public-secret key pairs. A keypair for signing (psk,ssk) and a keypair for encryption (pek,sek). The user u further holds private data PD_u which is solely known to u and which should be backed up.

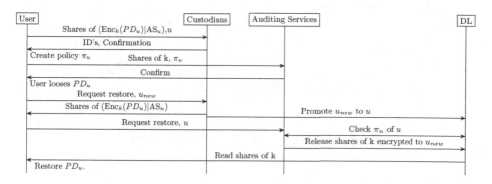

Fig. 1. Overview sequence diagram of AWARE.

Overview. The AWARE protocol (Fig. 1) consists of interaction from the user with his custodians and auditing services. The user chooses p auditing services and sends a share of his PD_u concatenated with the list of his auditing services and his public signing key to each of his n custodians. The user creates a policy π_u in which he specifies that x of y custodians are required to promote a new identity on the DL and the maximum amount of restore releases h. The user creates p auditing shares. He creates q key shares of the key k and adds $p - q$ fake shares. Subsequently, he distributes all auditing shares randomly over the p auditing services. The user receives ρ, the q auditing services holding a key share. In case of access loss to PD_u, the user approaches t custodians, requests his data and restores his encrypted PD_u and $\mathcal{AS}_u$. He approaches r auditing services from the ρ auditing services from $\mathcal{AS}_u$ and requests a restore. The auditing service checks the policy and only if it is met releases his share of k encrypted to the new identity of the user. The auditing service is aware of this new identity as it is promoted by the custodians on the DL. The user is then able to read the encrypted shares, decrypt them and reconstruct k. With the key k the user can decrypt his PD_u.

Initialization. To be fully self sovereign, the user is required to choose the system parameters. He has to choose $n = |\mathcal{C}_u|$ the total amount of custodians, $t \leq n$ the amount of custodians required for a restore, $p = |\mathcal{AS}_u|$ the total amount of auditing services, $q \leq p$ the total amount of auditing services holding a key share, $r \leq q$ the amount of auditing services required for a restore, and $k \xleftarrow{\$} \{0,1\}^l$ the key k of size l which must be generated uniformly random.

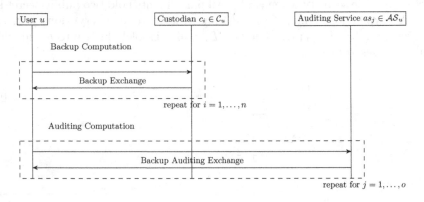

Fig. 2. Sequence diagram of our backup protocol.

Backup. The basic structure of our backup protocol is illustrated in Fig. 2. In the following we elaborate the details per step:

1. Backup Computation:
   - The user u encrypts his private data PD_u with the key k, $Enc_k(PD_u)$.
   - The user u appends $\mathcal{AS}_u$ and splits it

- $(Enc_k(PD_u)|\mathcal{AS}_u) \xrightarrow{ss_{(t,n)}} \{s_1(Enc_k(PD_u)|\mathcal{AS}_u), \ldots, s_n(Enc_k(PD_u)|\mathcal{AS}_u)\}$.

2. Backup Exchange, the user u meets with each custodian $c_i \in \mathcal{C}_u$ (for $i \in \{1, \ldots, n\}$):
   - The user u receives the public signing key psk_{c_i} of the custodian i.
   - The user u provides his public signing key psk_u and a share $s_i(Enc_k(PD_u)|\mathcal{AS}_u)$.

3. Auditing computation:
   - The user u chooses a policy, π_u.
     (a) psk_{c_i} for $i = 1, \ldots, x$ from which at least y must promote the user.
     (b) h, the maximum number of published restore releases.
   - The user u splits his key k, $k \xrightarrow{ss_{(r,q)}} \{s_1(k), \ldots, s_q(k)\}$.
   - The user u generates $p - q$ random fake shares f and appends them to his list of auditing shares $\mathcal{ASS}_u$, $\mathcal{ASS}_u = \{s_1(k), \ldots, s_q(k), f_1, \ldots, f_{o-q}\}$.
   - The user u performs a truly random permutation on $\mathcal{AS}_u$ to receive $Perm(\mathcal{AS}_u)$. The q servers holding a key-share are outputted as ρ.
   - The user u encrypts each auditing share appended with his policy π_u to the corresponding service in the permuted auditing service list, $Enc_{pek_{y_j}}(a_j|\pi_u)$ for $a_j \in \mathcal{ASS}_u$, $y_j \in Perm(\mathcal{AS}_u)$ and $j \in \{1, \ldots, o\}$.

4. Backup Auditing Exchange:
   - The IST_u is connected to an online device and each $Enc_{pek_{y_j}}(a_j|\pi_u)$ signed with his psk_u in the order of $\mathcal{AS}_u$ is uploaded to as_j.
   - The auditing service as_j confirms the receipt.

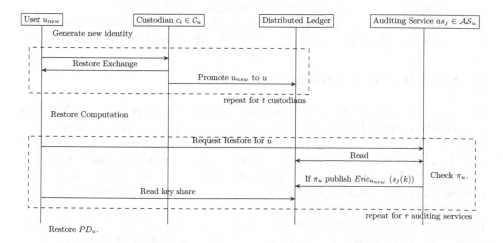

Fig. 3. Sequence diagram of our restore protocol.

Restore. Assuming that the user u looses access to his PD_u he needs to engage in a restore protocol. For this we assume a new identity u_{new} of the user as his old identity is lost. The basic structure of our restore protocol is illustrated in Fig. 3. In the following we elaborate the details per step:

1. Generate new identity:
   - The user generates a new key pairs $(psk_{u_{new}}, ssk_{u_{new}})$ and $(pek_{u_{new}}, sek_{u_{new}})$.
2. Restore Exchange:
   - The user u approaches a subset of t of his custodians and provides them with his new public encryption key $pek_{u_{new}}$.
   - The custodian c_i physically authenticates user u and provides him with his share, $s_i(Enc_k(PD_u)|\mathcal{AS}_u)$ for $i \in \{1, \ldots, n\}$.
3. Promotion:
   - Each of the t custodians promotes $pek_{u_{new}}$ for psk_u on the DL.
4. Restore Computation:
   - The user u reconstructs $Enc_k(PD_u)$ and $\mathcal{AS}_u$ from the t shares he received.
   - The user u approaches the auditing services holding a key share, by applying his low entropy information ρ.
5. Restore Auditing Exchange:
   - The user u request a key share from r auditing services.
   - If the auditing service $as_j \in \mathcal{AS}_u$ for $j \in \{1, \ldots, q\}$ receives a restore request for u, it checks the corresponding policy π_u and releases $Enc_{pek_{u_{new}}}(s_j(k))$ if the policy π_u is met.
6. Restore:
   - The user u reads the encrypted key shares on the DL.
   - The user decrypts r key shares with his $sek_{u_{new}}$ and reconstruct k. He uses it to decrypt the encrypted private data $Dec_k(Enc_k(PD_u)) = PD_u$.

4   Security-Risk Analysis

Security. The aim of AWARE is to allow the user u to conduct backup and restore self sovereignly. The authentication is conducted by carefully chosen custodians. The confidentiality and integrity of the data are maintained by choosing additional auditing services to audit the process of authentication and authorization. The AWARE protocol can be split into the sub-protocol conducted between the user and his custodians and the sub-protocol conducted between the user and his aware services. In our analysis we focus on both of the sub-protocols. For the protocol conducted between the user and his custodians it holds that if less than t custodians are compromised the private data's security is determined by the secret-sharing scheme used. For the protocol conducted between the user and his auditing services it holds that if less than r of the auditing services are compromised the key's security is also determined by the secret-sharing scheme used. If Shamir's secret sharing [27] is used the private data is information-theoretically secure if less than t custodians are compromised and the key is information-theoretically secure if less than r auditing services are compromised. Therefore, we assume for our analysis that t or more custodians are compromised and that r or more auditing services are compromised. We further assume that the custodians and auditing services do not collude and that ρ is only known to the user.

Integrity is the property of maintaining and assuring the accuracy and completeness of data over its entire lifecycle [17]. The custodians hold the shares of the private data encrypted with key k. The auditing services hold the shares of the key k. If t or more custodians are compromised they can restore the encrypted private data and can manipulate it, however, altering would render the encrypted private data undecryptable by k. Therefore, the accuracy and completeness of the private data is maintained and assured over its entire life cycle. If r or more compromised auditing services would manipulate the key k, the encrypted private data would be undecryptable and thus accuracy and completeness of the key k is also maintained and assured over its entire life cycle.

Confidentiality is the property that information is not made available or disclosed to unauthorized entities [17]. Our AWARE protocol makes use of secret sharing for the distribution of the encrypted private data PD_u to the custodians and the key k to the auditing services. If t or more custodians are compromised, the encrypted private data can be restored and is now protected by the security assumptions of the symmetric cipher used. To retrieve the key k an illegitimate restore attempt must be conducted. This attempt requires the compromised custodians to get the key k which will be logged on the DL. In this situation the user can engage. However, this is still insufficient to guarantee self sovereignty. The auditing services reply and proceed with the restore part of the AWARE protocol for a new identity, not distinguishing the user from an adversary. Therefore, we introduced auditing services holding fake shares and the maximum of potential restore releases h. The adversary is additionally required to choose r of the q auditing services holding a key share from the p auditing services in total. The chances to guess r auditing services from the q auditing services holding a key share from p auditing services in total without knowing ρ is $\prod_{i=0}^{h-1} \frac{q-i}{p-i}$. If we choose the strictest policy that the amount of allowed restore releases is equal to the amount of key shares required, thus fixing $h = r$, the chance to guess r key share holding auditing services is $\frac{q!(p-r)!}{(q-r)!p!}$. If r or more auditing services are compromised we have the same chance that these r auditing services holding key shares. Without compromised custodians, however, the adversary gets no information about PD_u and cannot even verify if the illegitimately restored key k' equals the key k.

Availability is the property that information is accessible and usable on demand by an authorized entity [17]. For the AWARE protocol this entails that at least t of the n custodians must be available and that r of the q auditing services must be available. It is, therefore, not enough to define that t or more custodians and r or more auditing services are compromised. The relevant aspect for availability is whether t or more custodians and r or more auditing services are compliant with the protocol. If so, the availability is guaranteed. If, however, less than t custodians or less than r auditing services are trustworthy the system locks itself. This is a denial of service (DOS) as the PD_u is not accessible anymore. By introducing h, the maximum of restore releases, the policy prohibits further publication of auditing shares which can result in an even earlier DOS. However, both DOS's are expected as they block an illegitimate restore attempt. During such a DOS, the user can be in one of two states: State one, the user is still in possession of his private data. Then there is no problem, he should simply choose more trustworthy custodians after seeing the auditing trail on the DL. State two, the user is not in possession of his private data, and the h published auditing shares contain less than r key shares. Then the protocol has locked access. When this situation occurs, the private data is inaccessible. This behavior is consistent with the requirements, that any entity other than the user has a very low likelihood of accessing the backed up private data while the user has a high likelihood. This high likelihood allows for lost access. Therefore, such an DOS is exactly what we are aiming for. If an illegitimate restore occurs locked access is the preferable state to identity theft and compromise. To prevent this still unpleasant situation users are advised to monitor restore requests on the DL to be aware of such illegitimate restore attempts and be able to engage in time.

Risk. Table 3 shows the numbers of our risk analysis. We conduct it with $t = 3$ of the $n = 5$ custodians being required to restore, as well as $r = 3$ of the $q = 5$ services being required for restore. The amount of legitimate restore responses is limited to $h = r$, and we choose $p = 100$ services in total. Our risk analysis's terminology and scale are based on the NIST 'Risk Management Guide' [28].

A *compromise* can concern the custodians, the shares stored at the custodians, the service, the low entropy information ρ or a combination of them. We assume a compromise if at least t custodians or shares are compromised. All compromises can either occur or not, except the compromise of the auditing services. Here we distinguish not occurring, the compromise of r services and the compromise of all services. We do this to account for the risk in a situation in which ρ is compromised. We further distinguish the custodian and the share, because a compromise of the custodians would enable the adversary to send sufficiently many valid promote message on the DL to conduct a restore, while a compromise of the shares would not. After calculating the risk rating for the five isolated compromises we calculate the risk rating of their mutual occurrence.

The *likelihood* is determined per isolated compromise. The low entropy information ρ of the user can be extracted by physical theft, social engineering or simply by a random guess. The likelihood of physical theft is zero as ρ gets only memorized by the user. The likelihood of social engineering can only be approximated. Even though the low entropy information is a novel concept, it can be compared to a user's password. Happ, Melzer and Steffgen found in [14] that 38.6% of the students they interviewed are willing to give up their password just by talking less than two minutes to female interviewers. In the case that a treat is provided directly before the password is asked, the likelihood rises to 47.8%.

Therefore, we decided to model the likelihood of social engineering with 0.4. The likelihood of a random guess is $\frac{q!(p-r))!}{(q-r)!p!}$ as all r service must be chosen correctly from all p services. Therefore, we assume it to be negligible if p is chosen properly. For the numbers used in our risk analysis the likelihood of a random guess is $\frac{5!(100-3))!}{(5-3)!100!} \approx 0.000062$. The share stored at a custodian can only be extracted by social engineering. This is the case as the device is assumed to be offline and the information is stored securely. If the device would be stolen, a full breach must be considered. Therefore, we determine the likelihood of just the share being compromised by 0.4. The share stored at a custodian and the secret signing key of the custodian can, however, be compromised by either social engineering or theft. The likelihood of social engineering is again 0.4. The likelihood of theft is harder to quantify. We set it to conservative 0.5, assuming that the chances are fifty-fifty. Those two events are not mutually exclusive, therefore, the accumulated likelihood of the custodian being fully compromised is 0.7. The compromise of a service is quite unlikely. However, we set it to the same conservative 0.5, again assuming that the chances are fifty-fifty as the data is out of control of the user. All other likelihoods used in the table are combinations of these base scenarios.

The impact can be low, medium or high. A high impact describes a situation in which all knowledge is accessible to the adversary (PD_u can be reconstructed). The medium impact describes a situation in which one piece of information is missing to the adversary. The low impact describes a situation in which more than one piece of information is missing to the adversary.

Seven mutual compromises result in a potential break of the system. Only one of them, however, has a risk rating which exceed *very low* by being *low*. The second *low* risk rating is from a moderate impact. It is crucial that both of these events include compromise of the custodians, thus compromise of the share and the capability to promote a new identity on the DL. The risk rating of just the compromise of the custodians is larger than the risk rating of compromise of the custodians and the low entropy information ρ, due to a higher likelihood. Compared to the other proposed solutions with the same likelihood assumptions it can be seen that the worst risk rating of the AWARE protocol is *low* with a risk rating of 13.71. It is close to the best risk rating of social backup and local backup. In Table 4 these risk ratings are presented. The risk of just trusting custodians is much higher with a *moderate* risk rating. Only the *low* risk rating of distributing the private data on local devices is slightly lower than our worst risk rating. However, the guarantees of local backup are highly dependent on its user and do not offer self sovereignty. Our AWARE protocol has a comparable low risk rating while enabling the user to be self sovereign by making use of trusted custodians, auditing service and the assumption that the user is capable of memorizing the low entropy information ρ. To guarantee self sovereignty, the user is required to hold some private information. We reduced its size from the arbitrary sized PD_u via a fixed size key to the size of ρ.

Table 3. Risk analysis for compromised custodians, shares, services, ρ and their combinations. The likelihood is determined as described in the text. The terminology and method are based on the NIST Risk Management Guide [28], the *risk rating* = likelihood * impact.

Compromised				Likelihood	Impact	Risk rating for t, r = 3 and p = 100	
Custodians	Shares	Service	ρ				
No	No	No	Yes	0.4 [14]	Low (10)	4	Very low
No	Yes	No	No	0.4^t	Low (10)	0.64	Very low
Yes	No	No	No	0.7^t	Medium (50)	17.14	Low
No	No	r	No	0.5^r	Low (10)	1.25	Very low
No	No	All	No	0.5^p	Medium (50)	$4 * 10^{-29}$	Very low
No	No	r	Yes	$0.4 * 0.5^r$	Medium (50)	2.5	Very low
No	No	All	Yes	$0.4 * 0.5^p$	Medium (50)	$1.58 * 10^{-29}$	Very low
No	Yes	No	Yes	$0.4^t * 0.4$	Medium (50)	1.28	Very low
No	Yes	r	No	$0.4^t * 0.5^r$	Medium (50)	0.4	Very low
No	Yes	r	Yes	$0.4^t * 0.5^r * 0.4$	High (100)	0.32	Very low
No	Yes	All	No	$0.4^t * 0.5^p$	High (100)	$5.05 * 10^{-30}$	Very low
No	Yes	All	Yes	$0.4^t * 0.5^p * 0.4$	High (100)	$2.02 * 10^{-30}$	Very low
Yes	No	No	Yes	$0.7^t * 0.4$	High (100)	13.71	Low
Yes	No	r	No	$0.7^t * 0.5^r$	Medium (50)	2.14	Very low
Yes	No	r	Yes	$0.7^t * 0.5^r * 0.4$	High (100)	1.72	Very low
Yes	No	All	No	$0.7^t * 0.5^p$	High (100)	$2.71 * 10^{-29}$	Very low
Yes	No	All	Yes	$0.7^t * 0.5^p * 0.4$	High (100)	$1.08 * 10^{-29}$	Very low

Table 4. Risk rating for social and device backup.

Compromised	Likelihood	Impact	Risk rating for t = 3	
Social backup	0.7^t	High (100)	34.3	Moderate
Local backup	0.5^d	High (100)	12.5	Low

5　Implementation

We implemented a simulation of the AWARE protocol[1].

We chose the high security level of our instantiation of the AWARE protocol to be 256-bit. The building block of symmetric encryption is instantiated as 256-bit AES [8] in Galois counter mode (GCM) [22]. The building block of the asymmetric encryption and decryption is instantiated as an integrated encryption scheme (ECIES) [20] of the symmetric AES256GCM and the P-521 elliptic curve being specified in NIST FIPS-186-4 [24]. The building block of signing and verifying signatures is instantiated as the elliptic curve digital signature algorithm (ECDSA) [18] over the P-521 curve. The building block of secret sharing is instantiated by Shamir's secret sharing [27] with a modulus of $2^{521} - 1$, the

---

[1] https://github.com/phil-jakubeit/aware.

13th Mersenne prime [31]. The random permutation of the auditing service list is realized by the Fisher-Yates-Durstenfeld random permutation [13].

5.1   Experimentation

We assume 1 KB of private data PD_u and an auditing service list $\mathcal{AS}_u$ consisting of the addresses and the public signing keys of the $p = 100$ auditing services. The address is 128-bit, the size of an IPv6 address [15]. The public signing key is 526-bit due to compression of the point on the P-521 curve. Thus is the service list about 8 KB. Due to formatting overhead the user and each of his custodians must exchange 24 KB in our simulation. The NFC specification [16] and serial infrared communication [3] allow a baud rate of 115,200 bit per second (14.4 B/s). With this baud rate the backup exchange and the restore exchange between a user and one custodian each takes less than 2 s.

The most cost intensive building blocks we use are the ECC computations on the P-521 curve and the generation of random coefficients for the secret sharing.

The most cost intensive operation of ECC is the scalar multiplication with a time complexity of $\mathcal{O}(n^{k+1})$ for $k = 2$ if ordinary school book multiplication is used and $n = 2^{521} - 1$, the order of the finite field. The implementation of the scalar multiplication under the P-521 curve on the low end ARMv6-M architecture by [19] is optimized for memory efficiency and takes about 84 million cycles. On a 48 MHz processor this equals about 1.7 s for one scalar multiplication. Even though the channel between a user and his custodian is secure one signature from the custodian and one verification from the user is required for the user to know the custodians capability to sign with his private key. This adds up to about 8 s but the required time can be decreased by using speed optimized implementations or a more powerful microcontroller. The secret sharing requires 521-bit randomness for each random coefficient. Due to the structure of Shamir's secret sharing we require $t - 1$ 521-bit strings. The built-in random number generator of an ARM cortex M4 with the ARMv7-M architecture is capable of generating a 32-bit random number every 40 cycles [2]. With $t = 3$ from our risk analysis 1042-bit of randomness are required. This can be generated in 1320 cycles, which takes about 0.0000275 s if the processor runs at 48 Mhz.

The communication with the DL has costs and is kept to a minimum. Each custodian writes a signed promotion message on the DL. It consists of the hex representation of the ASCII string "SSIAWARE-PROMOTION", the public signing key of the custodian, the public signing key of the user to restore and the public encryption key of the new user. The hex number requires 18-Bytes, each key requires 66-Bytes in its compressed form, and the signature consists of 132-Bytes. This adds up to 348-Byte of raw information. In our simulation we have up to 785-Bytes due to overhead from the serialized formatting.

The key k is 256-bit, but our secret-sharing scheme operates modulo the 13th Mersenne prime. Therefore, each share of the key can be up to 521-bit. The policy consists of two small integers, h and y and contains further x keys each of size 526-bit. Assuming $y = 3$ and $x = 5$, a complete message to an auditing service can be send in less than 3 KB and should be secured via TLS [10].

A signed restore release message consists of the hex representation of the ASCII string "SSIAWARE-RESTORE", the public signing key of the user to restore, the public signing key of the auditing service and the encrypted auditing share. The hex number requires 16-Bytes, each key requires 66-Bytes, the encrypted share also requires 66-Bytes, and the signature consists of 132-Bytes. This adds up to 280-Byte of raw information. In our simulation we have up to 1 KB due to serialized formatting.

6 Discussion

We achieved a high likelihood for the user to restore and a low likelihood for every other entity by requiring public commits to a DL.

Data can be written on any ledger. Exemplary for the Bitcoin (BC) ledger the data is concatenated, padded and extended with its RIPEMD-160 [11] hash. Then it is split into 20-Byte chunks and the minimum amount of BC is send to each 20-Byte chunk (BC address) [5]. The minimum amount of a single transaction is 0.00000547 BC and the fee per byte is 0.00000014 BC.

For the conservative amount of 785-Bytes in our simulation this equals 0.00032492 BC (3.04 Euro for 9348.66BC/Euro) for each promotion message. Each auditing service as_j that writes a restore release to the DL is must spend 0.0004278BC (3.95 Euro for 9348.66BC/Euro). The amount of custodians required for restore and the amount of auditing services required for restore directly translate to costs. Exemplary Fig. 4 shows that the amount of custodians directly translates to costs and to the risk rating of the AWARE protocol. The thresholds show that an increase in the number of custodians reduces the worst risk rating to *very low* with the tradeoff that the costs rise above 20 Euro. It also shows that less than 3 custodians imply a rise of the risk rating to *moderate*.

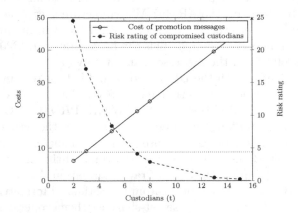

Fig. 4. Plot of the cost of promotion messages with varying t custodians and the worst risk rating of AWARE. The dotted lines indicate the threshold for the risk rating *Very Low* (0–4), *Low* (5–20) or *Moderate* (21–79) [28].

Other DL like the Ethereum ledger allow for smart contracts. Smart contracts can be used to write the promotion message and the restore release directly on the ledger. They can, however, also interact smart, thus performing gated re-encryption. Auditing services would be required to have a specific key per user. The user sends data to the smart contract which validates the policy and performs re-encryption in case of a valid restore request. This would shift the computation from the auditing services to the smart contracts for the increased price of computation on the DL, while granting compliance to the policy.

A private ledger (e.g. Hyperledger [29]) of trusted nodes could also be used. This decreases the cost to the power consumption of the auditing services. It must further be guaranteed that the ledger is accessible to any participant without authentication.

7   Conclusion and Future Work

Our AWARE protocol is built on physical trust relations towards custodians and handles a potential compromise by requiring online auditing on a DL. The exclusive information ρ in combination with the policy π_u empowers the user to be the only entity capable of restoring his backed up data with certainty. This makes the AWARE protocol the only self-sovereign backup-and-restore protocol. Backup-and-restore mechanisms in the literature make the trust assumption either towards a TA, towards other participants or towards devices. We make use of all these concepts, the auditing services, the custodians and the ISTs. However, in the AWARE setting the user is sovereign. The only trust assumption left is that the auditing services abide to the policy specified by the user. Future research can look into concepts of enforcing the policy (e.g. smart contracts [6] or trusted execution environments [25]). It is further desired to speed optimize ECC computations on low end 32-bit microcontrollers for security parameters of 256-bit.

The private data is held by the custodians and even in case of compromise of multiple custodians there is no possibility to retrieve the private data without notice. The auditing services involved are assumed to abide to the policy, therefore, either the symmetric cipher used (AESGCM256) must be broken or promotions on the DL are required to decrypt the private data. These promotions reveal the identity of the compromised custodians and the user can engage. The user remains in charge by being able to access the auditing log and perform the access authorization. By just holding ρ instead of his private data the user remains self sovereign.

References

1. Abraham, A.: Self-sovereign identity. Styria. EGIZ.GV.AT (2017)
2. Alkim, E., Jakubeit, P., Schwabe, P.: NEWHOPE on ARM Cortex-M. In: Carlet, C., Hasan, M.A., Saraswat, V. (eds.) SPACE 2016. LNCS, vol. 10076, pp. 332–349. Springer, Cham (2016). https://doi.org/10.1007/978-3-319-49445-6_19

3. Angerstein, J.: Serial infrared specification. http://berk.tc/intercon/irda/IrPHY_1p4.pdf
4. Steinberg, T., Pon, B., Locke, C.: Private-sector digital identity in emerging markets (2019)
5. CryptoGraffiti: Cryptograffiti (2019). https://cryptograffiti.info/
6. Christidis, K., Devetsikiotis, M.: Blockchains and smart contracts for the internet of things. IEEE Access **4**, 2292–2303 (2016)
7. ConsenSys AG: uPort (2017). https://www.uport.me/
8. Daemen, J., Rijmen, V.: The Design of Rijndael: AES-The Advanced Encryption Standard. Springer, Heidelberg (2013). https://doi.org/10.1007/978-3-662-04722-4
9. John, R., David, R., John, G.: The digitization of the world - from edge to core (2018)
10. Dierks, T.: TLS v 1.2 (2008). http://www.hjp.at/doc/rfc/rfc5246.html
11. Dobbertin, H., Bosselaers, A., Preneel, B.: RIPEMD-160: a strengthened version of rIPEMD. In: Gollmann, D. (ed.) FSE 1996. LNCS, vol. 1039, pp. 71–82. Springer, Heidelberg (1996). https://doi.org/10.1007/3-540-60865-6_44
12. European Commission: Data protection in the EU (2016). https://www.eugdpr.org/
13. Fisher, R.A., Yates, F.: Statistical Tables for Biological, Agricultural and Medical Research. Nature, Oliver and Boyd Ltd., London (1943)
14. Happ, C., Melzer, A., Steffgen, G.: Trick with treat–reciprocity increases the willingness to communicate personal data. Comput. Hum. Behav. **61**, 372–377 (2016)
15. Hinden, R.: IPv6 specification (2017). http://www.hjp.at/doc/rfc/rfc2460.html
16. International Organization for Standardization: Radio frequency parameters for communications at 13,56 MHz (2008)
17. International Organization for Standardization: ISO 27000 (2018)
18. Johnson, D., Menezes, A., Vanstone, S.: The elliptic curve digital signature algorithm (ECDSA). IJISS **1**, 36–63 (2001)
19. Liu, Z., Seo, H., Castiglione, A., Choo, K.-K.R., Kim, H.: Memory-efficient implementation of elliptic curve cryptography for the internet-of-things. IEEE TDSC **16**, 521–529 (2018)
20. Martínez, V.G., Encinas, L.H., et al.: A comparison of the standardized versions of ECIES. In: IAS. IEEE (2010)
21. Maurer, U.: Information-theoretically secure secret-key agreement by NOT authenticated public discussion. In: Fumy, W. (ed.) EUROCRYPT 1997. LNCS, vol. 1233, pp. 209–225. Springer, Heidelberg (1997). https://doi.org/10.1007/3-540-69053-0_15
22. McGrew, D.A., Viega, J.: The security and performance of the Galois/Counter Mode (GCM) of operation. In: Canteaut, A., Viswanathan, K. (eds.) INDOCRYPT 2004. LNCS, vol. 3348, pp. 343–355. Springer, Heidelberg (2004). https://doi.org/10.1007/978-3-540-30556-9_27
23. Miniwatts Data Group: World internet users and population stats (2019). https://www.internetworldstats.com/stats.htm
24. NIST: FIPS 186-4-Digital Signature Standard (DSS). NIST (2013)
25. Sabt, M., Achemlal, M., Bouabdallah, A.: Trusted execution environment: what it is, and what it is not. In: ISPA. IEEE (2015)
26. Sandhu, R.S., Samarati, P.: Access control: principle and practice. IEEE CM **32**, 40–48 (1994)
27. Shamir, A.: How to share a secret. Commun. ACM **22**, 133–138 (1979)

28. Stoneburner, G., Goguen, A., Feringa, A.: Risk Management Guide. NIST (2012)
29. The Linux Foundation. Hyperledger. https://www.hyperledger.org/
30. The Sovrin Foundation: Sovrin (2017). https://sovrin.org/
31. Weisstein, E.W.: Mersenne prime (2019). http://mathworld.wolfram.com/MersennePrime.html

Internet of Things

Automated Security Analysis of IoT Software Updates

Nicolas Dejon[1,2], Davide Caputo[1], Luca Verderame[1],
Alessandro Armando[1], and Alessio Merlo[1(✉)]

[1] DIBRIS - University of Genova, Genova, Italy
{nicolas.dejon,davide.caputo,luca.verderame,alessandro.armando,
alessio.merlo}@unige.it
[2] University of Technology of Compiègne, Compiègne, France
nicolas.dejon@etu.utc.fr

Abstract. IoT devices often operate unsupervised in ever-changing environments for several years. Therefore, they need to be updated on a regular basis. Current approaches for software updates on IoT, like the recent SUIT proposal, focus on granting integrity and confidentiality but do not analyze the content of the software update, especially the IoT application which is deployed to IoT devices. To this aim, in this paper, we present IoTAV, an automated software analysis framework for systematically verifying the security of the applications contained in software updates w.r.t. a given security policy. Our proposal can be adopted transparently by current IoT software updates workflows. We prove the viability of IoTAV by testing our methodology on a set of actual RIOT OS applications. Experimental results indicate that the approach is viable in terms of both reliability and performance, leading to the identification of 26 security policy violations in 31 real-world RIOT applications.

Keywords: IoT applications · Software Updates · SUIT · Model checking · Security policy

1 Introduction

The Internet of Things (IoT) is spreading into diverse application domains at an unstoppable pace: homes, hospitals, means of transportation, manufacturing -just to cite some- are all being affected by the coming of the IoT, and will significantly benefit from its adoption. IoT devices collect, exchange, and process data to support the dynamic and possibly even autonomous adaptation to new and/or evolving contexts. Due to changing requirements, the functionalities required by a device at deployment time is very likely to change in the future.

This work was partially funded by the Horizon 2020 project "Strategic Programs for Advanced Research and Technology in Europe" (SPARTA).

M. Laurent and T. Giannetsos (Eds.): WISTP 2019, LNCS 12024, pp. 223–239, 2020.
https://doi.org/10.1007/978-3-030-41702-4_14

The software stack of IoT devices, consisting of bootloader, operating system, and application(s), will need frequent updates for a number of reasons: to offer additional functionalities, to support new communication protocols, and/or to patch software bugs (including security vulnerabilities).

Securing the IoT software update process is key to the security of the IoT. To this end, the IoT ecosystem must be provided with the means to ensure the integrity of the software updates, i.e., that the updated software has not been tampered with by a malicious agent. The IETF IoT group is addressing the problem through the development of a new standard, Software Updates for Internet of Things (SUIT) [19], for the software update process of IoT devices. In SUIT, an IoT Software Maintainer (ISM) creates an update bundle, i.e., the firmware image (composed of an operating system and an application) holding the core logic of the IoT device. Then, the ISM uploads the updates to a distribution server, the Update Server (US), that dispatches the update to the devices using over-the-air (OTA) or wire technologies. The SUIT workflow has been designed to enforce the integrity and the confidentiality of the software update, thus providing end-to-end security between the author of the update (i.e., the ISM) and the device, even if an untrusted US mediates the process. This ensures a form of end-to-end security between the (trusted) ISM and the devices.

Unfortunately, even when a mechanism such as SUIT is in place and ensures the integrity of the software updates, there are no guarantees on the content of the update. This shortfall implies that an ISM may introduce, wittingly or not, an insecure software component that can compromise the security of the updated device. For example, the Zigbee Worm [25], triggered using a malicious firmware update, allowed the attackers to get full control over Philips Hue Smart Lamps.

In this paper, we present the *IoT Application Verification (IoTAV) Framework*, a novel analysis methodology that supports the automatic verification of security properties in applications running on IoT devices. Given an IoT device application in an executable format and a set of security properties, the framework tries to determine if the app meets the expected security properties. This is done by automatically (i) extracting the IoT app from the firmware image (without the need of source code), (ii) building a formal (i.e., mathematical) model of the app, and (iii) automatically evaluating a set of security properties (i.e., a security policy) by leveraging state-of-the-art model checking techniques. The framework enables the definition of security policies directly by the ISM or by trusted third-party entities, e.g., the network operator or the IoT device manufacturer.

IoTAV can be applied to both new and previously deployed devices. Moreover, it does not require the source code and, therefore, can be applied to third party applications whose source code is not available. As we will see later (cf. Sect. 3.5) it is almost independent of the hardware that will host and run the application. Finally, the framework complements and leverages current firmware updates workflows, including the new SUIT solution.

To demonstrate the effectiveness of the proposed solution, we developed a prototype implementation of IoTAV for the SUIT update process in the RIOT ecosystem [24]. Finally, we validated the prototype against a set of 31 real-world RIOT applications, thereby identifying 26 security policy violations.

Paper Organization. The rest of the paper is structured as follows. Section 2 introduces the major concepts of the IoT software update process and then details the SUIT standard, along with its security limitations. Section 3 describes our novel IoT Application Verification Framework for the automatic analysis of the applications contained in the IoT updates. Furthermore, it provides the specifications of a prototype implementation for the RIOT ecosystem. Section 4 discusses an assessment of IoTAV against real-world RIOT applications and presents the collected results along with a discussion on the current limitations of the approach. Section 5 analyzes the state-of-the-art proposals for securing IoT software updates and for analyzing IoT apps, thereby underlying the differences w.r.t. our approach. Finally, Sect. 6 provides some concluding remarks.

2   Software Updates for IoT Devices

The IoT software update process is an essential operation for maintaining a suitable level of efficiency and security of IoT devices. Over the last few years, the research community has been working on the definition of several IoT update processes [20], among which the software update for resource-constrained devices is still an open research challenge [1]. Resource-constrained devices, as specified in RFC 7228 [7], use microcontrollers (like the Arm Cortex-M) on which they run a real-time operating system such as Contiki, FreeRTOS or RIOT [14], just to cite a few. To this aim, several firmware update solutions have been proposed in the last years, like FOSE [11], The Update Framework (TUF)[1], and Uptane [21]. However, most of the proposed mechanisms are tied to specific operating systems or hardware architectures, and thus, they are not general-purpose.

To overcome such limitations, the Internet Engineering Task Force (IETF) is defining a standard for firmware updates called Software Updates for Internet of Things (SUIT) [19]. The main goals of SUIT are interoperability (w.r.t. the platform and the firmware distribution technology) and end-to-end security.

The SUIT standard, currently in draft status, includes a definition of the firmware update architecture [17], an information model [18], and a manifest description [16]. Hereafter, we define the firmware image as a binary file that contains the complete software stack of an IoT device (i.e., the OS and the IoT application), according to the terminology adopted by IETF [17]. The update process involves the IoT devices to be updated, the IoT software maintainer, and the Firmware Update Server, as sketched in Fig. 1.

The typical firmware update procedure works as follows: an IoT software Maintainer compiles the OS and the IoT app and generates a new firmware image. In the SUIT specification, firmware images comprise a manifest file that

---

[1] https://github.com/theupdateframework/tuf.

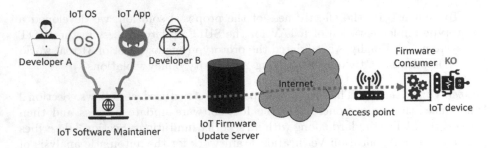

Fig. 1. A SUIT update scenario (inspired by [29]) where a developer is able to introduce a malicious app in the update pipeline.

embeds information such as the location of the firmware image for delivery, dependencies, cryptographic information, and device data. Both the firmware and the manifest are then published onto the IoT Firmware Update Server, which is responsible for storing the update and notifying the IoT devices about the availability of a new update. On the device side, the firmware update is handled by a firmware update module named Firmware Consumer, which retrieves both the manifest and the firmware image.

Upon receiving a notification from the IoT Firmware Update Server, the Firmware Consumer retrieves the manifest, checks the digital signature and the firmware sequence number to ensure the integrity and the freshness of the update image. If the verification succeeds, the IoT device pulls the firmware from the URI provided in the SUIT manifest, and stores the firmware image on the flash memory. The flash memory is divided into several memory regions (slots) containing (i) the bootloader and (ii) two slots, one containing the current firmware and the other is reserved for the update firmware. After the writing process, the bootloader reads the metadata from the firmware slots and chooses to boot the newest valid firmware. Using such an approach, an interruption in the update process (e.g., due to power loss) cannot cause the system to boot an invalid, corrupted or incompletely received image [29].

2.1   Security Issues in SUIT

The SUIT information model [18] defines a collection of security threats for the update process. As discussed in [29], such threats can be categorized into: (i) tampered firmware, (ii) firmware replay, (iii) offline device attack, (iv) firmware mismatch, (v) flash memory location mismatch, (vi) unexpected precursor image, (vii) reverse engineering, and (viii) resource exhaustion. Although the SUIT model suggests a set of security requirements and countermeasures, it is worth noticing that all these threats are related to the integrity and the confidentiality of the update process only, while the content of the update is inherently assumed as trusted. Therefore, the SUIT workflow allows an ISM to upload a firmware image containing security vulnerabilities or malicious behaviors. Furthermore,

SUIT allows the ISM to transfer its authority to another entity, e.g., a third-party developer, that can deliver to the ISM some components of a software update (e.g., the executable of the application to be updated) or triggers the update process directly. In this case, the ISM has no mechanism to assess the content of the external software components, and must fully trust the external entity.

For instance, consider the scenario depicted in Fig. 1. The ISM delegates two external developers (i.e., A and B) for updating the OS and the IoT application, respectively. Let us assume that developer A is honest (i.e., she dispatches a benign and reliable OS image), while developer B is malicious (i.e., she introduces a malware IoT application). According to the SUIT workflow, the ISM blindly composes the firmware image and dispatches the update to the Firmware Server. Then, the IoT device only verifies the authenticity and the integrity of the firmware image and installs the malware update. Such scenario depicts an actual and widespread attack vector, as the Philips Hue smart lamps security incident [25] and the Jeep Cherokee hack[2] have been carried out by injecting malicious software components inside the update process, without triggering any security enforcement mechanism.

To reduce the impact of unreliable updates, we argue that the SUIT update process needs to rely on a methodology to assess the security of the firmware image and in particular, of the IoT application. Such a methodology must be able to automatically evaluate the behavior of the firmware according to a set of security requirements, in order to allow the same ISM to deliver only validated and certified software updates. The security requirements can be defined directly by the same ISM, the IoT device manufacturer, or by a trusted third-party entity involved in the update process, like a Network Operator or a Device Operator, as defined in the SUIT standard.

We also argue that the methodology should work as a black box (i.e., without requiring the source code), in order to be systematically applied to any executable provided by third-parties. Finally, we argue that the analysis process must be carried out on the firmware image before it is submitted to the SUIT pipeline, in order to leverage the security mechanisms provided by SUIT to prevent any further modification of the image.

3   The IoT Application Verification Framework

In order to mitigate the aforementioned security concerns, we propose a novel verification solution called the **IoT Application Verification Framework** (IoTAV). IoTAV allows to automatically evaluate the security of the IoT applications included in firmware images in a black-box fashion. In details, IoTAV enables the definition of a set of security requirements, codified as a *security policy*, that are then automatically evaluated on the application executable using state-of-the-art model checking techniques. As depicted in Fig. 2, IoTAV can be seamlessly included in the existing update pipeline, like the one

---

[2] https://www.kaspersky.com/blog/blackhat-jeep-cherokee-hack-explained/9493/.

defined in SUIT. IoTAV is able to detect malicious updates (dashed arrows), thereby discarding those that doe n comply with the security policy and notifying the ISM, without affecting the normal operation in case of secure updates (solid arrows).

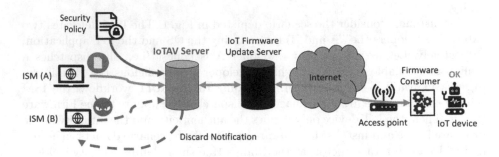

Fig. 2. SUIT update process with IoTAV. The IoTAV Server ensures that the IoT app bundled in the software update is compliant with the security policy.

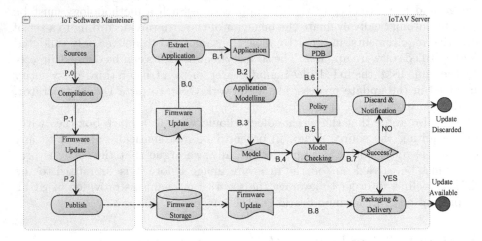

Fig. 3. The IoTAV verification workflow.

3.1   Formal Security Assessment Workflow

IoTAV features are granted by the workflow depicted in Fig. 3. Initially, the ISM compiles (P.0) and generates the firmware image update (P.1). Then, she publishes the executable (P.2) to the IoTAV Server, which stores the firmware update in a database (Firmware Storage). Then, an application extraction procedure is applied to the firmware image (B.0) to extract only the application part

(B.1). After that, the application executable goes through a modeling phase (B.2) that outputs the corresponding application model (B.3). Hence, the model is passed (B.4) to a verification process that checks its compliance against the security policy (B.5). Security policies are retrieved (B.6) from a policy database (PDB) handling policy instances that can be customized over the configuration of the single device. If the verification succeeds (B.7 → YES), IoTAV server executes a packaging procedure for the firmware (B.8). Finally, it bundles the system update following the regular SUIT publish procedure and notifies the IoT Firmware Update Server. Otherwise (B.7 → NO), IoTAV Server notifies the IoT Software Maintainer and discards the update. The notification contains the results of the verification process (i.e., which parts of the model violates the security policy and why).

3.2   Application Extraction and Modeling

The first step of the IoT app verification process is the *model generation*. To do that, IoTAV parses the firmware image and identifies the part of the executable related to the application logic. After that, the Application Modeling lifts the application machine code to a higher-level language, usually an Intermediate Representation (IR), by relying on a disassembler. From the IR, the service can then deduce the structure of the application program. The IoT Application Verification Framework builds a complete application model through a fruitful combination of Control Flow Graphs (CFGs), Call Graphs (CGs), and Inter-procedural Control Flow Graphs (ICFGs). A CFG is a directed graph made by nodes representing basic blocks, e.g., pieces of branch-less code, chained through edges to represent the control flow transfer. Although CFGs are widely used to model all the possible execution paths of a function call [28], they are able to represent the control-flow of a single procedure only. To overcome such limitation, IoTAV model generation procedure combines the CFGs of each procedure with the calling relationship between them, through CGs, thereby obtaining the ICFG of the whole application.

Algorithm 1 shows the pseudo-code of the ICFG construction algorithm. Each call site node is a root node of its own (local procedure) CFG. It is referenced in other computed CFGs since its procedure is called by the other ones. As a consequence, the *app_icfg* contains a list of the CFGs rooted at the *start_node* and at each *callee_node*, each related to another one by reference. Hence, by constructing the ICFG from an executable, IoTAV gets the structure of the entire application.

Nevertheless, since the IoT Application Verification Framework aims to describe the behavior of a system from a security standpoint, any operation which is not security-relevant is abstracted away. Therefore, the Application Modeling block records only security-relevant operations defined in the security policies, notably, file operations, cryptographic primitives, and network procedures. All irrelevant API (Application Programming Interface) calls that are invoked in a sequential way or in a conditional way (branches) are grouped and

Algorithm 1. Compute the ICFG from local CFGs

1: **procedure** ICFG CONSTRUCTION
2:     $app\_icfg \leftarrow []$
3:     $start\_node \leftarrow$ get the entry node
4:     $callees\_nodes \leftarrow$ get callees and callees of callees
5:     add local CFG of $start\_node$ to app_icfg
6:     **for** $callee\_node \in callees\_nodes$ **do**
7:         add local CFG of $callee\_node$ to app_icfg
8:     **end for**
9:     · **return** app_icfg
10: **end procedure**

---

then pruned. This way, IoTAV optimizes the application model for the model checking phase.

3.3 Policy Specification

A policy describes the properties that must hold in the model, while properties mirror a system description that can be formally expressed. In detail, the IoT Application Verification Framework allows the definition of security properties that need to be enforced in the IoT application once it is encapsulated inside the firmware update. Following the same approach of [3] and [2], IoTAV enables the definition of security policies on the interaction between the IoT application and the underlying OS in terms of API calls. Since the ICFG extracted from the application can be interpreted as a state graph, IoTAV uses Temporal Logic formulas, namely Linear Temporal Logic (LTL) [12] and Computational Tree Logic (CTL) [13]. An LTL formula describes a pattern for a sequence of events. Any actual sequence of events may match or not the pattern. Hence, one can express properties about the sequence of events with temporal operators. For example, from a given state, $\mathbf{F}p$ ("eventually") means the property p will *eventually* hold at some point in the future, while $\mathbf{G}p$ ("globally") means that the property p *always* holds in the future.

Instead, the Computation Tree Logic is based on a branching notion of time, meaning that its model of time is a tree-like structure in which the future is not determined. CTL considers different paths in the future, any one of which might be an actual path that occurs. Indeed, such a notion of time can represent the possible execution of a software program. In order to express if a property holds for all paths or some of them, two quantifier operators are introduced: the $\mathbf{A}$ operator ("for all paths") and the $\mathbf{E}$ operator ("there exists a path").

For example, the formula "$\mathbf{AG}p$" states that the property p should hold at each state of any path, whereas the formula "$\mathbf{EG}p$" states that there exists a path where the property p always holds (and eventually some paths that never hold property p).

Finally, IoTAV policies enable the definition of security properties in terms of a logical expression to be evaluated, as in the following example.

```
1 "never_fread" : A [G FRD=0];
```

Here, the sample policy bans any use of the *fread* C function. It states that along any path from the initial state, no state should set the *FRD* variable. In other words, the variable representing the *fread* function should never be part of the application model.

3.4   Model Checking

In order to verify the policy compliance of the IoT application, the IoT Application Verification Framework leverages model checking techniques that have been successfully applied to numerous real-world problems. Model checking can be mapped to a reachability problem, i.e., checking whether the model of the application cannot reach an undesirable state. Applying Temporal Logic policies to the model allows to verify some properties at any time (or state of the system). The model checking process ends up with a compliance result, that states whether the security policy is satisfied by the application model.

In order to prevent unbounded computations that are unacceptable in IoTAV workflow, the Model Checking module includes a timeout mechanism. Thus, the model checker produces three possible results: (i) YES – the model complies with the policy; (ii) NO - the model violates the security policy; or (iii) TIMEOUT (TO) – the time threshold has been reached.

One of the most critical issues in model checking is the so-called *state explosion problem* [10]. In order to check some properties, the model checker needs to explore the entire state space, which increases the complexity as the number of states grows large. Our security model addresses this problem by reducing the analysis to the sole security-sensitive operations, thus limiting the size of the corresponding model.

3.5   IoTAV Implementation

In order to evaluate the feasibility and effectiveness of the IoT Application Verification Framework, we developed a prototype implementation of IoTAV as a server appliance compatible with the SUIT update process for a RIOT ecosystem. It is worth noticing that, although the IoT Application Verification Framework is compatible with a generic SUIT update process, the focus of this prototype is the compliance with the current RIOT implementation.

SUIT in the RIOT Ecosystem. RIOT [5] is an open-source OS, based on a modular architecture built around a soft real-time micro-kernel. RIOT is structured in software modules that are aggregated at compile-time, around a kernel providing core functionality like process scheduling, inter-process communication, and threading. This approach allows building the complete system in a modular manner, including only modules that are required by the application at stake. One of these modules is the `application` module, which contains the IoT application.

RIOT implements the SUIT update described in Sect. 2. The RIOT update firmware is a bundle that contains both the OS and the IoT application in a single Executable and Link Format (ELF) file. The IoT Software Maintainer can (i) build the update, (ii) generate the corresponding manifest file, and (iii) push them to the IoT Firmware Update Server, by using a suit/publish command[3]. On the device side, after the board boots the new firmware, RIOT starts two threads: the idle thread and the main thread. The main thread is the first thread that runs and calls the `main` function. This function needs to be defined by the user application.

Application Modeling. Concerning static code analysis, the angr framework[4] is one of the most popular frameworks used in top-ranked teams of the DARPA Cyber Grand Challenge. It is a python-based binary analysis framework that currently supports the most common architectures, including x86, ARM, MIPS, and AMD, and it allows to retrieve the CFG of a program from its executable. IoTAV uses this tool to extract the CFG of each program procedure and to compute the overall ICFG. Since the entry point of the user application is the `main` function, the IoTAV computes the ICFG from there, which lets the analysis focus only on the application. For this, angr can be configured to begin the ICFG recovery directly from the `main` symbol in the program.

Policy Specification and Model Checking. PRISM (Probabilistic Symbolic Model Checker) [22] is one of the many existing model checkers. It is free, open-source, and it analyzes complex systems according to probabilistic behaviors. It also supports the model checking of non-probabilistic properties using LTL and CTL. The latter capability supports the definition of the IoTAV security policies. Indeed, the properties we would like to check with PRISM are the use of APIs and the call ordering in all execution paths. We mainly focus on APIs with a security meaning, because they are the only ones relevant in a security policy, notably any file operation or crypto primitive.

With non-probabilistic expressions, PRISM can also generate counterexamples and witnesses for further investigation on a failed property verification. Such a feature allows manual investigation as a post-process to determine the reasons that caused the policy check to fail.

Hence, the IoTAV Server embeds PRISM for the model checking phase, thereby adopting security policies in LTL and CTL. However, since the PRISM model checker needs to be fed with a model in its own PRISM language, we added a conversion block from the recovered ICFG to the PRISM language. PRISM can then compare these policies to the application model.

4   Experimental Evaluation

We carried out an experimental evaluation of IoTAV to prove the viability of our proposal and evaluate the impact on the SUIT update process. The experimental scenario is composed by an ISM which deploys updates verified by an

---

[3] https://github.com/RIOT-OS/RIOT/tree/master/examples/suit_update.
[4] https://github.com/angr/angr.

IoTAV in an IoT ecosystem made of RIOT-based devices. More specifically, the experimental setup is defined as follows.

IoT Applications. We took into consideration two sets of RIOT applications. The first one is composed of 21 RIOT sample applications available on the official repository[5], while the latter is made by 10 RIOT applications used for a demo dashboard[6] use case by the RIOT Development Team. In particular, the latter set contains a series of collecting nodes of environmental data (e.g., temperature, humidity, and pressure) that rely on CoAP [26] and MQTT [15] protocols to send their data to a real-time visualization dashboard.

SUIT Setup. We setup a standard SUIT environment composed by a Firmware Update Server connected over-the-air to a SAMR21 Xplained Pro evaluation board[7] equipped with RIOT OS Release 2019.07. Then, we deployed an IoTAV Server, according to the scenario depicted in Fig. 2. Finally, we simulated the ISM, thereby producing a set of firmware images for the update that are then pushed to the IoTAV Server to trigger the SUIT update process. In detail, each of the application under test is bundled with the OS on the evaluation board (i.e. RIOT OS Release 2019.07) to build the corresponding firmware image. Both the Firmware Update Server and IoTAV Server executes on two entry-level PCs equipped with Ubuntu 18.04.2 LTS, Intel Pentium (R) P6200 @2.13 GHz * 2, 4 GB of RAM and 50 GB HDD.

Security Policies. We defined a set of security policies describing three of the OWASP IoT Top 10 Vulnerabilities 2018[8]. The first two enforce the confidentiality of (i) the data transfer using the MQTT protocol and of (ii) the local file storage, as recommended in the *"Insecure Data Transfer and Storage"* - #7 OWASP Risk. The third policy enforces the exclusion of insecure or deprecated C functions in IoT apps, as suggested in the *"Use of Insecure or Outdated Components"* - #5 OWASP Risk.

Hence, we defined the following three PRISM policy expressions:

```
1  "mqtt_enc" : A [G MQPB=1 => (CPH_ENC=1 | AES_ENC=1 |
      CHA_ENC=1 | CHA_POLY_ENC=1)];
2  "st_enc" : A [G (FPRNT=1 | FWRT=1 | FPTS=1 | FPTC=1) => (
      CPH_ENC=1 | AES_ENC=1 | CHA_ENC=1 | CHA_POLY_ENC=1)];
3  "uns_c" : A [G SCPY=0 & SNCPY=0 & SCT=0 & SNCT=0 & SPRNT
      =0 & VSPRNT=0 & GTS=0 & MKPTH=0 & SPTH=0 & SCF=0 &
      SSCF=0 & SNSCF=0 & ATI=0 & ATF=0 & ATL=0];
```

The first expression (`mqtt_enc`) ensures that the data are encrypted when sent through MQTT using one of the following cypher algorithms `cipher_-encrypt`, `aes_encrypt`, `chacha_encrypt_bytes` or `chacha20poly1305_encrypt`.

---

[5] https://github.com/RIOT-OS/RIOT/.

[6] http://riot-demo.inria.fr.

[7] https://www.microchip.com/DevelopmentTools/ProductDetails/ATSAMR21-XPRO.

[8] https://www.owasp.org/index.php/OWASP_Internet_of_Things_Project.

Instead, the second expression (st_enc) grants that data are encrypted whenever they are written on a file through fprintf, fwrite, fputs or fputc C functions.

To represent both mqtt_enc and st_enc, we relied on the "=>" (implication) operator in PRISM which states that when the left side condition is satisfied, the right side should be satisfied as well.

Finally, the uns_C policy verifies that none of the insecure C functions (strcpy, strncpy, strcat, strncat, sprintf, vsprintf, gets, makepath, _splitpath, scanf, scanf, sscanf, snscanf, atoi, atof, atol) is used in the application.

4.1 Experimental Results

Table 1 summarizes the analysis results on the entire dataset. For each of the analyzed applications, we provide general details (name and Size of the executable), the execution times (Modeling time, Verification time, and Total time), and the results of the verification on the three policies. Since our analysis unveiled some vulnerabilities in the RIOT applications, we reported our findings to the RIOT Development Team.

Policy Verification Results. IoTAV was able to successfully analyze 28 out of the 31 IoT applications. Angr failed when trying to analyze the remaining three applications; as a consequence, IoTAV was not able to extract the model.

The outcome of IoTAV verification process showed that the *node_mqtt_-bmx280* application (belonging to the demo dashboard use case) does not comply with the mqtt_enc property, thereby indicating that the MQTT communication is unencrypted, and thus, the data are transmitted insecurely through the network. Since the source code of the application is available on Github[9], we both inspected the source code and tested the application to validate our findings. The manual analysis confirmed that data are published to an MQTT broker unencrypted. Besides, we were able to execute the node on the evaluation board. We successfully intercepted the plaintext data traffic sent by the application through the *tcpdump* tool. Also, the *emcute_mqttsn* application failed the mqtt_enc property as well.

Furthermore, IoTAV discovered that *lua_basic* and *lua_repl* applications do not comply with the st_enc policy, since they include some file storage operations without the adoption of any encryption support in place.

Finally, the experimental results show that the 71% of the dataset (22 out of 31) violate the uns_c, and thus adopting insecure or deprecated C primitives.

Notes on Performance. IoTAV successfully evaluated the applications of the dataset with a mean processing time of 191.2 s. The modeling generation phase takes on average 80% of the total processing time, while the model checking phase takes, on average, 20% of that time. The simplification and conversion phases have negligible impact on the global performance.

---

[9] https://github.com/future-proof-iot/riot-firmwares/tree/master/apps

Table 1. Execution times and policy verification results.

Applications	S [kB]	Time			Policies		
		M [s]	V [s]	Tot [s]	uns_c	mqtt_enc	st_enc
default	72.7	53.0	13.0	66.0	✗	✓	✓
ccn-lite-relay	335.2	169.0	138.0	308.0	✗	✓	✓
cord_ep	255.0	161.0	84.0	247.0	✗	✓	✓
asymcute_mqttsn	249.9	165.0	76.0	243.0	✗	✗	✓
saul_example	49.3	39.0	10.0	49.0	✗	✓	✓
ipc_pingpong	38.4	31.0	8.0	39.0	✗	✓	✓
hello_world	33.9	29.0	6.0	35.0	✗	✓	✓
timer_periodic_wu	43.8	37.0	11.0	48.0	✗	✓	✓
filesystem	107.1	100.0	18.0	118.0	✗	✓	✓
bindist	33.9	31.0	7.0	38.0	✗	✓	✓
ndn_ping	181.5	147.0	136.0	284.0	✗	✓	✓
gnrc_minimal	157.6	195.0	59.0	255.0	✗	✓	✓
nanocoap_server	184.1	312.0	123.0	436.0	✗	✓	✓
gcoap_example	249.9	427.0	171.0	600.0	✗	✓	✓
cord_epsim	195.9	337.0	140.0	479.0	✗	✓	✓
emcute_mqttsn	235.8	476.0	133.0	611.0	✗	✗	✓
gnrc_networking	282.3	606.0	185.0	792.0	✗	✓	✓
gnrc_tftp_example	286.6	638.0	208.0	848.0	✗	✓	✓
posix_sockets_example	240.3	664.0	195.0	861.0	✗	✓	✓
lua_basic	335.3	5003.0	1658.0	6668.0	✗	✓	✗
lua_repl	339.6	6099.0	1688.0	7794.0	✗	✓	✗
dashboard_riot_a8_m3	2400.0	1517.0	133.0	1652.0	✗	✓	✓
node_bmp180	3500.0	N.A.	N.A.	N.A.	N.A	N.A	N.A.
node_bmx280	3500.0	201.0	43.0	245.0	✓	✓	✓
node_ccs811	3500.0	N.A.	N.A.	N.A.	N.A	N.A	N.A.
node_empty	3400.0	137.0	29.0	167.0	✓	✓	✓
node_imu	2600.0	N.A.	N.A.	N.A.	N.A	N.A	N.A.
node_io1_xplained	3400.0	117.0	27.0	144.0	✓	✓	✓
node_leds	3400.0	112.0	27.0	140.0	✓	✓	✓
node_mqtt_bmx280	3400.0	110.0	34.0	144.0	✓	✗	✓
node_tsl2561	3500.0	179.0	35.0	214.0	✓	✓	✓

4.2 Limitations

The experimental results show both the effectiveness and the applicability of IoTAV in the SUIT update workflow, although its adoption comes with some restrictions. First, the evaluation techniques applied by IoTAV on the firmware image work with unstripped executables only, i.e., binaries containing symbols. Nevertheless, to the best of our knowledge, no tool is still able to extract CFGs without any available symbols that could otherwise be used in combination with our model extractor. Therefore, to overcome this limitation, we propose to add the possibility to strip the firmware only after the policy verification step. To this aim, the SUIT process for RIOT applications is still under active discussion and could eventually include this feature. In addition to that, the static evaluation of security policies may not cover all possible use cases for an IoT application. For example, if one security property requires to detect whether a file has been closed after being opened, the variable monitoring this property will still be set even if the file is later reopened, thereby potentially affecting the results of the analysis. To mitigate such issues, we are investigating the introduction of a runtime monitoring technique, by extending the approach in [4].

Finally, applications have been manually verified afterwards, with no false positives. However, we noticed that some applications are not expected to verify the policies, albeit the verification step succeeds. For example, this is the case of *asymcute_mqttsn*, an asynchronous MQTT-SN implementation, marked as meeting the `mqtt_enc` policy even if no encryption is used for the published data. This is due to the fact that the API *asymcute_pub* is not listed among the relevant APIs in the security policy. Such a result underlines how crucial is the definition of appropriate security policies to be used in the IoTAV to avoid false negatives.

5 Related Work

The increasing number of vulnerabilities found in IoT devices have raised the need for reliable methodologies for securing firmware updates. To this aim, the scientific and industrial communities have proposed different solutions. In [29], Zanberg et al. survey open standards and open source libraries that provide useful building blocks for secure firmware updates for resource-constrained IoT devices. The authors propose the design and the implementation of a prototype that leverages these building blocks. Bettayeb et al. [6] discuss security threats against firmware update for IoT devices and all available secure firmware update methods for IoT devices in the literature, like [20]. However, all of these works are focused only on providing end-to-end security between the IoT Firmware Update Server and the device, but they do not deal with the analysis of the IoT application.

On this topic, some proposals for static and dynamic analysis of IoT applications have been already put forward. Soteria [8] and IotSan [23] are static analysis systems that automatically extract a model of an IoT application and use a model checker to validate application-specific properties. However, they require the source code of the application. On the dynamic side, IoTGuard [9] is a policy-based enforcement system that monitors the execution of IoT applications. IoTGuard requires to instrument the source code to collect application data at runtime and build up a dynamic model that represents the runtime behavior of the application. The limitation of this approach is its invasiveness as well as the need to modify the business logic of the application. Previous solutions focus only on a single application, while SIoT [27] is the first tool that analyzes distributed IoT applications to detect buffer overflow attacks. The authors' idea is to look at a distributed IoT system as a single monolithic application.

Our proposal extends the current state of the art by allowing us to systematically verify the compliance of the binary code of IoT applications w.r.t. user-defined security policies without the need to modify applications.

6 Conclusion

In this paper, we introduced a novel methodology, called *IoT Application Verification Framework* (IoTAV), for the systematic assessment of IoT applications w.r.t. a set of given security properties. We applied such a methodology to the assessment of software updates in the IoT ecosystem. We proved the viability of our proposal experimentally by carrying out automatic analyses of RIOT applications on an actual deployment based on the SUIT update pipeline. The results yielded the identification of 26 security policy violations in 31 real-world RIOT applications.

As future work, we will deal with the limitations described in Sect. 4, at first. Then, the next step of our research will be to test the methodology on other IoT architectures, OSes and firmware update workflows. Finally, although we defined a set of policies based on the OWASP IoT Top 10 security risks, we argue that novel and more comprehensive security policies should be investigated and defined. To this aim, the interaction among IoT developers, network operators, and device manufacturers could lead to the definition of more sophisticated and widely-accepted security policies.

References

1. Padilla, F.J.A., Baccelli, E., Eichinger, T., Schleiser, K.: The future of IoT software must be updated. In: IAB Workshop on Internet of Things Software Update (IoTSU) (2016)
2. Armando, A., Costa, G., Merlo, A., Verderame, L.: Enabling BYOD through secure meta-market. In: Proceedings of the 2014 ACM Conference on Security and Privacy in Wireless Mobile Networks, WiSec 2014, pp. 219–230. ACM, New York (2014)
3. Armando, A., Costa, G., Merlo, A., Verderame, L.: Formal modeling and automatic enforcement of Bring Your Own Device policies. Int. J. Inf. Secur. **14**, 123–140 (2015)
4. Armando, A., Costa, G., Verderame, L., Merlo, A.: Securing the "bring your own device" paradigm. Computer **47**, 48–56 (2014)

5. Baccelli, E., et al.: RIOT: an open source operating system for low-end embedded devices in the IoT. IEEE Internet Things J. **5**, 4428–4440 (2018)
6. Bettayeb, M., Nasir, Q., Talib, M.A.: Firmware update attacks and security for IoT devices. In: Proceedings of the ArabWIC 6th Annual International Conference Research Track, ArabWIC 2019. ACM (2019)
7. Bormann, C., Ersue, M., Keranen, A.: Terminology for constrained-node networks. Internet Engineering Task Force (IETF), Fremont, CA, USA (2014)
8. Celik, Z.B., McDaniel, P., Tan, G.: SOTERIA: automated IoT safety and security analysis. In: Proceedings of the 2018 USENIX Annual Technical Conference (2018)
9. Celik, Z.B., Tan, G., McDaniel, P.: IoTGuard: dynamic enforcement of security and safety policy in commodity IoT. In: Network and Distributed Systems Security (NDSS) Symposium 2019 (2019)
10. Clarke, E.M., Klieber, W.: Model checking and the state explosion problem. Technical report (2011)
11. Doddapaneni, K., Lakkundi, R., Rao, S., Kulkarni, S., Bhat, B.: Secure FoTA object for IoT. In: 2017 IEEE 42nd Conference on Local Computer Networks Workshops (LCN Workshops) (2017). https://doi.org/10.1109/LCN.Workshops.2017.78
12. Gerth, R., Peled, D., Vardi, M.Y., Wolper, P.: Simple on-the-fly automatic verification of linear temporal logic. PSTV 1995. IAICT, pp. 3–18. Springer, Boston, MA (1996). https://doi.org/10.1007/978-0-387-34892-6_1
13. Goldblatt, R.: Logics of time and computation. Center for the Study of Language and Information, Stanford (1992)
14. Hahm, O., Baccelli, E., Petersen, H., Tsiftes, N.: Operating systems for low-end devices in the Internet of Things: a survey. IEEE Internet Things J. **3**, 720–734 (2015)
15. Hunkeler, U., Truong, H.L., Stanford-Clark, A.: MQTT-S - a publish/subscribe protocol for wireless sensor networks. In: 2008 3rd International Conference on Communication Systems Software and Middleware and Workshops (COMSWARE 2008) (2008)
16. IETF: Firmware manifest format (2019). https://tools.ietf.org/html/draft-moran-suit-manifest-01. Accessed 11 Sept 2019
17. IETF: Website of: A firmware update architecture for internet of things devices draft-ietf-suit-architecture-06 (2019). https://tools.ietf.org/pdf/draft-ietf-suit-architecture-06.pdf. Accessed 11 Sept 2019
18. IETF: Website of: Firmware updates for internet of things devices - an information model for manifests draft-ietf-suit-information-model-03 (2019). https://tools.ietf.org/html/draft-ietf-suit-information-model-03. Accessed 11 Sept 2019
19. IETF: Website of: Ietf suit draft architecture (2019). https://tools.ietf.org/html/draft-ietf-suit-architecture. Accessed 7 Aug 2019
20. Kolehmainen, A.: Secure firmware updates for IoT: a survey. In: 2018 IEEE International Conference on Internet of Things (iThings) and IEEE Green Computing and Communications (GreenCom) and IEEE Cyber, Physical and Social Computing (CPSCom) and IEEE Smart Data (SmartData) (2018)
21. Kuppusamy, T.K., DeLong, L.A., Cappos, J.: Uptane: security and customizability of software updates for vehicles. IEEE Veh. Technol. Mag. (2018). https://doi.org/10.1109/MVT.2017.2778751
22. Kwiatkowska, M., Norman, G., Parker, D.: PRISM 4.0: verification of probabilistic real-time systems. In: Gopalakrishnan, G., Qadeer, S. (eds.) CAV 2011. LNCS, vol. 6806, pp. 585–591. Springer, Heidelberg (2011). https://doi.org/10.1007/978-3-642-22110-1_47

23. Nguyen, D.T., Song, C., Qian, Z., Krishnamurthy, S.V., Colbert, E.J., McDaniel, P.: IotSan: fortifying the safety of IoT systems. In: CoNEXT 2018 - Proceedings of the 14th International Conference on Emerging Networking EXperiments and Technologies (2018)
24. RIOT: Riot-os (2019). https://www.riot-os.org. Accessed 7 Aug 2019
25. Ronen, E., Shamir, A., Weingarten, A.O., Oflynn, C.: IoT goes nuclear: creating a Zigbee chain reaction. IEEE Secur. Priv. **16**, 54–62 (2018)
26. Shelby, Z., Castellani, A.P., Bormann, C.: CoAP: an application protocol for billions of tiny internet nodes. IEEE Internet Comput. **16**, 62–67 (2012)
27. Teixeira, F.A., Pereira, F.M., Wong, H.C., Nogueira, J.M., Oliveira, L.B.: SIoT: securing Internet of Things through distributed systems analysis. Future Gener. Comput. Syst. **92**, 1172–1186 (2019)
28. Xu, L., Sun, F., Su, Z.: Constructing precise control flow graphs from binaries. Technical report, University of California (2009)
29. Zandberg, K., Schleiser, K., Acosta, F., Tschofenig, H., Baccelli, E.: Secure firmware updates for constrained iot devices using open standards: a reality check. IEEE Access **7**, 71907–71920 (2019)

Towards a Context-Aware Security and Privacy as a Service in the Internet of Things

Tidiane Sylla[1,3]([✉]) [iD], Mohamed Aymen Chalouf[2] [iD], Francine Krief[1] [iD], and Karim Samaké[3]

[1] University of Bordeaux, Bordeaux INP, CNRS, LaBRI, UMR 5800, 33400 Talence, France
`tidiane.sylla@u-bordeaux.fr`
[2] University of Rennes 1, CNRS, IRISA Lab, UMR 6074, 22300 Lannion, France
[3] University of Sciences Techniques and Technologies Bamako, Bamako, Mali

Abstract. Smart city is one of the most known Internet of Things (IoT) applications. The smart city services improve user's daily lives. However, security and privacy issues are slowing down their adoption. In addition, the characteristics of IoT devices, applications and users make security implementation of the considered applications a challenging task. To address these issues, we present, in this paper, a new context-aware security and privacy architecture for the IoT. Thanks to the "as a service" approach, this new architecture will be user-centric. It will also support known context-aware security issues: dynamicity, flexibility. In addition, it will address mobility, customization of security and privacy services, and support for generic IoT applications, particularly for smart city. To do so, a knowledge plane allowing effective management of context-awareness is proposed. A security and privacy plane allowing better implementation of context-aware security and privacy mechanisms is also proposed. This will be done through dynamic composition of context-based micro services. The role of the different components of these two planes are also described.

Keywords: IoT · Security · Privacy · Context-awareness · As a service · User-centric

1 Introduction

Internet of Things (IoT) applications enable advanced and intelligent services that make users everyday life easier. In this work, we are interested in the smart city field. It is a topical field and it includes a number of interesting IoT applications such as e-health, smart home, vehicular networks, etc. The implementation of smart city IoT applications and devices may involve risks related to the users's security and privacy (disclosure, espionage, theft, etc.). These problems have been addressed in a large number of works [1,9,11].

© IFIP International Federation for Information Processing 2020
Published by Springer Nature Switzerland AG 2020
M. Laurent and T. Giannetsos (Eds.): WISTP 2019, LNCS 12024, pp. 240–252, 2020.
https://doi.org/10.1007/978-3-030-41702-4_15

However, these solutions do not consider user's characteristics, such as privacy preferences, mobility, usability, etc. To overcome these problems, the emphasis should be on a user-centric approach. Due to its importance and relevance for IoT and other digital services, the European Telecommunications Standards Institute (ETSI) has adopted several standards [4]. Indeed, it allows users to play a central role in security and privacy. Thus, implementing security and privacy mechanisms according to some relevant information about users (e.g. contexts) and without their explicit intervention become necessary.

Furthermore, the security and privacy mechanisms specified in many research works are proposed or implemented to address specific security threat models to which the targeted system is exposed. Since the situation of a considered user could change due to many factors (e.g. mobility), the threat models will also change. Therefore, to ensure optimal security and address the detected vulnerabilities properly, the implementation of several security mechanisms is necessary according to different user situations.

Context-aware security and privacy is an effective way to implement user-centric security and privacy. It will allow to manage the threat models related to the users' frequent context changes. This is done by dynamically deploying security and privacy mechanisms that respond to the threat model characterizing user's current context without his intervention.

In this regard, different proposals have been introduced. However, to the best of our knowledge, none of these works propose a solution that meets the requirements: secure context-awareness management, privacy, authentication, access control and communication security. In addition, to meet next generation networks architecture requirements, security and privacy of the IoT could be based on the "**as a service**" approach. This allows it to provide flexibility, dynamicity, scalability, and better support for user mobility and heterogeneity [3].

That is why our work goes beyond existing works, by proposing a **Context-Aware Security and Privacy as a Service (CASPaaS)** based architecture. The main innovations of our work are the introduction of a knowledge plane, responsible for managing context-awareness through Machine Learning (ML) and Quality of Context (QoC), and a security and privacy plane, responsible for implementing mechanisms through the dynamic composition of context-based micro services.

The rest of the paper is organized as follows. Section 2 presents and compares related works. Section 3 describes our contribution. Finally, Sect. 4 concludes the paper and presents our further works.

2   Related Works

Context-aware security and privacy in the IoT has been the subject of several studies. In this section, we compare the different proposed solutions and point out the remaining challenges.

2.1 Proposed Solutions

A context-aware security and privacy solution in smart city IoT applications has been proposed in [11]. This solution implements context-based security policy management. It uses a combination of several contextual parameters (time, location, network, speed) for context perception. It allows the user to define some preferences (e.g. access control). The use of a combination of several contextual parameters can help to determine the context with greater precision. However, this paper has only focused on the implementation of policy-based security. It does not support the security of contextual information management. Thus, this mechanism is vulnerable to attacks of identity theft and fake location.

The solution described in [13] also implements context-aware security and privacy. Unlike the solution proposed in [11], the proposed context-awareness management system implements context information security. Nevertheless, Quality of Context (QoC) is not taken into account in these solutions. Thus, the contexts determined by these solutions can be subject to conflicts.

Context-aware privacy is complementary to context-aware security in the IoT. Therefore, in [11], the authors described a privacy mechanism based on pseudo-anonymization and delayed message delivery. Delayed message delivery can prevent user tracking (e.g. in geolocation). In [13], the authors presented a privacy system based on the anonymization of user's data. However, pseudo-anonymization and anonymization are vulnerable to inference attacks on user data. In [9], a context-aware security module offering privacy is described. However, the authors did not provide details on the technique used in this module.

In [2], the authors focused on context-aware authentication. The proposed mechanism uses a combination of username/password as an authentication factor, making it vulnerable to passwords attacks. In addition, the authors of [9] and [11] addressed authentication and access control. However, the context-aware security module proposed in [9] does not specifically define how authentication and access control are sensitive to the context.

In [13], the authors proposed an access control mechanism based on contextual access tokens. However, this mechanism does not enable user to dynamically define authorizations. Moreover, it does not have the needed flexibility to support the aforementioned features. In addition, the authorization management system is centralized, which can cause a single point of failure.

Context-aware communication security allows secure communications irrespective of whether the underlying networks are secured or not. However, none of the studied works proposed a mechanism for communication security.

2.2 Positioning

The above-described works propose context-aware security solutions in the IoT. Table 1 summarizes the comparison between these works. On the one hand, the support of the proposed contextual security and privacy mechanisms are mostly incomplete for the IoT. On the other hand, beyond these challenges, these works addressed the issues of context-aware security and privacy in a specific application field. In IoT, each user can have several devices and applications. Thus, proposing an architecture that allows to meet the requirements identified independently of smart city IoT applications and devices becomes necessary.

Table 1. Comparison of work that has proposed context-aware security and privacy solutions in the IoT

Works	C.A.S						
	C.A authentication	C.A authorization	C.A commu. security	C.A privacy	Context mgmt. security	As a service	ITU-T ref. arch. integration
[11]	Mentioned	Mentioned	No	Yes	No	No	No
[13]	No	Yes	No	Mentioned	Yes	No	No
[2]	Yes	Mentioned	No	No	No	No	No
[9]	Mentioned	Mentioned	No	Mentioned	No	No	No
[1]	No	Yes	No	Yes	No	No	No
[6]	No	No	No	Yes	No	No	No
Proposition	Yes	Yes	Yes	Yes	Yes	Yes	Yes

Furthermore, the need to move towards Software Oriented Architecture (SOA) in the IoT is growing. On one hand, this is mainly due to the fact that SOA enables component-based model. SOA allows designing a system into functional parts [3]. On second hand, next generation networks are essentially software defined. The architecture proposed supports context-aware security requirements. Moreover, it addresses challenges such as dynamicity, flexibility, mobility, customization, and support for generic IoT applications through secure API, particularly for smart city.

3 Context-Aware Security and Privacy as a Service Based Architecture

In this section, we give a detailed description of our contribution. We also highlight main challenges related to the architecture implementation.

3.1 Overview

An effective context-aware security and privacy needs a separation between the context-awareness management and the implementation of security and privacy mechanisms. Indeed, the separation of the intelligence (i.e, context-awareness) and the enforcement of security/privacy decisions enables more modularity and flexibility. Thus, these features enable more dynamicity and adaptability in offering security and privacy to users. Therefore, the proposed architecture is divided into two planes: **Knowledge Plane (KP)** and **Security and Privacy Plane (SPP)**. These planes will integrate ITU-T IoT reference architecture to provide context-awareness and adaptive security and privacy (See Appendix A).

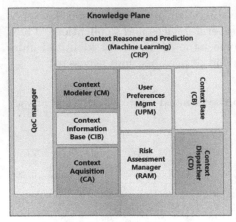 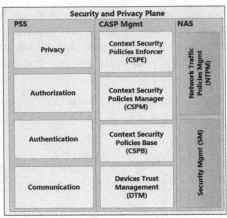

(a) Knowledge Plane   (b) Security and Privacy Plane

Fig. 1. Context-aware security as a service architecture

Thanks to the "as a service" approach, the architecture can be integrated into new service-oriented networks. Its addresses several challenges in securing the IoT (Sect. 2.2). Therefore, the modules composing the different planes are designed according to Virtual Network Function (VNF) requirements presented in [7]. As a result, security and privacy for IoT applications will be dynamic, flexible, customizable and user-centric.

The walking through example of our architecture operation will be the following. Bob is a diabetic patient living in a smart home. He is equipped with a smart watch, which continuously monitors his glucose level and daily activities. The hospital's smart healthcare system collects and processes Bob's health information in order to provide him with better healthcare and feeding.

3.2   Knowledge Plane

The Knowledge Plane (KP) (Fig. 1a) aims to provide specific and relevant context and related information (e.g. risk level and preferences) to the SPP. Based on this, the SPP will implement appropriate security and privacy mechanisms. It is composed of modules necessary for the management of context life cycle, i.e., context acquisition, modelling, reasoning and dissemination [12].

The first stage of context life cycle is context acquisition. The **Context Acquisition (CA)** module receives context information from trusted context sources (see Sect. 3.3). We refer by context source any device in the user's environment collecting context information. The CA module pre-processes (for example a raw GPS sensor data must be put in a format that represents geographical location) and stores context information, also called low-level context, in the **Context Information Base (CIB)**. For example, Bob leaves his house and is walking in the street. In this case, following low-level contexts are sent to the service: date and time, Bob's location, Bob's network and motion.

The next step in the context processing is context modelling. This is done by the **Context Modelling (CM)** module. Indeed, it represents the context in terms of context attributes, characteristics and **Quality of Context (QoC)** attributes. Then, the representation obtained is organized according to the chosen model. Different context models exist: the key-value model, ontology-based model, hybrid model, etc. [12]. The choice of a model depends on the its ability to meet the requirements of the context modelling and the target application domain. In the considered example, a key-value model is well adapted to the situation because of its simplicity and flexibility in modelling such a situation. These operations are performed in collaboration with the QoC module.

The QoC module aims to resolve conflicts in context determination. It is characterized by a set of parameters. First, the module computes QoC parameters (timeliness, reliability, completeness, importance) to measure the quality of the low-level context received. Then, the results of these measurements will be interpreted to determine the existence of conflicts. Depending on the type of detected conflict, it applies a set of policies to provide a context with a better-quality. For example, user's location sensing policy can be based on the up-to-dateness.

After context modelling, the next stage in context management is the context reasoning. Context reasoning is the process of deduction high-level context from several low-level context information. The output of the CM is used by the **Context Reasoning and Prediction (CRP)** module to determine the high-level context. Indeed, it infers on the low-level context information provided by the CM using a context reasoning technique. In Bob's case, the resulting high-level context will be: *"user is walking near the home"*. There are several context reasoning techniques, including ontology-based, machine learning, fuzzy logic, etc. In our architecture, supervised learning technique will be used by the CRP module, because of its good accuracy. The determined high-level context is first validated by the QoC module. Then, the resulting high-level context is stored in the **Context Base (CB)**.

Finally, the last stage of the context management is the dissemination of high-level contexts. Before context dissemination, the KP will assess the risk level and user's preferences associated with the context. These operations are performed by the **Risk Assessment Manager (RAM)** and the **User Preferences Management (UPM)** modules. Then, the context, risk level and user' preferences will be straightforward distributed to the SPP for making contextual security decision. This context distribution is done by **Context Dispatcher (CD)**. The main context consumer in the SPP is the **Context Security Policies Manager (CSPM)** (Sect. 3.3). The dissemination of context and related information to the CSPM is done through a publish/subscribe mechanism.

The RAM compute the risk level of a given context based on the threat model associated to that context. In the considered example, Bob is at a public garden with his friends. Bob's devices (smartphone, smartwatch) are connected to the public garden Wifi network. After the CD receives Bob's new context, it sends it to the RAM for risk assessment. The RAM assesses the given context risk based on its threat model (unsecure network, eavesdropping, etc.), so high security risk

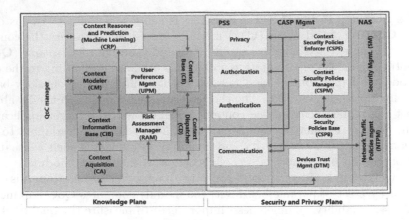

Fig. 2. CASPaaS modules and their interactions

in Bob's case. Next, the RAM returns to the CD Bob's context with the assessed risk level. When the CD receives the context risk level, it gets the corresponding user' preferences from the UPM and sends them to the CSPM. The SPP can use this new context and deploy appropriate security and privacy mechanisms. Thus, the KP provides the necessary intelligence to the SPP. Figure 2 illustrates interactions between the architecture components.

3.3   Security and Privacy Plane

The Security and Privacy Plane (Fig. 1b) addresses the identified context-aware security and privacy functional requirements. It is divided into three functional components: **Privacy and Security Services (PSS)**, **Context-Aware Security and Privacy Management (CASP Mgmt)** and **Network and Architecture Security (NAS)**.

The PSS and CASP Mgmt components constitute the core of the SPP. Indeed, the CASP Mgmt includes the modules in charge of contextual security policies management and security of context-awareness management. The PSS is composed of modules responsible for the enforcement of contextual security and privacy decisions taken by the CASP Mgmt. Finally, the NAS includes modules providing architecture and network security.

To provide secure context-awareness management, the architecture should be able to gather secured contexts from trusted user IoT devices. The **Device Trust Management (DTM)** is in charge of the management of contexts security and the trustworthiness of context sources. First, context sources will send encrypted context information to the DTM. A lightweight public key cryptography for IoT devices will be used to this end. Second, user's devices trustworthiness should be established for each exchange. This will be based on devices reputation. Device reputation will be assessed by computing the trustworthiness of context it has sent. Third, the user should be able to manage his devices ownership. The **Blockchain** can be leveraged to achieve these goals. This choice is motivated by its following features. Firstly, Blockchain-based decentralized PKI (Public Key Infrastructure) is well suited for IoT [5, 15]. Secondly, **smart contracts** features such as automated execution, transfer of property can help in automatic reputation assessment [10]. It can also allow the user to control his device's ownership.

A core element of the context-aware security and privacy is the management of contextual security policies. Thus, the **Context Security Policy Manager** (**CSPM**) is in charge of selecting the contextual security policy corresponding to a given context and related information (risk level, preferences). To do so, when the CSPM receives a context and related information, it gets the corresponding policy from the **Context Security Policies Base** (**CSPB**) and sends it to the **Context Security Policies Enforcer** (**CSPE**).

The contextual security policy describes the security and privacy mechanisms to be deployed in a specific context. The role of the CSPE module is to use the security policy provided by the CSPM to order the enforcement of appropriate security and privacy mechanisms. This enforcement will be done by the modules of the PSS component. When a **Contextual Security Policy** (**CSP**) has to be enforced, the CSPE will orchestrate the composition of micro services corresponding to the appropriate modules of the PSS component. For example, the CSP can dictate the enforcement of the following mechanisms: *two factor authentication, renew devices authentication keys, and secure communication.*

After the contextual security policy decision processing, the selected policy must be enforced by context-aware security and privacy mechanisms. Thus, the **Privacy**, **Authentication**, **Authorization** and **Communication** modules are responsible of implementing these mechanisms. Besides, APIs will be provided to ensure the genericity of the solution and its independence from the IoT applications. This will enable the developers to export the security task of their applications by calling the provided APIs.

The **Privacy** module will act as a privacy assistant. It will be able to continuously analyze the data coming from user's devices. Depending on the context, it informs user if there is a proven risk to his privacy. It also implements the rules provided by the CSPE.

The **Authentication** module is in charge of users and IoT devices. Thus, according to the rules provided by the CSPE, a type of authentication is proposed to the user (e.g. one factor, double factor). For a device, depending on the context, the session key can be renewed.

The **Authorization** module will manage resources access control. To this end, **Blockchain** can enables to define and manage the authorizations of an entity in a distributed way. This can be done according to the operation of an IoT application and based on user-centric approach. Indeed, an entity's authorizations must be represented in the form of tokens. Then it is entered in a smart contract registered in the Blockchain. Through the UPM, the user should be able to modify or revoke an authorization at any time. In all cases, the authorization is dynamically updated and implemented by the module.

Communication security is needed in some contexts, especially for unsecured networks. Thus, the **Communication** module role is, according to a context, to secure communications between devices and applications by enforcing the associated CSP. This can be done by implementing message security (payload) of the application layer. Indeed, the effectiveness of message security in providing secure communications to IoT devices over unsecured networks is proven [8]. Let's suppose that the hospital healthcare system needs to pull Bob's glucose level. Bob's context is *at the public garden*. For this context, the CSPM provides a CSP specifying *secure communication* and privacy to the CSPE. The result of that is the establishment of secure communications between Bob's smartwatch and the hospital's healthcare system prior to any data transmission. After secure communication's setup, Bob's glucose level is anonymized/obscured.

Finally, the architecture should be virtualized and deployed as a service. To this end, it must be secured in order to prevent possible attacks (e.g. denial of service). The role of **Security Management** (**SM**) is to ensure the security of the entire architecture. It implements a firewall and deep packet inspection for mitigating attacks against availability. It also addresses the user's mobility and devices heterogeneity. To do so, CSP rules will be sent to devices by leveraging SDN (Software Defined Network) capabilities.

The **Network Traffic Policy Management** (**NTPM**) module is responsible for transmitting rules to devices. It dictates to the SDN controller the traffic paths based on the results provided by the SM in case of an attack. The devices will then act as SDN agents, capable of applying and redirecting traffic at the request of a SDN controller. The SDN controller will receive commands from the architecture's mechanism implementation components. Please see Appendix B for an illustration of our architecture possible deployment in a network with an edge computing infrastructure.

4   Conclusion and Future Work

Context-aware security and privacy makes it possible to support the smart city IoT applications user's situations changes. We have identified important points that should be considered: intelligence, security services and privacy, dynamicity, flexibility, scalability, mobility, genericity, scalability.

In this sense, different solutions have been proposed. However, none of them have addressed the identified requirements. Hence, in this paper, these different approaches are described and compared, and a new architecture is proposed. This architecture, unlike the previous proposals, is designed based on "as a service" approach. It is composed of two planes. Essentially, a Knowledge Plane, using QoC, Machine Learning and Risk management and improving context-awareness, is proposed. Besides, the devices trust management within Security and Privacy Plane is proposed.

Future work will focus on the following points. The first objective is the implementation of the Device Trust Management module announced in Sect. 3.3. Then, we will implement the authorization management module based on the

Blockchain through a smart contract and contextual access tokens. This implementation will be based on the Hyperledger Fabric which is a Blockchain framework allowing the creation of smart contracts using Java language. Finally, we will perform a simulation of the architecture deployment in a 5G network and its performance evaluation will be performed.

Appendix A   ITU-T Reference Architecture Integration

The ITU-T IoT reference architecture integrates a transversal layer to ensure security across the different layers of the reference architecture[1]. Our proposed architecture aims to integrate this layer as a specific security capability in order to provide a context-aware security as a service for IoT. It also aims to integrate a knowledge plane in the ITU-T IoT reference architecture to enable context-awareness features for the management layer. Thus, our work will allow the ITU-T IoT reference architecture to support context-awareness feature, users security and privacy, while enabling the next generation networks integration. Figure 3 shows the integration of the proposed architecture into the ITU-T IoT reference architecture.

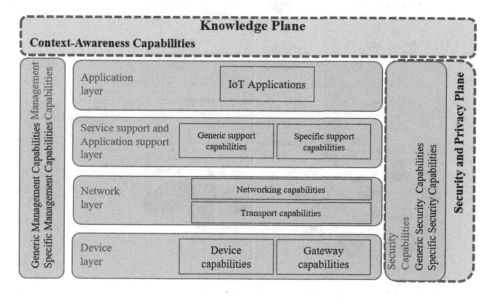

Fig. 3. ITU-T reference architecture integrating our proposed architecture

The management, control and data planes of the ITU-T IoT reference architecture need context-awareness capabilities to allow dynamic and flexible management of IoT networks (dynamic traffic steering, location-aware services, etc.). Therefore, the KP will be very useful for these planes of the ITU-T IoT reference architecture.

---

[1] ITU-T Recommendation Y.4000/Y.2060, 2012.

Appendix B   CASPaaS Underlying Network Architecture

New network architectures pave the way in the development of service-oriented computing, enabling the deployment of "as a service" architectures and virtualized environments in which only the necessary network function instances will be used when needed. They bring a new philosophy based on the transformations carried out in network architectures, essentially based on virtualization and network programming. They can thus support service-oriented computing, dynamic network programming through Software Defined Networking (SDN), Network Function Virtualization (NFV), Edge computing, etc.

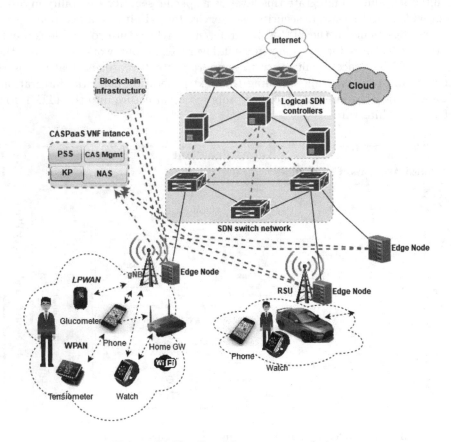

Fig. 4. CASPaaS architecture general view

Based on these technologies, our architecture can be implemented as VNF (Virtual Network Function). Then, it can be deployed instantly in the network, regardless of the user's location. This will ensure an optimal security and privacy levels for the user wherever he is. Thanks to VNFs and service function chaining, it will be possible to dynamically orchestrate the deployment of the service as close as possible to the user [14]. Moreover, these new network paradigms fit to ITU-T IoT reference architecture. Indeed, their Management and Orchestration plane can extend the management layer of the ITU-T IoT reference architecture (Fig. 4).

References

1. Alagar, V., Alsaig, A., Ormandjiva, O., Wan, K.: Context-based security and privacy for healthcare IoT. In: 2018 IEEE International Conference on Smart Internet of Things, Xi'an, China, pp. 122–128. IEEE (2018)
2. Ashibani, Y., Kauling, D., Mahmoud, Q.H.: A context-aware authentication service for smart homes. In: 2017 14th IEEE Annual Consumer Communications & Networking Conference (CCNC), Las Vegas, NV, USA, pp. 588–589. IEEE (2017)
3. Aubonnet, T., Amina, B., Lemoine, F., Simoni, N.: Controlled components for Internet of Things as-a-service. Open J. Internet Things (OJIOT) 2(1), 16–33 (2016)
4. Aubonnet, T., Lemoine, F., Cadzow, A., Dupré, B., Simoni, N.: User group; user centric approach in digital ecosystem. Technical report TR 103 438, European Telecommunications Standards Institute (ETSI), France (2019)
5. Axon, L., Goldsmith, M.: PB-PKI: a privacy-aware blockchain-based PKI. In: Proceedings of the 14th International Joint Conference on e-Business and Telecommunications, pp. 311–318 (2017)
6. Barhamgi, M., Perera, C., Ghedira, C., Benslimane, D.: User-centric privacy engineering for the Internet of Things. arXiv:1809.00926 [cs] (2018)
7. Boubendir, A., Bertin, E., Simoni, N.: Flexibility and dynamicity for open network-as-a-service: from VNF and architecture modeling to deployment. In: NOMS 2018–2018 IEEE/IFIP Network Operations and Management Symposium, Taipei, pp. 1–6. IEEE (2018)
8. Claeys, T., Rousseau, F., Tourancheau, B.: Securing complex IoT platforms with token based access control and authenticated key establishment. In: 2017 International Workshop on Secure Internet of Things, Oslo, pp. 1–9. IEEE (2017)
9. de Matos, E., Tiburski, R.T., Amaral, L.A., Hessel, F.: Providing context-aware security for IoT environments through context sharing feature. In: 2018 17th IEEE International Conference on Trust, Security and Privacy in Computing and Communications/12th IEEE International Conference on Big Data Science and Engineering, New York, NY, USA, pp. 1711–1715. IEEE (2018)
10. Mendiboure, L., Chalouf, M.A., Krief, F.: Towards a blockchain-based SD-IoV for applications authentication and trust management. In: Skulimowski, A.M.J., Sheng, Z., Khemiri-Kallel, S., Cérin, C., Hsu, C.-H. (eds.) IOV 2018. LNCS, vol. 11253, pp. 265–277. Springer, Cham (2018). https://doi.org/10.1007/978-3-030-05081-8_19
11. Neisse, R., Steri, G., Baldini, G., Tragos, E., Fovino, I.N., Botterman, M.: Dynamic context-aware scalable and trust-based IoT security, privacy framework. In: Vermesan, O., Friess, P. (eds.) Internet of Things - From Research and Innovation to Market Deployment. River Publishers Series in Communication, pp. 199–224. River Publishers, Gistrup (2015)
12. Perera, C., Zaslavsky, A., Christen, P., Georgakopoulos, D.: Context aware computing for the Internet of Things: a survey. IEEE Commun. Surv. Tutor. 16(1), 414–454 (2013)

13. Ramos, J.L.H., Bernabe, J.B., Skarmeta, A.F.: Managing context information for adaptive security in IoT environments. In: 2015 IEEE 29th International Conference on Advanced Information Networking and Applications Workshops, pp. 676–681. IEEE (2015)
14. Vilalta, R., et al.: TelcoFog: a unified flexible fog and cloud computing architecture for 5G networks. IEEE Commun. Mag. **55**(8), 36–43 (2017)
15. Won, J., Singla, A., Bertino, E., Bollella, G.: Decentralized public key infrastructure for Internet-of-Things. In: MILCOM 2018–2018 IEEE Military Communications Conference (MILCOM), pp. 907–913. IEEE (2018)

Author Index

Printed in the United States
By Bookmasters